SALAFI SOCIAL AND POLITICAL MOVEMENTS

Edinburgh Studies of the Globalised Muslim World

Series Editor: **Frédéric Volpi**, Director, Prince Alwaleed Bin Talal Centre for the Study of Contemporary Islam, University of Edinburgh

This innovative series investigates the dynamics of Muslim societies in a globalised world. It considers the boundaries of the contemporary Muslim world, their construction, their artificiality or durability. It sheds new light on what it means to be part of the Muslim world today, for both those individuals and communities who live in Muslim-majority countries and those who reside outside and are part of a globalised ummah. Its analysis encompasses the micro and the macro level, exploring the discourses and practices of individuals, communities, states and transnational actors who create these dynamics. It offers a multidisciplinary perspective on the salient contemporary issues and interactions that shape the internal and external relations of the Muslim world.

Published and forthcoming titles

A Political Theory of Muslim Democracy
Ravza Altuntaş-Çakır

Salafi Social and Political Movements: National and Transnational Contexts
Masooda Bano (ed.)

Islamic Modernities in World Society: The Rise, Spread and Fragmentation of a Hegemonic Idea
Dietrich Jung

Literary Neo-Orientalism and the Arab Uprisings: Tensions in English, French and German Language Fiction
Julia Wurr

edinburghuniversitypress.com/series/esgmw

SALAFI SOCIAL AND POLITICAL MOVEMENTS

National and Transnational Contexts

Edited by Masooda Bano

EDINBURGH
University Press

Edinburgh University Press is one of the leading university presses in the UK. We publish academic books and journals in our selected subject areas across the humanities and social sciences, combining cutting-edge scholarship with high editorial and production values to produce academic works of lasting importance. For more information visit our website: edinburghuniversitypress.com

Edinburgh University Press Ltd
The Tun – Holyrood Road
12 (2f) Jackson's Entry
Edinburgh EH8 8PJ

First published in hardback by Edinburgh University Press 2021

Typeset in 11/15 Adobe Garamond by
Servis Filmsetting Ltd, Stockport, Cheshire

A CIP record for this book is available from the British Library

ISBN 978 1 4744 7912 7 (hardback)
ISBN 978 1 4744 7913 4 (paperback)
ISBN 978 1 4744 7915 8 (webready PDF)
ISBN 978 1 4744 7914 1 (epub)

CONTENTS

Acknowledgements vii

Notes on Contributors ix

Glossary xiv

Series Editor's Foreword xix

Introduction: Salafism Today – A Break with the Past 1
Masooda Bano

PART 1 CHANGES IN SALAFI THOUGHT

1 Salafism: The Core Critiques 27
Hazim Fouad

2 In Today's Saudi Arabia: The State, the Society and the Scholars 44
Masooda Bano

3 Legitimising Political Dissent: Islamist Salafi Discourses on Obedience and Rebellion after the Arab Revolutions 61
Usaama al-Azami

PART 2 SALAFI MOVEMENTS ON THE GROUND

4 Quietist 'Scholastic' Salafism in Morocco since the Arab Spring 89
Guy Robert Eyre
5 Between *Da'wa* and Politics: The Changing Dynamics of Egypt's Ansar al-Sunna, 2011–13 114
Neil Russell
6 Salafi Leadership outside Saudi Arabia: Hakim al-Mutairi and the Umma Party of Kuwait 140
Kristin Diwan

PART 3 SALAFI JIHADISM AND INTER-GROUP COMPETITION

7 Wahhabi Salafism versus Islamic State: Age-old Traditions Appropriated by Modern-Day Terrorists 171
Abdullah bin Khaled al-Saud
8 Fratricidal Jihadism Revisited: The Complex Nature of Intra-jihadi Conflict 188
Tore Hamming
9 Ahrar al-Sham's Politicisation during the Syrian Conflict 222
Jérôme Drevon
10 Filling Gaps Left by the Muslim Brotherhood: Experience in Palestine 247
Belal Shobaki

Conclusion: Salafism in the Twenty-first Century 272
Itzchak Weismann

Index 287

ACKNOWLEDGEMENTS

This volume results from an international conference on the *Future of Salafism* that I co-hosted with the King Faisal Center for Research and Islamic Studies (KFCRIS), under the umbrella of a European Research Council (ERC) project, *Changing Structures of Islamic Authority and Consequences for Social Change: A Transnational Review* (European Union's Seventh Framework Programme [*FP7/2007–2013*] / ERC *grant agreement* no. [337108]). The conference would not have been possible without the generous financial contributions from both of these sources. I would like to thank Dr Saud al-Sahran, Director, KFCRIS, and Abdullah bin K. al-Saud, at the time Director of Research at KFCRIS, for their intellectual engagement with this project, for co-hosting the conference and taking active part in the selection of papers and shaping the details of the conference. I am also indebted to the KFCRIS's academic visitors' programme, which has facilitated my repeat research visits to Saudi Arabia since 2016. My very sincere thanks are also due to John Bowen, Robert Gleave, Stéphen Lacroix, Dietrich Reetz and Francis Robinson who acted as advisors on the ERC project (2014–19) and played active roles as chairs and presenters at the conference – one is lucky to have scholars such as these support one's intellectual endeavour; they raise the bar of the scholarly debate, while their presence acts as a magnet attracting other fine minds. Hugh Goddard and Itzchak Weismann, although not advisors on the project, played the same role – the generous intellectual contribution of the latter is visible, in particular, in the conclusion to this volume. Finally, I must also thank all the speakers at the conference, some of whose work features in this volume, and the members of the audience, many of whom were non-academics and present because of being 'practicing Salafis'. The active dialogue between the researchers and those who are subject of research made for an even livelier discussion.

Masooda Bano
University of Oxford
16 December 2020

NOTES ON CONTRIBUTORS

Usaama al-Azami is Departmental Lecturer in Contemporary Islamic Studies at the University of Oxford. He read his BA in Arabic and Islamic Studies at Oxford, and his MA and PhD in Near Eastern Studies at Princeton University. Alongside conventional academic studies, he has also studied a traditional *ʿālimiyya* curriculum at the Al-Salam Institute. He has a book monograph forthcoming, *Islam and the Arab Revolutions: The Ulama between Democracy and Autocracy*. His research and publications mainly focus on the way in which *'ulamā'* (Islamic scholars), have responded to the political upheavals marking the Arab world from the beginning of 2011. Dr al-Azami has also lived in the Middle East for five years, four of those in Saudi Arabia.

Masooda Bano is Professor of Development Studies in the Oxford Department of International Development (ODID) and Senior Golding Fellow at Brasenose College, University of Oxford. Her research has received funding from major research councils, including the European Research Council, the Economic and Social Research Council, and the Arts and Humanities Research Council. She is the author of *The Revival of Islamic Rationalism: Logic, Metaphysics and Mysticism in Modern Muslim Societies* (2020); *Female Islamic Education Movements: The Re-Democratisation of Islamic Knowledge* (2017); and *The Rational Believer: Choices and Decisions in* *the Madrasas of Pakistan* (2012). She has also edited *Modern Islamic Authority and Social Change*, Vols 1 and 2 (Edinburgh University Press, 2018); *Shaping Global Islamic Discourses: The Role of al-Azhar, al-Medina, and al-Mustafa* (Edinburgh University Press, 2015); and *Women, Leadership and Mosques: Changes in Contemporary Islamic Authority* (2012).

Kristin Diwan is a Senior Resident Scholar at the Arab Gulf States Institute in Washington. She works at the intersection of comparative politics and international relations, with an emphasis on social movements and political identity. Her current projects concern generational change, nationalism and the evolution of Islamism in the Arab Gulf states. Her articles have appeared in both academic and policy journals, such as *Geopolitics* and *Foreign Affairs*, and her commentary in prominent media such as the *New York Times*, *Financial Times* and *Washington Post*. Diwan teaches part-time at the George Washington University's Elliot School of International Affairs and was previously an assistant professor at the American University School of International Service. She holds a PhD in Government from Harvard University.

Jérôme Drevon is a Research Associate at the Graduate Institute of International and Development Studies (IHEID). He holds a PhD from Durham University and was previously a research fellow at the University of Oxford and the University of Manchester. Jérôme's research examines (mostly Islamist) non-state armed groups at the meso-level, including institutional, organisational and networking approaches. He is particularly interested in armed groups' trajectories in armed conflicts, especially the transformation of insurgents into more pragmatic and mainstream political actors. Jérôme has recently completed a book on Ahrar al-Sham's trajectory during the Syrian conflict, based on extensive field research in Syria and Turkey.

Guy Robert Eyre is a doctoral candidate in the Department of Politics and International Studies at the School of Oriental and African Studies (SOAS), University of London. Situated at the nexus of comparative politics, political theory and political anthropology, his work studies Islamic grassroots activism and politics in Morocco. Eyre is also a Teaching Fellow in the Department of Politics and International Studies at SOAS.

Hazim Fouad works as a Senior Researcher in Islamic Studies and as an Analyst for the Senator of the Interior in Bremen, Germany, in the Department on Countering Islamism. Prior to this, he worked at the London-based Institute for Strategic Dialogue for the Policy Planner's Network on Countering Radicalisation and Polarisation. In 2014 he published, together with Behnam T. Said, the first German anthology on Salafism. He has studied Near and Middle Eastern Studies in Bochum, Cairo and London and in 2019 received his doctorate with a thesis on 'Contemporary Muslim Criticism of Salafism' from the University of Kiel, Germany. He regularly delivers public lectures on the topics of radicalisation, domestic security and extremist ideologies, and he is a regular member of numerous expert panels and conferences concerning these topics. He is often interviewed by print media and appears on different radio and television broadcasts.

Tore Hamming holds a PhD in Political and Social Science from the European University Institute. In his research, Hamming specialises in Sunni Jihadism and particularly the internal conflict dynamics *between* and *within* jihadi groups. He has been a visiting researcher at CERI-Sciences Po, the Department of Politics and International Relations at the University of Oxford and the Danish Institute for International Studies (DIIS), as well as a non-resident fellow at the Middle East Institute and the International Centre for the Study of Radicalisation. Hamming's academic research has been published in *Perspectives on Terrorism*, *Terrorism and Political Violence* and the *CTC Sentinel*, while his analysis has appeared in a range of international journals. He currently blogs on Jihadica.com. Based on his work on jihadi groups, he has also testified in court cases against Danish foreign fighters joining the Islamic State in Syria and Iraq.

Neil Russell is an early-career scholar who recently completed his ESRC-funded PhD at the University of Edinburgh. For the past two years he has been a Teaching Fellow in Politics at Newcastle University, leading modules on Middle East Politics and International Relations. Focused on Egypt as a case-study, his doctoral dissertation examined the relationship between Islamic service provision and politics, with the delivery of social and religious services used as a lens to track changes in state-society relations since the revolutionary upheaval of 2011. Neil is currently developing a research project that will extend the findings of his doctoral work by conducting a comparative analysis of Middle East states' regulation of Islamic social and religious institutions since the 2011 Arab Uprisings.

Abdullah bin Khaled al-Saud is Associate Professor of Security Studies at the Naif Arab University for Security Sciences (NAUSS) in Riyadh, and an Associate Fellow at the International Centre for the Study of Radicalisation (ICSR), King's College London. From 2018 to 2020, he served as the Director of Research at the King Faisal Center for Research and Islamic Studies (KFCRIS). His research interests include Security Studies in general, with a focus on issues related to political violence, armed non-state actors, radicalisation and terrorism. In addition to having contributed several book chapters, al-Saud has published in a number of leading peer-reviewed journals in the field, such as *Terrorism and Political Violence* and *Studies in Conflict and Terrorism*. Al-Saud holds a PhD in War Studies from King's College London, an MA in International Peace and Security from King's College London and a BA in Law from King Saud University.

Belal Shobaki is the Head of the Department of Political Science at Hebron University, Palestine. He is a member of the Palestinian Policy Network. He has published on political Islam, identity and democratisation processes in Palestine. Shobaki lectures on the Palestinian political system, political analysis and Islamic political thought. He is also leading a team of researchers at Hebron University in a three-year project funded by the Erasmus+ programme, titled *Strengthening of National Research Capacity on Policy, Conflict Resolution and Reconciliation*. He has previously taught at An-Najah National University, Palestine, and at IIUM, Malaysia.

Itzchak Weismann is Professor of Islamic Studies and former Director of the Jewish-Arab Center at the University of Haifa. His research interests focus on modern Islamic movements and ideologies. He has published widely on the Muslim Brotherhood, Salafism, Sufism and jihadi organisations in the Middle East (especially Syria, Egypt and Saudi Arabia), in South Asia and worldwide. His latest monograph is *Abd al-Rahman al-Kawakibi: Islamic Reform and Arab Nationalism* (2015). He is also scientific editor of the Sahar (Crescent) series of translations into Hebrew of major modern Islamic texts.

GLOSSARY

ʿabāya or abaya	ʻcloakʼ; refers to a robe-like dress worn by women
al-ʿaduww al-qarīb	near enemy
ʿādil	equitable
Ahl-i Ḥadīth	*ḥadīth*-centric revivalist movement from nineteenth-century India
ʿaqīda, pl. *ʿaqāʾid*	Islamic creed, articles of faith
ʿaql	reason
Ashʿarī	one of the major Sunnī credal schools
bayʿa	allegiance
bughāt, sing. *bāghī*	rebels/rebel
bidʿa	blameworthy religious innovation
Dabiq	town in northeastern Syria; also the name of a journal produced by ISIL
daʿwa	proselytising, preaching of Islam
daʿwat al-khiṭāb	spoken *daʿwah*
al-daʿwa al-taṭbīqiyya	applied *daʿwah*
farḍ al-ʿayn	personal obligation
fatwa	a formal but generally non-binding statement on an issue or question related to Islamic law, given by a *mufti* (from *iftāʾ*, ʻadviseʼ)
fawḍā	anarchy

fikr	thought
fitna	temptation, disorder, civil strife
al-fitna al-kubrā	great schism
al-ghayb	the unseen
hadina sha'biyya	popular support
ḥadīth or hadith	reports describing the words, actions, or habits of the Prophet Muhammad
Hajj	the annual Muslim pilgrimage to Mecca
ḥākimiyya	God's sovereignty
Ḥanafi	Islamic legal school (*madhhab*) whose origins are attributed to Abū Hānifah (d. 767/150)
Ḥanbalī	Islamic legal school (*madhhab*) whose origins are attributed to Aḥmad ibn Ḥanbal (d. 855/214)
ḥarām	forbidden by Islamic law
al-haye al-islāmiyya	Islamic committee, institution, or body
ḥizbiyya	party politics, factionalism
ḥudūd	corporal punishments legislated in the Qur'ān
ḥuqūq	rights
ijmā'	consensus
ijtihād	the process of legal reasoning in which the jurist applies maximum effort in order to derive a ruling
inqisām	schism
al-'iṣyān al-madanī	civil disobedience
istiḥlāl	to deem something permissible
i'tiqād	belief
jabha	front or bloc
jāhiliyya	ignorance, often used to describe the 'ignorant' way of life of the Arabs before Islam
jā'ir	unjust
jamaa, pl. *jamaat*	a religious group or faction
juḥūd	to deny or reject something
kalam	Islamic theology
katā'ib	brigades

khawārij	'seceders', early sectarian group that revolted against the Caliph 'Alī ibn Abī Ṭālib (d. 661/40)
khilāfa	Caliphate
khurūj	rebellion
kufr	unbelief
kufr akbar	major unbelief that causes a person to be expelled from the fold of Islam
kufr aṣghar	minor unbelief
kufr bawāḥ	obvious and clear disbelief that is not open for interpretation or contestation
lūbbyāt	lobbies
ma'āhid al-shar'iyya	*sharī'a*-based institutions
madhhab, pl. *madhāhib*	'a path'; technically, an Islamic legal school of thought
majlis qiyādat al-thawra	council of the leadership of the revolution
majlis al-shūrā	assembly, advisory body
makhzan	privileged peoples from whom Moroccan state officials are recruited
Mālikī	a legal school of Islamic law (*madhhab*) whose origins are attributed to Mālik ibn Anas (d. 795/179)
manhaj	approach, method
maqāṣid	fundamental aims of the *sharī'a*
maṣlaḥa	welfare, common good
māturīdī	one of the major Sunnī theological schools
mīthāq sharaf thawri li-l-katā'ib al-muqātila	code of conduct for the fighting brigades
mudawwana	Moroccan family law
mubāḥ	permissible
mubtadi'	innovator
mujāhidīn	those who engage in *jihad*
murāja'āt	revisions
murtadd	apostate
muṭaawwi'	Saudi religious police

muwaḥḥidūn	those who affirm *tawḥīd*
nashīd	Islamic song
naṣīḥa	advice
naql	transmission
Qur'ān or Qur'an	the Islamic sacred book
Qur'ānic or Qur'anic	relating to the Qur'ān
ṣaḥāba	companion of the Prophet Muhammad
al-Ṣaḥwa al-Islāmiyya	'Islamic Awakening' of post-colonial politicised forms of religions in the latter twentieth century
al-salaf al-ṣāliḥ	pious predecessors; the first three generations of Muslims
al-salafī al-'ilmī	scholastic Salafi
sharī'a or shari'a	the ideal of Islamic law
Shāfi'ī	a legal school of Islamic law (*madhhab*) whose origins are attributed to Muḥammad ibn Idrīs al-Shāfi'ī (d. 820/204)
shahāda	testimony; testimony of faith; martyrdom
shūrā	consultation
siyāsat al-sharī'a	*sharī'a* politics
sunna	practice of the Prophet Muhammad
ta'āruḍ al-adilla	contradicting or conflicting proof-texts
ṭāghūt	one who goes beyond the limits set by God; in the Qur'ān, it refers to the idols that the pagans worshipped; among some modern groups, a pejorative applied to rulers who do not govern by *sharī'a*
takfīr	excommunication; declaring fellow Muslims to be outside the fold of Islam
takfīr al-mu'ayyan	declaring a certain individual a *kāfir*, an apostate or unbeliever
takfīr bi-l-naw'	declaration of *kufr* on specific words or deeds, but not on a specific person
taqlīd	imitation; following a legal school
al-tarbiyya wa-l-taṣfiyya	education and purification

ta'ṣīlī	foundational
tawāfuqiyya	organisational consensus, harmony
tawallī	alliance or loyalty to unbelievers
tawāṣulī	communicative teachings
tawḥīd	oneness of God
tawḥīd al-asma' wa-l-ṣifāt	oneness of Allah's names and attributes
tawḥīd al-rubūbiyya	oneness of Allah's Lordship
tawḥīd al-ulūhiyya	oneness of Allah's Divinity
'ulamā'	Islamic scholars
'umra	optional Muslim pilgrimage to Mecca that can be performed any time of the year; often referred to as lesser Hajj
al-'uqalā'	the sound of mind
uṣūl al-fiqh	Islamic legal theory (the 'roots' of *fiqh*)
wājib	obligatory
al-walā' wa-l-barā'	loyalty and disavowal
wāqi'	reality, the state of things as they are
zakāt or zakat	obligatory charity, one of the five pillars of Islam

SERIES EDITOR'S FOREWORD

Edinburgh Studies in the Globalised Muslim World is a series that focuses on the contemporary transformations of Muslim societies. Globalisation is meant, here, to say that although the Muslim world has always interacted with other societal, religious, imperial or national forces over the centuries, the evolution of these interconnections constantly reshapes Muslim societies. The second half of the twentieth century has been characterised by the increasing number and diversity of exchanges on a global scale bringing people and societies 'closer', for better and for worse. The beginning of the twenty-first century confirmed the increasingly glocalised nature of these interactions and the challenges and opportunities that they bring to existing institutional, social and cultural orders.

This series is not a statement that everything is different in today's brave new world. Indeed, many 'old' ideas and practices still have much currency in the present, and undoubtedly will also have in the future. Rather, the series emphasises how our current globalised condition shapes and mediates how past worldviews and modes of being are transmitted between people and institutions. The contemporary Muslim world is not merely a reflection of past histories, but is also a living process of creating a new order on the basis of what people want, desire, fear and hope. This creative endeavour can transform existing relations for the better, for example by reconsidering the relations between society and the environment. They can equally fan violence and hatred, as illustrated in the reignition of cycles of conflicts over sovereignties, ideologies or resources across the globe.

The series arrives at a challenging time for any inquiry into Muslim societies. The new millennium began inauspiciously with a noticeable spike in transnational and international violence framed in 'civilisational' terms. A decade of 'war of terror' contributed to entrench negative mutual perceptions across the globe while reinforcing essentialist views. The ensuing decade hardly improved the situation, with political and territorial conflicts multiplying in different parts of the Muslim world, and some of the most violent groups laid claim to the idea of a global caliphate to justify themselves. Yet, a focus on trajectories of violence gives a distorted picture of the evolution of Muslim societies and their relations with the rest of the world. This series is very much about the 'what else' that is happening as we move further into the twenty-first century.

Masooda Bano's edited collection, *Salafi Social and Political Movements*, sheds a much welcome light on the crucial processes that shape the contemporary trajectories of Salafi actors. Collectively, the essays presented in this work provide a set of interconnected insights articulating a three-pronged approach to the study of Salafism. Conceptually, this approach includes a historical and textual perspective on the core elements of discourse of these movements. This outlook is then complemented by a socio-political investigation of the praxis of these actors, mainly through an investigation of grassroots activism. Lastly but crucially comes a thematic focus that helps the reader contextualise better some of the more debated aspects of contemporary Salafism, namely the opposition and competition between different types of movements and the issue of violence framed as jihadism.

Individually, the chapters written by an excellent team of established and upcoming researchers provide a wealth of empirical material and rich analysis of the different actors and processes. The investigations of the evolution of Salafi thinking from an early Wahhabi core provide very useful historical perspectives that help the reader understand how the contemporary debates are shaped and why some issues are particularly problematic to solve today. Those focusing on the contemporary grassroots dynamics of these movements in Morocco, Egypt and Kuwait provide extremely useful illustrations and explanations of how a globalised Salafi discourse can be selectively embedded in very different parts of the Arab and Muslim world. The final focus on the role of violence in shaping the options of Salafi actors, in relation to one another and other societal forces in the post Arab uprisings context in particular, outlines the complexities of the use of violence by these movements.

Understanding the historicity of the answers provided by Salafism is crucial to appreciating the continuing relevance and influence of this current of thought and model of activism today. Their multifaceted discourses and practices are an important factor in the transformation of Muslim-majority and Muslim-minority societies. Considering both national and transnational dynamics, this collection provides the kind of interconnected perspectives and analyses that will enable the reader to fully appreciate the complexities of Salafi movements. By highlighting the interconnected evolution of the creed and the praxis of Salafism, the book constitutes a most useful foundation for future studies into these new globalised dynamics.

Frédéric Volpi
Chair in the Politics of the Muslim World
The University of Edinburgh

INTRODUCTION
SALAFISM TODAY – A BREAK WITH THE PAST

Masooda Bano

In October 2017, the Crown Prince of Saudi Arabia, Muhammad bin Salman, made a call for a return to 'moderate Islam'.[1] The statement came just a few weeks after the announcement of policy shifts in favour of social liberalisation, such as granting women the right to drive and the opening up of cinema halls.[2] Widely covered in the Western media, the announcement was greeted with applause as well as cynicism. Many, including those in senior ranks of the British government, interpreted it as a proof of the Crown Prince's ideological commitment to reform the Saudi state and promote social liberalisation;[3] cynics read it as a calculated move on his part to improve Saudi Arabia's image in the West.[4] Yet, despite attributing differing motives for this announcement, both sides shared an interpretation of the changes as the Saudi state's acknowledgement of the failure of Salafism. Traditionally criticised for enforcing extreme social conservatism, since the attacks on the Twin Towers in New York in 2001 Salafism has been subjected to a much graver allegation – namely, that of fuelling global Islamic militancy.[5] As we shall see in Chapter 1, for the other Sunni Muslim groups Salafism has historically been problematic due to its narrow notion of *tawḥīd* (oneness of God) which makes it easy to declare *takfīr* (excommunication; declaring fellow Muslims to be outside the fold of Islam) and impose textual rigidity, which is viewed as fuelling both sectarian violence and jihad, while simultaneously promoting a very dull and dry mode of living. It is therefore not surprising that a call for a return to moderate Islam by the future Saudi king was thus automatically interpreted as a move away from Salafism.

Reality, however, is more complex. As we shall see in Chapter 2, for the Crown Prince the call for a return to moderate Islam was in reality a condemnation of political Islam, the *Ṣaḥwa* movement, which had established roots in Saudi Arabia from the 1970s onwards.[6] However, even though the Crown Prince did not disavow Salafism, the conclusion drawn by Western observers was not entirely off the mark: Salafism as associated with Saudi Arabia is in retreat; the rigidity long associated with it is giving way to internal debate whereby areas of former consensus are now open to questioning. This shift is a product of the rapidly changing socio-economic realities within Saudi Arabia.[7] Not only is the Saudi state moving towards social liberalisation, thereby reversing many of the policies that led to Salafism being branded as a particularly rigid tradition: some scholars within the tradition have started to debate core theological positions formerly viewed as part of the established consensus. Furthermore, as we will see in Part II of this volume, Salafi *da'wa* movements in other countries, long viewed as the products of Saudi patronage, have by now developed vigorous local roots. The leaders of these movements are today providing strong intellectual leadership, limiting reliance on Salafi religious material exported from the Kingdom.

The chapters in this volume present timely insights into developments within contemporary Salafism and the changing priorities of the Saudi state, long held responsible for the emergence of Salafi networks around the globe. It is argued that at the heart of Salafism rests a deeply compelling ideal for a believing Muslim: the need to follow the first three generations of pious Muslims (*al-salaf al-ṣāliḥ*).[8] It is this basic principle that makes it an intellectually powerful movement capable of winning adherents, with or without Saudi support. However, as history has shown, all powerful religious movements have to adapt to the changing context if they are to retain adherents, and Salafism is no exception. The changing sensibilities of the Muslim populace in response to globalisation and socio-economic modernisation are obliging Salafism as a global Islamic reform movement to engage in a visible shift towards theological, social and/or political liberalisation; this shift in popular sensibilities is also the key force propelling changes in Saudi state policies. This volume captures this opening up of space for a greater degree of argumentation and debate than what was previously possible within the Salafi movements.

However, the volume also demonstrates that this opening up of space is not leading to a decline in jihadi mobilisation. The surge in Salafi-jihadi groups in the Middle East since the Arab Spring uprisings of 2011, examined in Part III of this volume, demonstrates that, in line with earlier evidence, jihadi mobilisation is more a product of strategic interests and contemporary political opportunities, and that Salafi Wahhabi teachings *per se* cannot be held responsible for inspiring movements such as al-Qaida or ISIS, or the array of jihadi groups that have emerged in countries such as Syria and Libya since the Arab Spring. The chapters in this volume propel the debate further by moving beyond the framework of strategic interest versus ideology to analyse jihadi mobilisation and highlight the need to understand its nuances: namely, how jihadi groups apply Wahhabi Salafi reasoning in order to legitimise jihad in ways that actually contradict the core teachings of official Saudi scholars; how the actual organisational structure of a jihadi organisation has a direct bearing on its ability to survive in a challenging context; how a complex mix of religious and political variables leads to violence among jihadi groups, undermining their collective mission (as seen in the case of Syria); and how the erosion of a credible political Islam movement to challenge state oppression can create space for Salafi jihadi movements.

To appreciate the core thesis of this volume – namely, that we are witnessing a visible increase in internal debate, and adaptation to local context, within Salafism – this introduction presents a detailed analysis of its origin and subsequent emergence as the most powerful and puritanical Islamic reform movement of the twentieth century; its core principles; its association with the Saudi state and Wahhabism; and its critics' core concerns. A detailed historical analysis of this movement is essential for an appreciation of the reasons why the old assumptions about Salafism need to be revisited today.

Salafism: Origins, Methods and Association with Wahhabism

Salafism is one of the most influential and talked-about Islamic movements today, yet its origin is very recent.[9] It was only in the 1970s that it began to become visible on the global stage. Its critics attribute its success entirely to Saudi oil wealth, which enabled the Saudi state to fund Salafi mosque and *daʿwa* networks around the world. Sponsoring the global Salafi networks is argued to help the Saudi royal family consolidate its soft power as the leader of the Muslim world.[10] Such readings are, however, simplistic and undermine the appeal of the Salafi *daʿwa*, its core theological beliefs and methodological principles.[11] Particularly problematic is that many of these claims assert a direct connection between Saudi Arabia, Salafi teachings and jihadi networks. Salafism, however, is a complex movement; as is the case with all influential movements, it is highly pluralistic. Salafi theology has inspired the very quietist and non-political Islamic movements involved primarily in *daʿwa* and personal piety (scholastic Salafis or Madkhalis), as well as those who have engaged in politics and the capture of state power with a view to imposing *sharīʿa* (political Salafis such as Surooris or Sahawis in Saudi Arabia, or the al-Nour Party in Egypt). Furthermore, Salafi interpretations of the Qur'ān and *ḥadīth* have been used by groups such as al-Qaida and ISIS (a tendency known as 'jihadi Salafism').[12] The differing approaches of al-Qaida and ISIS,[13] both espousing ideological commitment to Salafism, and the competition within Salafi jihadi groups in contexts such as Syria in themselves demonstrate the plurality within the movement. It is therefore important to examine the complex origins of Salafism, the distinctive features of its method as well as its creed in comparison with other Sunni groups, and the social, economic, and political life choices that it prescribes for its followers, in order to appreciate why this volume contends that we need to study Salafism through a new lens.

The Method of Reasoning

Much has been written about the distinctions between Salafism and other mainstream Sunni schools, but most scholars point to its emphasis on creedal purity.[14] However, equally important to an understanding of the distinctive aspects of Salafism compared with other Sunni groups is its method of reasoning in order to derive specific laws.[15] During the first three centuries of Islam, Muslim scholars focused on developing detailed methods to translate the principles of *sharīʿa* into specific laws that answer everyday questions.[16] By the tenth century, four Sunni *madhāhib* (schools of law) came to command an important position: *Shāfiʿī*, *Mālikī*, *Ḥanbalī* and *Ḥanafī*.[17] Each school evolved around the work of its founding scholar. Successive generations of scholars built on the work of the founding scholar to develop a distinctive methodological tradition in order to provide specific legal responses to emerging questions in the spirit of the Qur'ān and *ḥadīth*.[18] The emergence of these four Sunni schools of law led to the practice of *taqlīd*, whereby subsequent generations of scholars of each *madhhab* placed heavy emphasis on respecting the work of the earlier scholars in that tradition. There was at the same time a strong tradition of mutual respect among scholars of different *madhāhib*.[19] *Madhāhib*, as Tim Winter[20] notes, were developed as a science of Islamic jurisprudence (*uṣūl al-fiqh*) to provide consistent mechanisms for resolving any conflicts in a way that ensured that the basic ethos of Islam was not violated. Arguing that the term *ta'āruḍ al-adilla* (mutual contradiction of proof-texts) is one of the most sensitive and complex of all Muslim legal concepts, he notes: 'The *'ulamā'* of *uṣūl* recognised as their starting assumption that conflicts between the revealed texts were no more than conflicts of interpretation, and could not reflect inconsistencies in the Lawgiver's message as conveyed by the Prophet (PBUH)'.[21] Thus, the scholars within each *madhhab* focused on developing specific methods of reasoning for an interpretation of the law. He further notes how, as the *madhāhib* matured, an attitude of toleration and mutual respect among the scholars of the four schools became the norm. Along with it came an acknowledgement of the importance of respecting the role of scholarly classes who had specialised knowledge of the text and the language, as required of the *madhāhib*.

Compared to this emphasis on following the *madhāhib*, which was popular among other Sunni scholars (see the discussion concerning traditional scholars in the next chapter), the Salafi method argues for going back directly to the foundational texts, the Qur'ān and *ḥadīth*, instead of engaging with the dense body of literature associated with the four *madhhabs*.[22] In particular, it is against the idea of *taqlīd*, on the grounds that it leads to a blind following of the scholars in a given tradition. For the Salafis, direct engagement with the foundational texts and practices and sayings of the Prophet is key to regaining the lost glory of Islam. A return to the practice of the first three generations, as well as to learning from that period and the Qur'ān and *ḥadīth*, is deemed critical to putting Muslim societies on the straight path. The global success of Salafi *da'wa* illustrates the appeal of such a methodological approach.

Noting that the designation 'Salafi' is prestigious among Muslims because it claims an association with the oldest and thus most authentic version of Islam, Bernard Haykel[23] notes:

> Rather, it is Salafism's claim to religious certainty that explains a good deal of its appeal, and its seemingly limitless ability to cite scripture to back these up. A typical Salafi argument is that Salafis, unlike other Muslims, rely exclusively on sound proof-texts from revelations as the basis for their views, and they add the relevant verses or traditions every time they issue a judgment or opinion'.[24]

Its critics contend that such an approach opens the door for misinterpretation of Qur'ānic verses and *ḥadīth*. This, for instance, is one of the main reasons why Salafi method is claimed to fuel jihad: it is argued that jihadi organisations take Qur'ānic verses endorsing jihad out of context to legitimise their right to declare war and use violent methods which, according to traditional legal schools, violate Islamic principles. Chapter 1 records such critiques of Salafism by other Sunni groups in detail.

Saudia Arabia and the Emergence of Salafism

Contrary to the popular assumption that Saudi Arabia exported Salafism to the rest of the Muslim world, the reality is that the Salafi method of reasoning came to Saudi Arabia from outside:[25] from neighbouring Middle Eastern countries and South Asia. Wahhabi scholars do, in fact, follow the *Ḥanbalī madhhab*;[26] the adoption of the Salafi identity by the Saudi state was thus gradual. From inside the Middle East, the Salafi methodological influence came primarily from Egypt, and ironically from the work of Islamic modernists, in particular the work of Rashid Rida (1865–1935).[27] Holding the traditional *'ulamā'* responsible for stagnation within Islamic thought, modernist scholars such as Rashid Rida and his teacher, the famous Muhammad Abduh (1849–1905), argued for direct engagement with the Qur'ān and *Sunna* in order to find answers to the demands of the modern realities in which Muslims found themselves under colonial rule; they were against the practice of *taqlīd* and highlighted instead the importance of *ijtihād*.[28] In South Asia, a similar emphasis on direct engagement with foundational texts was advanced by the followers of *Ahl-i Ḥadīth*, a South Asian school of Islamic thought that places strong emphasis on the study of *ḥadīth* and is closely associated with

Wahhabism.[29] Unlike the Egyptian modernists, the *Ahl-i Ḥadīth* scholars were particularly conservative and literalist in their engagement with the text.[30] Both sides were influenced, however, by a shared concern about the decline of Islam, the challenges of modernity and colonialism, and the need to revive the glory of foundational Muslim societies.[31]

A young nation in the 1940s, with a weak educational infrastructure, Saudi Arabia easily absorbed these intellectual influences from abroad. Saudi scholars who had studied in Cairo or India in the late nineteenth or early twentieth century brought some of these influences back to Saudi Arabia.[32] Their influence was consolidated during the 1940s and 1960s when King Faisal gave refuge to many Islamic modernists and Muslim Brotherhood members fleeing from persecution at home.[33] As Saudi Arabia was at this time also starting to invest in the establishment of higher-education infrastructure, these migrating scholars secured senior positions within the newly emerging Saudi higher-education sector.[34] The International Islamic University in Medina, founded in 1961 and today seen as a primary base for promoting Salafi Wahhabi teachings among Muslim students from around the world, itself was shaped largely under the influence of prominent scholars from other Muslim countries.[35].

Some of these scholars, such as the *Ahl-i Ḥadīth 'ulamā'*, as mentioned earlier, had a natural affinity with the Wahhabi teachings, and thus the co-operation between them and the Wahhabi *'ulamā'* was seamless. For the Islamic modernists and political Islamists, the co-operation with the Saudi royal family had more complicated foundations. Modernist scholars, such as Rashid Rida, harboured genuine respect for the Saudi royal family, because it was more independent of Western influences than were the rulers in the other Middle Eastern countries.[36] These scholars were, however, critical of the literalist interpretation of the Qur'ān and *ḥadīth* by the Saudi Wahhabi *'ulamā'*.[37] Their collaboration with the Saudi state was thus premised on an optimistic assumption of their ability to counter the influence of the more conservative Wahhabi scholars.[38] On their part, the Saudi royal family opened the doors to these scholars, partly out of a sense of Muslim brotherhood and the tribal culture of hospitality. It was, however, also conscious that involving Muslim scholars from other regions in the newly evolving Saudi educational sector would help to win broad-based legitimacy, given the concerns shared by many Sunni scholars from different traditions about the strictness and rigidity that they all associated with the Wahhabi creedal beliefs.[39] Thus, what we understand today as being distinctive about the Salafi method of reasoning cannot be attributed to Saudi Arabia. In order to understand why today the terms Wahhabism and Salafism are mostly used interchangeably, and why Salafism is seen to be primarily a Saudi Arabian religious tradition, we need to understand how eventually it was the insistence of the Wahhabi *'ulamā'* on creedal purity, rather than the Islamic modernists' emphasis on reason-based engagement with the core texts, that came to dominate the Salafi writings and teachings. For this we first need a brief introduction to Wahhabism.

The Equating of Salafism with Wahhabism

Wahhabism refers to the eighteenth-century religious reformist movement led by Muhammad ibn 'Abd al-Wahab (1703–92), a Saudi religious scholar from the Najd region who forged a religious-political alliance with the House of Saud, one of the political clans in eighteenth-century Arabia. It was this alliance that eventually led to the establishment of modern Saudi Arabia in 1932.[40] Ibn 'Abd al-Wahhab was born in Najd into a scholarly family. After receiving education in 'Uyayna, a village near Riyadh, he began to travel to other regions, including Basra and Hijaz.[41] On his return home he started preaching an austere form of Islam which challenged many of the local religious practices. Central to his teaching was a strict notion of *tawḥīd* (divine oneness, or monotheism), which is the foundation of the Islamic faith.[42] Drawing on the work of Ahmad ibn Taymiyya (1263–1328), Wahhab argued that *tawḥīd* demands that faith in the oneness of God should not be treated as merely a matter of inner belief, which was the approach of classical Islamic scholars: it must be matched by action.[43] Making action integral to the notion of *tawḥīd* had critical implications: it made it easy to excommunicate fellow Muslims regarded as failing to observe the required level of ritual purity. Such a notion of *tawḥīd*, whereby observable actions and not just inner belief determine one's conviction in *tawḥīd*, in turn had other, more practical implications for the role of the state in regulating personal piety: the state acquired the authority to punish those who were seen as not observing their religious obligations, such as reciting the five daily prayers or giving *zakāt*, or those who were viewed to be indulging in practices that violate the oneness of God, such as venerating the saints.[44]

In return for the state taking responsibility for creating a social milieu conducive to the observation of individual piety, the religious scholars were to pledge their complete loyalty to it. Muhammad ibn 'Abd al-Wahhab's austere notion of *tawḥīd* thus had important implications not just for notions of individual piety, but for shaping the relationship between state and society; religion became an active part of the public sphere and also a major source of political legitimisation. It made excommunication (declaring *takfīr*) of fellow Muslims easier; it reduced the individual authority of the believer by giving the state the responsibility for regulating individual piety; and it encouraged political quietism in favour of authoritarian states as long as they provided the right societal framework for religious values to be upheld.

The teachings of ibn 'Abd al-Wahhab initially met with stiff resistance from the local Saudi scholars of the time, including his own brother as well as the local political authorities.[45] However, they found support within the House of Saud.[46] The resulting alliance proved mutually beneficial, as the Wahhabi use of *takfīr* enabled the Wahhabi scholars to endorse the wars that the House of Saud waged against other tribes and clans over two centuries, ultimately leading to the establishment of present-day Saudi Arabia in 1932. Madawi al-Rasheed maintains that Wahhabi *'ulamā'* used *takfīr* as a social-political tool in order to control social and political deviance, and to expand 'the political realm under the pretext of correcting the blasphemy of others'.[47] Drawing on the works of early Wahhabi scholars, including ibn 'Abd al-Wahhab's statements, she contends that these scholars viewed Muslims of their time as polytheists and thus in need of reform.[48] She also maintains that this process of *takfīr* was often driven by specific historical and political interests, rather than by theological concerns. While scholars agree that after the establishment of Saudi Arabia in 1932 the Saudi state, as well as the Wahhabi *'ulamā'*, became very cautious about the use of *takfīr* to legitimise war in order to gain authority in the eyes of Muslims from different Islamic traditions, the reason why modern jihadism is attributed to Salafism lies in that it is argued to draw on the very same Wahhabi teachings of *tawḥīd* and *takfīr* as were deployed by Wahhabi *'ulamā'* in the early period. As Maher notes, . . .

> *Takfīr* can seem like an archaic concept because it draws a line against those deemed to have left the Islamic faith, either voluntarily or through an act.

> For the global jihad movement it has become a valuable tool for the protection of Islam, a means of expelling those from the faith who are thought to be subverting it from within. As such, in its current constructions, the concept is used to license intra-Muslim violence – particularly in high sectarian environments.[49]

A related idea also attributed to Wahhabism that is deployed actively by jihadis to legitimise jihad against Muslims and non-Muslim targets alike is that of *al-walāʾ wa-l-barāʾ*. Put simply, this concept argues that one is a friend of those who are pious Muslims and against all those who are non-Muslims or Muslims who do not follow the strict ideal of *tawḥīd* as operationalised by ibn ʿAbd al-Wahhab. Maher explains:

> In its political and military contexts, the concept of *al-walāʾ wa-al-barāʾ* operates in a similar fashion to *takfīr*, as a tool of 'in-group' control which draws a line against those deemed to be outsiders. It forms a distinct delineation between the Salafi-Jihadi constructions of Islam and everything else, forming a protective carapace around the faith which guards against impurity and inauthenticity. Put this way, *al-walāʾ wa-al-barāʾ* is integral to the protection of Islam itself, just as *takfīr* is also used as a protective tool.[50]

As to why these core tenets of Wahhabi creed eventually became synonymous with Salafism instead of with the works of the Islamic modernist scholars, the answer rests in the unexpected outcomes of the Saudi state's decision to give refuge to Islamic modernist scholars and members of the Muslim Brotherhood from the 1960s onwards. The initial visits by Islamic modernists, such as Rashid Rida, to Saudi Arabia were followed by an influx of many Muslim Brotherhood members from the Middle East who were being persecuted by regimes in their home countries. Their political orientation led them to initiate political activism within Saudi Arabia, which particularly influenced the university-educated Saudi youth. This led to the birth of political Islam in Saudi Arabia (*al-Ṣaḥwa al-Islāmiyya*, Islamic Awakening), which, as explained later in this introduction, in the eyes of the Saudi royal family constitutes the real cause of religious radicalisation. An entirely unexpected outcome of the Saudi royal family's accommodation of the modernists and political Islamists, the *Ṣaḥwa* movement became a threat to the Saudi royal family as well as to the authority of the Wahhabi scholars. In order to de-legitimise the political Islamists, the Wahhabi scholars and the Saudi state actively tried to project themselves as the true guardians of the tradition of the *Salaf*.

This was particularly so as the label given by other Sunni groups to Saudi Islam was that of 'Wahhabi', which implied that Muhammad ibn 'Abd al-Wahhab had introduced a new school of Islamic law and, thus, is a *mubtadi'*(innovator). To the Wahhabi scholars, 'Wahhabism' was thus a derogatory term. Salafism, on the other hand, helped to assert a broad-based legitimacy, due to its claim to be emulating the first three pious generations of Muslims. Thus, in an attempt to reassert their religious authority, starting from the 1970s, the Wahhabi scholars and the Saudi state actively worked to claim the label 'Salafi'. They did so successfully by publishing writings that presented Wahhabi beliefs and practices as being according to the Salaf; Wahhabi *'ulamā'* were included among the biographies of the Salafs; primary religious texts were re-edited to highlight a historical link between the Salafi tradition and Wahhabism;[51] and foreign authors who wrote Salafi works with a pro-Wahhabi perspective were patronised.[52] It is due to this success that today Salafism is synonymous with Wahhabism and not with the work of the Islamic modernists or political Islamists who in the middle of the twentieth century actively self-appropriated the term.

Salafism and the Legitimisation of Jihad: The Saudi Perspective

As outlined in the preceding section, the Wahhabi conception of *tawḥīd* that makes it easy to ex-communicate Muslims or to declare war on non-believers, combined with the Salafi method of reasoning, is credited with helping jihadi groups to legitimise their actions.[53] Within Saudi Arabia, this attribution of Islamic militancy to the Wahhabi/Salafi way of thinking is, however, contested. The blame for promoting Islamic militancy is instead placed on the Muslim Brotherhood and the writings of its key ideologue, Syed Qutb. As argued in detail by al-Saud in Chapter 7, this position highlights the need for understanding how, among the Wahhabi followers, the teachings of the movement are divided between *ta'ṣīlī* (foundational) and *tawāṣulī* (communicative) teachings: the former consists of statements and declarations of creed, jurisprudence and rituals, through either authorship or annotations, and the latter comprises the many replies, epistles and discussions that engaged numerous past scholars of the movement. It is argued that the Wahhabi *manhaj* (path or approach) is captured in the former, and the study of these teachings shows that organisations such as ISIS do not fit within it. Among the differences highlighted are the fact that, unlike ISIS, Saudi Wahhabis have never aspired to, or advocated, the establishment of a caliphate; nor have the Wahhabis used the level of brutality displayed by Islamic State. In this view, it is not the Wahhabi writings but those of Syed Qutb[54] that help the current jihadis to legitimise their violence. In particular, reference is made to these organisations' practice of attacking leaders of Muslim states by drawing on the concept of *takfīr* in ways that run entirely contrary to the teachings of the Wahhabi scholars.

For the Wahhabi scholars, the notions of *ḥākimiyya* and what constitutes *kufr* (disbelief) have remained largely unchanged: in terms of *ḥākimiyya*, the scholars have maintained that the state can put in place new regulatory laws to meet the needs of the time, provided that they do not violate the *sharīʿa*; and as for *takfīr* on those who do not rule according to God's revelation and thus commit *kufr*, they argue for acknowledging *iʿtiqād* or *istiḥlāl* (the belief or conviction on the part of the ruler or legislator that a man-made law, while seemingly contradicting *sharīʿa,* may actually be a better choice and is in fact permissible in Islam) or *kufr aṣghar* (minor unbelief), neither of which should justify expelling the ruler from the realm of Islam. Al-Saud's chapter also emphasises the importance of appreciating the difference between two different types of *takfīr*: *takfīr bi-l-nawʿ* (declaration of *kufr* on specific words or deeds) and *takfīr al-muʿayyan* (declaration of a certain individual as *kāfir*, an apostate or unbeliever). While the former is argued to be largely uncontroversial among past and present Wahhabi scholars, the latter's application is seen to be very complicated among Wahhabi scholars, who argue that one cannot practise *takfīr al-muʿayyan* until all conditions (such as intent and free choice) are present and all barriers (such as ignorance or error) are absent, given that it can lead to a death sentence. They thus maintain that it is not an individual who can declare *takfīr*, but the ruler or the judiciary. If someone believes that a certain individual has committed an act of *kufr,* or apostasy, the only thing they should, or can, do is to disavow the deed in their heart or, if it is possible to do so without causing further harm, by their words; it is never the responsibility of the individuals to go beyond that and apply the rulings of *takfir*.

In Part III of this volume, we will see how there is some truth to both sides of the story. We will, however, also see how understanding the role of textual justifications only partly illuminates the process of jihadi mobilisation. While jihadi movements might invoke religious texts to win legitimacy in the eyes of their followers, their existence is equally due to explicit strategic interests or political grievances.

Salafism Today

Against this historical evolution and understanding of Salafism, the chapters in this volume highlight the need to appreciate that Salafism as a movement is undergoing a critical transformation. This is a result of the changing socio-economic dynamics within Saudi Arabia but equally a product of societal shifts within other Muslim countries and the growing independence of Salafi movements therein. While in some countries, self-identified Salafi movements might still adhere to the work of the Saudi scholars and the patronage of the Saudi state, in other countries, both in the Muslim-majority context and among Muslims in the West, Salafi movements and individual scholars are becoming quite independent of these influences, producing a rich literature of their own. The chapters in this volume are divided into three parts, in order to consider how the Salafi Wahhabi way of thinking and the rigidity associated with it is today under pressure at home and abroad. Together they show the malleability of Salafism. Salafis claim to represent timeless truth, but they have to operate in the specific socio-political contexts they inhabit. Top-down social opening in Saudi Arabia, bottom-up mobilisation in the Arab uprising, mobilisation for jihad in countries like Syria and a growing influence of globalisation on the attitudes of the Muslim youth is making Salafism open up to competing discourses.

Part I of this volume captures the shifts in Salafi thought as visible in the work of some reformist Salafi scholars who are arguing for social liberalisation, or greater political freedoms, and/or who are raising questions about foundational theological debates, including the very concept of *tawḥīd*, which is the bedrock of Wahhabi theology. The section also maps the socio-economic changes within Saudi Arabia that have made the ongoing social liberalisation an inevitable outcome, while also presenting a more detailed analysis of the challenges that other Sunni groups present to Salafism. Part II presents examples of Salafi *da'wa* movements in different country contexts to show how in a few places there is continued reliance on Saudi Arabia to provide intellectual leadership and finances, while in other contexts the Salafi movements are well-positioned to actually export Salafi ideals, due to a strong indigenous Salafi intellectual leadership and writings. Thus, irrespective of changes within Saudi Arabia, these movements can be self-sustaining. The chapters in this section also show how the traditional division between Salafi *da'wa* and political Salafism have become blurred in the Middle East since the Arab Spring. Part III in turn considers the connections between Salafism and jihad, to highlight how the links have always been tenuous, and how we need to appreciate that the political context and organisational structure, combined with a twisted application of religious reasoning, facilitate recruitment for jihadi organisations. Attributing jihadism to Salafi modes of thinking or Saudi funding is thus counter-productive. Such an approach avoids focusing on the real political, organisational and strategic factors that shape the working of jihadi groups.

Part I: Changes in Salafi Thought

The three chapters in Part I map the new debates emerging within the Salafi scholarly sphere that are critically examining issues which until recently were regarded as settled: social conservativeness; a narrow definition of *tawḥīd*; and loyalty to the ruler. While the work of Salafi scholars, such as Salman al-Awda, who led the *Ṣaḥwa* movement starting from the 1970s, is already familiar to many, the recent questioning by a prominent Salafi scholar of the Salafi conception of *tawḥīd*, the foundation of its theology and the Saudi state's own push towards social liberalism are marking a major shift from the past. The chapters thus demonstrate how the pressure for reform is coming from within the state as well as from within the ranks of the respected Salafi scholars. To fully understand the implications of the ongoing shifts within Salafism, it is useful to understand first why Salafism has been challenged across time by Sunni groups and continues to be challenged even today. Thus, in the first chapter in this section, Hazim Fouad captures the critiques of Salafism as voiced by various Sunni groups. Based on interviews and writings of scholars viewed as representative of traditional Sunni *madhāhib*, as well as of Sufi *ṭarīqahs* and Islamic modernists, this chapter recaptures why the Salafi Wahhabi way of thinking is to date viewed as an aberration by other Sunni groups, and why these groups insist on labelling Saudi Salafism as a modern phenomenon not representative of the authentic Islamic scholarly tradition. Developing understanding of these traditional critiques of Salafism is key to appreciating why the ongoing shifts recorded in this volume are important.

In Chapter 2, I build on the analysis that I presented in *Modern Islamic Authority and Social Change*, to map the changing societal dynamics within Saudi Arabia that are prompting the Saudi state to promote greater social freedoms. Drawing on fieldwork in Saudi Arabia, this chapter shows how a complex set of socio-economic changes are triggering the ongoing shifts. In particular, this chapter considers the views of the educated urban youth (men as well as women), who are seen to constitute the primary support base for the ongoing social-reform agenda of Crown Prince Muhammad bin Salman. The chapter also focuses on the work of two contemporary Salafi scholars, one operating within Saudi Arabia, Hatim al-Awni, and the other based in the USA, Yasir Qadhi, who each have a strong individual following among Salafi Muslims and who are arguing for greater individual autonomy in the area of theology as well as everyday life choices for Muslims. This chapter considers the arguments advanced by these scholars in favour of greater social freedoms or greater individual autonomy in interpreting religious obligations than what has historically been the norm within the Saudi Salafi tradition.

In Chapter 3, Usaama al-Azami considers the work of Salman al-Awda (b. 1956) and Muhammad al-Hasan Wuld al-Dadaw (b. 1963) to illustrate how these prominent Salafi scholars legitimised the notion of political rebellion from within a Salafi framework in the context of the Arab Spring. The chapter shows how these scholars counter the traditional position of the official Saudi Salafi establishment, which argues for obedience to the ruler at all costs, in order to avoid the risk of *fitna* (civil strife). Al-Azami shows how these scholars use the same Islamic sources as those used by the official Saudi Salafi establishment – but in defence of the public's right to engage in political protests against unrepresentative regimes. Not surprisingly, the Saudi state has shown less tolerance for these scholars than for those arguing in defence of greater theological freedom or social liberalisation, the latter of which is in fact in line with the Saudi state's own agenda. Thus, while the ongoing changes are partly triggered by the Saudi state, there are also new discourses and debates emerging due to self-reflection by prominent Salafi scholars.

Part II: Salafi Movements on the Ground

The chapters in Part II present case-studies of Salafi *da'wa* movements in three Muslim-majority countries. These chapters cover contexts where Salafi groups are still reliant on Saudi support, as well as contexts where they are quite independent. By presenting detailed studies of Salafi movements in these Muslim-majority countries, the volume shows how the leaders of some of these movements are producing publications and religious material that have a wide readership in Salafi circles, not only in their own countries, but also among Saudis. The removal of Saudi support might weaken the Salafi groups that are reliant on it, but Salafism as a movement has developed strong indigenous roots in most countries. Further, we see also a great deal of pragmatism on the part of the leaders to expand the scope of their activities when opportunities become available: thus, in the post-Arab Spring context Salafi *da'wa* movements turned to politics in ways not traditionally associated with them. We also see that even in other contexts, just like the Saudi state, Salafi movements are becoming conscious of the need to move away from the textual rigidity that historically marked Saudi Salafi reasoning.

In Chapter 4, Guy Eyre explores how, even in the case of Morocco, quietist Salafi groups attempted to take advantage of the space that emerged in the political arena, even if it proved to be only a momentary phenomenon. The chapter shows how, in response to the nationwide protests in Morocco on 20 February 2011, in order to avert further mass protests the state tried to release some of the quietist Salafis from prison and invited others back from exile. Using year-long ethnographic fieldwork in Marrakech and lectures available on social media, Eyre considers the case of two Salafi quietist scholars who came out in support of political protests and endorsed Islamic parties, contrary to their pre-2011 positions, thereby demonstrating tactical acumen on their part to expand the scope of their activities. However, the chapter also shows that they reverted to their former positions when the grip of the state and their patrons, especially the Saudi state, tightened.

In Chapter 5, Neil Russell traces the responses of Salafi networks in

Egypt since the Arab Spring, to examine why al-Sisi's government persecuted Ansar al-Sunna, a quietist Salafi *da'wa* network, while it did not target political Salafi movements such as the al-Nour Party and Dawa Salafiyya. Noting that the latter two movements avoid persecution because of their support for the *coup d'état* of 3 July 2013, Russell argues that Ansar al-Sunna became a target of state oppression because, while staying out of electoral politics, it did support Islamic political activism, irrespective of party orientations. Ansar al-Sunna sought to promote the 'collective identity' of the Islamic movement above individual factional interests, to further the electoral prospects of both the Muslim Brotherhood and the Salafi alliance. By supporting this broad-based Islamic activism, it posed a threat to the al-Sisi regime in a way that the al-Nour Party and Dawa Salafiyya did not. Ansar al-Sunna effectively became a political interest group representing Egypt's Islamic movement in the electoral sphere. This does demonstrate that, while we have seen increasing polarisation among Salafi groups since the Arab Spring, there are some who have had the vision to look beyond narrow group interests and forge an alliance for strengthening the defence of Islam against the secular forces in society. These groups have also shown the pragmatism necessary to change their quietist orientation and engage in politics when opportunities have become available.

In Chapter 6, Kristin Diwan considers the Hizb al-Umma Party in Kuwait and situates it within the current regional politics of the Middle East. The analysis in this chapter draws on the writings and activities of Hakim al-Mutairi, the leader of the Umma Party. It elaborates on the expansion of his ideas and the Umma network into Saudi Arabia. It also maps the role of the Umma Party in other regional political tensions, especially Syria. Among other things, the chapter illustrates how Salafi writers and figures outside Saudi Arabia have influenced Salafi networks within Saudi Arabia and beyond. The flow of Salafi discourse has never been uni-directional: Saudi Arabia has imported Salafi discourses evolving in other Muslim countries as much as it has exported them.

Part III: Salafi Jihadism

The chapters in this section show how Salafi jihadism has proliferated across the Middle East since the Arab Spring, as many quietist Salafi movements have moved into politics or even espoused jihad, troubled by state oppression in contexts such as Syria. The chapters in this section, however, record a great deal of inter-group competition within Salafi jihadi groups, whereby strategic interests, as opposed to ideology alone, shape their operational strategies. As a result, in contexts such as Syria, Salafi jihadi groups are competing with each other rather than joining hands, thereby undermining their ability to focus on the actual enemy. Further, the volume shows that the weakening of the Muslim Brotherhood has also contributed to the rise of Salafi jihadism, which has often moved in to fill the gap.

In Chapter 7, Abdullah al-Saud presents a detailed critique of the idea that Wahhabi-Salafi teachings are responsible for modern global jihadi networks. Comparing the position of ISIS with the Wahhabi *manhaj*, al-Saud demonstrates major contradictions between the two. The chapter presents a detailed analysis of the traditional Saudi position that attributes the birth of modern Islamic militancy to the Muslim Brotherhood, rather than to the Wahhabi creed. Focusing on the political quietism associated with Wahhabi scholars, the chapter illustrates how the principles of *takfir* have been misappropriated by the jihadi groups to legitimise jihad against Muslim rulers. The chapter thus presents the counter-narrative to the popular perception that links Wahhabi creed and Saudi funding to the spread of jihadi networks. It is important to note that to some the analysis presented in this chapter could appear like an apology piece for the Saudi regime. The reason for its inclusion is that most researchers and students do not understand the difference between Salafi jihadi thought as advanced by the Salafi Wahhabi scholars and how it is operationalised by the numerous jihadi groups. This volume is thus distinct in attempting to present both sides of the debate.

In Chapter 8, Tore Hamming complicates the role of religious conviction in mobilisation for jihad, by asking why Salafi jihadis kill each other. Despite being inspired by the same ideology, they end up engaging in internal fights that weaken them. Existing literature indicates that extreme ideologies or strategic differences are responsible for generating inter-group conflict. Hamming, however, notes that since 2013 inter-group conflicts are evident even among jihadi groups that share the same theological outlook and strategic goals. The chapter contends that the jihadi in-fighting in Syria in the period between 2013 and 2018 offers a microcosm of examples illustrating how different issues can lead to conflict between groups. He presents a fourfold typology of protagonists of this in-fighting: hegemony seekers, unitarians, opportunists and isolationists.

In Chapter 9, Jérôme Devon also examines the proliferation of Salafi armed groups since the Arab Spring uprising in 2011. Considering the case of Ahrar al-Sham, which was the main alternative to the al-Qaida-oriented Jabhat al-Nusra, this chapter analyses how these jihadi groups strategise to cooperate or compete with other Islamist groups. The author identifies three factors as influencing these strategies: a group's level of political institutionalisation from the perspective of having a clear strategy; its ability to work with other Islamist militant groups and states; and the nature of its relationships with the population. The analysis is based on extensive interviews with members of Ahrar al-Sham and other jihadist groups operating out of Turkey. The chapter shows how a narrow focus on the ideology of these groups ignores the fact that in contexts of civil war their adaptation to structural factors becomes more important in shaping their strategies.

In the final chapter of the volume, Belal Shobaki examines changes within the political outlook of Hamas, whereby it has moved away from a religious and non-reconciliatory discourse to the adoption of a more democratic outlook, a discourse that is open to forming political partnerships with secular and Marxist parties, and a political settlement with the Israeli occupation. Shobaki shows how the softening of Hamas's political outlook has disappointed some of its followers, making them drift towards the combative stance urged by Salafi jihadism. The other factors leading to the emergence of Salafi jihadism in Palestine include the decline of the Muslim Brotherhood in the entire region after the Arab Spring, as well as the absence of more moderate Salafi political movements in Palestine. Developments in the region since the Arab Spring have thus also led to an increasing polarisation within the Islamic groups in Palestine, while creating increased space for jihadi networks.

These ten empirically rich chapters, which draw on fresh fieldwork at a number of different sites, help to illustrate how Salafism today needs to be studied through a new lens. Capturing the core contentious of these chapters, in the volume's conclusion Itzchak Weismann thus notes a visible weakening of the more rigid forms of Salafism associated with Wahhabi creed and a revival of its earlier version, which was open to accommodating pluralistic interpretations.

Notes

1. 'Crown Prince says Saudis want return to moderate Islam', *BBC News*, 25 October 2017, https://www.bbc.co.uk/news/world-middle-east-41747476 (accessed 23 October 2019).
2. Martin Chulov, 'Saudi Arabia to allow women to obtain driving licenses', *The Guardian*, 26 September 2017, https://www.theguardian.com/world/2017/sep/26/saudi-arabias-king-issues-order-allowing-women-to-drive (accessed 23 October 2019). Since then, the state has made further concessions which in the past would have been highly contentious: the relaxation of rules concerning male guardianship of women (Bethan McKernan, 'Saudi Arabia "planning to relax male guardianship laws"', *The Guardian*, 11 July 2019, https://www.theguardian.com/world/2019/jul/11/saudi-arabia-planning-to-relax-male-guardianship-laws [accessed 23 October 2019]); and allowing unmarried foreign couples to share a hotel room (in a bid to promote tourism): Julia Buckley, 'Saudi Arabia Allows Unmarried Couples to Share Hotel Rooms', *CNN*, 17 October 2019, https://edition.cnn.com/travel/article/saudi-arabia-unmarried-couples-female-travelers/index.html (accessed 23 October 2019).
3. Since then, the Crown Prince's suspected involvement in the murder of the Saudi journalist Jamal Khashoggi in the Saudi Embassy in Istanbul has greatly compromised his international standing.
4. Saudi Arabia and Salafism are routinely blamed for promoting jihadi networks, not only by Western observers, but by many Muslim scholars and members of the lay public.
5. As Roel Meijer notes in the influential volume that he edited on *Global Salafism: Islam's New Religious Movement*, ed. Roel Meijer (Oxford: Oxford University Press, 2014), before the September 11 attacks in 2001 there was limited interest in Salafism among scholars overseas. Since then, however, there have been published a number of monographs and collected works that provide in-depth analysis of Salafi movements in various country contexts.
6. *Al-Ṣaḥwa al-Islāmiyya* (Islamic Awakening) is an indigenous political movement that began in Saudi Arabia under the influence of scholars and activists from the rest of the Middle East and combined political activism with local religious discourse.
7. Masooda Bano, 'Saudi Salafism amid Rapid Social Change', in *Modern Islamic Authority and Social Change, Volume 1: Evolving Debates in Muslim-Majority*

Countries, ed. Masooda Bano (Edinburgh: Edinburgh University Press, 2018), 127–49.

8. The first three generations of Muslims making up the Salaf consisted of the following: the Prophet's companions (*ṣaḥābas*), the last one of whom died in 690; the *tabiʾīn*, the last one of whom died in 750; and the *tabiʾ tabiʾīn*, the last one of whom died in 810. Shiraz Maher, *Salafi-Jihadism: The History of an Idea* (London: C. Hurst & Co., 2016).
9. See the chapters in Meijer, *Global Salafism*, for a good introduction to the core tenets and historical evolution of Salafism. See Chapters 5–7 in Bano, *Modern Islamic Authority and Social Change, Volume 1*, for an in-depth historical analysis of Wahhabism and Salafism, the relationship between the state-society and the scholars in Saudi Arabia, and the position of reformist Salafi scholars on contemporary issues. On the latter, see also Pooya Razavian, 'Yasir Qadhi and the Development of Reasonable Salafism', in *Modern Islamic Authority and Social Change, Volume 2: Evolving Debates in the West*, ed. Masooda Bano (Edinburgh: Edinburgh University Press, 2018), 155–79.
10. As the guardian of the two holy mosques, the Saudi state is in a privileged position to claim traditional Islamic authority.
11. See Meijer's edited volume *Global Salafism* for a good summary of the Salafi creedal beliefs and methodological principles, as well as their appeal.
12. Joas Wagemakers, 'The Transformation of a Radical Concept', in Meijer, *Global Salafism*, 81–106.
13. ISIS has adopted much more violent tactics and established a state.
14. Bernard Haykel, 'On the Nature of Salafi Thought and Action', in Meijer, *Global Salafism*, 33–57.
15. Scholars often assert that an emphasis on creed, rather than method, is the most distinctive element of Salafism. See Haykel, ibid. But starting with creed associates Salafism too closely with Wahhabism. As will be argued below, Salafism has a more complex origin.
16. Wael B. Hallaq, *Sharīʿa: Theory, Practice, Transformations* (Cambridge, New York: Cambridge University Press, 2009). For a simpler introduction to the evolution of the *sharīʿa* and the main *madhāhib*, see Raficq S. Abdulla and Mohamed M. Kesharjee, *Understanding Sharia: Islamic Law in a Globalised World* (London: I. B. Tauris, 2018).
17. There existed many competing approaches in the initial period; see Abdulla and Kesharjee, *Understanding Sharia.* Of these, four survived and became formally recognised schools of law across the Sunni Muslim world.

18. For the derivation of specific law from the principles of *sharīʿa*, see Hallaq, *Sharīʿa*, and Abdulla and Kesharjee, *Understanding Sharia*.
19. Hallaq, *Sharīʿa*; Abdulla and Kesharjee, *Understanding Sharia*.
20. Abdal Hakim Murad, *Understanding the Four Madhhabs* ([n. p.]: Muslim Academic Trust, 1999).
21. Ibid.
22. Haykel, 'On the Nature of Salafi Thought'.
23. Ibid.
24. Ibid, 36.
25. For a detailed analysis of this argument, see Nathan Spannaus, 'Evolution of Saudi Salafism', in Bano, *Modern Islamic Authority, Volume 1*, 150–71.
26. David Commins, *The Wahhabi Mission and Saudi Arabia* (London: I.B. Tauris, 2012).
27. 'Rashid Rida, Muhammad', in *The Oxford Dictionary of Islam*, ed. John L. Esposito; *Oxford Islamic Studies Online*, http://www.oxfordislamicstudies.com/article/opr/t125/e1979 (accessed 23 October 2019).
28. Islamic modernism is an approach associated most noticeably with the work of scholars such as Muhammad Abduh, Jamal ad-Din al-Afghani and Muhammad Rashid Rida, who tried to reconcile Islam and modern values associated with Western civilisation. Operating against the tension of the colonial period, these scholars differed from the traditional *ʿulamāʾ* as well as from secular groups. They argued for adopting Islam as the guiding framework, while simultaneously defending the adoption of Western institutions and values in areas where they were optimal. This adaptation was argued to be essential for ensuring that Islam remained relevant for all times. For a detailed analysis of the modernists' influence on Salafism and the eventual shift to more puritanical Salafism, see Itzchak Weismann, 'A Perverted Balance: Modern Salafism between Reform and Jihād', *Die Welt des Islams* 57 (2017), 33–66; Itzchak Weismann, 'New and Old Perspectives in the Study of Salafism', *Bustan: The Middle East Book Review* 8/1 (2017), 22–37.
29. Mariam Abou Zahab, 'Salafism in Pakistan', in Meijer, *Global Salafism*, 126–42; Spannaus, 'Evolution'.
30. Abou Zahab, 'Salafism in Pakistan'.
31. Spannaus, 'Evolution'.
32. When studying at al-Azhar, the Saudi scholars tried to search for more direct connections between Ḥanbalism and Wahhabism. In India, they had a natural alliance with *Ahl-i Ḥadīth* due to their similarly literalist approaches to the text and also their shared concerns about Sufism. Nabil Mouline, *The Clerics of*

Islam: Religious Authority and Political Power in Saudi Arabia (New Haven: Yale University Press, 2014); Spannaus, 'Evolution'.

33. In the 1950s and 1960s, the Islamists were persecuted by the secular and socialist regimes that came to power in many Middle Eastern countries upon the withdrawal of the colonial powers. For details of how Saudi Arabia acted as a refuge for Islamists from all over the Middle East during this period, see Stéphane Lacroix, *Awakening Islam: The Politics of Religious Dissent in Contemporary Saudi Arabia*, trans. George Holoch (Cambridge, MA: Harvard University Press, 2011).
34. Ibid.
35. Michael Farquhar, *Circuits of Faith: Migration, Education, and the Wahhabi Mission* (Palo Alto: Stanford University Press, 2016).
36. Spannaus, 'Evolution'.
37. Henri Lauziere, *The Making of Salafism: Islamic Reform in the Twentieth Century* (New York: Columbia University Press, 2016); cf. Samira Haj, *Reconfiguring Islamic Tradition: Reform, Rationality, and Modernity (Cultural Memory in the Present)* (Palo Alto: Stanford University Press, 2011), esp. 67–108; Albert Hourani, *Arabic Thought in the Liberal Age 1798–1939*, 2nd edn (Cambridge: Cambridge University Press, 1983); Malcolm Kerr, *Islamic Reform: The Political and Legal Theories of Muhammad 'Abduh and Rashid Rida* (Berkeley, CA: University of California Press, 1966).
38. In 1927, Rida defended the modernist interpretations of Qur'ānic text, which were challenged by a leading Wahhabi scholar, on the grounds of securing social benefit for contemporary Muslims. He provided the Wahhabi scholars with copies of his own exegesis of the Qur'ān, *Tafsīr al-Manār*.
39. Commins, *The Wahhabi Mission*; Spannaus, 'Evolution'.
40. For details on the alliance between the House of Saud and the House of Wahhab, see Commins, *The Wahhabi Mission.*
41. Ibid.
42. Conversion to Islam requires committing to worship of one God and acknowledging Muhammad as his last prophet.
43. Haykel, 'On the Nature of Salafi Thought'.
44. Mouline, *The Clerics of Islam.*
45. Spannaus, 'Evolution'.
46. The House of Saud was one of the rival tribal factions always competing for control over the region of Najd. For details, see Commins, *The Wahhabi Mission.*

47. Madawi al-Rasheed, *Contesting the Saudi State: Islamic Voices from a New Generation* (Cambridge: Cambridge University Press, 2007), 37.
48. Ibid, 267.
49. Maher, *Salafi-Jihadism*, 71.
50. Ibid, 111.
51. Commins, *The Wahhabi Mission*; Spannaus, 'Evolution'.
52. Khaled Abou El Fadl, *The Great Theft: Wrestling Islam from the Extremists* (New York: HarperCollins 2005), 72–74; Spannaus, 'Evolution'.
53. Maher, *Salafi-Jihadism*.
54. In this line of reasoning, it is maintained that Qutb's focus on *jāhilī*s was developed by Muhammad Abdul Salam Faraj, the main ideologue of the Egyptian extremist group *Tanzim al-Jihad* and the author of the 1980 tract, *Jihad: The Absent Obligation*, to argue for the excommunication of all Muslim rulers, thus paving the way for armed rebellion. Faraj maintained that such a rebellion has become a personal duty for every Muslim, in order to establish the caliphate and institute God's *ḥākimiyya*. He stressed that the priority is to fight the enemy at hand (the apostate rulers), rather than the distant enemy (Israel).

PART I

CHANGES IN SALAFI THOUGHT

1

SALAFISM: THE CORE CRITIQUES

Hazim Fouad

While claiming to represent the authentic Islam, the Islam of the *Salaf*, Salafism has from the beginning been challenged by other Sunni groups. Rather than being seen as an authentic representation of the Islamic tradition, Salafism is perceived as a modern invention, a new sect formed by Muḥammad ibn 'Abd al-Wahhab in the eighteenth century. This chapter analyses the critiques that other Sunni Muslim groups direct against Salafism: traditional *'ulamā'* who follow one of the four Sunni *madhāhib* and the *māturīdī* or the *ash'arī kalām* (theology); Sufis; modernists; and reformists.[1] It draws on books, essays and videos of scholars from these traditions. The traditionalist voices are captured through the work of scholars from al-Azhar University, Dar al-Ifta and the Ministry of al-Awqaf in Egypt, as well as that of individual *'ulamā'* such as Said Ramadan al-Buti (d. 2013) and Muhammad ibn Alawi al-Maliki (d. 2004)[2], and some associated with the website *Marifah.info*. For other traditions, the analysis draws on the work of the members of a Sufi order and of individual scholars. Understanding in some detail these traditional critiques of Salafism, which are also referred to in the volume's introduction, will help us to better appreciate the importance of the ongoing shifts within Salafism, which are then mapped out in the remaining chapters of this volume.

Traditional *'Ulamā'*

The major reproach against the Salafis from a traditionalist point of view is their allegedly insufficient theological and legal qualifications. Traditional *'ulamā'* believe that safeguarding the correct interpretation of religious texts relies on a methodology that has been in use for over a millennium. This methodology is taught in a long-term process via the traditional institutions of Islamic learning. It includes the observance of the higher objectives of Islamic law (*maqāṣid*), a comparison among the views of all four Sunni schools of law on a certain topic and the consultation of legitimate sources of Islamic law beside the Qur'ān and the Sunnah, in order to reach a contemporary judgement.[3] The Salafi method of taking a singular *ḥadīth* as a basis for the finding of justice is regarded as deficient. Neglecting the opinions of the law schools leads, in the eyes of the traditionalists, to the formulation of absolute positions regarding matters where, in fact, there exists a plurality of opinions. In their view, most topics of disagreement concern legal questions (*masā'il fiqhiyya*) and not matters of *ʿaqīda* as claimed by Salafis. The excessive imposition of prohibitions by, and the seclusive tendencies of, Salafis are rejected since Islam is supposed to facilitate the lives of the believers and let them become productive members of the societies in which they live.[4]

The traditionalist scholars also make extensive references to Qur'ān and *ḥadīth* collections, but in their writings, they want to demonstrate their superiority in the interpretative process. They thus also engage with the work of scholars who are unequivocally accepted by Salafis, such as Ibn Taymiyyah (d. 1328), to prove that the Salafis have misunderstood them. The claim of the *Salaf* to represent *the* Islam by calling themselves *Salafiyy*ūn is regarded as presumptuous by traditionalists. The legitimacy of their point of view is denigrated by calling them 'modern-day *Ahl al-Ḥadīth*', 'stern zealots' (*mutashaddidūn*), or even 'Pseudo-Salafis' (*mutasallifūn*).[5]

Traditionalist scholars present *Salafiyya* as a modern movement within Islam, one that only represents a minority of Muslims.[6] The latter is taken to be proof enough that the Salafis' understanding of Islam is incorrect, since several authentic *ḥadīth* point to the fact that it will always be the majority of Muslims who are on the right path. The 'victorious group' (*al-firqa al-nājiya/al-ṭāʾifa al-manṣūra*) can therefore never be a minority group among Muslims.[7] Salafis in return accuse the traditionalists of 'blindly' following a *madhhab* and the opinions of their imams, something against which they warn. They hold that Muslims should learn, instead, to access the primary sources directly in order to see whether a certain *fatwa* is in accordance with Islam.[8] This notion is fiercely contested by the traditionalists who argue that the founders of the *madhāhib* are not taken to be infallible. They were humans who might have erred, but that does not compromise their scholarly achievements. It is completely unacceptable to question a scholar who is superior in learning:

> What the Imāms have, or may have, said regarding having their respective fatwas rejected in the face of evidence found against that particular fatwa, does not concern us non-scholars here on the low level of *taqlīd*, but, rather, it applies to their elite class of pupils who do possess the distinctions of *mujtahid fi madhhab* (*mujtahid* within the methodological scope of that school of thought and interpretation).[9]

The core message of Islam was certainly obvious and easy to understand for everybody. It is another matter, however, to derive rulings from the scriptural sources. While the texts are indeed free of error (*maʿṣūm*), their comprehension by the human interpreter is not.[10] When examining historic arguments, the accusations against the reform movement of Muhammad Abduh (d. 1905) stand out. The movement's questioning of following the system of the legal schools (*taqlīd*), together with its advocacy for independent legal reasoning (*ijtihād*), had been picked up by modern-day Salafis with quite unintended outcomes, as discussed in the introduction to this volume.[11] While the Wahhabi movement might have contentious theological views in the eyes of traditionalist scholars, at least it upheld the *Ḥanbalī madhhab*. The modern *Salafiyya* was, in contrast, heterodox from a theological as well as an Islamic legal point of view.

The views of Al-Maliki and Al-Buti, partially shared on the *Marifah* website, in particular focus on the work of ibn Taymiyya. Al-Maliki quotes several statements of ibn Taymiyya in order to prove their compatibility with traditionalist positions. Al-Buti also ranks ibn Taymiyya as an outstanding scholar, but one who diverged numerous times from the consensus of *Ahl al-Sunna*.[12] Al-Buti and al-Maliki seem to regard themselves as sufficient authorities and see no need to refer to other contemporary scholars in order to legitimise their viewpoints. Al-Buti has managed to establish himself as the most prominent traditionalist voice in Syria, without the perception of being as closely connected to the regime as the grand *muftī*.[13] Al-Maliki, meanwhile, was able to capitalise on his background as a member of a respected family of religious scholars in Mecca.[14] The comparatively young authors publishing on the *Marifah* website, by contrast, rely much more on the statements of better-known scholars, as well as medieval authorities, in order to add legitimacy to their discourse.

Sufi *Ṭuruq*

This section explores the critique levelled by actors on the Sufi spectrum. One may object that the differentiation between traditionalism and Sufism is artificial since Sufism is part and parcel of traditionalist thought. Although this is by and large correct, there are differences both in the arguments that the two strands make against Salafi Islam and in the ways in which they generate religious authority. Ahmad al-Tayyib might also be a Sufi, but his authority is mainly derived from being Shaykh al-Azhar and not from being a Sufi. In turn, the heads of different Sufi *ṭuruq* might be portrayed as great legal scholars, but their authority also rests on their alleged spiritual genealogy to the Prophet Muhammad (*silsila*) and their ability to receive direct inspiration from God (*ilhām*). There is a long history of Sufi criticism against Salafism; the *ṭarīqa* under scrutiny in this section is the transnational *tarīqa al-Nāẓimiyya*.[15]

When analysed, the criticism found in documents from scholars of this *ṭarīqa* can be divided into two broad thematic categories.[16] The first is a comprehensive defence of Sufism and of ritual practices declared as deviant by the Salafis. This is accomplished by quoting extensive passages from the Qur'ān and the *ḥadīth*. These quotes are followed by statements by medieval scholars who are portrayed as having interpreted the primary sources in the same way as the authors of the documents. The second set of arguments focuses on critiquing Salafi practices. These arguments partially mirror the critique of the traditionalists, especially when it comes to the correct interpretation of the attributes of God. The aim is to ascribe anthropomorphic tendencies to the Salafis, which have been commonly regarded as heretical throughout

Islamic history. If the Salafis have been disqualified on theological grounds, so the logic goes, then there is no need to engage with other points of their critique of traditional *'ulamā'* and Sufi understandings of Islam, especially those that might be more challenging to refute. The Salafis are portrayed as a marginal sect that, like all other sects in Islamic history, is doomed.[17]

A clear shift of emphasis can be discerned between the Sufis and the traditionalists when it comes to discussing the status of the Prophet. The accusation that Salafis are defaming Muhammad by stressing the point that he was merely a human being cannot be found as explicitly in the documents of the traditionalists. The reason for this is the spiritual closeness to the Prophet ascribed to the Sufi *shuyūkh*, which is more than often explained in ways that transcend the human intellect. If the *shaykh* is the living representative of the Prophet, there must be no difference between the veneration of Muhammad and of him.[18] The Sufis criticise several Saudi scholars for being 'slavishly loyal to the Saudi oligarchy', which in their view is everything but a truly Islamic government.[19] The Saudi scholars' derision of celebrating the *mawlid* is regarded as hypocrisy, given that the same scholars participated in the celebration of a 'Muḥammad ibn 'Abd al-Wahhab Week' in Saudi Arabia back in 1980. Further points of criticism concern the alleged tampering with works of classical jurisprudence, inappropriate language towards other Muslims and being influenced by Western philosophical concepts – such as the idea that all knowledge can be obtained from books: 'The delusion that "no Islamic knowledge is hidden from me if only I decide to find it in the books", is the Westernized belief of the 'Salafis' who rebel against the idea of having an Imam of fiqh or tasawwuf [. . .]'.[20] The same text goes on to argue that real Islamic knowledge is taken and understood not from books – as is taught by Jewish and Christian professors in non-Muslim academies – but from Allah's *awliya*', the scholars of knowledge who are the full beneficiaries of the Prophet.

It might reasonably be assumed that this harsh rhetoric is due to the fact that the Sufis face much more pressure from the Salafis than do traditional *'ulamā'*. In fact, there is no general Salafi critique of traditional *'ulamā'*. In comparison, we find numerous books written by Salafis that reject Sufism as a whole.[21]

The generation of authority through textual material remains ambiguous.

It seems somewhat peculiar to first criticise the science of the *ḥadīth*s and the merits of studying books, by using *ḥadīth*s that have been declared as authentic by exactly this science. From the perspective of the authors, however, this is logically consistent: if even the luminaries of the *fuqahā'* had declared that the *awliyā'* are superior to them, who should remain to object? Assuming that the statements of the *shuyūkh* are binding for the *murīdūn* through their spiritual bond (*rābiṭa*), it seems surprising that there are hardly any comments from Shaykh Nazim himself in the books analysed. It seems convincing, therefore, that the target groups of this kind of literature are non-members or even critics of the *Nāẓimiyya*, especially those who accept no arguments not related to a quote from the Qur'ān or the Sunnah.

Modernist Scholars

For the purposes of this essay, modernists are defined by their critical attitude towards the *'ulamā'*. They do not necessarily consider themselves as belonging to one of the four Sunni *madhāhib*, and some advocate choosing (*takhayyur*) or combining (*talfīq*) different legal opinions. For the purpose of an *ijtihād* that fits modern concerns, the consultation of secular laws as well as Western political, legal and philosophical concepts is allowed in their view. They also regard many of the ancient theological discussions as futile given the current challenges facing the *ummah*. Although they do not regard concepts such as representative democracy, human rights (including women's rights), as well as the freedom of press and of expression to be in conflict with Islam, they should not be perceived simply as 'pro-Western', which is an accusation levelled at them by both traditional *'ulamā'* and Islamists. Many of them are in fact highly critical towards Western foreign policy and the treatment of Muslim minorities in Western countries.

This section summarises the analysis of statements from three prominent Egyptian modernists whose views are frequently covered in the media: Islam Buhairi, Ahmad Abduh Mahir and Ibrahim Isa. All three differentiate between a man-made Islamic tradition (*turāth*), which developed historically, and the immutable holy Qur'ān. *Fiqh* should not be regarded as an essential component of the religion, since 'what has been written down by human intellect can never be regarded as [a part of] religion' (*mā kutiba min 'aql bashar lā yumkin an ya'udd dīnan*).[22] It must not be sacralised (*taqdīs*). These modernists regard neither the consensus of the *'ulamā'* (*ijmā'*) nor the classical collections of *ḥadīth*s as being able to answer all contemporary questions of importance to Muslims. The Salafi presentation of these collections as divine commandments is challenged, since these collections have not been revealed by God, but compiled by humans who lived centuries after the Prophet. If these early Muslims were able to decide which reports were to be included and which refuted, then modern Muslims – whose knowledge of the world far exceeds the intellectual horizons of al-Bukhārī and other *muḥaddithūn* – are much more entitled to do so.[23] The benchmark for such a reform would be contemporary ethics, which can be derived from the Qur'ān – if properly understood. This attitude underlines the point that the discourse of the modernists is exclusivist insofar as it posits an objective reading of the Qur'ān. Interpretations that differ from those of the modernists are not regarded as possible alternatives, but simply as being wrong.

Compared to the critique of Salafism by traditionalists and Sufis, modernists make more use of sociological than of theological arguments. The reduced use of religious technical vocabulary is due to their critical stance towards the classical Islamic sciences, especially in the field of *ḥadīth*. For modernists, human dignity and the use of reason serve as the benchmark for the interpretation of religious texts. They generate authority by attaching to a Western-dominated *Zeitgeist*, which regards certain forms of corporal punishment as well as discrimination based on ethnicity, gender or religion as archaic. Muslims who argue otherwise, they assert, have misunderstood the core message of the Qur'ān, which is mercy for all humanity. This way of argumentation makes the modernist discourse vulnerable, insofar as both Salafis and traditionalists accuse them of merely wishing to please the West. The Salafis notably contend that arguments which are not based on Islamic primary sources are to be rejected *a priori* – a view highly contested by modernists. When the Salafi Walid Ismail questions Ahmad Mahir in a TV debate by asking 'Which scholar has ever said something similar to what you are putting forth here?' (*mīn min al-Fuqahā' āl al-kalām illī ḥaḍritak bit'ūl*), the latter laconically responds: 'I am the scholar [by myself]' (*anā l-faqīh*)!'[24]

For modernists, the Salafi interpretation of Islam, which is permeated by images of the enemy, is the leading cause of the political violence plaguing the Islamic world. In the words of Ibrahim Isa, 'All their preaching is full of hatred' (*kull da'watihā karāhiya*).[25] Modernists believe that only a rigorous reform of the Islamic discourse could stop the spread of religiously justified violence. This is why they perceive the increased political participation of Salafis in Egypt as a threat. These scholars convey their views via the numerous TV channels and programmes broadcast throughout the country and often also run their own YouTube channels.

It is, however, important to note that the primary targets of the modernists' criticism in contemporary Egypt are actually the traditionalists, whom they hold responsible for the 'backwardness' of the Muslim world. In the words of Islam Buhairi, 'al-Azhar is the source of all evil, the Salafis are mediocre'.[26] From this viewpoint, it is the lack of initiative on part of traditional *'ulamā'* to undertake reform, a lack of initiative that has caused many problematic aspects of the legal texts to remain untouched. This in turn provides the Salafis with a religious justification for their outdated opinions, since the traditional *'ulamā'* have never distanced themselves from the critical passages of the legal heritage (*turāth*). As long as the Salafis can rely on texts that have been declared as sacrosanct by *'ulamā'*-led religious establishments, such as al-Azhar, they can continue to impress the uneducated masses. Although modernists acknowledge that there are several individuals among the *'ulamā'* who have enlightened views, they question their ability to assert themselves. They argue that the only solution is to do away with the shackles of traditional hermeneutics and to start a fresh interpretation of the religious primary sources in order to reach appropriate conclusions for modern challenges.

Reformist Scholars

This category is made up of Muslim intellectuals in the Western diaspora. These individuals do not form a homogenous group, and all have a different emphasis within their reform projects. Still, their aims are similar to an extent that it seems legitimate to put them under one label vis-á-vis their critique of Salafism. They have all been trained in both traditional Islamic and Western secular institutions of higher education. This background makes them familiar with both discursive worlds and their references. They do not see a contradiction between a Muslim identity, which is grounded in an adaptable Islamic tradition, and being a citizen of a non-Muslim secular nation-state. They are attacked by both critics of the majority population, who regard their views as being still too conservative, and by traditional *'ulamā'* and Islamists alike, who say that they have become too liberal. For reformists, the problem is not with the tradition itself, but with the contemporary Muslims' understanding of it. The tradition possesses all the tools conducive to a constant, ongoing renewal, but this process has been stopped for historical and political reasons. They seek a radical reform of the tradition through the means of the tradition itself. This section summarises the analysis of their arguments against Salafism, based on books, articles and video appearances.[27]

For reformists, the Salafi approach to the sources of Islamic law is methodically highly questionable. Like the traditionalists, reformists regard ultra-conservative Salafi Islam as well as ultra-liberal modernist Islam as the undesirable result if Muslims do away with the tradition.[28] In clear contrast to the traditionalists, however, the reformists criticise the Salafis for their degradation of women and their refusal to engage in critical thought. They also stress the fact that the classical *maqāṣid* have to be further developed to meet contemporary needs. Because of the Salafis' literalism, so the reformists contend, they forget the higher aims of Islam and persevere in a kind of formalism, which is intellectually shameful. Their exclusivism and aggressive attitude towards other Muslims as well as non-Muslims is not only wrong from an ethical and theological perspective, it is also counter-productive with respect to *da'wa*. The simplicity of Salafi Islam might be highly attractive for young people in a phase of disorientation, and its growth in the Muslim diaspora is proof of this phenomenon. However, at the end of the day, Salafism does not provide any real tools for young Muslims to deal with the challenges they are facing in their everyday life, and it leads to a kind of defeatism and victimhood.[29] The intellectual stagnation of Salafism blocks the urgently needed reform of Islamic thought and reinforces the prejudices of the non-Muslim majority populations against Islam.

The methodology of the arguments presented in the documents is highly diverse. The reformist authors utilise legal, theological, political and historical, as well as sociological arguments. This diversity is an expression of their educational background, for they have been influenced by the Islamic as well as the Western history of ideas. They regard the exclusion of concepts from Western humanities in Islamic legal thought and exegesis as a major problem in dealing with the historical heritage of Islam: 'The objectives and methodologies of Shari'ah have not been developed to meet contemporary advances in epistemology, hermeneutics, or social theory'.[30] At the same time, reference to the tradition is a *sine qua non* for reform, because otherwise both the authenticity and the acceptance of any Islamic reform project is doomed to fail: 'Such interpretations, produced from within, defended and argued in the light, and in full respect, of the texts, will alone be able to rival "immediate" acceptance of literalist readings [. . .].'[31]

The context of being situated in the diaspora plays a large role in the documents of the reformists. For them, religion has to be helpful in the daily lives of its worshippers and must not be concerned with abstract theological questions only. In order to change the lamentable state of large parts of the *umma*, Muslims have to increasingly deal with questions pertaining to the lived-in world. There exist numerous examples of reformist arguments from a sociological perspective, asserting that Salafism offers no solutions to pressing, contemporary religious and societal questions. Although only a minority of Muslims worldwide would define themselves as belonging to the Salafi trend, its methodology and discourse seems to have penetrated the mainstream. As the famous scholar, Khaled Abou El Fadl notes . . .

> In fact, I would go as far as to claim that the Wahhābī methodology has been transplanted to schools ideologically at odds with Wahhābism, such as Sufi schools of thought. For instance, if one examines the works of Sufis such as Nuh Ha Mim Keller or Hisham al-Kabbani, one notices that while the positive determinations are different, the methodology is substantially the same. In the methodology of individuals not affiliated with the Wahhābī school one finds that all legal problems yield a definitive, singular determination in which the law of God is searched, discovered and clearly asserted for all times to come. Put differently, one notices that the earmark of contemporary approaches to Islamic law [. . .] is the certainty of results, incontrovertibility of conclusions, and the unequivocalness of the asserted determinations. The end result is that the subtlety and richness of the Islamic legal heritage is largely absent in the contemporary age.[32]

The authority of the reformist authors is derived from their position in their academic settings. Through their scholarly position as Muslim intellectuals they are actively forming the discourse of and on Islam. Their critiques are legitimised by the fact that all of them have been trained in traditional Islamic sciences, which provides them with the methodology and terminology necessary for acceptance from more conservative segments of the Muslim community. At the same time, they are able to monitor and to comment on academic discourses in the Western world; something that sets them apart from the traditionalists. This intellectual discourse of a Muslim elite may at the same time, however, be their Achilles' heel, since it might be perceived as too aloof and detached from the daily questions of ordinary Muslims in the West, let alone the Islamic world. Bearing in mind that one of the main attractions of Salafism lies in the straightforwardness and simplicity of its message, this could be an obstacle to the wider reception of their work. When Khaled Abou El Fadl was asked whether he was able to publish the main arguments in a short version of one of his books, he replied by saying: 'I do not believe, however, that I have the ability to further simplify this work without rendering it into an ineffectual and meaningless work'.[33]

All of this makes it likely that the documents are targeted at non-Salafi Muslims as well as non-Muslims who shall be confronted with an alternative interpretation of Islam. The focus on contemporary societal issues of this world would probably lead Salafis concentrated on the correct performance of rituals to merely shrug their shoulders. From the Salafi perspective, Muslims have to fulfil God's commandments irrespective of their individual living situation. The value of theological correctness is not measured by its utility for everyday life. For this reason, the discourses of the reformists and the Salafis seem to bypass each other to a large extent.[34]

Conclusion

There exists a large corpus of anti-Salafi publications from a Sunni perspective. However, Salafism is not faced with a unified front of critics. They not only differ in their method of argumentation but are also highly sceptical towards each other's interpretative approaches. Traditionalists and Sufis both criticise the modernists for mirroring the Salafi approach of directly accessing the texts without using a proper method, which in their view leads to an arbitrary exegesis. Modernists, in turn, accuse the traditionalists of holding similar outdated views as the Salafis, which are rooted in prescriptions they describe as holy, but which were developed in a completely different age and context.

This leads to the question of authority. It would be naïve to believe that the persuasiveness of the messages is only dependent on the objective plausibility of their arguments. It is at least to the same degree contingent on the credibility of its proponents. This is why paying attention to the socio-political context and the power relations in which texts are produced is so important.[35] The traditional *'ulamā'* in the Islamic world can benefit from the resources provided to them by the institutions with which they are associated. The prestige of century-old madrasas adds legitimacy to their discourse, which is often portrayed as state-sanctioned, 'official' Islam. The connection to the state and its support, however, can be damaging to the reputation of the traditionalists – as, for example, in the case of al-Azhar[36] – in the eyes of anyone who is opposed to a regime that they regard as unjust and therefore un-Islamic.

The Sufi *ṭarīqa* analysed here may be perceived as more independent, although it is vehemently opposed to any revolt against incumbent regimes. Its members (*murdīdūn*) will not question the positions of the *shaykh* in any case, since the order holds that the head of a *ṭarīqa* yields absolute spiritual authority. It is exactly this obedience that is contested by both Salafis and other currents of the Muslim spectrum. The modernists in Egypt rely on television programmes and the internet in order to challenge the dominance of traditionalist and Salafi discourses on Islam. The popularity of these programmes and the number of followers online indicate that parts of the Muslim community seem to sympathise with their radical attitude towards a tradition that they regard as ossified and moribund.[37] The reformers can finally benefit from their prestigious positions in institutions of higher learning in the West. They serve as role models for young Muslims and as living examples that faith-oriented work can also lead to success in a non-Muslim majority country. At the same time, it might be asked if and to what extent Salafism may appeal to more disadvantaged social strata as being a more authentic representation of Islam than that of a 'Westernised' Muslim elite.

Notes

1. This chapter presents a synopsis of the findings of my doctoral dissertation titled 'Zeitgenössische muslimische Kritik am Salafismus: Eine Untersuchung ausgewählter Dokumente', available both as a book and online via the library of the University of Kiel: https://macau.uni-kiel.de/servlets/MCRFileNodeServlet/dissertation_derivate_00008418/2019_fouad_dissertation.pdf (accessed 1 November 2019).
2. Said Ramadan al-Buti and Muhammad ibn Alawi al-Maliki are highly revered Islamic scholars. Shaykh al-Buti, a Syrian, was known as the 'Shaykh of the Levant'; al-Maliki, who hailed from a family of scholars from Saudi Arabia, was known as the great *mujaddid* (one who brings about renewal of religion) of the twentieth century.
3. Although not uniformly accepted, these are the consensus of the *'ulamā'* (*ijmā'*), analogical reasoning (*qiyās*), the statements of the companions (*ṣaḥāba*), the closing of the means that can lead to evil (*sadd al-dharī'a or dar' al-mafāsid*), the deeds of the people of Medina during the time of the Prophet, *ḥadīth* that were transmitted by a follower (*aḥādīth mursala*) and juristic discretion (*istiḥsān*). See Ali Jum'a, *Al-Mutashaddidūn: Manhajuhum ... wa-munāqashat ahamm qaḍāyāhim* (Cairo: Dār al-Muqaṭṭam li-l-Nashr wa-l-Tauzī', 2011), 62.
4. Muhammad al-Ghazali (d. 1994), an al-Azhar trained traditionalist scholar who was initially associated with the Muslim Brotherhood, regards the chains of transmission (*isnād/asānid*) of *ḥadīth*s that prescribe an ascetic way of life as being weaker than those that encourage an active way of life and the accumulation of wealth. See Muhammad Al-Ghazali, *Al-Sunna al-nabawiyya bayna ahl al-fiqh . . . wa-ahl al-ḥadīth* (Cairo: Dār al-Shurūq, 2011), 136–39. Compare this with the statement by the Salafi preacher Bilal Phillips: 'Believers are principled individuals, sticking by their beliefs and practices regardless of how odd they may seem or how lonely and isolated the society may make them'. *Facebook* post, 23 June 2013, www.facebook.com/DrBilalPhilips/posts/10151653209889089?fref=nf (accessed 10 November 2016).
5. For the first two terms, see Al-Ghazali, *Al-Sunna*, and Jum'a, *Al-Mutashaddidūn*. For the term *mutasallifūn* (literally, 'those who pretend to follow the *Salaf*'), see Ahmad Mahmud Karima, *Al-Salafiyya bayna l-aṣīl wa-l-dakhīl* (Cairo: Dār al-Kutub al-Ṣūfiyya, 2012).
6. This is the main argument in Sa'id Ramadan al-Buti, *As-Salafiyya: Marḥala zamaniyya mubāraka lā madhhab islāmī* (Damascus: Dār al-Fikr, 1988).

7. The discussion revolves around two seemingly conflicting *ḥadīth*s. The first states that the *ummah* will split into 73 sects, only one of which will be saved. It is to be found in different variations in the collections of Abū Dāwūd (d. 889) in the book of *sunna* in the chapter 'The Explanation of the Sunnah (*sharḥ as-sunnah*)'; al-Tirmidhī (d. 892) in the book of faith in the chapter 'What Has Been Reported on the Fragmentation of the Ummah' *(mā jāʾa fī iftirāq hādhihī l-ummah*); and ibn Mājah (d. 887) in the book of *fitna* in the chapter 'The Fragmentation of Peoples' (*iftirāq al-umam).* It is reported neither by al-Bukhārī (d. 870), nor by Muslim (d. 875). The other *ḥadīth* reports Muhammad to be saying that the *umma* will never unite upon error and if you find yourself in disagreement you should stick to the majority. It is found in the collection of ibn Mājah, in the book of *fitna*, in the chapter 'The Majority' (*al-sawād al-aʿẓam*).
8. 'Abu Ḥanifah said: "If my word contradicts the Qur'an and sunna you should abandon it" [. . .] Imam Ahmad [. . .] said: "Follow nobody in your religion! Follow only our Prophet and things narrated by his companions! [. . .] Do not follow me, or Shafi'i, Malik [. . .] Awza'i [. . .] or [. . .] Thawri [. . .] but make use of the sources from which they derive their teaching!"'; Ahmet Kanlıdere, 'Abdullah Bubi', in *Modernist Islam, 1840-1940: A Sourcebook*, ed. Charles Kurzman (Oxford, New York: Oxford University Press, 2002), 236.
9. Tahir Mahmood Kiani, 'Taqlīd: Trusting a Mujtahid', *Marifah*, 2007, http://marifah.net/articles/taqlid-tahirkiani.pdf (accessed 9 January 2017).
10. Saʿid Ramadan Al-Buti, *Al-Lā-madhhabiyya: Aḫṭar bidʿa tuhaddidu l-sharīʿa al-islāmiyya* (Damascus: Maktabat al-Fārābī, 2005), 145.
11. Compare this argument with a quote by the historian Indira Gesink: 'Muhammad 'Abduh never intended that ordinary people perform ijtihād for legal issues, only for matters of personal belief, but his arguments developed a life of their own in the popular press'. Indira Falk Gesink, *Islamic Reform and Conservatism: Al-Azhar and the Evolution of Modern Sunni Islam* (London, New York: Tauris Academic Studies, 2010), 233.
12. 'Lā nukaffiru Ibn Taymiyya lakin Muḥammad Ibn ʿAbd al-Wahhāb lau staṭāʿa an yuzīla l-qubba al-ḫaḍra [sic] wa-wājihat qabr an-nabiyy la-faʿala' [Video], *YouTube*, 29 September 2015, www.youtube.com/watch?v=vXF9hjJS6Q0 (accessed 6 March 2017).
13. Things changed obviously with the Syrian uprising, where al-Buti clearly declared his solidarity with the Assad regime. See Thomas Pierret, 'Syrian Regime Loses its Last Credible Ally Among the Sunni Ulama', *Syria Comment*, 22 March 2013,

www.joshualandis.com/blog/syrian-regime-loses-last-credible-ally-among-the-sunni-ulama-by-thomas-pierret/ (accessed 10 January 2017).

14. Seraj Hendricks, H. A. Hellyer and Ahmad Hendricks, *A Sublime Way: The Sufi Path of the Sages of Makka* (Western Cape, South Africa; Louisville, KY: DYI, Fons Vitae, 2018).
15. In my doctoral dissertation, I also analyse the arguments by the primarily Egypt-based *tarīqa* al-ʿAzmiyya.
16. The objects of study are the seven-volume *Encyclopedia of Islamic Thought* and *The 'Salafi' Movement Unveiled*, both published by Hisham Kabbani, who is leading the movement in North America. See also Gibril Fouad Haddad, *Albani & His Friends: A Concise Guide to the Salafi Movement* (Birmingham: AQSA Publications, 2009).
17. Hisham Kabbani, *The 'Salafi' Movement Unveiled* (Mountain View: As Sunna Foundation of America, 1997), 100.
18. Two anthropological studies state that many members of the *Nāẓimiyyah* regard the head of the *ṭarīqa* as the living embodiment of the Prophet. See Tayfun Atay, *A Muslim Mystic Community in Britain: Meaning in the West and for the West* (Bremen: Europäischer Hochschulverlag, 2012), 49; Simon Stjernholm, 'The Centre of the Universe: Shaykh Nazim and his Murids in Lefke, Cyprus', *Journal of Muslims in Europe* 4 (1) (2015), 41.
19. Haddad, *Albani & His Friends*, 54.
20. Kabbani, *The 'Salafi' Movement Unveiled*, 110–11.
21. Richard Gauvain, 'Egyptian Sufism under the Hammer: A Preliminary Investigation into the Anti-Sufi Polemics of ʿAbd al-Rahman al-Wakil (1913–70)', in *Sufis and Salafis in the Contemporary Age*, ed. Lloyd Ridgeon (New York: Bloomsbury Publishing, 2015), 33–57.
22. 'Maʿa Islām Buḥairī al-ḥalqa al-thāniya ʿashr Istikhdām al-salafiyyīn li-l-maʿārīḍ li-l-kidhb wa-l-nifāq Faqaṭ ʿalā #l-Qāhira wa-l-Nās' [Video], *YouTube*, 10 July 2014, www.youtube.com/watch?v=YkIC7IuyXVA (accessed 1 September 2018).
23. 'Maʿa Islām Buḥairī ḥalqa 23 kāmila, Al-Tanwīr wa-maʿrakat al-tanwīr" [Video], *YouTube*, 8 July 2015, www.youtube.com/watch?v=YW_LXSrzzpg (accessed 17 September 2018).
24. 'Sīra wa-Tafattaḥat maʿa ʿIzzat al-Bandārī ḥalqa 17-11-2017 Al-Fikr al-salafī wa-fauḍā l-fatāwā' [Video], *YouTube*, 17 November 2017, www.youtube.com/watch?v=N0MyRQDamAA (accessed 26 September 2018).
25. 'Maʿa Ibrāhīm ʿĪsā | Al-Azma al-iqtiṣādiyya . . . Al-Fikr al-wahhābī al-salafī wa-stibāḥat al-qatl 4 Dīsambar' [Video], *YouTube*, 5 December 2016, www.youtube.com/watch?v=RiCtLudiVRg (accessed 3 October 2018).

26. 'Islam Beheiry: Al-Azhar is the Source of All Evil, the Salafis are Mediocre', *Egypt Independent*, 16 June 2015, www.egyptindependent.com/news/islam-beheiry-al-azhar-source-all-evil-salafis-are-mediocre (accessed 18 December 2016).
27. The individuals whose publications were subject to the analysis in this section are Khaled Abou El Fadl and Yasir Qadhi from the US, Tariq Ramadan from Switzerland and France, respectively, and Mouhanad Khorchide from Germany.
28. 'Our Time Our Challenges: Ultra Conservative vs. Ultra Liberalism - Dr. Yasir Qadhi' [Video], *YouTube*, 19 September 2015, www.youtube.com/watch?v=aSY5TioFiO8 (accessed 18 October 2015).
29. See Khaled Abou El Fadl *The Great Theft: Wrestling Islam from the Extremists* (New York: Harper On, 2007), 95; Tariq Ramadan, *Western Muslims and the Future of Islam* (Oxford: Oxford University Press, 2004), 5; Mouhanad Khorchide, *Gott glaubt an den Menschen: Mit dem Islam zu einem neuen Humanismus* (Freiburg, Basel, Wien: Herder, 2017), 215.
30. Khaled Abou El Fadl, *Speaking in God's Name: Islamic Law, Authority, and Women* (Oxford: Oneworld Publications, 2001a), 111.
31. Tariq Ramadan, *Radical Reform: Islamic Ethics and Liberation* (Oxford: Oxford University Press, 2009), 191.
32. Khaled Abou El Fadl, *And God Knows the Soldiers: The Authoritative and Authoritarian in Islamic Discourses* (Lanham, MD: University Press of America, 2001), 174.
33. Ibid, 96. Without the appendix, the book consists of 91 pages.
34. Every chapter in my dissertation entailed a subchapter of Salafi responsa to the criticisms of the traditionalists, Sufis, modernists and reformists, respectively. At this point, it shall suffice to say that there were far fewer rejoinders to the critiques by modernists and reformists, probably because the Salafis regard them as being westernised to such an extent that occupying oneself with their specific arguments becomes superfluous: they and their works are therefore rejected *a priori*.
35. Sergiu Balan, 'M. Foucault's View on Power Relations', *Cogito* 2 (2012), 55–61.
36. Masooda Bano, 'Al-Azhar University: A Crisis of Authority', in *Modern Islamic Authority and Social Change, Volume 1: Evolving Debates in Muslim Majority Countries*, ed. Masooda Bano (Edinburgh: Edinburgh University Press, 2018), 55–78.
37. The official Facebook account of al-Azhar has 86,429 'Likes': www.facebook.com/AlAzharUniversity/ (accessed 17 May 2019); Islam al-Buhairi's account

has reached 100,194 'Likes': www.facebook.com/ma3islam.behery/ (accessed 17 May 2019). Although al-Azhar certainly possesses other ways and means to reach its target audience, it is still remarkable that an individual is able to surpass an entire institution in terms of followers.

2

IN TODAY'S SAUDI ARABIA: THE STATE, THE SOCIETY AND THE SCHOLARS

Masooda Bano

In early 2016, I was undertaking fieldwork in Saudi Arabia as part of my research project on *Changing Structures of Islamic Authority and Social Change: A Transnational Review*. Premised on the observation that globalisation, ease of travel, as well as improved internet, media and mobile technology have facilitated the spread of liberal values around the globe, the Muslim world being no exception, the project aimed to understand how leading Islamic scholarly platforms with global followings are responding to the changed sensibilities of their followers, especially young people. The four Islamic scholarly traditions that were the special focus of this study consisted of Saudi Salafism, the al-Azhar mosque and university network in Egypt, the Directorate of Religious Affairs (*Diyanet*) in Turkey and the South Asian Deoband tradition. The fieldwork in Saudi Arabia was thus part of the effort to map the extent and nature of societal change and to understand the responses of the Wahhabi Salafi scholars to ongoing social changes in Saudi society. As part of this fieldwork, I also held a meeting with officials in the General Entertainment Authority, a newly established institution working directly under the supervision of Crown Prince Muhammad bin Salman.[1]

Facilitated by the King Faisal Center for Research and Islamic Studies, this meeting was important for its potential to provide crucial insights into the nature and extent of the social reform agenda envisioned by the Crown Prince. This was so because the promotion of tourism and entertainment opportunities constituted a critical component of the economic diversification strategy presented in the Vision 2030,[2] even though such a strategy directly challenged existing social norms. As expected, interviews in the Entertainment Authority indicated a push for social liberalisation, in particular an emphasis on providing the public with more forms of social entertainment. The rationale provided by the officials for this initiative was economic: since Saudi citizens spend large sums of money on entertainment in neighbouring Gulf states, part of the Vision 2030 agenda was to keep this money within Saudi Arabia. The immediate priority of the Entertainment Authority was to open cinema halls, host public concerts and plan mega theme parks. Yet, despite acknowledging the full backing of the Crown Prince, during the discussion the officials repeatedly acknowledged the need to roll out these programmes at a gradual pace, to avoid provoking a reaction from the conservative elements in Saudi society. They were keeping a tab on popular sentiments by closely monitoring the Twitter feeds concerning the proposed programmes. Identifying the pace of change that would be acceptable to a majority of the public was thus one of their key tasks. While theme parks were seen as an easy sell to all segments of society, mixed concerts (attended by women as well as men) were an example of a form of entertainment that was viewed as contentious.

That Saudi Arabia is undergoing a socio-cultural transformation has been clear to scholars who have been doing fieldwork in Saudi Arabia in recent years. *Saudi Arabia in Transition: Insights on Social, Political and Economic Religious Change*, edited by three scholars[3] with a long-standing engagement with Saudi Arabia as well as Salafism, gives an excellent insight into the changing socio-economic and political dynamics that are occurring within Saudi society, despite its apparent resistance to reform. Noting that outsiders have often seen Saudi Arabia as a 'combustible mixture of religious zealots, rebellious Bedouins, and rich oil sheikhs',[4] the editors of the volume set out to highlight the processes of change across the socio-economic and political domain. They attribute such misconceptions about Saudi society to the scarcity of scholarship on Saudi Arabia, itself the result of the until recently limited opportunities for foreign researchers to carry out fieldwork. Among the factors propelling the current changes, they note the changing line of succession whereby the last of the sons of King Abdulaziz al-Saud (1875–1953) is in power, and a mechanism has to evolve in order to transfer power to the third generation; the youth bulge, which is creating pressure for increased job opportunities, especially when oil-based revenues are becoming unpredictable since the decline in prices in 2016–18; popular demands for some kind of participation and representation in governance; and increased political tensions in the region, especially with Iran and its extension into Yemen.

Saudi Arabia in Transition showed how, alongside its courting of religious authorities, the Saudi state has grounded its political legitimacy on more secular bases and acted as a force for modernisation and development. King Abdullah bin Abdulaziz al-Saud, who ruled from 2005 to 2015, in particular played a major role in initiating certain programmes which have directly contributed to the ongoing social changes. In addition to founding the King Abdullah University of Science and Technology (KAUST), which provides high-quality education in scientific fields and is the only Saudi university to offer co-education, he also initiated an international scholarship scheme equally open to women and men. The widespread access to higher education open to women in Saudi Arabia today is one of the best examples of the major societal transformations over the past few decades, given that primary schools for girls had not been introduced until the 1960s and were resisted by many communities.[5] Since then the opportunities for Saudi women to pursue higher education have been completely transformed; 35 per cent of Saudi women aged 25–34 hold a post-secondary degree, compared with 3 per cent Saudi women aged 55–74. Further, their rate of participation is higher than that of men: only 28 per cent of Saudi men aged 25–34 hold a post-secondary degree.[6]

During my own fieldwork with women at universities in Riyadh and Jeddah, I have found them to be highly articulate, with high professional aspirations and markedly Western tastes in terms of style and dress.[7] Most acknowledge the support of their male family members (fathers, brothers, husbands) in their pursuit of their educational and professional aspirations. During my fieldwork, most recognised the King Abdullah international scholarship scheme that enables women to pursue higher education overseas as a game changer.[8] The returning graduates come home not just with foreign degrees but also with a healthy exposure to Western liberal sensibilities. This increase in educational opportunities has been combined with access to the internet since the late 1990s, and more recently with access to the latest mobile phone apps.[9] A majority of the Saudi youth is thus as well connected to the global culture as are their counterparts in other parts of the world.

The most forceful example of the growing pressure from within Saudi society (and from many members of the royal family alike) to relax social norms preceding the current reforms came in the curtailing of the powers of the *muṭaawwiʿīn* (religious police) in 2016. The immediate trigger for this change was the video clip of a Saudi *muṭaawwa* trying to force two young women into a van to take them to a police station, for some apparent transgression of accepted moral behaviour outside a shopping mall in Riyadh, which went viral on social media and Twitter.[10] The government ruling to abolish the powers of the *muṭaawwiʿ* to take people into custody was, however, not a response to this single event but the result of slowly increasing pressure from the public and the more progressive members of the royal family to remove such forced restrictions on individual behaviour.

Despite recording these changes, most scholars were of the view that the pace of social liberalisation will be slow, in line with the conservative ethos of broader Saudi society and Salafi Wahhabi social conservatism. The conclusion that I drew at the end of my interview with officials in the Entertainment Authority was the same: while promoting a social reform agenda, the state is keen to ensure that the pace of change takes into account the conservative ethos of Saudi society. Thus, for example, mixed-sex concerts would not be a reality for some time, because the officials noted strong resistance to the idea in the Twitter chats that they were following. In the immediate future, the focus seemed to be on holding same-sex concerts, featuring a female singer performing for a female audience, and vice versa.

Thus, most scholars on Saudi Arabia, even those writing about the ongoing changes, have been taken by surprise by the speed of social reforms that the Crown Prince Muhammad bin Salman has been announcing since late 2017 and, equally, by their steadily expanding scope. In October 2017, the Crown Prince announced the new policy of allowing women the right to drive, while at the same time announcing the opening up of cinema halls. In December 2017, the first mixed concert took place and was very well attended. During my fieldwork in 2016 and early 2017, the issue of women's right to drive was a subject of constant debate in the Saudi newspapers, but there were no indications of an imminent shift in policy. At the launch of Vision 2030 in April 2016, when asked about this issue, the Crown Prince's response was that change had to be gradual: 'We just need to remember that securing women's rights in the West was also a long process'.[11]

Yet, barely one year later, the ban on women's right to drive was lifted – a policy that for decades had been closely associated in popular Western media with the rigidity of Wahhabi Salafi Islam. Two years after the initial announcement of these reforms, policies restricting women's mobility and their wider social participation have been relaxed further. The male guardianship rule, which made women dependent on their male family members when travelling overseas or undertaking activities in the economic sphere, has been amended:[12] Saudi women can now travel overseas without a male guardian. During my fieldwork in 2019, the foreign workers in Saudi Arabia were of the view that, given the unexpected speed of change, it would not be long before the policy requiring women to wear *ʿabāya* would also be removed. Whether or not the policy is actually changed, the widespread public expectation that this shift is also imminent reflects the highly unexpected nature of the approved reforms. Given the changes already announced, now anything seems possible: not tomorrow, but today.

Salafi Wahhabi social conservatism is thus visibly under pressure in today's Saudi Arabia. Allowing women the right to drive, relaxing male-guardianship requirements and opening up mixed-sex cinema halls and mixed-sex concerts all represent a major push-back against Salafi Wahhabi prescriptions on social organisation. So is the recent announcement by the Saudi state that unmarried foreign couples will be allowed to share hotel rooms, in a bid to promote foreign tourism.[13] More importantly, the weakening of the power of the religious scholars is also visible in the way in which these policies are being approved. Unlike in the past, there are only limited attempts, if any, by the Saudi state to legitimise these reforms by seeking religious scholars to issue fatwas to endorse them. Most of these policies are being announced in a matter-of-fact manner, which suggests that the state feels no need to pretend to have secured religious legitimacy. The state's ability to push through these reforms and the relative lack of resistance on the part of the religious scholars indicate a weakening in the appeal of the Salafi Wahhabi conceptualisation of the social sphere, even in one of the most conservative Muslim societies.

What factors have contributed to these changed social attitudes, and why are religious scholars tolerating this challenge to their authority?

Response of the State Scholars

The fact that the Crown Prince does not hesitate to use absolute repression to curb any form of resistance is an obvious reason why scholars are choosing to stay quiet about the ongoing changes, however much they might detest them.[14] But the real reasons for their tolerance of this reform agenda rest in the changing dynamics of the mutual dependence between the House of Saud and the House of Wahhab, which in the past has safeguarded their respective political and religious authority.[15] Historically, the Wahhabi scholars provided religious legitimacy to the Saudi royal family in return for preserving the privilege to regulate the religious domain. Thus, political and economic matters remained mainly in the hands of the state, while the religious authority dictated policies related to the social and educational spheres.[16] But, for this division of authority to work, the religious authority had to have real influence over the perceptions and actions of the public. Only a religious authority with the ability to shape public perceptions of right and wrong can enhance the political authority of a regime.[17] The relative acquiescence of the Salafi Wahhabi scholars that we are witnessing today is in fact reflective of the more fundamental shifts in Saudi society whereby, as noted in the preceding section, the religious authorities, in general, are losing ground. This does not imply a decline in belief – although some surveys do indicate growing secular propensities within the Saudi public, as elsewhere in the Middle East[18] – but a relative shift away from the very rigid readings of the texts.

This view, voiced by many during my fieldwork, was confirmed by the overwhelming support that Muhammad bin Salman's reforms have received from young Saudis. During my interviews in Saudi Arabia, there was unanimous agreement that among young people aged 15–30, male as well as female, the Crown Prince was extremely popular. Muhammad bin Salman's popularity among the youth has thus made the scholars still more aware of their eroding societal base. As one respondent commented, 'the scholars realise that religious authority is under pressure not just in Saudi Arabia but across the Muslim world. Their choice is thus pragmatic. They realise that, despite its shifting priorities, the Saudi state is still more religious in outlook than what they see of the states in the surrounding region'.

Such an approach is also not inconsistent with the traditional position of the Wahhabi scholars, which argues in favour of pledging obedience to the ruler in order to avoid any risk of *fitna*. As noted in the introduction to *Saudi Arabia in Transition*, the Salafi Wahhabi scholars draw on the work of ibn Taymiyya to argue that following an oppressive ruler is better than the chaos that could result from rebellion. This theoretical position, which critics equate with encouraging political quietism and support for dictatorial regimes (see the next chapter for a detailed discussion of this point), has gained increased legitimacy in the eyes of the scholars and even members of the public after seeing the chaos that emerged in countries such as Syria and Libya after the Arab Spring. The destruction and instability that has followed there after the Arab Spring has thus reinforced the Wahhabi scholarly consensus on political quietism. This is particularly so because, while clearly violating the traditional dominance of the *'ulamā'* in defining the rules for regulation of the social sphere, the state is making no intervention in the domain of *'aqīda,* which is the core of Wahhabi teachings. All policy reversals related to the Salafi Wahhabi positions concern regulation of the social sphere, especially around the mixing of the sexes; the actual teaching of Islamic *'aqīda* still remains a preserve of the Wahhabi scholars.[19]

Thus, when the Crown Prince made the famous statement in October 2017 promising to make Saudi Arabia return to 'moderate Islam',[20] he was not suggesting abandoning the Wahhabi theological debates in favour of the more rationalist-leaning *māturīdī* or *ash'arī* schools of theology, or revisiting the Salafi method of reasoning to define laws for current times. Instead, he was explicitly attacking the *Ṣaḥwah* movement and the political radicalism that the Saudi state associates with it (see Chapter 7). Salman al-Awda, one of the key leaders of the *Ṣaḥwah* movement, has been in prison and under threat of the death penalty since 2017.[21] The weak foundation of the case against him has led even Western human-rights groups to take up his case internationally. However, he remains in a Saudi prison and under duress. Under pressure, the Wahhabi scholars are therefore of the view that it is important to preserve the domain over which they are still being given complete control – namely, the teachings of the *'aqīda*.

Response of the Independent Scholars

While the above helps to explain the responses of the traditional Wahhabi scholars and their acceptance (partly forced and partly pragmatic) of the ongoing social reforms, it is important to appreciate that the shifts in public sensibilities that have made the ongoing social reforms popular are also influencing the attitudes and approaches of the scholars themselves. There is an increasing plurality of viewpoints among Salafi scholars. Issues that formerly were part of the established consensus are now open to discussion, including the foundation of the Wahhabi concept of *ʿaqīda*. In addition, everyday questions that present a conflict between observing Islamic rulings and living by the expectations of a modern society, as faced by Muslims especially in the West, are leading some Salafi scholars to draw different conclusions, following the same Salafi method of reasoning. The work of Hatim al-Awni in Saudi Arabia and that of Yasir Qadhi in the USA is noteworthy in this context. Both are self-identified Salafi scholars, albeit from different generations.

Yasir Qadhi, an American Muslim and graduate of al-Madina University, who later earned a doctorate at Yale University and is now a faculty member in the USA, as well as a popular Salafi scholar in American Salafi circles, presented a paper on the contribution of Hatim al-Awni at the conference on which this volume is based. In his paper, he highlighted the importance of al-Awni's efforts to open up critical space for debate within Salafism. For him, al-Awni's contributions are important to study because of the status he enjoyed within the Salafi scholarly sphere and because of his family lineage.[22] He was a student of Nasir al-Din al-Albani (1914–99), has taught in a number of Saudi universities and has also written extensively on *ḥadīth* science and law. In Qadhi's view, al-Awni's critique of dominant Wahhabi Salafi teachings about *ʿaqīda* is particularly important because it is coming not from an external opponent, but rather from one who achieved fame and prestige from within the ranks of conservative Salafism and who is an admirer of ibn Taymiyya.[23] Also, it is important because his criticism is actually being given airtime, generating discussion and being endorsed as well as refuted in forums and internet chat rooms. Although critical of the Wahhabi doctrine, al-Awni has not adopted any political stance against the Saudi dynasty, which has helped him to have continued access to media platforms where he can openly air his views.[24] The fact that he has been able to command public space while presenting theologically sensitive critiques of the Najdi doctrine is evidence of a growing plurality within Saudi religious spheres and a growing tolerance of this within the Saudi royal family.

As Qadhi highlights, al-Awni's main focus is on establishing the importance of tolerance and deliberation within the domain of *'aqīda*. In a detailed analysis of al-Awni's key writings on the subject, Pooya Razavian presents a detailed analysis of his contribution to exposing the limits of Wahhabi thought from within.[25] Al-Awni argues for space for more open dialogue and discourse and for freedom of conscience. In doing so, he critically engages with the Wahhabi understanding of two key concepts also mentioned in the introduction to this volume: *takfīr* and *al-walā' wa al-barā'*. In his writings he tries to demonstrate how key Wahhabi texts end up endorsing the use of *takfīr* that plays into the hands of the jihadis. A Wahhabi text that he has critiqued in great detail is *Al-Durar al-sanīyah fī al-ajwibah al-najdīyah* (The Glittering Pearls of the Najdi Response), a collection of the writings of Wahhabi scholars from the time of ibn 'Abd al-Wahhab until the mid-twentieth century.

This book, which is considered an essential reference in Saudi religious scholarship,[26] is known to have inspired certain influential jihadis, but the fact that it has the potential to inspire jihadism is normally denied by Wahhabi scholars. Critiquing this approach, al-Awni accuses them of complacency concerning the jihadis' agenda. He goes so far as to refer to them as dormant members of ISIS (*al-dā'ishīyūn al-qa'dah*) who are waiting for an opportunity to implement their vision of *takfīr*.[27] His contention is that the subject of *takfīr* is central to this text, and that the scholars' denial is deliberate. Al-Awni's two influential works on the subject of *takfīr* include *Takfīr ahl al-shahadatain* (Excommunicating the People of Two Witnesses), which presents an analysis of the permissibility and possibility of excommunicating other Muslims, and *Al-'Ibadah*: *Bawābat al-tawḥīd wa bawābat al-takfīr* (Worship: The Gate of Tawhid and the Gate of Takfir).

Apart from presenting a detailed critique of the Wahhabi reading of *tawḥīd*, al-Awni has also criticised Wahhabi readings of the concept of *al-walā' wa-l-barā'*. As noted in the introduction to this volume, the notion *al-walā' wa-l-barā'* requires that Muslims must be loyal to those who defend *tawḥīd* and disown those who do not. Al-Awni acknowledges the importance of this concept but places heavy emphasis on the use of moderation, tolerance and mercy in its application.[28] This means that in practice he checks many of the potential applications of *al-walā' wa-l-barā'* by the jihadi groups: 'Muslims cannot force non-Muslims to believe in Islam;[29] Muslims are bound to honour any contracts or deals that they have with non-Muslims;[30] and, that it is *ḥarām* for Muslims to kill any non-Muslims who are abiding by their contracts and the conditions of *dhimmah*'.[31] His view is that Muslims have to protect the basic human rights of non-Muslims,[32] and that they have to treat people of all religions, not just fellow Muslims, with justice and kindness.[33] Further, al-Awni argues that an action that might contravene the concept of *al-walā' wa-l-barā'* would indeed be a sin, but it does not make the doer of that action a non-believer.[34] This is so because the concept of *al-walā' wa-l-barā'* is based on one's beliefs, and only God knows what is inside a person's heart; thus, actions do not reveal actual levels of inner belief. Such a position poses a fundamental challenge to the Wahhabi notion of *tawḥīd* which, as explained in the introduction to this volume, makes action central to showing commitment to *tawḥīd*.

Thus, al-Awni presents an example of a radical reformer from within the senior ranks of the scholars within the tradition, one who is questioning the very foundation of Wahhabi doctrine of *'aqīda*. The fact that his silence on political issues helps him to avoid any state repression does not detract from the fact that within Saudi society there is now some space for debating the very foundation of Wahhabi theology. The media outlets do keep inviting him back suggesting a consistent audience for his views.

At the same time, Yasir Qadhi himself serves as a good example of a Salafi scholar taking a fresh analytical perspective on critical issues from within the Salafi religious sphere. Qadhi's work is notable because he is a graduate of al-Madina University and a self-identified Salafi scholar who enjoys great popularity on the speaking circuits among Muslim youth in the USA. He is at the same time comfortable with his American identity and plays a critical role in helping young Muslims in the USA resolve the tensions that they often feel between being a devout Muslim and being an American national. Unlike al-Awni, Qadhi has therefore focused more of his work on providing new answers to critical everyday questions for young Muslims living in the West, instead of focusing on deeper conceptual debates on *'aqīda*. Yasir Qadhi has tried to address many critical questions concerning sensitive topics such as same-sex marriage laws in America, approaches to liberal citizenship and respect for the law of the state when Muslims are in a minority.

In order to argue for new interpretations, he uses various conservative historical fatwas to show how they led to a negative socio-political or economic outcome for Muslim societies. The conclusions that Qadhi draws on contemporary social problems show how the same Salafi methodology can be used to justify radically different positions, as was the case with the work of Islamic modernists and that of Wahhabi Salafi scholars. Qadhi is using Salafi methods of reasoning to convince Muslims in the West to respect the secular constitution of the country of which they are nationals; not to try to impose their values on non-Muslims, just as they would not like people of other religions imposing their values on them; and to be tolerant of socio-religious pluralism in society. Thus, while al-Awni presents an example of a scholar defending increased deliberation and tolerance at the level of foundational creedal beliefs, Qadhi is complementing these efforts by applying the same logic of respect for a plurality of thought to finding answers to contemporary challenges that enable young Muslims to stay loyal to their religious tradition yet be confident members of their societies.

Having written his doctoral thesis on ibn Taymiyya's attempt to reconcile reason and revelation,[35] Qadhi notes that, unlike other *Ḥanbalī* scholars, he read the work of those who disagreed with his standpoint, both philosophical and theological texts. While ibn Taymiyya is viewed by most as being opposed to rational inquiry, Qadhi presents him as a scholar 'who redeems *'aql* (reason) while keeping *naql* (text) supreme'.[36] Defending such an approach whereby text remains supreme while allowing space for rational reasoning, Qadhi's approach to addressing contemporary legal questions is important because it advocates unchanging loyalty to what he views as being clear in the text (for example, a complete Islamic ban on homosexuality), while allowing for debate on other issues (such as participation in democracy and Western democratic institutions). He is also open about the evolution of his own understanding of Salafism and admits to having moved away from mainstream Salafism due to the refusal of most Salafi scholars to engage with issues at an intellectual level. Such an approach, he contends, is incompatible with the needs of the current times. To date, Qadhi defends the Salafi method of engaging directly with the source text of the Qur'ān and *ḥadīth* as being more effective in understanding Islam than a reliance on the interpretations of a group of scholars. However, he engages with the same foundational texts in ways different from the traditional Salafi Wahhabi scholars, thereby often reaching dramatically different conclusions about how young Muslims should respond to contemporary issues.

As Razavian notes, Qadhi's position can best be viewed as a move towards 'reasonable Salafism': an approach to the interpretation of texts whereby scholars recognise the need to bear in mind the lived experiences of Muslims when determining legal rulings. He interprets traditional Salafi conservatism as being reluctant to bring change in Islamic law, even when Islamic law provides the scholars with the tools for reasoning and adapting the laws to contemporary needs. Drawing on historical evidence, he shows how such an approach can cause harm to the development of Muslim societies. In his own writings, he has thus addressed questions and issues that pose a challenge to traditional conservative views, such as how to recognise evolution as a scientific truth but at the same time to justify God's intervention; how to obey laws of the secular state that might clash with Islamic rulings; or how to be active participants in modern democracies despite their Western origin.

Conclusion

This chapter has tried to map the pressures on Salafism as a highly socially conservative and theologically rigid religious tradition. The Saudi state is visibly distancing itself from Wahhabi Salafi social conservatism, although not questioning foundational creedal beliefs. The attempt to reposition itself as a socially progressive state is, however, making the Saudi state also endorse increased liberalisation in areas which are linked to Wahhabi creedal beliefs. Thus, in my own fieldwork I have found less aggressive attempts to discourage visitors coming for the Hajj and *'umra* from visiting the graves of the *ṣaḥābas*. The reforms geared towards social liberalisation are critical to convincing the West of the Saudi state's social reform agenda, when it comes to successfully repositioning itself in the eyes of Muslims around the world, especially the young, showing that increased tolerance in interpretation of creedal beliefs becomes equally critical.

It is thus perhaps not surprising that al-Awni has continued to be given space in the media, despite openly attacking Wahhabi foundations of *'aqīda*, which irks the scholars. Where matters remain unchanged are in the area of political liberalisation, as it would mean sharing political authority. As in the case of any political elite, the Saudi royal family is keen to resist the diffusion of its political authority as long as it possibly can. It is thus not surprising that it is the *Ṣaḥwa* scholars that are imprisoned and threatened with death sentences. However, it must be recognised that even on the political front the royal family is feeling the pressure for creating platforms that give the public some sense of political participation. As one member of the royal family noted, it could slowly lead to the establishment of some form of elected assembly, working under royal guidelines.

Thus, in this period of dramatic socio-economic shifts within Saudi Arabia and the visibly weakening power of the Wahhabi Salafi scholars in their home base, one might be tempted to predict a semi-demise of Salafism as a global movement. That, however, would be an erroneous conclusion stemming from a historically faulty assumption which associates the global spread of Salafism over the past five decades primarily with Saudi oil money. As we shall see in the chapters in Part II and Part III of this volume, while the Saudi state or scholars might be connected to Salafi movements around the globe and in some cases might even pour in financial aid, the Salafi movements in most contexts today have developed strong indigenous roots. Irrespective of the ongoing shifts within Saudi Arabia, the future of Salafism as a global movement remains relatively secure, as many within the movement are driven by their independent commitment to the Salafi ideals. What we are witnessing in these movements, however, is a growing space for plurality and adaptation to changing local societal and political contexts, just as we have documented with reference to the writings of Yasir Qadhi and al-Awni in this chapter. In a similar vein, the next chapter shows how the *Ṣaḥwa* scholars, who arguably were the first ones to push the limits of Wahhabi Salafi consensus from within, continue to build a counter-discourse against political quietism by using Salafi methods and texts.

Notes

1. *General Entertainment Authority Website*, https://www.gea.gov.sa/en/ (accessed 30 October 2019).
2. Vision 2030 is an ambitious plan for socio-economic reform, launched by the Crown Prince Muhammad bin Salman in 2016. Also referred to as the National Transformation Program, it is presented by the Crown Prince as a 'bold yet achievable blueprint for an ambitious nation. It expresses our long-term goals and expectations and it is built upon our country's unique strengths and capabilities. It guides our aspirations towards a new phase of development – to create a vibrant society in which all citizens can fulfil their dreams, hopes and ambitions to succeed in a thriving economy'. *Vision 2030 Kingdom of Saudi Arabia Website*, https://vision2030.gov.sa/en (accessed 30 October 2019). The focus of the plan is on economic diversification, moving away from a dependence on oil. Independent reviewers, however, remain critical of its feasibility and scope.
3. Bernard Haykel, Thomas Hegghammer and Stéphane Lacroix (eds), *Saudi Arabia in Transition: Insights on Social, Political, Economic and Religious Change* (Cambridge; New York: Cambridge University Press, 2015).
4. Ibid., 1.
5. Masooda Bano, 'Saudi Salafism amid Rapid Social Change', in *Modern Islamic Authority and Social Change, Volume 1: Evolving Debates in Muslim Majority Countries*, ed. Masooda Bano (Edinburgh: Edinburgh University Press, 2018), 127–49.
6. Dalia Fahmy, '5 Facts about Religion in Saudi Arabia', *Pew Research Centre*, 12 April 2018, https://www.pewresearch.org/fact-tank/2018/04/12/5-facts-about-religion-in-saudi-arabia/ (accessed 30 October 2019).
7. Bano, 'Saudi Salafism'.
8. Over 70,000 Saudi students have already benefited from the King Abdullah Scholarship scheme. The scholarship covers tuition fees as well as living costs for the full duration of the academic programme at leading universities in the USA, UK, Europe, Canada and Australia. 'King Abdullah Scholarship Program to Continue for Five Years to Come', *Ministry of Education Website*, https://www.moe.gov.sa/en/news/Pages/an74.aspx (accessed 30 October 2019).
9. Bano, 'Saudi Salafism'.
10. Ibid.
11. 'Deputy Crown Prince Backs Women Driving', *Arab News*, 23 April

2016, http://www.arabnews.com/featured/news/914356 (accessed 12 June 2017).

12. A royal decree issued in August 2019 allows Saudi women the right to travel overseas without seeking permission from a male guardian. They can now also request the issuance of official documents – for example, to register a marriage, divorce, or childbirth – and act as legal guardian of children. Emma Graham-Harrison (and agencies), 'Saudi Arabia Allows Women to Travel without Male Guardian's Approval', *The Guardian*, 2 August 2019, https://www.theguardian.com/world/2019/aug/01/saudi-women-can-now-travel-without-a-male-guardian-reports-say (accessed 30 October 2019).
13. Julia Buckley, 'Saudi Arabia Allows Unmarried Couples to Share Hotel Rooms', *CNN*, 7 October 2019, https://edition.cnn.com/travel/article/saudi-arabia-unmarried-couples-female-travelers/index.html (accessed 23 October 2019).
14. The strong perception that the Crown Prince himself was involved in ordering the murder of Jamal Khashoggi in the Saudi Embassy in Istanbul, as well as the brutal method of the killing, has created fear among activists. The execution of 37 individuals in April 2019, many of them charged with promoting extremist ideologies, has had a similar impact. 'Saudi Arabia Executes 37 in Connection with Terrorism', *Al Jazeera*, 27 April 2019, https://www.aljazeera.com/news/2019/04/saudi-arabia-executes-37-connection-terrorism-190423140531849.html (accessed 30 October 2019). Critics believe that many of those executed were simple political activists.
15. David Commins, *The Wahhabi Mission and Saudi Arabia* (London: I. B. Tauris, 2012).
16. Nabil Mouline, *The Clerics of Islam: Religious Authority and Political Power in Saudi Arabia* (New Haven: Yale University Press, 2014).
17. Bano, 'Saudi Salafism'.
18. As noted by Faisal Devji in an article for *The New York Times*, the 2012 Gallop international survey recorded 5 per cent of Saudis identifying themselves as atheist and 19 per cent declaring themselves not to be religious. Faisal Devji, 'Conversions from Islam in Europe and Beyond', *The New York Times*, 17 August 2017, https://www.nytimes.com/2017/08/15/opinion/islam-conversions.html (accessed 30 October 2019).
19. Further, the Salafi Wahhabi *'ulamā'* can sustain their sectarian narrative against the Shi'i. This anti-Shi'i discourse, which is integral to Salafi teachings, is in line with the Saudi regime's anti-Iran discourse.
20. Martic Chulov, 'I Will Return Saudi Arabia to Moderate Islam, Says Crown

Prince', *The Guardian*, 24 October 2017, https://www.theguardian.com/world/2017/oct/24/i-will-return-saudi-arabia-moderate-islam-crown-prince (accessed 30 October 2021).

21. Tamara Qiblawi, 'MBS Once Sought Advice from This Cleric: Now Saudi Prosecutors Want Him Executed', *CNN*, 25 July 2019, https://edition.cnn.com/2019/07/25/middleeast/saudi-cleric-sheikh-salman-al-awda-intl/index.html (accessed 30 October 2019); 'Amnesty: Saudi Cleric Ouda Faces Possible Death Penalty for Peaceful Activism', *Middle East Monitor*, 27 July 2019, https://www.middleeastmonitor.com/20190727-amnesty-saudi-cleric-ouda-faces-possible-death-penalty-for-peaceful-activism/ (accessed 30 October 2019).
22. Yasir Qadhi, 'Reformation or Reconstruction: Dr Hatem al-Awni's Critiques of Wahhabism', paper presented at *The Future of Salafism* conference, University of Oxford, 5–7 December 2018.
23. Ibid.
24. Ibid.
25. The analysis of al-Awni's and Qadhi's own writings presented in this section draws heavily on the research carried out on these two scholars as part of the project *Changing Structures of Islamic Authority and Social Change: A Transnational Review*. For detailed analysis of the work of these two authors, see Christopher Pooya Razavian, 'Post-Salafism: Salman al-Ouda and Hatim al-Awni', in *Modern Islamic Authority and Social Change, Volume 1: Evolving Debates in Muslim Majority Countries*, ed. Masooda Bano (Edinburgh: Edinburgh University Press, 2018), 172–94; Christopher Pooya Razavian, 'Yasir Qadhi and the Development of Reasonable Salafism', in *Modern Islamic Authority and Social Change, Volume 2: Evolving Debates in the West*, ed. Masooda Bano (Edinburgh: Edinburgh University Press, 2018), 155–79.
26. Stéphane Lacroix, *Awakening Islam: The Politics of Religious Dissent in Contemporary Saudi Arabia*, trans. George Holoch (Cambridge, MA: Harvard University Press, 2011), 321.
27. Razavian, 'Post-Salafism'.
28. Ibid.
29. Ibid.
30. Ibid.
31. Ibid.
32. Ibid.
33. Ibid.
34. Ibid.

35. Yasir Qadhi, 'Reconciling Reason and Revelation in the Writings of Ibn Taymiyya (d. 728/1328): An Analytical Study of Ibn Taymiyyah's "Dar' Al-Ta'arud"' (doctoral dissertation, Yale University, 2013).
36. Razavian, 'Yasir Qadhi'.

3

LEGITIMISING POLITICAL DISSENT: ISLAMIST SALAFI DISCOURSES ON OBEDIENCE AND REBELLION AFTER THE ARAB REVOLUTIONS

Usaama al-Azami

In a *Washington Post* article from 1 November 2018, a journalist interviewed people in rural Saudi Arabia about the brutal murder of Saudi journalist Jamal Khashoggi a month earlier by agents in the Saudi consulate in Istanbul. This murder set off a global media storm that was still ongoing at the time of the interview. The *Post*'s journalist comes across a young man by the name of Mohsin Muhammad al-Mohsin who, having recently graduated from university in Riyadh, is seeking employment as a teacher of religion. His response to the Khashoggi affair is interesting on a number of levels. The twenty-six-year-old begins by saying that the killing was a 'mistake', and that the media was lying about it. The murder still concerned him because it contravened Islamic norms but, like many of his compatriots, al-Mohsin expressed his support for the Crown Prince Muhammad bin Salman, even if he were found to be guilty of ordering the killing of his countryman. What is of interest to the present chapter, however, is an observation in this connection made by al-Mohsin. Presenting a narrative of his interview, the *Post* quotes him thus: '"People should not disagree with their leaders, no matter what", [al-Mohsin] said, rubbing red prayer beads in his right hand. "There is an Islamic saying: 'To be patient and live with an unjust leader for 50 years is better than to live without a leader for one day'"'.[1]

This Islamicate saying and others like it have a long pedigree in Islamic thought. Something resembling this particular statement is mentioned by the Saudi Salafi movement's most important premodern antecedent, ibn Taymiyya (d. 1328), who notes in his *Majmū' al-fatawa* that 'the sound of mind (*al-'uqalā'*) have stated: "sixty years of a tyrannical ruler is better than a single night without a ruler"'.[2] But statements like these go back far earlier in the Islamic tradition. A similar saying is attributed to the early jurists Mālik b. Anas (d. 795) and Sufyān al-Thawrī (d. 778), by the North African Mālikī scholar Qāḍī 'Iyād b. Mūsā (d. 1149), as follows: 'Tyrannical rule of seventy years is better than a leaderless *ummah* for a moment of the day'.[3] Going even further back in time, one finds such a sentiment attributed to the companion of the Prophet and notable military commander who conquered Egypt, 'Amr b. al-'Aṣ (d. 664). In advice he gave to his son, as reported by al-Tabarānī (d. 971), he notes: 'Outrageously tyrannical rule is better than perpetual civil war'.[4] Such views are not uncommon in the contemporary Middle East, as is illustrated by the frequency of their citation in fatwas, online discussion forums and new media, such as YouTube.[5]

In the wake of the Arab revolutions, however, the meaning of these sentiments have become highly contested. At the heart of this contestation is the question of whether these statements, the roots of which lie in Prophetic teachings, imply absolute obedience in the face of the worst imaginable oppression, or whether they are to be understood simply as a statement of the obvious, namely that political authority is often a necessary evil – a position that allows for opposition to its evils without calling for its abolition in principle. This and related questions are considered in the course of the present chapter. Specifically, I study the key concepts of obedience (*ṭā'a*) and rebellion (*khurūj*), as articulated in the statements and writings of three prominent scholars with close links to Saudi Arabia, two of whom are Islamist Salafis who supported the Arab revolutions, and one of whom is a prominent non-Salafi who has emerged as one of the revolutions' most noteworthy opponents. This chapter deliberately takes as its primary focus the two pro-revolutionary scholars, since its purpose is to present a vista into the world of dissident Salafism. Due to space limitations, I do not consider the discourse of the non-Salafi anti-revolutionary scholar addressed below at the same level of depth as I afford the two pro-revolutionary Salafi scholars.[6]

Three Scholars on Obedience and Rebellion

In recent years, the concepts of obedience and rebellion in Islamic political thought have gained salience in societies directly affected by the Arab revolutions. These concepts may be conceived of as two ends on a spectrum of attitudes towards political authority. Between these two poles, one finds an idea that is more difficult to pinpoint using a single term in the language of the premodern Islamic scholarly tradition – namely, the notion of protest or non-violent revolution. This could approximate scriptural notions such as commanding right and forbidding wrong (*amr bi-l-maʿrūf wa-l-nahy ʿan al-munkar*), advising rulers (*naṣīḥa*) or, to use a concept borrowed from the modern Western lexicon, civil disobedience (*al-ʿiṣyān al-madanī*).[7] It is important to note that, in this spectrum, 'rebellion' is conceived of as necessarily violent. The English word 'rebellion' implies as much in its primary meaning according to authoritative English dictionaries.[8] By contrast, it should be noted that the term 'revolution' does not lexically necessitate physical violence in the English language or in the conception of the scholars considered here. These concepts, and their scriptural bases, are addressed in what follows, in relation to the post-Arab revolutionary public engagements of three scholars – Muhammad al-Dadaw, Salman al-Awda and Abdallah bin Bayyah.[9]

The first of these, Muhammad al-Hasan Wuld al-Dadaw (b. 1963), is a Mauritanian scholar who is Salafi in his theological leanings – he prefers the label 'Ḥanbalī' – and Islamist in his political leanings. Born a Bedouin in the western Mauritanian desert, he studied informally but extensively with prominent scholars from his extended family and is noted for his remarkable memory. After pursuing undergraduate studies in Mauritania, he went on to earn a master's degree at Imam Muhammad ibn Saud Islamic University in Riyadh. Currently he is one of the trustees of the Qatar-based International Union of Muslim Scholars (IUMS) which, after the Arab revolutions, became the focal point of Islamist scholarly activism in support of the revolutions.

Salman al-Awda (b. 1956) is a prominent Saudi Salafi scholar with a long career in Islamist activism, as part of what is known as the Saudi *Ṣaḥwa* movement.[10] Born in Burayda in the al-Qasim region of north-central Saudi Arabia, he pursued extensive informal and formal Islamic studies up to the doctoral level and also taught at the above-mentioned Imam Islamic University. He is also one of the current trustees of the IUMS but, since September 2017, he has been imprisoned in Saudi Arabia in a crackdown on dissenting voices by the crown prince, Muhammad bin Salman (b. 1985). In addition to his being subject to torture, the Saudi state currently seeks the death penalty against him.[11]

Finally, Abdallah bin Bayyah (b. 1935) is a highly regarded Islamic scholar and one-time politician. Born in eastern Mauritania, he is acknowledged by his contemporaries as a learned Islamic jurist, and he has held senior positions in past Mauritanian governments, including as the country's vice president in the 1970s. Bin Bayyah's career in Mauritanian politics ended with the military coup of July 1978, after which he relocated to Jeddah, Saudi Arabia, where he has remained ever since as a professor of jurisprudence at King Abd al-Aziz University. From its founding in 2004 until his resignation in September 2013, he was a vice president of the IUMS. Since then, he has 'defected' to set up royalist counter-institutions to the IUMS in the UAE, most notably the Forum for Promoting Peace in Muslim Societies (FPPMS).[12]

These scholars have naturally long known each other, all of them having lived in and frequented Saudi Arabia. They have long shared institutional links through the IUMS; Bin Bayyah served as a member of Salman al-Awda's doctoral committee in 2004, and the latter has written and spoken of him in adulatory terms in subsequent years.[13] Al-Dadaw, for his part, has praised Bin Bayyah in the past as one of the five great Islamic jurists of present-day Mauritania.[14] After the Arab revolutions, however, and particularly after the Egyptian coup of 2013, these relationships appear to have come to an end. This state of affairs has no doubt been reinforced by Bin Bayyah's silence towards the Saudi authorities after the crackdown on all independent voices in Saudi Arabia in late 2017. The figures arrested included al-Awda, but also younger Saudi scholars with links to al-Dadaw, such as al-Dadaw's regular host Adil Banama (b. 1974) on the now defunct Islamist-oriented Saudi satellite channel *4Shabab*. Both Banama and the channel's owner Ali al-Umari (b. 1973) – a friend of al-Dadaw and al-Awda – were arrested by the Saudi authorities in late 2017 and remain indefinitely incarcerated.[15] Al-Umari is, in fact, also a past student of Bin Bayyah, and as in the case of al-Awda, Bin Bayyah sat on al-Umari's doctoral committee. As of writing in late 2019, Bin Bayyah's website still contains a glowing endorsement of the shaykh written by all three imprisoned scholars.[16] His royalist orientation towards the Saudis and the Emiratis has thus been a cause for some disquiet among his erstwhile friends.

A relatively straightforward typology of the scholars vis-à-vis the concepts under discussion thus suggests itself: scholars who were in favour of the Arab revolutions, specifically al-Dadaw and al-Awda, and scholars who were opposed to them, namely Bin Bayyah. In what follows, I will consider the arguments presented by these scholars in favour of their conceptions of obedience and rebellion. These arguments are built around a set of Qur'ānic verses and *ḥadīth*s, some of which may be seen as providing a basis for the kinds of quietist statements with which this paper began.

The most relevant and oft-cited verse in this context is 4:59, which reads, 'O you who believe, obey God and obey the Messenger and those in authority among you, but if you are in dispute over any matter, refer it to God and the Messenger, if you truly believe in God and the Last Day'. One of the most important *ḥadīth*s in this context is to be found in the two most significant collections in the Sunni canon – those of al-Bukhārī and Muslim. In this *ḥadīth*, the companion 'Ubādah b. al-Ṣāmit (d. 654/5) states:

> We pledged allegiance to the Messenger of God, peace be upon him, to hear and obey in difficulty and ease, whether we like it or not, even if others are preferred over us, and that we would not contest the authority of those in power unless you see clear disbelief for which you have a proof from God, and that we would stand for or speak the truth wherever we may be without fear, for God's sake, of the critic's criticism.[17]

Several other *ḥadīth*s are cited by the scholars, as I will present in the discussion below, but the verse and *ḥadīth* cited above provide the core material for framing the issues at hand.

The first of these issues is that it is clear that the concept of obedience to authority (*ṭāʿa*) finds its origins in the Qur'ān. The disagreement pertains to how that obedience manifests in practice, and how to deal with disagreements if they arise. The Qur'ān suggests here that disagreements are taken up by consulting God and his Prophet, and this is understood by authoritative

Sunni scholars as referring to consulting the Qur'ān and Sunnah. The Sunnah, of which the *ḥadīth* literature is the primary repository, provides a number of *ḥadīth*s, including that cited above. This *ḥadīth* suggests, as other *ḥadīth*s further clarify, that a Muslim's obedience to their rulers is rendered even if one dislikes it, and that there apparently is no scope for subversive dissent. Yet, the *ḥadīth* suggests that other forms of dissent may be called for, for it demands 'speaking or standing for the truth' whatever the circumstance. It is inconceivable within Sunni theology that this could have led to any form of opposition on the part of the companions to the Prophet himself, but subsequent rulers to whom one has pledged allegiance could conceivably be the locus of such truth-telling. This is suggested in a *ḥadīth* that is narrated in the *Mustadrak* of al-Ḥākim al-Naysābūrī (d. 1014), in which the Prophet states: 'The master of the martyrs is Ḥamza b. ʿAbd al-Muṭṭalib, and a man who stands up to a tyrannical ruler, commands him [to right] and forbids him [from wrong], so he kills him'.[18]

This brief presentation of some of the key pieces of evidence should make clear that much hinges on how this evidence is interpreted. It is to such interpretations that we shall now turn. In what follows, I will first present the ideas of the two pro-revolutionary scholars before turning briefly to the thought of Bin Bayyah. Since al-Dadaw began addressing these issues first, in satellite TV shows in 2011 that continued through 2014, I will begin with his treatment of these matters, followed by that of al-Awda, who treats these matters somewhat more systematically in a short book published in 2012. Selections from Bin Bayyah's royalist reading of the scriptural sources follow the pro-revolutionary perspectives of al-Awda and al-Dadaw. In the main, these are from his writings published from 2013 onwards. As noted earlier, since the present chapter focuses on Salafis, the non-Salafi Bin Bayyah's thought is not dealt with in as much detail as that of the other two scholars.

Pro-revolutionary Islamic Discourses on Obedience

Al-Dadaw addresses the issue of obeying one's rulers in a number of TV shows from 2011 onwards. In one such show the presenter, Adil Banama, who often plays devil's advocate in discussions, presents a series of canonical *ḥadīth*s that appear to promote absolute obedience to one's rulers. One such *ḥadīth* is found in al-Bukhārī and reads: 'Whoever obeys me, obeys God, and whoever disobeys me, disobeys God. Whoever obeys the commander/ruler [*amīr*] has obeyed me, and whoever disobeys the commander/ruler has disobeyed me'.[19]

On the surface, the obedience appears unconditional, but al-Dadaw suggests that such *ḥadīth*s must be read in the context of the other *ḥadīth*s and verses that pertain to the issue. He notes that obedience to one's rulers is upheld as a norm inasmuch as it accords with obedience to God and his messenger, as is made explicit in other *ḥadīth*s such as: 'There is no obedience to be rendered in disobedience [to the Creator]. Obedience is only rendered in that which is right [*ma'rūf*]'.[20] However, if this is the case, then obedience is indeed an obligation (*wājib*) according to al-Dadaw. This, he argues, is simply necessary for the proper running of affairs. Indeed, he asserts, every country operates in accordance with this principle, since insubordination would simply lead to anarchy (*fawḍā*).[21]

Al-Dadaw also highlights that this 'obedience' is derivative of obedience to the Prophet, since the pertinent Qur'ānic verse highlights that obedience is of two classes. In 4:59, the Qur'ān states: 'O you who believe, obey God and obey the Messenger and those in authority among you'. Citing an oft-repeated principle with respect to this verse, al-Dadaw notes that absolute obedience is due to God and his messenger, while the verse does not say 'and *obey* those in authority among you'. Rather, he notes that the phraseology of the verse makes clear that the obedience due to 'those in authority' is derivative of obedience due to the messenger. In the case of the latter, one may not disobey him, but in the case of rulers, one may disobey in cases of commands that are contrary to the teachings of the messenger. This derivative or lesser nature of the obedience due to rulers is a common refrain in the writings of Sunni commentators on this verse.[22] Al-Dadaw also adds that in the Prophet's lifetime, obedience, presumably of a derivative kind, was due to any governors he appointed. After his death, this authority was passed on to his caliphs and their governors. Such authority derives from the authority of the Prophet, but its derivative nature, according to al-Dadaw, renders it weaker than the direct authority of the Prophet. Yet, one who obeys such authority when it is in line with Prophetic teachings is thereby obeying the Prophet and may expect to be rewarded in the hereafter accordingly.[23]

Al-Dadaw's interviewer next cites a similar *ḥadīth* exhorting obedience to one's rulers, which is found in both al-Bukhārī and Muslim. It reads: 'Whoever dislikes [*kariha*] something about their ruler should exercise patience, for no one rebels against authority by even a hand span [*kharaj min al-sulṭān shibr*^an^], dying in that state, except they die a pagan [*jāhilī*] death'. In response to the suggestion by the presenter that this is a dire warning against any form of opposition to one's rulers, al-Dadaw avers that this *ḥadīth* is specifically about rebellion, that is *armed* insurrection, which he notes is prohibited (*muḥarram*) with respect to a Muslim ruler. Al-Dadaw provides a concise definition of 'rebellion' as he discusses this *ḥadīth*. He defines it as follows: 'attempting to remove the political authorities by force of weapons' (*al-khurūj al-sa'y li-khal' al-sulṭān bi-l-quwwa wa-l-silāḥ*); he adds that directing weapons towards the political authorities is prohibited.[24] Such armed rebellion is rejected by a majority of Muslim jurists, although this position was not settled in the earliest period of Islam.[25] Thus, al-Dadaw may be viewed here as upholding the post-formative Sunni stance against armed rebellion as a general rule.

Salman al-Awda's most systematic treatment of the topics of rebellion, protest and obedience may be found in his short 2012 work entitled *As'ilat al-thawra* which, by the author's own admission, represents his rudimentary ruminations on these issues. His engagements in other forms of media and social media are less systematic, and in the present chapter I will therefore focus exclusively on his book. Like al-Dadaw, al-Awda is at pains to highlight the nuance of the scriptural tradition as necessitating a careful weighing of different scriptural sources and the manner in which they have been understood by scholars throughout history in a variety of contexts. This is why, he suggests, one finds difference of opinion as to the legal status of rebelling against oppressive and immoral rulers, with some jurists saying that it is prohibited, while others call it obligatory and still others say it is legally neutral (*mubāḥ*).[26] Despite the nuance of the scriptural tradition on these issues, he argues that there has been a tendency in official circles to present a 'one-sided' perspective on the relationship between the ruler and the ruled. He characterises this as an occasional tendency to almost deify the ruler (*ta'līh al-ḥākim*). As we shall see below, al-Awda's description of one-sided readings of scripture could be applied to Bin Bayyah's subsequent portrayal of the tradition.[27]

Al-Awda notes that obedience to one's ruler is ultimately contingent on freely and willingly pledging allegiance (*bay'a*) to the ruler, given that such a pledge forms a contractual obligation, and such contractual obligations are predicated on voluntary compliance in the *sharī'a* as a matter of consensus (*ijmā'*). The Qur'ān (4:29) stipulates that sales contracts must be on the basis of mutual consent, and so, he argues, such contracts as a pledge of allegiance must be so *a fortiori*. Like al-Dadaw, al-Awda also affirms that obedience to one's rulers is indeed enjoined in the scriptural tradition, but in keeping with a long tradition of commentary on such matters he notes that this is plainly not a slavish or absolute form of obedience. Rather, it is obedience that is counterbalanced by a duty to advise the ruler on the part of the ruled.[28]

Citing Qur'ān 4:59, al-Awda highlights how the verse requires one to respond to disagreements with one's rulers by exhorting: 'And if you are in dispute over any matter, refer it to God and the Messenger, if you truly believe in God and the Last Day'. Thus, al-Awda argues that the verse itself places God and his messenger as the final arbiters in any disputes, rather than highlighting obedience as an absolute matter. Al-Awda also stresses that similar sentiments are found in canonical *ḥadīth*s. To this end, he cites the same canonical *ḥadīth* of 'Ubādah b. al-Ṣāmit that we saw earlier. The paradigmatic pledge of allegiance found within it, so al-Awda points out, is notable in that it combines both a commitment to obedience to the ruler and to speaking the truth without fear of criticism.[29] In his estimation, another *ḥadīth* in al-Bukhārī and Muslim also highlights this fact. He cites a report in which the Prophet states the following: 'A Muslim must hear and obey [their rulers] in what they like and dislike, unless they are commanded to sin. If they are commanded to sin, there is no hearing and obeying'.[30] At the heart of his discussion lies the contention already stated: that the Islamic scholarly tradition, as a matter of consensus, recognises that contracts require both parties to enter them freely and willingly, something that applies, in al-Awda's view, to any pledge of allegiance to a ruler.

Thus we find that both al-Awda and al-Dadaw share similar approaches to the question of obedience to one's rulers. In this connection, al-Dadaw also presents a discussion of rendering obedience when one perceives an injustice towards oneself on the part of the ruler. On the question of how to deal with such a perceived injustice, al-Dadaw considers the statement of the companion, Ibn Mas'ūd (d. 652/3), who reportedly counselled a younger contemporary thus: 'If the Imam [that is, caliph] is just [*'ādil*], then he is rewarded, and you must be thankful; but if he is unjust [*jā'ir*], then he is sinful, and you must be patient'. Al-Dadaw argues that in Ibn Mas'ūd's historical context, the 'injustice' mentioned here was a reference to 'preferential treatment' given to some over others. More specifically, he argues that this *ḥadīth* is relating a historical exchange in which Ibn Mas'ūd is discussing the appropriate attitude to be adopted towards a caliph who bears the mantle of the Prophet's political authority (*khalīfat Rasūl Allāh*). Ibn Mas'ūd is addressing someone who wishes to rebel against the third caliph, 'Uthmān (d. 656), due to the perception that the latter was nepotistic in awarding administrative posts. Al-Dadaw affirms the historical fact that 'Uthmān had appointed some of his relatives, who were not companions, to posts over senior companions, due to his exercising his administrative discretion in accord with his judgement (*ijtihād*) on the matter.[31]

He adds, however, that giving preferential treatment is something that the Prophet warned his companions they would be confronted with after his passing, and his advice to them was that they should be patient in the face of such *athara*. In addition to the *ḥadīth* of 'Ubādah b. al-Ṣāmit mentioned earlier, here al-Dadaw appears to be referring to another *ḥadīth* that is related in both al-Bukhārī and Muslim, in which the Prophet says: '"There will be *athara* after me, and things that you find objectionable (*umūr tunkirūnahā*)". [The companions] asked: "O Messenger of God, what do you command one who experiences this?" He replied: "You should fulfil your obligations, and ask God for what is due to you"'.[32]

Given the specific context of these *ḥadīth*s, however, al-Dadaw argues that patience in the face of perceived oppression is not an absolute principle – although the *ḥadīth*'s exhortations did apply vis-à-vis the third caliph since, in other respects, the state was legitimate. For patience to be the appropriate response to injustice, he argues, the state should be operating in an otherwise healthy fashion with all the concomitants that that entails. These, as al-Dadaw lists *extempore*, are: that the state is secure, that God's *sharī'a* and *ḥudūd* are being upheld, and that the caliph is not intrinsically an unjust ruler, aside of the perceived injustice of awarding appointments preferentially. Besides this, he adds that people's rights should be upheld, freedoms should be afforded to the populace, and the state should be able to maintain its power and authority. Al-Dadaw thus narrowly circumscribes the Prophet's exhortations to patience in the face of *athara* as referring to patience vis-à-vis the preference of others over oneself in the ruler's allocation of state administrative posts – something that could appear unobjectionable even in modern democracies.[33]

On Commanding Right and Forbidding Wrong

On the issue of whether one may criticise a ruler, al-Dadaw considers the statement attributed to the companion, Abū al-Dardā' (d. c. 652), in the *Shu'ab al-Iman* of al-Bayhaqī (d. 1066) –namely, that '[t]he first manifestation of hypocrisy (*nifāq*) in a man is his attacking (*ṭa'n*) his Imam'. Once again, al-Dadaw argues that this is a sound principle in general, but not an absolute one. It applies only to the caliph and, even with respect to him, the tradition does not prevent opposing or correcting the caliph. Rather, al-Dadaw states that the Prophetic principle of sincere advising (*nuṣḥ*, *naṣīḥah*) necessitates that the ruler is corrected if he makes mistakes.[34] If the mistakes are commissioned in public, then he should be corrected publicly, and private mistakes should be addressed privately. None of this constitutes an attack in his view. In this connection he gives the example of 'Alī, who publicly contravened the then Caliph 'Uthmān's prohibition of conducting the Ḥajj in a particular manner.[35]

The type of 'attack' that is being warned against in Abū al-Dardā's statement is, according to al-Dadaw, verbal abuse (*shatm*), defamation (*tashwīh*), rebellion (*khurūj*) and efforts to unseat the incumbent authority (*al-sa'y li-'azlihī*). Yet, even here, he argues that *shatm* is not absolutely prohibited, as is clear from the behaviour of companions vis-à-vis political authorities. As an example, he notes from authoritative *ḥadīth* collections that when Bishr b. Marwān (d. c. 693), the caliph's cousin and governor in Iraq, gave a sermon in which he raised his hands in prayer, one of the companions, 'Umarah b. Ruwayba (d. c. 690), considered this action to be a reprehensible innovation (*bid'a*) and verbally attacked him, saying: 'May God disgrace (*qabaḥa*) these little hands! I saw the Prophet on his pulpit, and he never did any more than this'. He then raised the index finger of his right hand. Al-Dadaw suggests that this rather severe insult from a companion qualifies the otherwise sound statement from Abū al-Dardā'.[36]

By extension, with respect to protest, al-Dadaw argues that such acts do not constitute rebellion. Rather, he maintains that protesting should be viewed as in keeping with the *ḥadīth* of 'Ubādah b. al-Ṣāmit cited earlier, which emphasises the need to 'stand for or speak the truth wherever [one] may be, without fear, for God's sake, of the critic's criticism'. This, al-Dadaw argues, was the practice of the companions, including vis-à-vis the caliphs, and the obligation of defending Muslims against oppressive rulers is, he claims, a matter of consensus.[37] Ultimately, al-Dadaw concludes, the Arab revolutions that are taking place for the most part without the bearing of arms – he made these remarks in mid-2011 –do not constitute rebellion (*khurūj*).

In his conclusion to a four-episode treatment of democracy on *4Shabab* recorded in late 2011, al-Dadaw presents a summary of his assessment of the Arab revolutions and the question of whether or not such revolutions constitute rebellion. As might be expected from his earlier remarks regarding the meaning of *khurūj*, he rejects the suggestion that protesting and demanding one's rights in a peaceful manner can be viewed as rebellion. Yet, on the question of rebellion, he notes that not all Arab rulers are the same. Those who are just, loved by their citizens and uphold the *sharī'a* are legitimate rulers against whom one may not rebel. But if this is not the case, then this does not apply. Al-Dadaw then proceeds to list certain conditions that, if present, would in fact obligate rebellion (*wujūb al-khurūj*):

> [A ruler] who is an unjust tyrant (*ja'ir ẓālim*), does not adjudicate on the basis of the Sharī'ah (*la yuḥakkim Shar' Allāh*) and does not judge using the Book of God (*lā yaḥkum bi-Kitāb Allāh*); nor does he claim any connection to the religion of God. He does not claim that he is the Caliph or Imam or one who applies any of God's *ḥudūd*. [In his time as ruler] he is not known to have applied even one of God's *ḥudūd*. He does not treat as *ḥarām* what God has prohibited (*lam yuḥarrim mā ḥarram Allāh*), but rather treats as halal what God has prohibited (*aḥall mā ḥarram Allāh*), including fornication (*zinā*), interest (*ribā*) and enormities (*fawāḥish*). One is obligated to rebel against (such rulers).[38]

This list is in some ways quite striking. It could be viewed as an invitation to rebel against most Muslim rulers in modern times, given that hardly any make claims of being the caliph or can claim to uphold all of these values consistently. Yet, al-Dadaw's praise a few minutes later of the then Saudi king, Abdullah bin Abd al-Aziz (d. 2015) – who did not claim to be a caliph – for his support for the Syrian people against Bashar al-Assad (b. 1965) suggests that he is not necessarily making a subversive political statement when discussing the obligation of rebellion under certain conditions. It is possible to interpret his statement as indicating that a ruler who combines all of the flaws listed should be rebelled against with force of arms, at least in theory.

Contending with a *Ḥadīth* Enjoining Obedience

In the remaining discussion of al-Dadaw and al-Awda's ideas, we shall find that, when it comes to responding to one particularly challenging canonical *ḥadīth*, the two scholars adopt contrasting strategies to arrive at similar results. An oft-cited *ḥadīth* in defence of tyrannical rule is one that contains the purported exhortation from the Prophet to the companion Hudhayfa b. al-Yamān (d. 656) to 'hear and obey [your ruler] even if he lashes your back and takes your wealth'.[39] On its surface, this suggests that, even when a ruler contravenes basic *sharī'ah* norms, a Muslim is required to remain obedient. Al-Dadaw disagrees, arguing that taking a single line from a *ḥadīth* without its broader context is misleading. In the typical manner of a scholar of *ḥadīth*s, he notes that there are shorter and longer versions of this *ḥadīth* in various canonical collections of variable reliability. He argues that the context is made explicit when one considers the full range of these reports.

Accordingly, he avers that the fuller versions of this *ḥadīth* found in the *Musnad* of Aḥmad b. Ḥanbal (d. 855) clarify that the context of the *ḥadīth* is one in which the Prophet is informing Hudhayfa of how to conduct himself in times of social breakdown and civil strife. Al-Dadaw highlights a phrase in the longer versions of the *ḥadīth* that provides what he considers to be crucial context: 'If there is a Caliph of God on the earth' (*fa-in kāna li-Llāh yawma'idh*^{in} *fī al-arḍ khalīfa*) in such times of civil strife, then you must be obedient to him, 'even if he lashes your back and takes your wealth'.[40] But if there is no such caliph, he contends, then no such obligation exists. Concomitantly, he argues that the *ḥadīth* cannot be used to support claims of the absolute authority of a tyrant who does not specifically qualify as a caliph – which considerably narrows the scope of application for such a *ḥadīth* in the present day, given that there has been no widely accepted caliphal claimant for roughly a century. Al-Dadaw states elsewhere, in the context of the pretentions of ISIS to the caliphate, that the status of being a caliph is not simply conferred on any claimant to it but must be affirmed by the *umma* on the basis of legitimate procedure.[41]

In a separate interview, al-Dadaw makes an important additional note regarding the *ḥadīth*. He asserts that the statement 'even if he lashes your back and takes your wealth' cannot be seen as implying that the ruler is engaging in such behaviour without legitimate justification. That is to say, the *ḥadīth* cannot reasonably be understood as meaning 'even if he takes your wealth illegally [*bi-l-ḥarām*]'. Al-Dadaw asserts that no past scholar has ever made such a claim. Drawing on Ibn Ḥazm (d. 1064), al-Dadaw suggests that this is as outrageous as saying the Prophet would say something like: 'You must be obedient, even if [your ruler] rapes your wife'. After all, he argues, the Prophet has stated in other *ḥadīth*s: 'A person who is killed defending his wealth is a martyr' (*man qutila dūn mālih fa-huwa shahīd*); 'A person who is killed defending his family [*ahl*] is a martyr'; and 'A person who is killed defending his honour [*'irḍ*] is a martyr'.[42]

Salman al-Awda also addresses the controversy pertaining to this *ḥadīth*, but he considers the version found in *Ṣaḥiḥ Muslim*, which contains an exhortation to obey one's ruler, 'even if your back is hit and your wealth is taken'.[43] Al-Awda's written treatment is different from al-Dadaw's *extempore* response to a question on a live TV show, most notably in that the former's approach is to criticise the variant of the *ḥadīth* containing this particular phrase as unsound. He notes that, although the original *ḥadīth* is to be found in both al-Bukhārī and Muslim, only one narration of Muslim's contains the particular phrase that speaks of being hit and robbed. This variant is also one of the few *ḥadīth*s in Muslim's *Ṣaḥiḥ* that has been critiqued by subsequent scholars, notably by Dāraqutni (d. 995) among premodern scholars and by Muqbil al-Wadi'i (d. 2001) in the modern period.

Unlike al-Dadaw, al-Awda does not explore the narrations in the *Musnad* of Aḥmad, which are deemed mostly sound by al-Dadaw and the editors of the *Musnad*, but like al-Dadaw in his 2013 interview, al-Awda highlights that this *ḥadīth* conflicts with the unquestionably sound *ḥadīth* regarding the martyred status of one who dies defending their wealth from robbers. Al-Awda additionally points out that the *ḥadīth* in which the Prophet declares

'Whoever dies defending his wealth is a martyr' is considered to be unimpeachable in its authenticity by scholars including al-Munāwī (d. 1621) and al-Kattani (d. 1927), by virtue of being widely transmitted (*mutawātir*). He thus argues for disregarding the problematic version of the *ḥadīth* in *Ṣaḥiḥ Muslim* altogether.[44] Al-Dadaw's and al-Awda's approaches both have the result of neutralising a potentially problematic *ḥadīth* – the former's through interpretation, the latter's through disqualification. Both are substantive engagements with the tradition. As suggested by the case of Bin Bayyah, such substantive engagements are less common among prominent defenders of a doctrine of absolute obedience to rulers.

The Arguments of a Counter-revolutionary Scholar

Those scholars who opposed the Arab revolutions generally appear to present less scripturally fastidious arguments. The only such scholar whose arguments I will consider here, namely Abdallah bin Bayyah, is an Islamic legal theorist (*uṣūlī*). His apparent inability to escape a fairly theoretical orientation, even in his public-facing advocacy, makes his discourse somewhat vague. The relatively unsystematic nature of his arguments on the points raised by al-Dadaw and al-Awda makes it difficult to pinpoint how he would respond to their arguments. My treatment of his discourse will reflect this. On the question of obligation to render obedience to one's rulers, however, it is clear that he holds such an obligation to be virtually absolute. Bin Bayyah's discourse on political matters is interesting, not only for what he says, but also for what he leaves out. As with any public figure active on social media addressing concerns that have arisen after the Arab revolutions, there is something to be said about his careful avoidance of any substantive engagement with the absence of political freedom and the pervasive repression that forms the backdrop of the context in which he operates. As noted earlier, despite, or perhaps because of, being based in the Saudi port city of Jeddah, he has remained completely silent about the systematic imprisonment of scholars in the country, many of whom were personally close to him.

Early on in the Arab revolutions, Bin Bayyah expressed repeated reservations about them, noting that he did not encourage revolution.[45] He did this while he was still a senior member of the Islamist-dominated organisation International Union of Muslim Scholars. He resigned from the IUMS in September 2013, two months after the Egyptian coup, with Saudi and UAE support, removed the democratically elected but unpopular Muslim Brotherhood government three weeks after the massacres at Rabaa and al-Nahda squares of 'likely more than 1,000' protestors, according to Human Rights Watch.[46] While the website of his erstwhile institution, the IUMS, had during this period become a veritable anti-coup pulpit with a constant stream of condemnations directed towards the Egyptian army, Bin Bayyah's website remained studiously quiet. In the months prior to these massacres, his website had been publicising his close cooperation with the UAE government, and so it was not altogether surprising that he went on to establish the Forum for Promoting Peace in Muslim Societies (FPPMS) in early 2014, under the explicit sponsorship of the UAE's foreign minister, Abdullah bin Zayed, thereby openly becoming an official scholar of the UAE.[47] It is around this time that Bin Bayyah's discourse became most explicitly hostile to notions such as democracy and protest. In the present discussion, I focus on documents from the inaugural meeting of the FPPMS in 2014. This UAE-sponsored forum's proceedings contain Bin Bayyah's full keynote address, a shortened version of which was presented in Abu Dhabi in March 2014.[48]

Bin Bayyah on (Absolute) Obedience

Notably for our purposes, Bin Bayyah's discussion of the notions of obedience, rebellion and protest are rarely grounded explicitly in scriptural sources. Rather than extensively citing verses and *ḥadīth*s, Bin Bayyah speaks in general terms of the principle of obedience (*ṭāʿa*) being affirmed by the *'ulamā'* on the basis of authentic *ḥadīth*s. Unlike al-Dadaw's or al-Awda's treatments already described, which affirm the authenticity of most of these *ḥadīth*s but then seek to contextualise their meaning in light of the apparently conflicting implications of the principles of obedience and truth-telling, Bin Bayyah engages with them very differently. Instead of citing specific verses or *ḥadīth*s, he appears to take for granted that they imply absolute obedience and then proceeds on this operative assumption to argue that rendering such absolute obedience to one's rulers does not actually imply surrendering to oppression (*istislām li-l-ẓulm*) or defeat (*inhizām*). This is because relinquishing one's rights on the basis of the Qur'ānic exhortation to 'Repel evil with that which is best' (23:96) is a way to 'seek justice in a way that is less unjust and more merciful'. It is a way of claiming the moral high ground that is closer to the way of the Prophets and more likely to reform tyrants (*akthar najā'a fī iṣlāḥ al-ẓālim*).[49]

If this seems counter-intuitive, Bin Bayyah does not provide any argument that would obviate this concern. Rather, he speaks of those who 'mock talking about obedience' as being unaware of a number of considerations. These include the scholarly agreement (*ittifāq*) regarding the numerous authentic *ḥadīth*s concerning obedience as recorded by such scholars as ibn Ḥajar al-'Asqalānī.[50] Bin Bayyah argues that such people as reject the necessity of obedience are also not sufficiently cognisant of the need to prevent bloodshed, which is a serious matter in Islam; nor do they heed the importance of preserving the common good of the community (*jamā'a*) whose interests may be lost in potential civil strife (*fitan*, sing. *fitna*) that results from a lack of obedience.[51] By speaking in general terms about scripture, Bin Bayyah does not have to contend with the substance of the arguments of scholars like al-Awda and al-Dadaw, who readily accept the importance of *ṭā'a* and the authenticity of its scriptural bases, but put forward alternative conceptions that they view as preserving fealty to the texts while undermining claims that they may be used to justify autocracy and oppression.

Bin Bayyah's discourse regarding the necessity of obedience is interesting in that it places the responsibilities of preventing social breakdown as a consequence of speaking out against oppression fully on those who are being oppressed. His discourse does not countenance critique of the oppressor under any circumstances. If one considers Bin Bayyah to not be an impartial scholar, but rather a state functionary, this makes perfect sense. It is his job to address the masses with the religious arguments necessary to prevent them from rebelling against his employers. In this regard, he is akin to a party spokesperson rather than an independent authority, but he portrays himself, given his high scholarly rank, as an impartial commentator grounded in scripture. This only makes him more effective at his job as a state official who is undertaking public relations work for his employers, the UAE, and by extension, his state of residence, Saudi Arabia.

Bin Bayyah against Democracy

This also provides context for Bin Bayyah's excoriation of democracy in his keynote speech.[52] Selectively drawing on certain Western authors' condemnations of the evils of democracy, he notes that 'democracy is the best of the worst', and that it is only suitable for 'societies that are prepared for it'. This arguably Orientalist comment will prove important a few paragraphs later when Bin Bayyah declares: 'In societies that are not ready, the call for democracy is essentially a call for war'. Given all its terrible flaws, he asks rhetorically: 'Is it not our right and obligation to find a better political solution than democracy and to establish a system based on the principles of consultation (*shūrah*) [sic] and higher justice?'[53] What that system is, he does not elaborate in any detail here, nor anywhere else in his writings. Bin Bayyah, in keeping with his role as a representative of the UAE rulers, is saying enough to undermine democracy, but not enough to propose any concrete alternative to autocracy.

Of the various concepts considered in this paper, Bin Bayyah only addresses two relatively directly: obedience and rebellion. On these, he is able to give a clear statement of support for the former and rejection of the latter. There is a complete absence of any discussion of protest – or to use scriptural parlance, *naṣīḥa*, or commanding right and forbidding wrong vis-à-vis one's rulers. This allows Bin Bayyah to present the dispute as one between those calling for peace – that is, the autocrats and those who support the status quo – versus those calling for war – that is, those violently rebelling against the order and precipitating civil war in a misguided quest for justice. As Bin Bayyah represents the powerful side of the conflict between the autocrats and the Islamists calling for democracy and limited government, he can afford to simply ignore the other side of the argument without much consequence. However, this means that, in terms of substance, his treatment of the issues under discussion may be viewed by an outside observer as worthy of study in terms of its socio-political function, but not necessarily as an interesting development in Islamic intellectual history.

Conclusion

In the foregoing, I have sought to present two dissident voices in contemporary Salafism vis-à-vis the Arab revolutions and the religio-political debates that they occasioned. Most Salafis, especially within the Saudi establishment, have tended to evince considerable hostility towards the ideas brought forth by the Arab revolutions, most notably those that place limits on the absolute authority of rulers. By studying the thought of two Islamist Salafis, namely Muhammad al-Dadaw and Salman al-Awda, I have tried to demonstrate that a scripturally grounded alternative to the political quietism of traditional Salafism has emerged after the Arab Spring, one that has provoked the ire of autocratic regimes throughout the Middle East. Such regimes have responded by imprisoning the scholars who have vocally supported the revolutions, and also by patronising counter-revolutionary scholars such as Abdallah bin Bayyah. This highly regarded jurist, although not himself a Salafi, has historically garnered the respect of the Salafi scholars cited in this chapter. In the brief consideration of his ideas presented above, his purpose is clear, even if his arguments are not consistently so. Bin Bayyah aims at undermining the pro-revolutionary scholars by arguing that the obedience owed to one's rulers is absolute, and that notions like democracy are ultimately destructive to the welfare of Arab societies. However, Bin Bayyah's engagement with the tradition in the context of modernity comes across as more superficial and less persuasive than that of his ideological competitors, who anchor their arguments in the scriptural tradition while not rejecting Western concepts such as democracy or the suggestion that popular revolution can lead to democratisation.

In many respects, modern Salafi scholars like al-Dadaw and al-Awda are attempting to shift the ground of the discourse in ways that may be seen as resembling the norms of Western traditions of political free speech. Al-Dadaw does not make any Western inspiration behind such demands explicit in his discussion of the notions of obedience and protest, although elsewhere he does not shy away from explicitly borrowing from the West, with appropriate Islamic adaptation, namely vis-à-vis the concept of democracy.[54] In his post-revolutionary discussions regarding obedience and rebellion, his discourse suggests that he views the resources within the Islamic scriptural and scholarly tradition to be sufficient for developing healthy Islamic political norms in the modern context. Al-Awda is willing to more explicitly appeal to the European experience of the last few centuries which, for him, illustrate the political possibilities that revolutionary action can give rise to over the longue durée. In this respect, he highlights that the French revolution experienced multiple phases and republics over many decades before there emerged what we would recognise as modern France with its legal protections guaranteeing certain political freedoms.[55]

The perspectives of al-Dadaw, al-Awda and Bin Bayyah are alternative interpretations that ultimately arise from the same source texts. These texts do circumscribe the range and nature of possible Islamic interpretations, but they do not lock in a single interpretation as is demonstrated by the differing perspectives in the foregoing. It is likely that the outcome of the disagreement, which has become a violent one with Bin Bayyah's royalist viewpoint being backed by the force of autocratic states in the Middle East, will be decided in the short term through a combination of scholarly argumentation and on-the-ground political considerations. In the long term, however, it is probably the arguments that will play a more decisive role. In this respect, it would appear that much more will need to be done by the counter-revolutionary camp in the modern context to make their interpretation of the scriptural sources palatable to modern Muslims. The admittedly limited range of evidence presented above suggests that the arguments of Islamic scholars calling for greater political freedom and accountability currently carry the day in the intellectual space. Crucially, it remains to be seen whether they can actualise any of their aspirations in a political context in which such voices appear unable to find dependable political backing.

Notes

1. Kevin Sullivan, 'In the Saudi Countryside, Khashoggi's Death Seems Remote and Royal Involvement Far-Fetched,' *The Washington Post*, 11 January 2018, www.washingtonpost.com/world/in-the-saudi-countryside-khashoggis-killing-seems-remote-and-royal-involvement-far-fetched/2018/10/27/083e9bc6-d920-11e8-8384-bcc5492fef49_story.html?utm_term=.79c393b36b6a.
2. Ibn Taymiyyah, *Majmuʿ al-Fatawa* (Medina: Majmaʿ al-Malik Fahd, 2004), vol. 30, 136.

3. Qadi ʿIyad bin Musa, *Tartib al-madarik wa-taqrib al-masalik li-maʿrifat aʿlam madhhab malik* (Rabat: Wizarat al-Awqaf wa-l-Shu'un al-Islamiyya, 1983), vol. 3, 326. The text may be accessed here: https://archive.org/stream/FP37029/03_37031#page/n326/mode/2up. Interestingly, a version of this tradition was cited by the American Muslim scholar Hamza Yusuf, a week after the attacks of 11 September 2001. See http://islam.uga.edu/hamza.html. Hamza Yusuf would, subsequent to the Arab revolutions of 2011, work closely with the UAE government to support autocratic rule in the Middle East in the interest of regional stability. In this regard, he reflects the orientation of his teacher Abdallah bin Bayyah, whose ideas we will consider below. For a brief discussion of these and other scholars' responses to the Arab revolutions, see Usaama al-Azami, 'Neo-Traditionalist Sufis and Arab Politics: A Preliminary Mapping of the Transnational Networks of Counter-Revolutionary Scholars after the Arab Revolutions', in *Global Sufism: Boundaries, Structures, and Politics*, eds Francesco Piraino and Mark Sedgwick (London: Hurst, 2019), 225–83.
4. Abu al-Qasim al-Tabarani, *al-Muʿjam al-Kabir*, ed. Hamdi al-Salafi (Cairo: Maktabat Ibn Taymiyya, 1983), vol. 20, 214. One modern scholar deems this tradition to be extremely weak in its attribution to ʿAmr. See www.ahlalhdeeth.com/vb/showthread.php?p=2330004.
5. For fatwas from the Qatari website Islamweb.net, including one published two days after the fall of the longstanding Egyptian president, Hosni Mubarak, see http://fatwa.islamweb.net/fatwa/index.php?page=showfatwa&Option=FatwaId&Id=149387, www.islamweb.net/fatwa/index.php?page=showfatwa&Option=FatwaId&Id=195253, http://fatwa.islamweb.net/fatwa/index.php?page=showfatwa&Option=FatwaId&Id=216631; for Salafi online forums, see www.tasfiatarbia.org/vb/showthread.php?t=11049 and www.dd-sunnah.net/forum/showthread.php?t=13583; for a YouTube video by a Salafi scholar uploaded in 2013, see https://youtu.be/ChZO-QeUvEw.
6. I hope to address anti-revolutionary Islamic thought in greater detail elsewhere. Some preliminary reflections may be found in al-Azami, 'Neo-Traditionalist Sufis and Arab Politics', and al-Azami, "Abdullāh bin Bayyah and the Arab Revolutions: Counter-Revolutionary Neo-traditionalism's Ideological Struggle against Islamism', in *The Muslim World* (2019).
7. I use the term 'scripture' and its derivatives to refer to the Qur'ān and *ḥadīth* literature.
8. This is the case in the dictionaries of Oxford and Cambridge. The Merriam-Webster dictionary highlights violence in its secondary meaning of the word.

9. In this chapter, I spell Bin Bayyah's name according to his own usage in the English language.
10. For a comprehensive study of this movement, see Stéphane Lacroix, *Awakening Islam: The Politics of Religious Dissent in Contemporary Saudi Arabia* (Cambridge, MA: Harvard University Press, 2011).
11. See https://genevacouncil.com/en/2019/06/06/gcrl-sends-urgent-appeal-to-the-un-special-rapporteurthree-scholars-at-imminest-risk-of-death-in-record-executions-this-month-in-saudi-arabia/.
12. For a more detailed discussion of his resignation from the IUMS and move towards the UAE, see al-Azami, "Abdullāh bin Bayyah and the Arab Revolutions'.
13. See https://vb.tafsir.net/tafsir3931/#.W91ml2j7RPY, www.aljazeera.net/encyclopedia/icons/2016/3/23/%D8%B3%D9%84%D9%85%D8%A7%D9%86-%D8%A7%D9%84%D8%B9%D9%88%D8%AF%D8%A9, www.salmanalodah.com/popups/print_window.aspx?article_no=30383&type=3&expand=1.
14. https://youtu.be/zZtlhvZW1Ek.
15. Al-'Umari has also been subject to torture according to news reports. See www.middleeastmonitor.com/20190111-rights-group-cleric-ali-al-omari-brutally-tortured-in-saudi-prison/.
16. For al-ʿUmari's praise of Bin Bayyah on the latter's website, see http://binbayyah.net/arabic/archives/336, for Banama's see http://binbayyah.net/arabic/archives/326, and for al-Awda's, see http://binbayyah.net/arabic/archives/319.
17. In Arabic, this *ḥadīth* reads: *Bāyaʿnā Rasūl Allāh, ṣallā Allāh ʿalayhi wa-sallam, ʿalā al-samʿ wa-l-ṭāʿa fī al-ʿusr wa-l-yusr wa-l-manshaṭ wa-l-makrah wa-ʿalā athara ʿalayna wa-ʿalā an-la nunāziʿ al-amr ahlahu illā an taraw kufr*[an] *bawāḥ*[an] *ʿindakum min Allah fīh burhān wa-ʿalā an naqūm aw naqūl bi-l-ḥaqq aynamā kunnā wa-lā nakhāfu fi-Llāh lawmat lāʾim*. This is the fullest version of the *ḥadīth*. For variants, see Ahmad bin Hanbal, *Musnad*, eds Shuʿayb al-Arnaʾut et al. (Beirut: Muʾassasat al-Risala, 2001), vol. 24, 411–15.
18. The *ḥadīth* is deemed *ṣaḥīḥ* by al-Ḥākim al-Naysabūrī, al-Khātib al-Baghdādī (d. 1071) and al-Albani (d. 1999) and deemed *ḥasan* by Abu ʿAbd-Allah Mustafa bin al-ʿAdawi (b. 1954). See al-ʿAdawi, *Al-Sahih al-musnad min fadaʾil al-sahaba* (Khobar: Dar Ibn ʿAffan, 1995), 184–86.
19. See https://youtu.be/Q0SCr_MOvis, published on YouTube on the *4Shabab* official channel, 25 September 2013.
20. This *ḥadīth* is narrated by both al-Bukhārī and Muslim. For a discussion of

the *ḥadīth* in an unrelated fatwa, see https://islamqa.info/ar/answers/162423/هل-يطيع-والدته-في-اخذ-القرض-الربوي.

21. See https://youtu.be/Q0SCr_MOvis.
22. There are many instances in the premodern scholarly tradition where this is highlighted. See, for example, the following two authors who are admired by Salafis: Ibn Hajar al-ʿAsqalānī, *Fath al-bari sharh Sahih al-Bukhari* (Beirut: Dar al-Maʿrifa, 1959–60), vol. 13, 111–12. The text may also be accessed here: www.islamweb.net/newlibrary/display_book.php?idfrom=13058&idto=13215&bk_no=52&ID=3928. Ibn Abi al-ʿIzz al-Hanafi, *Sharh al-ʿaqida al-tahawiyya* (Beirut: Muʾassasat al-Risala, 1990), 542–43.
23. See https://youtu.be/Q0SCr_MOvis.
24. See https://youtu.be/Q0SCr_MOvis. Incidentally, the counter-revolutionary former grand mufti of Egypt, ʿAli Gomaa (Jumʿa), has similarly argued that rebellion is necessarily armed rebellion (*al-khurūj maʿnāhu* [. . .] *al-khurūj al-musallaḥ*). See https://youtu.be/52DMpHZBxE4?t=27m16s.
25. For a discussion on this issue that is less resolute in its rejection of armed rebellion against a Muslim ruler, see http://fatwa.islamweb.net/fatwa/index.php?page=showfatwa&Option=FatwaId&Id=216631. See also Khaled Abou El Fadl, *Rebellion and Violence in Islamic Law* (Cambridge, UK: Cambridge University Press, 2001).
26. Al-Awda, *Asʾilat al-thawra* (Beirut: Markaz Nama li-l-Buhuth wa-l-Dirasat, 2012), 142.
27. Ibid., 142–43.
28. Ibid., 139–55.
29. Ibid.
30. Ibid., 140.
31. See https://youtu.be/Q0SCr_MOvis.
32. Ibid.
33. Ibid.
34. See https://youtu.be/gVYeWD8DIXA?t=2629. Al-Dadaw does not use gender neutral language, which is generally rare in Arabic. Elsewhere, however, he argues that besides a caliph, a head of state could be a woman. See https://youtu.be/QQ1-01iSA84?t=8m04s.
35. The nature of the disagreement is not made clear in this instance, although al-Dadaw repeats the story in more detail in another episode. See https://youtu.be/gVYeWD8DIXA?t=2629.
36. See https://youtu.be/Q0SCr_MOvis.

37. For a Salafi criticism of the historic soundness of one of the reports he uses as evidence for this, see www.sahab.net/forums/index.php?app=forums&module=forums&controller=topic&id=139629. On the apparent inaccuracy of his claims of consensus that Muslims must stand up for the rights of any Muslim who has been oppressed by a ruler, see www.kulalsalafiyeen.com/vb/archive/index.php/t-36457.html. These criticisms slightly weaken, but do not seem to seriously undermine al-Dadaw's overall argument.
38. See https://youtu.be/gVYeWD8DIXA?t=2565 (uploaded 13 August 2011)
39. See https://youtu.be/KuUC7PkTtTE?t=2789 (uploaded 13 August 2011).
40. The *extempore* recollection of al-Dadaw does not perfectly match the wording of the *ḥadīth*s, but the overall sense is accurate. The *ḥadīth*s may be found in Aḥmad, *Musnad*, vol. 38, 421–26.
41. See https://youtu.be/fcvQamvf_3g.
42. See https://youtu.be/G_F5KV2m5zA.
43. 143ff. The wording cited by al-Awda, drawn from Muslim's *Ṣaḥīḥ*, is slightly different from that of the version addressed by al-Dadaw, as reflected in their respective translations.
44. Al-Awda, *As'ilat al-Thawra*, 143–45.
45. For a more detailed treatment of the issues addressed in this paragraph, see al-Azami, "Abdullāh bin Bayyah and the Arab Revolutions'.
46. See 'All According to Plan: The Rab'a Massacre and Mass Killings of Protesters in Egypt,' *Human Rights Watch*, 8 December 2014, www.hrw.org/report/2014/08/12/all-according-plan/raba-massacre-and-mass-killings-protesters-egypt.
47. The website presents Bin Zayed as the Forum's official sponsor, giving the impression that it is not averse to seeing itself as a foreign policy project of the UAE. See www.peacems.com/en/about.peace/sponsor.message.aspx
48. See Bin Bayyah, *In Pursuit of Peace* (Abu Dhabi: Forum for Promoting Peace in Muslim Societies, 2014). The full version may be found in PDF form in Arabic, French and English in a single document online: https://drive.google.com/open?id=1TOts39QzfEg-QQGZ-I0WD731KlSy_nL7.
49. Bin Bayyah, *In Pursuit of Peace*, 35 (Arabic text), 22 (translation).
50. Ibid. The work of ibn Ḥajar's referenced in Bin Bayyah's footnotes more or less contradicts his statement, although elsewhere ibn Ḥajar – along with the vast majority of *ḥadīth* scholars, including those like al-Awda and al-Dadaw – do indeed affirm the authenticity of the *ḥadīth*s concerning obedience, as noted earlier with respect to al-Awda and al-Dadaw. Contrary to Bin Bayyah's

presentation of the issue, however, they do not understand such obedience to be virtually unconditional.

51. Ibid.
52. Bin Bayyah provides a more thorough condemnation of democracy in other writings, which I hope to consider elsewhere.
53. Bin Bayyah, *In Pursuit of Peace*, 34 (Arabic text), 21–22 (translation).
54. See https://youtu.be/QQ1-01iSA84?t=5m14s.
55. Al-Awda, *As'ilat al-thawra*.

PART 2

SALAFI MOVEMENTS ON THE GROUND

4

QUIETIST 'SCHOLASTIC' SALAFISM IN MOROCCO SINCE THE ARAB SPRING

Guy Robert Eyre

The popular uprisings that swept through Tunisia, Egypt, Bahrain, Yemen and Libya in 2011 and 2012 also swept through Morocco, leading to the unprecedented nationwide '20 February' protests. These protests also marked the beginning of new evolutions within Morocco's Salafi community[1] – Salafis, who had essentially been banned from the public sphere by the Moroccan regime since the 2003 Casablanca bombings (orchestrated by jihadi-Salafis), quickly resurfaced as significant players. Many former Salafi-jihadi leaders, whom the Moroccan regime released from prison between 2011 and 2013,[2] took advantage of the new (albeit limited) political openings. Some began to officially support the palace and the new 'democratic process' after years of rejecting the monarchy's legitimacy and espousing violent insurrection. Several prominent Salafi *shuyūkh* publicly endorsed the main Islamist party in the country, the 'Justice and Development Party' (Hizb al-Adala wa-l-Tanmiya – henceforth, PJD). Others (including Shaykhs Abou Hafs and Abdelkarim al-Chadli) joined the smaller Islamist 'Renaissance and Virtue Party' (Hizb al-Nahda wa-l-Fadila) and called on Salafis to join existing legal political parties[3] in order to engage in party politics. Several other more 'activist' Salafi leaders (most notably Mohammed Fizazi) continued to campaign for the establishment of a first Moroccan Salafi political party, modelled on the Egyptian al-Nour Party.[4]

This chapter contributes to the growing scholarship that demonstrates that, despite the rigidity typically associated with Salafi reasoning, it is in fact malleable.[5] In Morocco, new (and changing) political opportunities saw Salafis rethink their positions on political participation and political activism. Furthermore, these shifts in Salafi reasoning were not accepted uncritically by other Salafi scholars and their followers. Instead, such revisions provoked dynamic debates and contestation over ideas and, ultimately, ideological tensions and divisions within these Salafi scholarly communities.

This chapter demonstrates this based on the case of the 'quietist', Marrakech-based, 'scholastic Salafi' (*al-Salafiyya al-'ilmī*) 'Association for the Quranic Call and for the Sunnah' (Jamaat al-Dawa ila al-Quran wa-l-Sunna) – popularly referred to as Dor al-Quran – and its founder Muhammad bin Abdul Rahman al-Maghraoui (b. 1948) in light of the nationwide '20 February' protests in the country.

While the events of the so-called 'Arab uprisings' since 2011 have led to a greater interest in new Salafi politicians and Salafi political activism, as well as jihadi-Salafi networks, as the 'balance of power within the wide Salafi spectrum [. . .] shifted in their favour', the more 'quietist' ideal-type, once 'considered to be a kind of standard norm defining Salafism' and enjoying a 'kind of precedence' over the other Salafi trends, should not, as Bonnefoy argues, disappear from the 'academic radar' as they remain important actors.[6] It is important to also understand how quietist Salafis contended with the challenge of the emergence of popular power across the region, as well as their ability to react to changing circumstances as they (ultimately) sought to resist new trends of Salafi politicisation.[7]

Salafism in Morocco has received little scholarly attention, despite the dramatic evolutions within these circles since 2011 and the close-up, detailed and rich contextual fieldwork that the now safer and relatively open research environment offers. Existing scholarship on Salafis in Morocco (and particularly since 2011) largely focuses on the re-integration of former detainee jihadi-Salafis into public and political life since 2011. This scholarship – particularly Masbah's important work[8] – shows how these figures entered politics in large part to avoid state harassment and improve their legal standing, employment and financial prospects. However, there has been very little academic study of Shaykh al-Maghraoui and Dor al-Quran[9] – arguably the most prominent and important Salafi organisation in Morocco and the largest quietist Salafi network in the kingdom – and the dramatic evolutions and divisions it underwent between 2011 and 2016.

This chapter draws on a large range of Salafi literature (including books, YouTube videos of lectures, online statements, and media interviews and comments), a tranche of Moroccan media sources and articles, as well as in-depth interviews with Salafi figures. This chapter argues that, following his return to Morocco in early 2011, Maghraoui suddenly disavowed his traditional rejection of participation in formal politics and protests, and that his discourse increasingly referenced more societal and political, rather than simply doctrinal, issues. This was part of his own strategy to secure the reopening and survival of Dor al-Quran and came in response to changing opportunities and pressure from the Moroccan regime, rather than on the basis of any substantive ideological revision regarding politics itself.

Yet, while several prominent Salafi figures from within Dor al-Quran – most prominent amongst them, Hammad al-Qabbaj – underwent substantive ideological revision vis-à-vis political participation, protests and procedural democracy, the closure of Dor al-Quran's remaining headquarters in 2013 by the Moroccan authorities saw Maghraoui quickly revert to his pre-2011 positions on these issues. The 2013 closing down of Maghraoui's association also stirred the already existing internal debates and fissions within Dor al-Quran, between a clique of Salafi figures centred on al-Qabbaj and the more traditionalist followers of Maghraoui, over the legitimacy of participation in formal politics and protests. These internal divisions became irreconcilable by August 2013, following Maghraoui's support of the Saudi king's position on the military coup in Egypt. Al-Qabbaj and some of his followers left Dor al-Quran and engaged in greater political activism, ultimately (albeit unsuccessfully) attempting to enter parliamentary politics through the Islamist PJD party in the 2016 legislative elections.

Finally, this chapter argues that, because the '20 February' movement did not substantively challenge the Moroccan regime nor throw the political sphere wide open (unlike the scale of the protests and political openings in Egypt, Tunisia and Syria, for example), political opportunities for Salafis to rise to prominence in Morocco were more limited. The 'evolution' of Salafism in Morocco since 2011 is thus somewhat different from developments elsewhere in the region; as Masbah importantly notes,[10] they have neither formed their own political parties, nor run for political office in elections (as occurred in Egypt), nor have they radicalised (at least not on the scale of Tunisia or Libya) and carried out (sustained) political violence, such as attacking Sufi shrines and US embassies.[11] The Moroccan regime (or *makhzen*)[12] has instead prevented the formation of a Salafi political party, actively prevented attempts by Salafi figures to run for parliamentary seats and ensured that only individual Salafi figures, rather than Salafi associations or groups, can join political parties – and even then only small parties, rather than larger (Islamist) parties, particularly the ruling PJD.

Dor al-Quran before 2011

The purist *salafiyya* trend in Morocco emerged in the 1970s, with the founding of Dor al-Quran in 1976 by Shaykh al-Maghraoui, a native of the province of al-Rashidiyya in eastern Morocco. Maghraoui himself was a student of the Islamic University in Medina, where he completed a master's degree and a doctorate on Salafi doctrine (*ʿaqīda*) before returning to Morocco. Throughout the 1980s and 1990s, as increasing numbers of Moroccan students travelled to universities in Saudi Arabia,[13] and with the help of financial support from the Gulf, nine Dor al-Quran centres were established under Maghraoui in Marrakech, and more than fifty centres affiliated to Maghraoui's association mushroomed throughout the country. Maghraoui was supported by the Moroccan regime (or *makhzen*) and allowed to work through mosques and various associations in spreading his *daʿwa* (call to Islam, or proselytising), as the regime worked to counterbalance perceived domestic challenges from leftist movements, Islamist groups and Shiʿi currents.[14]

Yet, this period of Dor al-Quran's co-existence with, and deployment by, the regime came to an end in the early 2000s, with the 2003 suicide bombings in Casablanca by Salafi-jihadi networks.[15] The event marked a watershed moment in Salafi-state relations in Morocco. A widespread crackdown on jihadi militancy,[16] and Salafi networks more broadly, followed.[17] Approximately 7,000 persons were detained and 1,500 arrested and sentenced for their alleged role in the attacks.[18] By 2004, the regime had launched a comprehensive set of reforms that sought to openly assert and stress the monarchy's hegemony over the religious field[19] and to underscore King Mohammed VI's status as sole representative of Islam in the country.[20] State control of public religion and the religious sphere – in effect, the 'bureaucratization of Islam'[21] – had become a 'national security imperative'. The regime also more actively promoted a 'moderate' and 'tolerant', official 'Moroccan Islam', centred around the notions of Sufism, Mālikism[22] and Ash'arism,[23] challenging Salafi religiosity. Working to directly restrict what it perceived as the influence of Saudi Wahhabi Islamic trends and Arabia's religious influence within the country, the regime seized Salafi educational materials[24] and in 2003 closed various schools associated with Wahhabism, including all of Dor al-Quran's centres in Marrakech, except for its headquarters.[25]

Several years later, in 2008, Maghraoui posted a *fatwa* (Islamic legal opinion)[26] stating that marriage was permissible in Islam for girls as young as nine years old.[27] The *fatwa* was considered a challenge to both the new Moroccan family law (*al-Mudawwana*) that the king had introduced in 2004 and to the state's claim to the exclusive authority to issue *fatwa*s through the official High Scientific Council (*Majlis al-'Ulamā' al-'Alā*), which also strongly rebuked him.[28] In response, the regime in that year closed 67 Dor al-Quran centres throughout the kingdom, many of them following Maghraoui's association,[29] and Maghraoui and his family left for Saudi Arabia where they remained in voluntary exile until 2011.[30]

The '20 February' Protest Movement and Maghraoui's Return to Morocco in 2011

Inspired by the wave of popular anti-regime protests in Egypt and Tunisia, between 240,000 and 300,000 mostly young Moroccans in more than fifty urban centres across the country took to the streets under the banner of the '20 February' movement, in order to air their grievances and push for substantial political and economic reform.[31] The protests involved a broad range of actors, including many from political parties and organisations that were largely outside the formal political process,[32] and sporting different ideological colours (including the partially-banned Islamist movement of the Justice and Spirituality Association [*Jamaat al-Adl wa-l-Ihsan*, henceforth AJS] and also leftists)[33] that directly challenged the Moroccan regime's policy of gradual reform. Unlike other protests in the region, however, they challenged neither the 'monarchical form of the state', nor the position of King Mohamed VI.[34]

The Moroccan regime immediately engaged in a campaign of releasing prominent Salafi preachers and their followers, many of whom had been sentenced for their roles in the 2003 Casablanca bombings, in order to pacify former Salafi hardliners and their followers and to isolate them from the protests. The regime also considered Salafis a 'popular counterweight'[35] to the potential Shi'i sectarian threat that it saw spreading from Iran.[36] A deal was also reached by the regime with Maghraoui to return to Morocco in early April, on the condition that he did not join the '20 February' protests.[37] The authorities also required Maghraoui to support its reformist agenda through advocating its 2011 constitutional reform referendum and to help combat low voter-turnout by calling on Moroccans to participate in the 2011 parliamentary elections, which the regime brought forward from 2012 in the hope to appease the protest movement and forestall its momentum. The *makhzen*'s reconciliation with Maghraoui was also likely an attempt to isolate (quietist) Salafis and particularly the grassroots youth from the protests[38] and to deploy Maghraoui's traditional fervent antipathy[39] towards the AJS, prominent as it was in the 20 February protest movement, in order to undercut the AJS's appeal to more conservative social groups in the country.[40] The regime's new policy thus offered Maghraoui, and Morocco's Salafis more generally, an opportunity to return to the public sphere from which they had been largely excluded since 2003.[41]

Maghraoui soon abandoned his pre-2011 exclusive discursive concern with *al-tarbiyya wa-al-taṣfiyya* (education and purification) and instead publicly voiced his opinion in the ongoing political debate through a number television and newspaper interviews, as well as appearances in symposia alongside Salafi and non-Salafi figures. It is in this context that Maghraoui's position on political participation, protests, the '20 February' movement and Islamist networks in the kingdom first shifted. Despite the opposition to the 20 February protests by some Salafi *shuyūkh*, Maghraoui disavowed his historical rejection of protests and demonstrations as impermissible and prone to facilitate chaos and *fitna*. Under Islam, he contended, demonstrations in countries 'based on Islamic rules and [which] apply them'[42] are not permissible. However, in countries not based on Islamic rules and in which demonstrations are legally permitted (by which he meant, *inter alia*, Morocco), 'there is no doubt that there is benefit from demonstrations', on the condition that 'the demonstrations are called to the truth and Islam' and do not 'raise slogans that contradict Islam and contradict the guidance of the Qur'ān and Sunnah' and are 'warned [. . .] from falsehood, bloodshed, and adultery, and violating of property'.[43] Despite his initial opposition to the protests, he also publicly described it as 'a blessed movement' and noted that any call to better people's lives and the country's future and any call 'for reform, justice and freedom within the limits of Islamic *sharī'a* is welcome', and that 'we call upon it to be successful'.[44]

Maghraoui's combative and highly critical attitudes towards the AJS also softened. He stated that the role of the AJS in the protests, and of the youth participating in the '20 February' movement more generally, would flourish insofar as 'they reach consensus on preaching to goodness and piety'.[45] Maghraoui instead directed vitriol at the 'Moroccan left and atheists', which he likened to a 'Hiroshima bomb', saying that they 'spread absolute poverty, moral ruin and with all evil carried by the devil'.[46] In another media appearance, Maghraoui again reaffirmed the permissibility of the protests on the condition that they did not involve blasphemy, the mixing of men and women, and the sabotage of facilities and buildings.[47] Protests, he maintained, 'are a means like any other kind of means of avowing the good and disavowing the bad [*amr bi-l-ma'ruf wa naheey 'an al-munkar*] and as a means of advising people'.[48] Maghraoui's new discourse increasingly focused on more societal and political issues and also referenced citizenship rights. He contended that 'people have rights [*al-ḥuqūq*], and there is injustice [*al-dhulum*]. How will this injustice be rectified and how can these rights be realized if people don't come together, and try to develop these peaceful means that are organized [. . .] There is no one against nor nothing that prevents this matter [. . .]'.[49]

As part of Maghraoui's arrangement with the regime, he also publicly supported the 1 July 2011 constitutional reform referendum.[50] In doing so, for the first time he argued that electoral participation and the ballot box were legitimate practices. He called on Moroccans to register and vote to pass the new constitutional amendments proposed by the monarchy,[51] and he released a statement that justified Dor al-Quran's official support for the amended constitution, by praising 'the provisions of the Constitution to explicitly promote the status of the Islamic religion in the Moroccan identity'.[52] The statement itself concluded with a 'renewed call for the reopening of the role of the Qur'ān in accordance with the requirements and requirements of the new constitution'.[53] Concerned to both protect and even expand the Islamic identity of the Moroccan state and society and to confront secular threats, the statement also called on 'all officials, scholars [*'ulamā'*] and practitioners in the field of *da'wa* to work hard for the further activation of the requirements of the Constitution relating to the Islamic identity at the level of legislation, politics, the economy and culture'.[54] Maghraoui also emphasised the need to 'continue to call for the status of Islamic law in the system of legislation' in the country.[55]

Maghraoui's public attitude towards other Islamist groups, and particularly the PJD, had also become more positive and conciliatory after years of harsh public rebuke for their involvement in politics and doctrinal innovation (*al-bid'a*). In 2011 and 2012 he instead spoke of the 'advice and guidance for good [*al-khayr*]' that he had received from his 'students and friends' from the PJD, including senior figures such as Abdullah Benkirane and Mustafa Al-Ramid. '[W]e may disagree with them in many methodological and doctrinal issues [. . . but] [w]e advise each other [. . .]', he concluded.[56]

Dor al-Quran also rapidly broadened its activities from focusing on only *al-tarbiyya wa-l-taṣfiyya* to also exerting more direct political influence and demonstrating a new openness to political participation by, *inter alia*, publicly calling on all Moroccans to vote in the 25 November 2011 parliamentary elections. Officially, Dor al-Quran maintained that it had not sided with any particular party but rather supported all and any political party that would show people 'honesty and [would] benefit' Moroccans.[57] In more private gatherings among his Salafi followers, however, Maghraoui urged people to vote for the PJD specifically.[58] The arrangement between Maghraoui and the PJD was highly practical: Maghraoui would secure additional votes for PJD candidates running for parliamentary seats in Marrakech and strengthen the PJD's Islamic credentials, in return for the support of the PJD and its associated social movement, the Movement of Unity and Reform (Harakat al-Tawhid wa-l-Islaḥ), in contesting the regime's decision to close Dor al-Quran centres. Maghraoui's appeals to his supporters are thought to have contributed to the PJD winning various parliamentary seats in Marrakech and the Tensift El-Haouz region for the first time in its history.[59]

There is reason to think that in 2011 and 2012 the *makhzen* was also reluctant to expend too much political capital, forestalling this reconciliation between Dor al-Quran and the PJD. Both the PJD and Dor al-Quran broadly positioned themselves against the Arab Spring uprisings and 20 February protests (despite Maghraoui's comments above) and, therefore, were important allies for a regime on the defensive and determined to ensure political support from Morocco's conservative Islamic social milieu.

In December 2011, after the PJD had won 107 out of 395 seats in the parliamentary elections – the largest number of seats of any party and the biggest haul of its political life – a delegation of senior Dor al-Quran Salafi figures (including Maghraoui, and two prominent protégées of his, Adil Reffouch and Hammad al-Qabbaj) visited the new PJD Prime Minister Abdullah Benkirane's home in Rabat,[60] in order to thank the PJD for its role in supporting Dor al-Quran's call for the reopening of its centres.[61] In March 2012, Mustafa al-Ramid, the new PJD Minister of Justice and Public Freedoms, also publicly visited Maghraoui at Dor al-Quran. Maghraoui announced the filing of an appeal with the local authorities against the closure, and al-Ramid pledged to continue pushing for the reopening of Dor al-Quran.[62] Prominent Dor al-Quran *shuyūkh*, including Maghraoui, also spoke at regional PJD-run symposia throughout 2012. Maghraoui would continue to praise the PJD's 'political reform', stating his 'hope for my brothers [in PJD] for all the best, because their power and success are ours. They are still the best at what they do and deserve our support and encouragement'.[63] As the PJD continued to push for the reopening of the rest of the Dor al-Quran centres through its connections to the *makhzen* and new political influence as the largest party in parliament, Maghraoui again publicly endorsed PJD parliamentarian Ahmed al-Motassedeq in a 4 October 2012 re-election for the parliamentary seat of Gueliz, Marrakech.[64]

Maghraoui's new openness to electoral participation and political cooperation with the PJD was most likely a strategy to secure the survival of his Salafi association and the reopening of its many centres in the new, open political environment of 2011 and 2012. Yet, his engagement with parliamentary politics was not accompanied by any political programme relating to, for instance, matters of the economy or societal issues. Instead, it pursued largely purist aims – the Islamisation of society (in a Salafi sense) and, mostly notably through the Dor al-Quran campaign in support of the 2011 constitutional referendum, to further influence legislation in Morocco regarding the Islamic nature of the state and society. Maghraoui's political participation was also in many ways a reactionary means of challenging or precluding what Maghraoui considered to be not only secular, but also Sufi and Shi'a challenges to the place of (Salafi) Islam in Morocco.

Following the May 2011 bombing of the Argana Café in the historic centre of Marrakech,[65] Maghraoui also began to explicitly denounce violence and, participating in parts of the regime's discourse, articulated Dor al-Quran's loyalty to and support for the monarchy, while denouncing all links between terrorism and Salafism. The 'true army of Dor al-Quran', Maghraoui argued, 'raises its hands to God during these dark nights and prays with tears asking God to protect the king and the country'.[66]

In response to Maghraoui's support for the regime's constitutional reform agenda in 2011, several Dor al-Quran centres were reopened by the Ministry of Interior on 9 November.[67]

Deepening Dissent within Dor al-Quran in 2012

In 2012, the prominent Dor al-Quran Shaykh Hammad al-Qabbaj published a book entitled *Foresight and Deliberateness* (*Al-Istabsar wa-l-To'da*). Maghraoui wrote the introduction. The book attempted to prove the legitimacy of participation in political governance under a political system involving violations of *sharī'a* and argued that democracy has provisions that are at the core of *sharī'a*. Therefore, so al-Qabbaj wrote, there is no harm in accepting democracy and 'benefiting' from some of its principles in political participation at the procedural level – that is, with regard to elections, voting and parliament – and at the level of gatherings, demonstrations, sit-ins and strikes. Salafis are duty-bound to not leave the political arena empty, al-Qabbaj argued, and must instead contend with their 'secular' opposition in all domains and spaces so that broader areas of policy-making are influenced by Islamic principles.

The book caused considerable debate among the *shuyūkh* and students of Dor al-Quran. A clique of other Salafi *shuyūkh* and students at Dor al-Quran, most notably 'Adil Reffouch, supported many of these ideas. However, the majority of Dor al-Quran *shuyūkh* and followers were not convinced by this new logic and instead reaffirmed Maghraoui's traditional stance towards democracy as lack of belief and (at least direct) political participation as deviation.

In late June 2013, however, the Ministry of Interior suddenly closed all (five) of Maghraoui's Dor al-Quran centres in Marrakech and a total of seventy of the Dor al-Quran centres associated with Maghraoui throughout Morocco, on the grounds that Dor al-Quran had failed to 'submit to the laws governing' educational associations.[68] As relations between the regime and the PJD began to deteriorate from early 2013 onwards, many saw the closure as a punitive decision in response to the growing relations between Dor al-Quran and the PJD; specifically, Maghraoui's supporting the PJD in the 2011 parliamentary elections, rather than a royally sponsored party,[69] such as the Authenticity and Modernity Party (Hizb al-Asala wa-l-Muasira),[70] and his reaction to al-Qabbaj's politicised writings.[71]

When Maghraoui subsequently ordered the dispersal of a sit-in and mass rally of more than 15,000[72] Dor al-Quran supporters protesting the closure on Friday, 28 June 2013,[73] there was great anger within Dor al-Quran circles that a firmer and stronger response had not been taken by the association's leadership.[74] Ongoing internal debates and divides over the issue and legitimacy of political participation, procedural democracy and alliances with (Islamist) political parties intensified, increased by suspicions within Dor al-Quran that al-Qabbaj's political writings were one of the reasons for the state's decision to close the centres.[75] Al-Qabbaj's shifts in Salafi reasoning, I argue, were not uncritically embraced by other Dor al-Quran scholars and attendees, but instead involved intense contestation over ideas that would, ultimately, produce implacable fissures within Maghraoui's association.

The Poem that Shook Dor al-Quran

On 18 August 2013, four days after the massacres at the pro-Morsi and anti-coup sit-ins at Rabaa al-Adawiyya and al-Nahda in Egypt, and the Egyptian Salafi al-Nour party's support for the Egyptian military, ideological cleavages within Dor al-Quran deepened further.[76] As Maghraoui remained in Saudi Arabia, the senior Dor al-Quran shaykh, Shaykh Adil Reffouch, published a poem titled *O Custodian of the Two Holy Mosques* (*Ya Khādim al-Ḥaramayn*), which directly criticised the Saudi King, Abdullah bin Abdulaziz Al Saud, for supporting the military coup in Egypt and the violent crackdown on the sit-ins.[77] Maghraoui, reaffirming his loyalty to the Saudi establishment, announced that the poem did not represent Dor al-Quran's position and called on Reffouch to withdraw the text and apologise to the Saudi king. Reffouch refused. Soon, al-Qabbaj declared his support for Reffouch's stance and, in protest over Maghraoui's uncritical defence of the Saudi monarchy's position, resigned from Dor al-Quran, together with Reffouch.[78] In an open letter, al-Qabbaj also berated the Saudi king for separating 'ethics from politics' and supporting the coup.[79] While criticising the Muslim Brotherhood's 'mistakes in political practice, especially in governance', al-Qabbaj observed that 'no matter how we disagree with them, we do not condone and accept the injustice [. . .] inflicted on them'.[80] Al-Qabbaj also took part in a demonstration in the Moroccan capital, Rabat, in August 2013, side-by-side with members of the AJS and the PJD, to protest the crackdown on the Rabaa al-Adawiyya sit-in.

Through late August and September 2013 Maghraoui, while under pressure to remain aligned with his patrons in the Gulf, tried to find a compromise between the different factions within Dor al-Quran.[81] On his return to Morocco later that summer, however, his mind was made up. Maghraoui also largely abandoned his discourse from 2011 and 2012 concerning matters of social (in)justice and politics. In late 2013, he instead proclaimed in a public statement that Dor al-Quran's 'approach is not to go into contemporary politics, which we see far from legitimate politics [*al-siyāsa al-shara'iyya*] [. . .] And if we had participated in it [politics] in a particular period of time, it was meant to disavow what is forbidden [*nahy 'an al-munkar*], and it was not a deviation from our approach or abandonment of our call'.[82] Maghraoui also argued that the introduction he had written to al-Qabbaj's 2012 book *Foresight and Deliberateness* had been neither a pretext nor an excuse to expand Dor al-Quran's activities into activities that he in fact did not want to pursue.[83] The Dor al-Quran founder also argued that the objective of his *manhaj* (method) had in fact never entailed involvement in protests, demonstrations and sit-ins, since these activities 'have only resulted in unrest and strife, bloodshed and hatred for Muslims'.[84] Quoting a verse (āya) from *Surat al-Nūr* (Verse of Light) (Qur'ān 24:39), Maghraoui contended that politics was an 'illusion', 'a mirage in the desert which the thirsty man deems to be water; until when he comes to it he finds it to be naught'.[85] Instead, he called on his followers to return to gaining knowledge about the Qur'ān and the Sunna – 'to spread knowledge until the ignorant becomes knowledgeable'.[86]

By 2015, Maghraoui had also renewed his traditional critique and harsh rebuke of other Islamist groups. He publicly distanced himself from al-Qabbaj and Reffouch, and also from the PJD, through 'explicit speech acts'[87] of defamation and critique.[88] At a speech at the funeral for a local Salafi scholar in Marrakech, he publicly instructed al-Qabbaj to keep away from Dor al-Quran and to not speak of it again. Maghraoui also denounced the PJD and the Muslim Brotherhood as 'supporters of the *rawāfid* and friends of *bid'ah*' and as 'followers of the delusions of Hassan al-Turaby, Sayid al-Qutb and Hassan al-Banna'. Referring to the PJD and al-Qabbaj, he observed that '[they have] ministerial portfolios and parliamentary seats, and we have only these graves'. He also depicted the AJS as 'evil' adjuncts of Shi'i groups in Iran.[89] Partly under pressure from the *makhzen* to help combat voter abstention, Maghraoui did, however, continue to publicly call on Moroccans to participate in the 2015 local and regional elections, as well as in the 2016 parliamentary elections. He initially refused to openly support any particular party, stating instead that Dor al-Quran affirms its support 'for all honest actors in the service of Islam and our homeland, and we call on people to vote for the best of them in order to achieve the increase the good and reduce evil'.[90] Al-Qabbaj, by contrast, called on Moroccans to vote for the PJD in the local and regional Marrakech elections and criticised the PAM, accusing it of being 'violators of Islamic principles'.[91]

The Emergence of *Ibn Tashfin* and Al-Qabbaj's Politicisation

In May 2015, Reffouch and also al-Qabbaj founded a new Salafi association in Marrakech, named the Ibn Tashfin Institute for Modern Studies and Heritage Research and Intellectual Creativity (Mo'asat Ibn Tachfeen lil-Dirasat al-Mu'asira wa-l-Baht al-Turathiyya wa al-Ibda' al-Fikry).[92] In contrast to Dor al-Quran, the Ibn Tashfin Institute does not 'reform society through lessons and Islamic education'.[93] Rather, as a research centre, it produces reports and studies on religious, cultural and political matters.[94] The nature and range of issues that al-Qabbaj's regular articles and videos – published through his personal website, social media handles and the Ibn Tashfin Institute's website[95] – concern include matters of social injustice in Morocco, the legitimacy of political participation and protests, and regular commentary on parliamentary matters and international politics.

From 2013 onwards, al-Qabbaj strengthened his connections with the PJD. He was also appointed a member of the National Dialogue Committee on Civil Society (Comité de Dialogue National sur la Société Civile) by the then PJD Minister of Parliamentary Relations and Civil Society, Habib al-Choubani, in March 2013; through this committee, al-Qabbaj also campaigned for greater rights and social support for disabled Moroccans.[96] With the collapse of relations between Maghraoui and the PJD, the PJD leadership chose al-Qabbaj as their candidate for the Gueliz-Annakhil seat in the centre of Marrakech for the 7 October 2016 parliamentary elections.[97] Al-Qabbaj agreed and formally supported the PJD's campaign platform. In line with this, his public discourse made increasing reference to matters of economic reform, fighting corruption within institutional politics and mitigating the social problems of unemployment and illiteracy.[98]

Al-Qabbaj's parliamentary aspirations were to be disappointed, however. By 16 September 2016, the Ministry of Interior rejected his candidature on the grounds that he had previously assumed several positions 'against the basic principle of democracy [. . .] and through the expression of extremist ideas that encourage racism, hatred, and violence in Moroccan society'.[99] While al-Qabbaj furiously challenged the decision, Maghraoui publicly called on Moroccans to vote for the candidate who would best serve the country and re-affirmed that Dor al-Quran was 'not inclined towards the PJD nor to PAM'.[100] Maghraoui also urged Moroccans who would not vote to get better informed about who to vote for, arguing that political disengagement endangers the future of the country, thus underscoring the importance of being engaged in politics. Many observers considered this to be in line with the state's policy of combatting voter abstinence.[101]

As the two favourites in Marrakech for the legislative elections, the PAM and the PJD, competed over the Salafi electoral base, rumours of a new secret alliance between Maghraoui and the PAM surfaced.[102] A recording was circulated just two days before the elections, purporting to show Maghraoui at a private meeting arguing to Dor al-Quran attendees that they had a 'responsibility' to vote for 'whomever is the best for us and for our *da'wa*'.[103]

Maghraoui 'strongly' called on his followers to help the PAM and to 'ask anyone you know to ask his relatives and friends to vote for the PAM anywhere in Marrakech. Dor al-Quran will open its doors soon'.[104]

When Dor al-Quran was then reopened by a decision of the Ministry of Religious Endowments and Islamic Affairs in late September 2016, just days before the 7 October general election,[105] many, surprised by the coincidence of the timing, sensed the direct involvement of the monarchy in the reopening.[106] Maghraoui, however, rejected the allegations that Dor al-Quran had exchanged Salafi votes in support of the royalist PAM for the reopening of the association.[107]

Conclusions

This chapter has mapped how the oldest and largest quietist, 'scholastic' Salafi network in Morocco, Dor al-Quran, contended with the challenge of popular power in the form of the 20 February protest movement in 2011. In doing so, this chapter has argued that, following Maghraoui's 2011 return to Morocco from self-imposed exile in Saudi Arabia, he broke from his traditional concern for only matters of *al-tarbiyya wa-al-taṣfiyya* and personal piety, and instead developed a new discourse that engaged with societal and political issues and questions of social (in)justice. While these latter issues largely remained secondary to questions of doctrine and *da'wa*, Maghraoui also abandoned his pre-2011 rejection of demonstrations and electoral and political participation as *bid'a*. In contrast, he argued that demonstrations were beneficial and permissible in countries such as Morocco, which were not based on Islamic rule and in which said protests were legal. Maghraoui also described the 20 February protests as 'blessed' and 'welcome'. Dor al-Quran's position on Moroccan Islamist parties and associations (particularly the PJD and the AJS) also took on a more positive and conciliatory tone. It sought to exert more direct political influence and demonstrated a new openness to electoral and political participation more generally by, *inter alia*, publicly calling on all Moroccans to vote in the 2011 constitutional reform referendum (as part of an attempt to curry favour with the *makhzen* that had closed Maghraoui's centres in 2008) and also in the 25 November 2011 parliamentary elections. Privately, Maghraoui also urged voters to support the Islamist PJD. As this chapter has contended, Maghraoui's new openness to electoral participation and political cooperation with the PJD was most likely a strategy to secure the *da'wa* activities and survival of his Salafi association by exchanging Salafi votes for the PJD's support in coaxing the *makzhen* to reopen Dor al-Quran centres in the city. Maghraoui's political participation was also a 'reactionary' means of challenging what he considered to be not only secular, but also Sufi and Shi'i, challenges to the place of (Salafi) Islam in Morocco.

In this way, the case of Moroccan Salafis (and Dor al-Quran specifically) demonstrates how, despite the inflexibility that academic literature often associates with Salafi thought, it is in fact malleable and open to revision. In Morocco, new (and changing) opportunities saw some of Maghraoui's protegés, such as Shaykh al-Qabbaj and Shaykh Reffouch, substantively rethink their positions on political participation and political activism, marking the beginning of a new, more politicised trend within the Moroccan Salafi landscape. Yet, these evolutions in al-Qabbaj's and Reffouch's reasoning were not uncritically accepted by other Dor al-Quran scholars and their followers, including Maghraoui himself. Instead, growing tensions between different factions within the association over the legitimacy of political participation and protests came to a head over the issue of the military coup that unseated Mohammed Morsi in Egypt in 2013 and the Saudi regime's position on this. A public spat ensued between Reffouch and al-Qabbaj, who criticised the Saudi king, and Maghraoui, who reaffirmed Dor al-Quran's solidarity with the Saudi regime (with whom Maghraoui was determined to maintain his good relations). Within days, Reffouch and al-Qabbaj and their followers resigned from the association. By 2015 they had established the Ibn Tashfin Institute, a new, rival Salafi association in Marrakech. Al-Qabbaj would also (unsuccessfully) attempt to run as a parliamentarian under the PJD's electoral platform in the 2016 parliamentary elections.

Following the closure of Dor al-Quran in 2013 by the regime, Maghraoui also increasingly re-adopted many of his pre-2011 positions. He soon resumed his traditional lambasting of the PJD (and also the AJS) and, arguing that Dor al-Quran's *manhaj* did neither entail political participation nor legitimise involvement in protests after all, he urged his followers to return to focusing on *al-tarbiyya wa-l-taṣfiyya* only. However, Maghraoui still continued to encourage Moroccans to participate in the 2015 and 2016 elections and, while he by and large refused to officially support any particular party, he exhorted his followers to vote for a number of royalist parties, including the PAM, forging a secret alliance with the latter in return for the reopening of two of his centres.

Since opportunities for Salafis to rise to prominence in Morocco were fairly limited – the 20 February protest movement neither seriously challenged the Moroccan regime, nor threw the political sphere wide open – the experience of Morocco's Salafis since 2011 is thus somewhat distinct from developments elsewhere in the region, as this chapter has suggested. As Masbah observes, Salafis in Morocco have neither formed their own political parties, nor run for political office in elections (as occurred in Egypt), nor have they radicalised (at least not on the scale of Tunisia or Libya) and carried out (sustained) political violence (such as attacking Sufi shrines and US embassies).[108] The regime has also ensured that only individual Salafi figures, rather than Salafi associations or groups, have been able to join political parties.

Notes

1. See, for example, Henri Lauziere, 'Post-Islamism and the Religious Discourse of Abd Al-Salam Yasin', *International Journal of Middle Eastern Studies* 37 (2005), 241–61; Mohammad Masbah, 'Moving towards Political Participation: The Moderation of Moroccan Salafis since the Beginning of the Arab Spring', *SWP Research Paper* (2013).
2. Imad Stitou, 'How Morocco Plans to Contain its Salafists', *Al-Monitor* (2015), www.al-monitor.com/pulse/originals/2015/06/morocco-salafist-sheikhs-regime-isis.html (accessed 14 October 2016).
3. Sanaa Karim, 'Morocco's Salafis: In Search of a Comprehensive Solution', Carnegie Endowment International Peace (2013), http://carnegieendowment.org/sada/?fa=51812 (accessed 31 May 2016).
4. Jibreel Delgado, 'Post-Islamist Transformations in Morocco', *Sociology of Islam* 3 (2015), 125–45.
5. See, for instance, Stéphane Lacroix, 'Between Revolution and Apoliticism: Nasir al-Din al-Albani and his Impact on the Shaping of Contemporary Salafism', in *Global Salafism: Islam's New Religious Movement*, ed. Roel Meijer (Oxford: Oxford University Press, 2014), 58–80; Roel Meijer, 'Commanding Right and Forbidding Wrong as a Principle of Social Action: The Case of

Jama'a al-Islamiyya', in Meijer, *Global Salafism*, 189–220; Joas Wagemaker, 'The Transformation of a Radical Concept: Al-Wala' Wa-l-Bara' in the Ideology of Abu Muhammad al-Maqdisi', in Meijer, *Global Salafism*, 81–106.

6. Laurent Bonnefoy, 'Quietist Salafis, the Arab Spring and the Politicization Process', in *Salafism Arab Awakening: Contending with the People's Power*, ed. Francesco Cavatorta and Fabio Merone (London: Hurst, 2016), 205–18.
7. Ibid.
8. Mohammad Masbah, 'Salafi Movements and the Political Process in Morocco', in *Salafism After the Arab Awakening: Contending with the People's Power*, ed. Francesco Cavatorta and Fabio Merone (London: Hurst, 2017); Masbah, 'Moving towards Political Participation'.
9. The one major study of Dor al-Quran is Aboullouz's sociological study of Salafism in Morocco between 1971 and 2004. Through extensive (undercover) ethnographic fieldwork with the 'traditional Salafi' trend associated with Maghraoui's Dor al-Quran network in Marrakech, he studies rural Salafi youth from the Sous Valley, broader shifts in modes of religiosity in Morocco and weakening traditional modes of religiosity. He also studies the emergence of jihadism in Morocco. Elsewhere, Delgado looks at the historical and social background of Salafism in Morocco, arguing that the trend has long been changing 'in relation to competing and collaborating Islamist trends as well as toward the Moroccan government'. See Abdelhakim Aboullouz, *The Salafi Movements in Morocco (1971–2004): A Socio-Anthropological Study* (Beirut: Markaz Dirasat al-Wahda al-'Arabiya, 2009); Delgado, 'Post-Islamist Transformations'.
10. Mohammad Masbah argues that Morocco's Salafis 'are neither fully recognized as political actors nor do they work illegally or use violence'. See Masbah, 'Moving towards Political Participation', 7.
11. The Argana Café bombing by an al-Qaida-inspired network in Marrakech in 2011 and the killing of two Scandinavian women near Imlil in the Atlas Mountains (close to Marrakech) in 2019 by an allegedly ISIS-inspired network are notable exceptions.
12. A term in Morocco for the ruling elite, centred on the monarchy, high-ranking military figures, elite businessmen, local notables and bureaucrats.
13. Aboullouz, *The Salafi Movements in Morocco*; Abdelhakim Aboullouz, 'The Role of the Islamic University in Madinah in Reproducing the Religious Ideology of Moroccan Salafi Activists', *Arab Journal of Political Science* 25 (Winter 2009). Masbah also helpfully cites this paper. See Mohammad Masbah, 'Between

Preaching and Activism: How Politics Divided Morocco's Salafis', 2019, https://mipa.institute/5615 (accessed 14 July 2019).

14. Mohammad Darif, في مسار العلاقة بين الدولة والتيار السلفي, www.maghress.com/almassae/153383, 2012 (accessed 8 March 2019); Aboullouz, 'The Role of the Islamic University'.
15. Anneli Botha, 'Terrorism in the Maghreb: The Transnationalisation of Domestic Terrorism', Institute of Security Studies Monograph (2008), 236; Carlos E. Jesús, 'The Current State of the Moroccan Islamic Combatant Group', *CTC Sentinel* (March 2009), 2, 3; Jeffrey Palmer, 'The Death of Moroccan Exceptionalism: A Brief History of Moroccan Salafi Jihadism and Current Jihadist Trends', *Jihadology* (2014), https://jihadology.net/2014/09/05/the-clear-banner-the-death-of-moroccan-exceptionalism-a-brief-history-of-moroccan-salafi-jihadism-and-current-jihadist-trends/ (accessed 19 February 2021).
16. Raymond Hinnebusch, 'Change and Continuity after the Arab Uprising: The Consequences of State Formation in Arab North African States', *British Journal of Middle Eastern Studies* 42 (2015), 12–30.
17. Francesco Cavatorta, 'Neither Participation nor Revolution: The Strategy of the Moroccan Jamiat al-Adl wal-Ihsan', *Mediterranean Politics* 12 (2007), 381–97.
18. Botha, 'Terrorism in the Maghreb'; Palmer, 'The Death of Moroccan Exceptionalism'.
19. Michael J. Willis, 'Containing Radicalism through the Political Process in North Africa', *Mediterranean Politics* 11 (2006), 137–50.
20. Sami Zemni, 'Moroccan Post-Islamism: Emerging Trend or Chimera', in *Post-Islamism: The Changing Faces of Political Islam*, ed. Asef Bayat (Oxford University Press, 2013), 134–56.
21. Ann Marie Wainscott, *Bureaucratizing Islam: Morocco and the War on Terror* (Cambridge University Press, 2017), x.
22. One of the four major Sunni schools (or *madhāhib*) of jurisprudence.
23. One of the orthodox schools (*madhāhib*) of theology in Sunni Islam.
24. Wainscott, *Bureaucratizing Islam*, 85.
25. Maghress, تأجيل النظر في دعوى»جمعية الدعوة إلى القرآن والسنة» ضد وزير الداخلية, www.maghress.com/almassae/20565, 2009 (accessed 19 July 2018).
26. Under the title 'The legal age for marriage', 'Fatwa no. 371'. Maghraoui published it on his personal Facebook page on 12 August 2008.
27. Maghress, الشيخ المغراوي يفتي بجواز زواج بنت 9 سنوات, www.hespress.com/videos/8344.html, 2009 (accessed 2 November 2018).

28. Samir al-Hamady, السياسة تفرّق شمل السلفيين في المغرب, www.ssrcaw.org/ar/print.art.asp?aid=419466&ac=1, 2014 (accessed 19 July 2018).
29. Harakat al-Tawheed w-al-Islah, دار القرآن في مواجهة العاصفة, http://alislah.ma/oldwebsite/%D8%A2%D8%B1%D8%A7%D8%A1-%D9%88%D8%AA%D8%AD%D9%84%D9%8A%D9%84%D8%A7%D8%AA/%D9%82%D8%B6%D8%A7%D9%8A%D8%A7-%D9%88%D8%A2%D8%B1%D8%A7%D8%A1/2013-07-05-14-22-39, 2013 (accessed 10 July 2018).
30. HesPress, المغراوي: التظاهر في بلد الإسلام غير جائز في الأصل, www.hespress.com/interviews/30395.html, 2011 (accessed 2 November 2018).
31. Zemni, 'Moroccan Post-Islamism'.
32. Michael J. Willis, *Politics and Power in the Maghreb: Algeria, Tunisia and Morocco from Independence to the Arab Spring* (Oxford University Press, 2014), 152.
33. Irene Fernández Molina, 'The Monarchy vs. the 20 February Movement: Who Holds the Reins of Political Change in Morocco?' *Mediterranean Politics* 16 (2011), 435–41.
34. Ibid.
35. Masbah, 'Between Preaching and Activism'.
36. Vish Sakthivel, 'Are Morocco's Political Salafists Committed to Peace?' *Washington Institute Research Paper* (2013), www.washingtoninstitute.org/policy-analysis/view/are-moroccos-political-salafists-committed-to-peace (accessed 22 August 2016).
37. Despite the '20 February' movement's call for Moroccans to boycott the nationwide referendum, on 1 July the new constitution was ratified (according to the Ministry of the Interior, 98.5 per cent of voters supported the amendments) and replaced the 1996 constitution. The amendments defined Morocco as a 'parliamentary constitutional monarchy', re-characterised the figure of the monarch as inviolable (rather than 'sacred') figure, emphasised equality between men and women, and confirmed Amazigh as an official state language. It also broadened the parliament's powers, stipulating that the sovereign no longer has the right to appoint the prime minister at his own discretion, instead requiring the king to appoint the head of the government from the political party with the most seats in the House of Representatives. However, the new constitution did not challenge the position of the monarch as an executive and ultimate political decision-maker in the country. See Emanuela Dalmasso and Francesco Cavatorta, 'Political Islam in Morocco: Negotiating the Kingdom's

Liberal Space', *Contemporary Arab Affairs* 4 (2011), 484–500; F. Biagi, 'The Pilot of Limited Change: Mohammed VI and the Transition in Morocco', in *Political and Constitutional Transitions in North Africa: Actors and Factors*, ed. Justin Frosini and Francesco Biagi (2014), 50.

38. M. Masbah, 'Salafi Movements and the Political Process in Morocco'.
39. For example, in the 1990s, Maghraoui published a book titled *Benevolence in Following the Sunnah and Qur'an, Not in Repeating Men's Mistakes* (الإحسان في اتباع السنة والقرآن لا في تقليد أخطاء الرجال) in which he criticises and responds directly to Abdessalam Yassine's book *Benevolence and Men*. See also Darif, في مسار العلاقة بين الدولة والتيار السلفي, for more on Maghraoui's pre-2011 rhetoric towards the AJS and Yassine.
40. See the comments of Professor 'Abd El-Raheem Manar al-Slymy of the Mohammed V University in Morocco: Alhurra Channel, عودة محمد المغراوي إلى المغرب, www.youtube.com/watch?v=QUWIvUM8epw, 2011 (accessed 19 February 2021).
41. Masbah, 'Moving towards Political Participation'.
42. Medi1 TV, تقريرحول الشيخ محمد المغراوي, www.youtube.com/watch? v=vEDaihYzHJI (accessed 19 February 2021).
43. Ibid.
44. Ibid.
45. HesPress, المغراوي: التظاهر في بلد الإسلام غير جائز في الأصل.
46. Ibid.
47. Youtube, الشيخ محمد المغراوي والمظاهرات, www.youtube.com/watch?v=J5An0npmf1Q, 2014 (accessed 19 February 2021).
48. Ibid.
49. Ibid.
50. al-Hamady, ةسايسلا قّرفت لمش نييفلسلا يف بـرغـملا.
51. DarcoranChannal, ةوعد خيشلا يوارغملا ةبراغملا لوقل ةملك قحلا يف روتسدلا, www.youtube.com/watch?v=PIU-r39W-v4, 2011 (accessed 19 February 2021).
52. Maghraoui, بيان بخصوص مشروع الدستور الجديدبيان بخصوص مشروع الدستور الجديد, www.facebook.com/notes/180913391966643/?__tn__=HH-R (accessed 2 November 2018).
53. Ibid.
54. Ibid.
55. Ibid.
56. HesPress, المغراوي: التظاهر في بلد الإسلام غير جائز في الأصل.

57. Ibid.
58. For example, the PJD ideologue Bilal al-Taleedy recalls attending a 2011 lecture in which Maghraoui urged people to vote for the PJD (interview with the author in Rabat, 28 February 2018).
59. The PJD was also probably keen to forge an alliance with Maghraoui in order to strengthen its Islamic credentials through association with Maghraoui's traditionalist Salafi stance (see, for example, Professor 'Abderaheem Manar al-Slymy,'s comments at www.youtube.com/watch?v=QUWIvUM8epw). See also Mohammad Masbah, 'Moving towards Political Participation'; Perspectives Med, 'Cooptation politique des salafistes: Le PAM est-il intervenu pour la réouverture des écoles de Maghraoui?', 2016, www.perspectivesmed.ma/cooptation-politique-salafistes-pam-intervenu-reouverture-ecoles-de-maghraoui/ (accessed 11 July 2018).
60. Dor al-Quran, لقاء وفد التنسيقية المغربية لجمعيات دور القرآن بوزير العدل والحريات في مكتبه, https://www.facebook.com/notes/979397832529922, 2012 (accessed 2 November 2018).
61. Hiba Press, بنكيران يستقبل دعاة والنشطاء السلفيين . يتقدمهم المغراوي, www.maghress.com/hibapress/76575, 2011 (accessed 15 October 2011).
62. Al-Fur'any, التسجيل الكامل لزيارة الوزير مصطفى الرميد لدار القرآن الكريم, www.youtube.com/watch?v=eMtfwbBSNgE, 2012 (accessed 19 February 2021).
63. This was during a symposium as part of the local branch of youth wing of the PJD (6–8 July 2012). Maghraoui spoke alongside the well-known PJD figure and mayor of Marrakech, Mohammed al-'Araby Bilqayed, رأي المغراوي في نهاري و الغزيوي و العدالة و التنمية, www.youtube.com/watch?v=VaSzX3VMNBo, 2012 (accessed February 2021).
64. Maghress, مغرس : حالة المغرب بعد'الاختبار السياسي' لحزب العدالة والتنمية في الانتخابات الجزئية, www.maghress.com/hespress/64327, 2012 (accessed 2 November 2018).
65. On 28 April 2011. Seventeen people were killed. Moroccan state investigators argued that the bombing was carried out by a group led by Adil al-Othmani who, while he had no direct formal relations with al-Qaida, had been inspired by the network.
66. Youtube, كلمة الشيخ المغراوي في ساحة الكتبية من زوايا متعددة, www.youtube.com/watch?v=qavYGcGD0pA, 2011 (accessed 2 November 2018).
67. Harakat al-Tawheed wa-l-Islah, الداخلية ترفع قرار إغلاق عن دار القرآن سيدي يوسف بمراكش, www.alislah.ma/%D8%A3%D8%AE%D8%A8%D8%A7%D8%B1/%D8%A3%D8%AE%D8%A8%D8%A7%D8%B1-%D8%AC%

D9%85%D8%B9%D9%88%D9%8A%D8%A9/%D8%AF%D8%A7%D8%B1-%D8%A7%D9%84%D9%82%D8%B1%D8%A2%D9%86-%D8%B3%D9%8A%D8%AF%D9%8A-%D9%8A%D9%88%D8%B3%D9%81-%D8%A8%D9%85%D8%B1%D8%A7%D9%83%D8%B4, 2012 (accessed 11 July 2018).

68. Maghress, سلطات مراكش تفتح 'دور القرآن' وسط اتهامات للشيخ المغراوي, www.hespress.com/politique/322206.html, 2016 (accessed 15 July 2019).
69. Masbah, 'Salafi Movements and the Political Process in Morocco'.
70. The PAM party was founded in August 2008 by Fouad Ali El Himma, a close friend and former classmate of King Mohammed VI and former deputy Minister of the Interior.
71. Morocco World News, 'Closing of Marrakesh's Quranic Schools: A Miscalculated Decision', *Morocco World News*, www.moroccoworldnews.com/2013/07/96727/closing-of-marrakeshs-quranic-schools-a-miscalculated-decision, 2013 (accessed 10 July 2018).
72. Maghress, احتجاج ضد محاولة إعادة إغلاق دور القرآن بمراكش, www.maghress.com/attajdid/106880, 2013 (accessed 10 July 2018).
73. Kech24, هذا ما خلفه قرار إغلاق دور القران بمراكش، ويونس بنسليمان ل'كش"24 قرار الإغلاق تعسفي وليس له اي سند قانوني, shorturl.at/jwHT8, 2013 (accessed 10 July 2018).
74. Kech24, قصيدة رفوش القشة التي قسمت ظهر جمعية المغراوي, shorturl.at/crIN1, 2017 (accessed 11 July 2018).
75. Assabah, جماعة المغراوي أمام ثلاثة خيار ات, www.maghress.com/assabah/46209, 2013 (accessed 2 November 2018).
76. HesPress, يا خادمَ الحرمينِ, www.hespress.com/opinions/86950.html, 2013 (accessed 14 July 2019).
77. Ibid.
78. Hammad al-Qabbaj, استقالة واحتجاج, www.facebook.com/kabbadj.hammad/posts/550829234966334/, 2013 (accessed 15 July 2019).
79. HesPress, 'القبّاج يوجه رسالة غضب إلى ملك السعودية و'العربية' و'السلفيين', www.hespress.com/orbites/87691.html, 2013 (accessed 2 November 2018).
80. Ibid.
81. Masbah, 'Salafi Movements and the Political Process in Morocco', 173.
82. Mohammad al-Maghraoui, بيان الشيخ محمد بن عبد الرحمن المغراوي: هذا منهجنا، وهذه دعوتنا. هوية بريس, http://howiyapress.com/2822-2/, 2014 (accessed 2 November 2018).

83. HesPress, الشيخ المغراوي يرفض السياسة والمظاهرات لإثارتها 'الفتن والمحن', www.hespress.com/orbites/153611.html, 2014 (accessed 15 July 2019).
84. Ibid.
85. HesPress, الشيخ المغراوي يرفض السياسة والمظاهرات لإثارتها 'الفتن والمحن.
86. Ibid.
87. Judit Kuschnitzki, 'The Establishment and Positioning of al-Rashad: A Case Study of Political Salafism in Yemen', in *Salafism After the Arab Awakening*, ed. Cavatorta and Merone (London: Hurst, 2018).
88. le360, المغراوي: القباج أكبر المفسدين والبيجيدي أتباع ضلالات وبدع, http://ar.le360.ma/politique/93997, 2016 (accessed 15 July 2019).
89. Ibid.
90. Marrakech Press, المغراوي: الملك لم يتدخل لفتح دور القرآن ولا صلة لنا بـ'البّام', http://marrakechalaan.com/article-137987, 2016 (accessed 11 July 2018).
91. Yabiladi, حماد القباج: التصويت على حزب العدالة والتنمية واجب شرعي والبام والاستقلال يمسان بالدين الإسلامي, 2016, https://ar.yabiladi.com/articles/details/38598/undefined (accessed 2 November 2018).
92. Hammad al-Qabbaj, موقع الأستاذ حماد القباج | مؤسسة ابن تاشفين. موقع الأستاذ حماد القباج, https://kabbadj.com/?p=1779, 2015 (accessed 11 July 2018).
93. Interview by the author with Hammad al-Qabbaj in Marrakech, 12 December 2017
94. Interview by the author with Hammad al-Qabbaj in Marrakech, 12 December 2017
95. See, for example, https://kabbadj.com/ and https://ar-ar.facebook.com/itf.ma/?ref=nf
96. Howiya Press, لجنة الحوار الوطني حول المجتمع المدني.. مدرسة للوطنية الحقة. هوية بريس, http://howiyapress.com/3753-2/, 2014 (accessed 2 November 2018).
97. AlYaoum24, 2016 ,لماذا رشح 'البيجيدي' السلفي 'القباج' في لوائحه لانتخابات سابع أكتوبر, www.alyaoum24.com/694845.html (accessed 19 February 2021).
98. Kabbadj TV, مشاركة القباج في مهرجان العدالة والتنمية, www.youtube.com/watch?v=EMdGvNoN6_c, 2016 (accessed 19 February 2021).
99. H. al-Qabbaj, سالة مفتوحة إلى صاحب الجلالة الملك محمد السادس نصره الله, www.facebook.com/kabbadj.hammad/posts/1109388319110420:0, 2016 (accessed 15 July 2019).
100. Ibid.
101. Marrakech Press, المغراوي: الملك لم يتدخل لفتح دور القرآن ولا صلة لنا بـ'البّام'.
102. Ibid.

103. Kech TV, 2016 ,المغراوي يدعو طلبة وأئمة دور القرآن بمراكش للتصويت على البام, www.youtube.com/watch?v=aHhldHlJYM4 (accessed 19 February 2021).
104. Ibid.
105. Perspectives Med, ‘Cooptation politique des salafistes’.
106. Maghress, سلطات مراكش تفتح ’دور القرآن‘ وسط اتهامات للشيخ المغراوي.
107. Marrakech Press, ‘المغراوي: الملك لم يتدخل لفتح دور القرآن ولا صلة لنا بـ’البّام’.
108. Masbah, ‘Moving towards Political Participation’.

5

BETWEEN *DA'WA* AND POLITICS: THE CHANGING DYNAMICS OF EGYPT'S ANSAR AL-SUNNA, 2011–13

Neil Russell

On 23 December 2013, the Egyptian government seized the assets of 1,055 Islamic associations with alleged Muslim Brotherhood ties, under the premise that they had been exploited as a means of generating support for the banned organisation.[1] Despite this campaign purportedly targeting the social base of the Brotherhood, the list also included branches of other prominent Islamic associations, among them the Salafi group Ansar al-Sunna. The decision to include one of Egypt's most prominent Salafi associations is a curious one, for despite the politicisation of Egypt's Salafi scene after 2011, Ansar al-Sunna was a notable exception, declaring its continued commitment to *da'wa* (but support for wider Salafi politicisation). Furthermore, the main political Salafi actor in this period, the Nour Party – together with its parent organisation, al-Dawa al-Salafiyya – escaped persecution due to its support for the 3 July coup d'état in 2013 (an act in which Ansar al-Sunna followed suit).[2] Why then – given Ansar al-Sunna's decision in 2011 to eschew potentially risky and contentious participation in electoral politics, the continued acceptance post-2013 of politicised Salafism and Ansar al-Sunna's professed fealty to Sisi's new regime – did it become a target of the wider crackdown on the Brotherhood and Egypt's Islamic movement? Moreover, what lessons does the case-study of Ansar al-Sunna offer for our understanding of the relationship between Salafism and political processes?

This chapter examines the changing dynamics of Ansar al-Sunna's activities in Egypt's transitional period between 2011 and 2013, considering what role it played in Egypt's newly politicised Salafi scene. Based on a review of Egyptian newspaper articles and the statements and speeches of Ansar al-Sunna leaders, it argues that, despite not forming a political party, Ansar al-Sunna – and others who opted against formal politicisation – revised their view on the relationship between *da'wa* and politics, in order to reformulate their understanding of *da'wa* to include engagement in political activism. In their advocacy, Ansar al-Sunna rose above narrow partisan Salafi affiliations to promote the collective identity of the Islamic movement against the secular forces in the political sphere. This confounds assumptions of rigidity typically associated with 'quietist' Salafi scholarly networks such as Ansar al-Sunna and demonstrates how the distinction between 'quietist' and 'activist' Salafism can be overly pronounced.[3] On the one hand, Ansar al-Sunna remained 'quietist' in the sense that it decided against forming a political party, instead declaring its intention to concentrate on *da'wa*. On the other hand, its reinterpretation of the meaning of *da'wa* led to it effectively becoming a political interest group on behalf of Egypt's Islamic movement across electoral cycles during the transitional period.

This chapter demonstrates Ansar al-Sunna's adaptability and change between 2011 and 2013, both organisationally and ideationally, in four areas. First, Ansar al-Sunna took advantage of the political opportunity presented by the deposal of Mubarak and the ensuing instability, to expand its activities both in its traditional domain of *da'wa* as preaching, as well as in the area of service provision. By extending beyond strictly scholarly pursuits to engage in types of social activism more typically associated with other Islamists such as the Brotherhood, the case of Ansar al-Sunna shows how 'activist' need not only be viewed through the lens of formal political processes. Second, Ansar al-Sunna took further advantage of the opportunity to extend its organisational links with other Islamic actors, forming advisory bodies to counter non-Islamic influence during the transitional period. The formation of the Sharia Body of Rights and Reformation (SBRR) and the Shura Council of Scholars would bring together figures from Ansar al-Sunna with those from al-Gamiyya al-Shariyya, another major *da'wa* organisation that did not form a political party, as well as al-Dawa al-Salafiyya, the Muslim Brotherhood and al-Gamiyya al-Shariyya. In taking this opportunity, Ansar al-Sunna showed a willingness to step outside their traditional networks to further the cause of the Islamist movement more generally, rather than factional Salafi interests alone.

Third, ideational adaptation also complemented these organisational links, with increasing alignment between the discourse of Ansar al-Sunna and that of other Islamic associations regarding the relationship between *daʿwa* and politics. No longer viewing *daʿwa* as being distinct from politics, as had been the case in more restrictive periods, both Ansar al-Sunna and al-Gamiyya al-Shariyya began to blur the boundaries of what constitutes each field, leading to political advocacy being accepted as a form of *daʿwa*. This shows that, despite opting against formal politicisation and remaining 'quietist', Ansar al-Sunna nevertheless underwent ideational change in response to the more open political environment. Fourth and finally, this chapter shows how these revised ideas received practical implementation during electoral cycles across the transitional period. During the March 2011 referendum on constitutional amendments, the 2011/12 parliamentary elections and the 2012 presidential elections, Ansar al-Sunna framed the political choices facing voters as a religious duty (*wājib*) and/or a performance of *shahāda*, thus being equated with a demonstration of one's faith.

Egypt's Salafi scene has been the subject of much scholarly inquiry since the uprisings of 2011. A number of works have sought to explain the decision by previously 'apolitical' movements to institutionalise politically, by forming political parties and fielding candidates in the parliamentary elections of 2011 and 2012.[4] The focus of these works is on the three Salafi parties that formed in 2011: al-Nour, al-Islah and al-Fadila. There is acknowledgement of the debt that modern Salafism owes to Ansar al-Sunna, but mainly passing reference to its role post-2011, such as its receipt of 296m EGY in foreign donations from Gulf state donors. Reflecting the focus on formal political participation, some contrast the 'apolitical' stance of Ansar al-Sunna to that of al-Dawa al-Salafiyya and the Nour Party.[5] Meanwhile, others have highlighted their 'historically' apolitical stance, contrasting it with their 'involvement' in the political process post-2011 and Ansar al-Sunna's endorsement of participation for the wider Salafi movement in electoral politics.[6] Again, this positional shift is highlighted as an isolated point, rather than forming part of a specific, detailed study.

The most in-depth analyses of Ansar al-Sunna are found in studies by Steven Brooke,[7] Richard Gauvain[8] and, to a lesser extent, el-Meehy.[9] In trying to understand the 2013 seizure of Islamic associations, Brooke assesses the organisational capacity of Ansar al-Sunna's social welfare network, giving reference to links between Ansar al-Sunna branches and the Freedom and Justice Party (FJP) politicians regarding welfare provision. In a similar vein, el-Meehy has shown how Ansar al-Sunna became intimately involved in the market to distribute gas cylinders amidst national shortages in 2011. Gauvain, meanwhile, has outlined the positions of leading Ansar al-Sunna shaykhs regarding the virtuousness of the uprisings and the question of political participation, while in the postscript of his 2013 book, *Salafi Ritual Purity*, he discusses the importance of coalitions and advisory groups alongside political factions in trying to implement *sharī'a* to its fullest extent. This chapter aims to expand on the organisational links and activities referred to by Brooke and el-Meehy, providing more detail during electoral cycles, while also shedding more light on how ideational justifications intersected with these organisational developments.[10] In doing so, it aims to provide a fuller account of the activities and shifting dynamics of Ansar al-Sunna post-2011, as well as to contribute to an important and understudied aspect of Egyptian Salafism in a crucial period of its history and development.

Ansar al-Sunna: Founding, Organisational Structure and Post-2011 Expansion

Egyptian Salafism comprises various fragmented strands; according to Gauvain,'the most important of which is, indisputably, Ansar al-Sunna'.[11] It was established in 1926 by an Azharite scholar, Shaykh Muhammad Hamid al-Fiqqi, who had been a student of the influential Islamic reformer Rashid Rida.[12] Al-Fiqqi's initial affiliation was with al-Gamiyya al-Shariyya, which had been formed more than a decade prior, in 1912, and was one of the first new Islamic associations in Egypt to call for the revival of the *sunna* and confronting *bid'a* (innovation) in religious practices in the country. Against a background of colonial encroachment, al-Gamiyya al-Shariyya sought to counter the displacement of Islamic law from public life and the path of national education, as well as a perceived campaign of westernisation that included calls for the liberation of women and minimising the status of *sharīʿa* law in social, political and economic fields.[13] Yet, for al-Fiqqi, al-Gamiyya al-Shariyya had not countered forcefully enough these perceived corrupting innovations, and he differed in his interpretation of the attributes of God, in particular, in his doctrinal closeness to *Ahl al-Sunna*. The result was the formation of a new association, Ansar al-Sunna, focusing on worship and behaviour, stressing strict adherence to *tawḥīd* (the oneness of God) and particularly scathing of Sufism.[14] The more scripturalist motivations of Ansar al-Sunna were reflected in its activities, with behaviour and piety being prioritised over the more service-oriented activities of al-Gamiyya al-Shariyya – a trend that has continued into the contemporary period.

Although Ansar al-Sunna and al-Gamiyya al-Shariyya would embark on their own paths, their trajectories would overlap across historical periods. Under Nasser they would be targeted as part of his attempts to dominate civil society by imposing strict regulations on voluntary associations.[15] The entire management board of al-Gamiyya al-Shariyya was dissolved in 1966, only being allowed to resume its work under a new regime-appointed chairman, General Abdelrahim Amin, who would keep close watch over its activities.[16] Three years later, the assets of Ansar al-Sunna were seized due to their political activities, and the group was forced to merge with al-Gamiyya al-Shariyya for several years.[17] After regaining its autonomy, Ansar al-Sunna tempered its political involvement under successive regimes, partly due to the influence of increased ties with the Wahhabi clergy of Saudi Arabia. Ansar al-Sunna scholars have travelled and lived in the kingdom since the 1960s, with the ideas of the quietist Saudi figure Rabi al-Madhkali becoming increasingly prominent within the group. This led to a refusal among the group's leaders to engage in any anti-regime activism. Notably, Ansar al-Sunna's leader Abdullah Shakir even said in 2010 that he supported the hereditary secession of Gamal Mubarak to the presidency.[18] In contrast to al-Gamiyya al-Shariyya, who had developed increasing collaboration with the Brotherhood in terms of charitable work, the trajectory of Ansar al-Sunna was to adopt a decidedly quietist position under Mubarak, with its method being mainly textual and academic, promoting debate over Islamic legal issues among its scholars and theologians.[19]

Organisationally, Ansar al-Sunna is second only to al-Gamiyya al-Shariyya in terms of its size and scope. Yet, with more than 200 branches and 3,000 mosques under its umbrella, it is the largest Salafi network in Egypt.[20] In addition, thirty-two preacher training institutes offer courses of between two and four years, while Ansar al-Sunna also promotes its doctrine and Qur'ānic learning outside of Egypt through its Centre for African Education, with particular prominence in Sudan. In terms of social welfare programmes, the Orphan Sponsorship Project is claimed to benefit 12,000 families. Meanwhile, its magazine, *al-Tawhid*, distributes 100,000 copies monthly. These activities have made Ansar al-Sunna one of the most prominent Islamic associations in Egypt. While the balance of those activities has traditionally been weighted more towards scholastic endeavours, an examination of the tumultuous period after Mubarak's deposal in 2011 reveals that, despite deciding against institutional politics, the group nevertheless took advantage of the instability of this period to expand the scope and nature of their activities. In this period, we see that not only did Ansar al-Sunna seize the opportunity to expand in their traditional areas of strength, such as *da'wa* in the form of proselytising and preaching, but they also made a significant expansion in their service-provision apparatus.

The aftermath of the Arab Uprising provided one of the main factors enabling the expansion of Ansar al-Sunna's activities: the end of security checks resulting from the dissolution of State Security Investigations (SSI, Mubaḥith Amn al-Dawla) – the main security and intelligence apparatus of the Ministry of Interior, and its department specialising in religious-based activism, *al-nashāṭ al-dīnī*. In collaboration with the Ministry of Awqaf, SSI had monitored and kept surveillance over private mosques with detailed lists of worshipers, their activities and associations – and inclusion on these lists could lead to detention or worse.[21] With the units responsible for monitoring Islamist activism disbanded, the security services withdrew from their previous role in monitoring the affairs of mosques, providing a vacuum in which Egypt's Islamist movement could contest for control of the religious sphere and its institutions. Social movement theory recognises such 'political opportunity structures' as constituting changes in the institutional structure of the state, which provides an opportunity for civil society activity to emerge.[22] This may result from a reduction in the state's 'policy implementation capacity', in which its power to implement policies – such as those of the security services – erodes.[23] The instability that resulted from the uprisings created just such changes in the institutional structure of the Egyptian state and, consequently, opportunities for actors such as Ansar al-Sunna to expand the nature and scope of their activities.

In an interview with the Kuwaiti magazine *al-Furqān*, Ansar al-Sunna's leader, Dr Abdullah Shakir, explained how his movement was able to take advantage of this political opportunity structure resulting from the security vacuum to expand their activities:

> It is well known that there were different types of restrictions exerted over *da'wa* during the previous regime. After the end of the regime, we began to reformulate the work of *da'wa* once again, and one of the most important sectors we have focused on is *ma'āhid al-shar'īyah*, where we have expanded the establishment of *da'wa* institutes which graduate preaching specialists. These institutes were present before, but were weak and few, the reason being that the security services did not allow their establishment in many places. With thanks to God, after the demise of this system, we started to expand the establishment of these institutes. As the state security apparatus' checks ended, the movement of preachers became wider to the places we could not reach and which were deprived of *da'wa* with sheikhs being forbidden from going to them. Now, we are moving all over Egypt.[24]

Freed from the penetration of state security, Ansar al-Sunna proceeded to extend their organisational infrastructure. According to Ansar al-Sunna's website, the relatively few preaching training institutes described by Shakir have grown and now number thirty-two, offering courses of between two and four years long. Shakir explained further in the interview that new Ansar al-Sunna branches were established in the villages of Upper Egypt and the Sinai, with *da'wa* 'caravans' being deployed to reach the more remote areas. In addition, Qur'an memorisation workshops were expanded, previously having been limited under Mubarak due to restrictions over youth gatherings of Islamists, and now number more than 200. Ansar al-Sunna thus seized the opportunity to expand their reach across Egypt in areas where Islamic activism had been restricted, thus broadening the scope of their activities in areas forbidden under the previous regime.

Further capitalising on these new-found opportunities, Ansar al-Sunna also expanded their service-providing infrastructure in the form of 'popular committees' (*lijān sha'biyya*), aided by the donations of LE 296 million (USD 49 million) from Kuwaiti and Qatari charities. This novel form of grassroots mobilisation had emerged among youths largely as a secular response to the departure of police from Egypt's streets amid the protests, providing security for the community in their absence. In many cases, however, the committees of Islamic associations would outlast those of their secular counterparts, in part due to their basis on pre-existing networks of organisation. In a May 2011 statement, Ansar al-Sunna confirmed its involvement as a 'supervisor' of PCs, 'in all provinces to maintain the security and stability of the country during the current period'.[25] In a study on PCs, el-Meehy outlines how Ansar al-Sunna's operations in this area expanded from the provision of neighbourhood security to include the distribution of goods, such as gas cylinders, during periods of acute shortages.[26] Yet, the provision of these cylinders was also observed during the parliamentary elections, when both Ansar al-Sunna and candidates from the FJP were able to accumulate and distribute them via mosques. Ansar al-Sunna's entry into areas of service provision more typically associated with the Brotherhood shows not only a shift away from its previous focus on scholarly pursuits, but also a more 'activist' direction in the way in which these distribution networks were politicised during electoral cycles.

Coalition Building in Egypt's Islamic Movement after 2011

Beyond the development of its organisational infrastructure, Ansar al-Sunna and others took advantage of the political opportunity structure to establish stronger ties across Egypt's Islamic movement. When presented with such opportunities, actors who identify shared values, goals and interests often seek to formalise that solidarity through coalition-building in pursuit of achieving common goals.[27] During the transitional period, the issue of identity was central for many Islamic associations, leading to their seeking cooperation and coordination with one other, rather than with secular and/or liberal groups, in a display of national unity. Reflecting this primary concern, on 8 February 2011, two days before Mubarak's departure, al-Dawa al-Salafiyya in Alexandria organised what was dubbed the 'first Salafi conference' under the slogan 'Egypt's Islamic identity' (*huwiyat masr al-islamiyya*). The conference was attended by a large number of Salafis and formed the precursor for further demonstrations held across the country in the following days and weeks, aimed at showcasing the strength of Salafism in the country.

These displays of collective Islamic identity would lead to the creation of two new bodies to provide legal opinions on issues arising during the transition. The first was the Sharia Body of Rights and Reformation (*al-Haya al-Sharia lil-Ḥuquq wa al-Iṣlah*), which positioned itself as an umbrella group for Egypt's various Islamic factions and sought to counter non-Islamic influence. Formed in July 2011, it included ten senior scholars and activists from Ansar al-Sunna, al-Dawa al-Salafiyya, al-Gamiyya al-Shariyya and the Muslim Brotherhood, as well as several Azharite imams. Among the most prominent founding members were Yasser Borhamy, vice-president of al-Dawa al-Salafiyya; Talaat al-Afifi, who was a senior figure in al-Gamiyya al-Shariyya and who would go on to serve as Minister of Awqaf in Muhammad Morsi's cabinet; as well as Abdullah Shakir from Ansar al-Sunna. Within a year its membership included more than 100 prominent figures and incorporated more factions such as al-Gamiyya al-Islamiyya; another notable later addition was the Brotherhood's deputy supreme guide, Khairat al-Shater. The ethos of the body was that of a collective seeking to further the cause of the Islamic movement; it was summed up by Borhamy thus:

> The aim of participating in this front is the formation of a Salafi Islamist bloc, in a sentence, to multiply the spectrum against secularist attempts to exploit the opportunity to modify some of the articles in the constitution and rob the will of the *ummah*, and amend or cancel the second article in the constitution which reads, 'an Islamic *sharī'ah* reference'.[28]

Borhamy's description illustrates the way in which Egypt's Islamic movement developed a degree of collective identity during this early stage, recognising the shared purpose of Islamists as a whole, rather than the factional interests of individual parties, particularly when juxtaposed with non-Islamist actors. As we shall see, this theme of shared purpose would become particularly strong during electoral cycles and was promoted particularly strongly by Ansar al-Sunna and al-Gamiyya al-Shariyya.

The second body of note was the Shura Council of Scholars (Majlis Shūrā al-'Ulāma'), established by senior figures within Ansar al-Sunna, tasked with providing legal opinions on the 25 January revolution and its aftermath, and making regular forays into political debates. The council was led by Ansar al-Sunna's leader, Abdullah Shakir, with Muhammad Hassan – a prominent and influential preacher due to his appearances on the popular satellite channel al-Nas TV and also a prominent figure within al-Dawa al-Salafiyya – as his deputy. Other members included Gamal al-Murakabi, Ansar al-Sunna's former leader; the Islamic scholar Muhammad Hussein Yacoub, a vocal supporter of the newly formed Salafi party, al-Asala; Shaykh Ali Nais, who was elected to the People's Assembly as part of the Nour Party; and Sayyid Abdul Azzim, a prominent al-Dawa al-Salafiyya leader in Alexandria. The council thus comprised a number of prominent Salafi figures and, although dominated by Ansar al-Sunna, also represented other important Salafi movements as well as its political parties. The transitional period thus provided an opportunity for Egypt's Islamists – both Salafi and, to an extent, Brotherhood – to unite under their common Islamic identity, through demonstrations and eventually formal organisations in an attempt to maximise the role that Islam would play in the new Egypt. While this demonstrates some organisational convergence among Islamic associations, by looking at their newly interpreted positions on *da'wa* and politics, we can observe alignment along ideational lines also.

Revising the Relationship between *Da'wa* and Politics

Despite expanding its activities after 2011 and establishing more organisational ties with other groups, Ansar al-Sunna decided not to form a political party, as some of its contemporaries had done. Initially, following Mubarak's departure, it appeared that the opposite might be the case. In an interview with *Asharq al-Awsat*, Muhammad Hassan stated that the stage through which Egypt was passing necessitated religious scholars to take action, to direct people towards what they believe to be in the best interests for the country. Accordingly, he declared that Ansar al-Sunna would establish its own political party and field candidates for both houses of parliament.[29] Ultimately, Ansar al-Sunna decided against formal political institutionalisation – yet it was not rejected as a legitimate avenue to take for others. The first statement from the Shura Council of Scholars, issued on 19 March 2011, outlined its position on the issue of political participation:

> We do not see any legal impediment to political participation in the People's Assembly, the Shura Council [upper house of parliament], and the local councils, because it is a means of enabling *da'wah* and spreading it among the different segments of society [. . .] We prefer scholars and preachers not to run for themselves so as not to distract them from *da'wah*, but rather to support those who adopt the issues of Islam and the interests of the nation. We call on Muslims to vote in the presidential elections for those who see it as more adopting the issues of Islamic law and the interests of the nation.[30]

In choosing to prioritise *da'wa* over political participation, Ansar al-Sunna did not eschew politics, as was its tradition, but rather encouraged wider participation in the electoral field as a means of its advancement. This reflects Lacroix's observation of al-Dawa al-Salafiyya's view of politics as being a 'purely instrumental approach' that is 'based on what was perceived to be in the interest of the Salafi Da'wa'.[31] As well as establishing the legal permissibility of political participation in this service of their wider mission, the statement also includes a subtle reformulation of what *da'wa* constitutes. In stressing that scholars who remain outside of politics should also support those Islamists who do run for political office, the Shura Council sanctions engagement in political advocacy in the service of Islamist candidates in the electoral arena.

The second Shura Council statement, issued on 16 April 2011, moves further in the direction of promoting cooperation and collaboration between the different trends of the Islamic movement.[32] It recommended that *da'wa* organisations establish working committees in each governorate, combining representatives from different factions to cooperate over common goals. Here the reformulation of *da'wa*'s meaning is extended to include organisational cooperation and collaboration between different Islamic associations. The Shura Council, with Ansar al-Sunna its dominant actor, thereby outlined a framework for a politicised *da'wa* that would be exercised across the Islamic movement. When we look at the statements of other Islamic associations on these same issues, we can identify a similar trend.

For its part, al-Gamiyya al-Shariyya adopted a similar position on political participation, but was more forthright in specifying the way in which it viewed *da'wa* and political participation as reinforcing one another. This is evidenced by a small booklet that the group issued in September 2011, outlining its position towards politics and titled 'The vision of al-Gam'iyya al-Shar'iyya in Joint Islamic Action and Party Politics' (*Ru'yat al-gam'iyya al-shar'iyya fī al-'amal al-islāmī al-mushtarak wa al-siyāsa wa al-ḥizbiyya)*. The booklet explained how the changing environment post-Mubarak had necessitated a change in approach for Islamists more generally, but even for those who would forgo formal political participation:

> The fall of this regime has become a door to power in Egypt, open to all for the first time in decades. The scales have tipped and the conditions have changed so it has now become a duty [*wājib*] for Islamists to race against time so that the events do not miss or overtake them [. . .] Al-Gam'iyya al-Shar'iyya considers party politics to be one of the developments which is necessary to achieve the interests of Muslims through a comprehensive vision of *da'wah* [. . .] The vision of al-Gam'iyya al-Shar'iyya in party political actions stems from its overall vision of joint action [*al-'amal al-mushtarak*] [. . .] *da'wah* is the base and party politics is a branch. You cannot talk about the branch in isolation from the base. Working in party politics at this stage has become a duty and for Islamists there are two directions. First, avoid spoilage by closing the door to non-Islamists to prevent them from reaching power. Second, achieving interest and bringing benefit with the arrival of those who establish Islamic rule.[33]

With the fall of Mubarak, entry into the political process is characterised as a 'duty' (*wājib*) for the Islamic movement, as it represents a genuine opportunity to establish a state governed by Islamic law. Despite choosing to remain in the area of *da'wa*, the booklet makes clear that al-Gamiyya al-Shariyya no longer viewed this work as being distinct from politics. Instead, they held that *da'wa* and politics are two branches of the same tree and cannot be considered in isolation from one another. Thus, 'joint Islamic action' implies that *da'wa* may advance the cause of Islam in politics, just as, in turn, politics may advance the cause of *da'wa* in the social fields. Al-Gamiyya al-Shariyya's leader, al-Mahdy, would later expand on this idea, identifying three fields of *da'wah*: the 'spoken *da'wah*' (*da'wat al-khitab*, proselytising/education), 'applied *da'wah*' (*al-da'wa al-tabtiyya*, service provision) and, finally, the work of party politics (*ḥizbiyya*).[34] In al-Mahdy's vision, different factions should work together to identify the areas in which they would specialise, while also working together to coordinate their activities.

The reformulation of the meaning of *da'wa* adopted by both Ansar al-Sunna and al-Gamiyya al-Shariyya is significant for how we view formerly 'quietist' Salafis. Even though they did not enter formal politics themselves, they reformulated their method of *da'wa* so that it may be used in the service of Islam in the political sphere. In addition, the Shura Council's position on *da'wa* and politics and al-Gamiyya al-Shariyya's notion of joint Islamic action also reflects 'frame alignment' among Islamic associations during this period. Snow et al., for example, discuss how convergence among social movements can take place when an 'ideologically congruent frame' is shared over a particular issue.[35] This is demonstrated in Ansar al-Sunna's and al-Gamiyya al-Shariyya's revised positions on the meaning of *da'wa*, which, as we will now see, was exercised in their political advocacy during the three electoral cycles of the transitional period.

Political Advocacy during Electoral Processes

1. The March 2011 Referendum on Constitutional Amendments

On 19 March 2011, a referendum was held over a package of nine constitutional amendments dealing mainly with the conduct of elections and the powers of the presidency. For Islamists, securing a 'yes' vote was favourable for two reasons. First, approving the amendments would facilitate a quick timetable for parliamentary elections, in which both the Brotherhood and the newly formed Salafi parties would be well-placed to succeed ahead of secular and liberal parties, due to their superior resources and mobilising power. The second reason is not readily apparent when looking at the detail of the amendments, for no specific reference to religion is made. This, in fact, is the very point. Article 2 of Egypt's constitution, amended under Anwar Sadat in a previous referendum in 1980, states: 'Islam is the religion of the State, Arabic is its official language, and the principal source of legislation is Islamic jurisprudence'. This article is key for Egypt's Islamic movement, and thus Article 2 became a central issue in the debate over the drafting of the constitutional amendments.[36] The fear among Islamists was that drafting a new constitution may lead to the removal of this article, and with the proposed amendments leaving it alone and making no reference to it, they became vocal supporters of a 'yes' vote.

Although mobilisation for the 'yes' vote was led by Islamists such as the Brotherhood, Islamic associations outside the political field were also actively campaigning to support it. Revisiting Ansar al-Sunna's Shura Council of Scholars' first statement, we find the following proclamation:

> We call on Muslims not to delay by voting to approve the constitutional amendments [. . .] because its advantages outweigh the negatives [. . .] The nation [. . .] will not allow anyone to change the second article of the constitution, or change it in any future formulation of the constitution.[37]

As with outlining their position on *da'wa* and politics, Ansar al-Sunna would again be joined in its new-found political activism by al-Gamiyya al-Shariyya, with its resources being mobilised on several fronts in advocating for a 'yes' vote. On 16 March, from its main headquarters in the al-Jalaa Mosque in the Ramses district of Cairo, al-Gamiyya al-Shariyya held a seminar under the title 'The Need to Vote Yes in the Referendum over the Constitutional Amendments'.[38] Al-Mahdy told the assembled religious scholars and journalists that going out to vote was a 'religious duty' (*wājib shar'ī*). It also appears that al-Gamiyya al-Shariyya imams used their Friday sermons to urge worshippers to vote this way.[39] Furthermore, three days before the poll, the group sought a national audience with a front-page advertisement in *al-Ahrām*, Egypt's most widely circulated newspaper, stating that the January 25 revolution was a gift from God that had to be protected. In a key section the advert read:

> The entire leadership of the association considers it to be an *Islamic duty* that every Egyptian voice their agreement to the amendments as a first step towards the later formulation of a complete constitution [. . .] We see giving up on this duty as a negative thing rejected by Islam.[40]

The emphasis on doing one's duty reflects a common rationale among Islamic associations during the transitional period, equating a political decision with a religious act. Such an intervention by an ostensibly non-political group was striking, garnering much criticism in the secular/liberal camp, including by the Nobel Laureate Muhammad El-Baradei, who in a tweet condemned the action as 'scary and suspicious'.[41] Yet, in a television interview responding to the criticisms, al-Mahdy was assiduous, stressing further that this *wājib* for Muslims was tantamount to performing the *shahāda*, the first of the five pillars of Islam, and the basic statement of faith that Muslims are expected to recite to demonstrate their commitment to their religion.[42] As we shall see later, Islamic associations repeated this justification in subsequent electoral cycles, equating political acts with the basic tenets of faith.

Framing the referendum as a 'religious duty', implying that a 'no' vote would mean that citizens had somehow committed a violation of their religion, was an interpretation shared widely by other Islamic associations in their advocacy ahead of the referendum. Al-Dawa al-Salafiyya, for example, urged citizens to vote for the amendments based on the fact that 'positive engagement' would be the most effective path for the implementation of *sharī'a* law. In particular, they stated that the amendments were positive precisely because they did not try to overturn Article 2, which would be the implication of a 'no' vote.[43] Preachers used their sermons to stress the religious duty of voting 'yes', while al-Dawa al-Salafiyya shaykhs in Alexandria erected banners in its streets referring to the 'religious duty' of voting 'yes'.[44] In the Manufiyya governorate, meanwhile, al-Gamiyya al-Salafiyya rented cars and broadcast propaganda from loudspeakers, once again putting up banners that read 'Voting yes is a religious duty'.[45]

What we see, then, is a convergence of the positions of Egypt's Islamic associations, including those who decided against formal politicisation, on a shared position towards the 2011 constitutional amendments and its framing as a political act fulfilling a religious duty. The shared beliefs of several actors led to a unified Islamist position, or 'frame alignment', towards the constitutional amendments. As the issue became debated in the public sphere, the particular interpretation of voting 'yes' as a 'religious duty' became *diffused* across the discourse of these actors, be they formally 'apolitical' groups such as Ansar al-Sunna and al-Gamiyya al-Shariyya, or those with newly formed political parties, such as al-Dawa al-Salafiyya.

2. Parliamentary Elections, November 2011–February 2012

With the parliamentary elections beginning in November 2011, Egyptians would have the first opportunity to vote for their representatives in the political arena since Mubarak's departure. At the time, Egypt's parliament was a bicameral system, consisting of a lower house, the People's Assembly, and an upper chamber, the Shura Council.[46] The elections for the People's Assembly began on 28 November 2011, with further rounds of voting continuing into the New Year; voting for the Shura Council got underway at the end of January 2012 and lasted one month. The 'collective identity' of Egypt's Islamic movement was on full display in mobilising support for Islamist candidates in each of the voting cycles. On 6 November 2011, in the city of Sohag, for 'Eid al-Aḍḥā, the Muslim Brotherhood, al-Gamiyya al-Islamiyya, al-Gamiyya al-Salafiyya and al-Gamiyya al-Shariyya formed a union called the Islamic Action League (Rābiṭat al-'Amal al-Islāmī) to unite in prayer in the city's main square.[47] However, what was billed as a prayer meet turned into an electoral platform, as the 15,000 in attendance witnessed the presentation of the programmes of various Islamist candidates for parliament.

The use of religious ceremonies as platforms to disseminate electoral propaganda appeared to be widespread. Imams in thousands of Salafi mosques used their Friday sermons to urge worshippers to favour candidates calling for the application of Islamic law in their electoral programmes and promising to maintain the religious identity of the state.[48] In one such case, the imam of a al-Gamiyya al-Shariyya-affiliated mosque in Asyut urged worshippers and citizens via loudspeakers to give their votes to Islamist parties and not to liberal or secular parties.[49] Despite their historical closeness to the Brotherhood, al-Gamiyya al-Shariyya mosques were commonly found to be propaganda outlets for Nour Party candidates – either as the starting point for rallies for specific candidates, or as sites distributing the electoral paraphernalia of candidates – as outlined by observers who tweeted about them.[50] Similar occurrences were observed in local Ansar al-Sunna branches, where candidates from the FJP cooperated to provide medical services in constituencies during electoral periods.[51]

Links between political candidates and Ansar al-Sunna also took other forms. The more prominent candidates of the Islamic Alliance, such as

Abdel Moneim el-Shahat, the official spokesperson of al-Dawa al-Salafiyya in Alexandria, tended to run in electoral districts electing an individual candidate. Other, lesser-known figures, such as al-Nour's candidate in Mansoura, Hazem Shoman, and al-Asala's candidate, Mamdouh Ismail, were placed on wards using an electoral list system. To boost their profile, the logos of Ansar al-Sunna and al-Gamiyya al-Shariyya were positioned at the head of their electoral lists distributed to voters.[52] It is not clear whether either association officially sanctioned this; however, considering the use of their offices for other campaigning activities, it seems unlikely that this would have occurred without their knowledge. Indeed, both Brotherhood and al-Nour candidates were observed plugging their affiliations with Ansar al-Sunna in their biographical statements.[53] The social capital of these Islamic associations was thereby used in an attempt to bolster support for Islamist candidates.

Islamic associations also promoted a strategic rationale in the fielding of Islamist candidates for the elections. Despite the Muslim Brotherhood's presumed dominance, the pluralisation of the party system nevertheless led to the fragmentation of Islamist parties. Alongside the FJP, a further eleven parties with an Islamic reference contested parliamentary seats.[54] Concerned about a split in the Islamic vote, which would benefit secular/liberal parties, both Ansar al-Sunna and al-Gamiyya al-Shariyya advocated for parties to cooperate to ensure multiple Islamist candidates did not contest the same constituency. Ahead of the second phase of the parliamentary elections, the deputy leader of Ansar al-Sunna's Shura Council of Scholars, Muhammad Hassan, delivered the Friday sermon to 20,000 worshippers from the al-Gamiyya al-Shariyya mosque in the city of Mansoura in the Dakahlia governorate. He stated: 'I do not want to see competition in the second round of voting between Islamists because competition breaks the Islamic voice to the benefit of others'.[55] Hassan advocated a tactical alliance, whereby different Islamist parties would cooperate to ensure only a single Islamist candidate ran in a constituency. Al-Gamiyya al-Shariyya also issued statements demanding only one Islamist candidate, with their shaykhs stressing the necessity of unity, so that their voice would not be dispersed, giving secularists the chance to rule the country.[56] This demonstrates how Ansar al-Sunna and al-Gamiyya al-Shariyya approached their political activism through the lens of a collective

Islamic identity, rather than political factionalism with their closest ideological bedfellows.

The SBRR also embarked on the task of encouraging strategic voting, asking for the leaders of the FJP, Salafis and al-Azhar to coordinate with each other during the elections.[57] In particular, they implored the FJP and al-Nour to make mutual concessions in seats decided as individual districts, rather than electoral lists. SBRR member Dr Hisham Nodah declared that competition between a Brotherhood candidate and another Islamist in the presence of a rival against the application of Islamic law is considered *ḥarām*. Initially it seemed that their calls were heeded, as after forming an electoral alliance with al-Asala and al-Fadila, al-Nour indicated that similar coordination with the FJP was also being sought, facilitated by the SBRR. Despite the formation of a joint committee to discuss the proposals, according to Nadar Bakar, a member of the al-Nour supreme body, the FJP refused to give up seats to al-Nour, even though al-Nour had offered to concede three seats in return. In the end, both would run without mutual concessions.

Here we see that Islamic associations such as Ansar al-Sunna and al-Gamiyya al-Shariyya, who by themselves did not have a formal stake in the race, were more likely to urge the adoption of tactical voting and strategic candidate selections as part of a coordinated effort reflecting the collective identity of the Islamic movement. These associations had promoted a religious cleavage before considerations of the political platforms of individual parties. Yet, for the parties themselves, the temptations of electoral competition would ultimately prevent the realisation of this expression of Islamic collective identity to the full.

3. Presidential Elections, May 2012

The fissures that emerged during the parliamentary elections among rival Islamist parties resurfaced when they were confronted with settling on a candidate for president. In the build-up to the vote, there was an initial degree of enthusiasm for continuing the cooperation and collaboration outlined in previous sections. In March 2012, al-Dawa al-Salafiyya launched an initiative for coordination among the different groupings to agree on one candidate, in order to ensure that votes for Islamists were not fragmented.[58] Among those supporting the initiative was Egypt's official religious body, al-Azhar, the

Muslim Brotherhood, Ansar al-Sunna, al-Gamiyya al-Shariyya, al-Gamiyya al-Islamiyya, the SBRR and the Shura Council of Scholars, with the Islamist parties – the FJP, al-Nour, al-Asala and the Building and Development party – also indicating their support. The previous levels of coordination proved to be a step too far, however, as unlike in the parliamentary elections, the need to settle on a single candidate led to disagreement over who would be the most suitable.

Choosing the right candidate meant weighing normative goals against pragmatic considerations. Who was most likely to implement the fullest vision of Islamic law, but also succeed in a run-off against a non-Islamist candidate? If the Brotherhood were to field a candidate, then the likelihood was that they would be victorious. Yet, the reformist ideology of the Brotherhood led to concerns in the Salafi camp over who best represented their vision. Thus, the Salafi-dominated SBRR was the first to demand that the Muslim Brotherhood nominate Khairat al-Shater, who was a senior member in the body. Ansar al-Sunna, meanwhile, called for the nomination of the Salafi Shaykh Hazem Salah Abu Ismail. For al-Dawa al-Salafiyya, Ismail's brand of 'revolutionary Salafism' would not secure victory against a non-Islamist candidate.[59] They then took the surprising move of supporting the former Brotherhood member and 'liberal Islamist' Abdel Monem Abul Futuh. The only faction not to name a specific candidate was al-Gamiyya al-Shariyya, who stated only that they stand with the 'Islamic trend' and that 'it is important that the banner of Islam be raised by the person chosen by the people'.[60] The matter was somewhat settled by default, however, with the disqualification from running of Abu Ismail and al-Shater, who was the Brotherhood's initial choice, for technical reasons. The result was the surprise nomination of Muhammad Morsi, an experienced yet uncharismatic parliamentarian, as the Brotherhood candidate for the presidency.

When the second round of voting pitted Morsi against Ahmed Shafik, an experienced minister in various National Democratic Party cabinets under Mubarak, the realignment of the Islamic movement towards the shared goal of an Islamist presidency was resumed. With the disqualification of Abu Ismail, Ansar al-Sunna also urged their followers to support Morsi, on the basis that he now represented the best chance of advancing *sharīʿa* in Egypt.[61] In their statement of support, the Shura Council of Scholars stated that

Egypt's Muslims would be performing *shahāda* in voting for Morsi, reflecting al-Mahdy's invocation of this idea during the referendum on constitutional amendments. This frame was shared in the discourse of other preachers who campaigned under the banner of the SBRR ahead of the ballot. A mass rally was held in the square outside of Giza's main train station, under the title 'How to choose the next president?'[62] Talaat al-Afifi, a al-Gamiyya al-Shariyya figure who would become Minister of Awqaf under Morsi, addressed the crowd and stated that the choice of the president is a '*shahāda* and we are entrusted with it' and that the '*shahāda* is obligatory and the people should not abandon it'.[63] Al-Afifi went on to make explicit the parallel between voting as a *shahāda* and the act of the traditional *shahāda*, 'a worship in which a man draws closer to his God'. The framing of political choices as a *shahāda* was therefore diffused across successive electoral cycles and adopted by Ansar al-Sunna and al-Gamiyya al-Shariyya, as well as by al-Afifi, who would become the most senior religious appointee in the FJP cabinet.

The episode of choosing and backing an Islamist candidate for president shows that, when faced with an issue over which the individual group's ideological preferences emerge, such as during the selection of a single candidate, the fissures between the different factions are more likely to present themselves. But when the matter returned to promoting the Islamist movement as a whole, Islamic associations reverted to their approach of promoting a religious cleavage, as the fault lines of the fight returned to those of the secular-religious divide.

Conclusion

This chapter argues that Ansar al-Sunna became a target of state oppression because, while staying out of electoral politics, it did support Islamic political activism, irrespective of party orientations. Ansar al-Sunna sought to promote the 'collective identity' of the Islamic movement above individual factional interests, to further the electoral prospects of both the Muslim Brotherhood and the Salafi alliance. By supporting this broad-based Islamic activism, it posed a threat to the al-Sisi regime in a way that the al-Nour Party and al-Dawa al-Salafiyya did not. Ansar al-Sunna effectively became a political interest group representing Egypt's Islamic movement in the electoral sphere. This does demonstrate that, while we have seen increasing polarisation among Salafi groups since the Arab Spring, there are some who have shown the vision to look beyond narrow group interests and forge an alliance for strengthening the defence of Islam against the secular forces in society. These groups have also shown the pragmatism to change their quietist orientation and engage in politics when opportunities have become available. Removed from partisan politics, Islamic associations such as Ansar al-Sunna and al-Gamiyya al-Shariyya aligned their discursive frames through the equation of political choices with one's religious duty.

Carrie Wickham has recognised this framing strategy previously in the Egyptian context. In her study of how young students in Egypt's universities were recruited to the Islamic movement in the 1980s and early 1990s, Wickham describes how 'Islamists framed activism as a moral "obligation" that demands self-sacrifice and unflinching commitment to the cause of religious transformation'.[64] In particular, the Brotherhood 'asserted that every Muslim is obligated to contribute to the task of Islamic social and political reform'.[65] While the similarities are clear in terms of the discursive frame, there are important differences in their deployment in the contemporary context. First, in Wickham's example, specific groups like the Muslim Brotherhood adopted this frame to increase participation in their own movement, whereas in 2011–12 a multitude of Islamic actors aligned towards a similar interpretation as a means of furthering the cause as a whole. Second, this framing was exercised not to compel recruits to join the Islamic movement only, but to compel Muslims more broadly to participate in a particular way in the political process in the service of their religion. This case thus demonstrates the half-way house between *daʿwa* and politics occupied by Salafi associations such as Ansar al-Sunna, and how their increasingly politicised forms of activism may nevertheless continue to eschew the traditional parameters of party politics in favour of a superlative ideal that takes an instrumental view of political power.

Notes

1. Rania al-Abd, '*Tajmīd ʾamwāl 1055 jamʿiyya <ikhwāniyya>*', *al-Akhbar*, 28 December 2013, https://al-akhbar.com/Arab/62617 (accessed 17 June 2019).
2. Mohamed Nagi, 'Al-Sisi meets with Islamists', *Daily News Egypt*, 4 August 2013,

www.dailynewsegypt.com/2013/08/04/al-sisi-meets-with-islamists/ (accessed 17 June 2019).

3. Wagemakers has stressed that distinguishing between expressions of Salafism as 'quietist' and 'political' is overly pronounced, when in fact two *manahij* (methods) often overlap. See Joas Wagemakers, 'Revisiting Wiktorowicz: Categorising and Defining the Branches of Salafism', in *Salafism After the Arab Awakening: Contending with the People's Power*, ed. Francesco Cavatorta and Fabio Merone (New York: Oxford University Press, 2016), 7–24.
4. Mokhtar Awad, 'The Salafi Dawa of Alexandria: The Politics of A Religious Movement', Hudson Institute, 14 August 2014, www.hudson.org/research/10463-the-salafi-dawa-of-alexandria-the-politics-of-a-religious-movement-; Jacob Høigilt and Frida Nome, 'Egyptian Salafism in Revolution', *Journal of Islamic Studies* 25 (2014), 33–54; Stéphane Lacroix, 'Sheikhs and Politicians: Inside the New Egyptian Salafism', Brookings Institution, 2012, www.brookings.edu/~/media/research/files/papers/2012/6/07-egyptian-salafism-lacroix/stephane-lacroix-policy-briefing-english.pdf; Bjørn Olav Utvik, 'The Ikhwanization of the Salafis: Piety in the Politics of Egypt and Kuwait', *Middle East Critique* 23 (2014), 5–27.
5. Omar Ashour, 'From Bad Cop to Good Cop: The Challenge of Security Sector Reform in Egypt', Brookings Institution, 2016, www.brookings.edu/wp-content/uploads/2016/06/Omar-Ashour-English.pdf.
6. Nathan J. Brown, 'Islam and Politics in the New Egypt', Carnegie Endowment for International Peace, 2013, https://carnegieendowment.org/files/islam_politics.pdf; William McCants, 'The Lesser of Two Evils: The Salafi Turn to Party Politics in Egypt', Brookings Institution, 2012, www.brookings.edu/wp-content/uploads/2016/06/0501_salafi_egypt_mccants.pdf.
7. Steven Brooke, 'Islamic Groups' Social Service Provision and Attitudinal Change in Egypt', Combating Terrorism Center at West Point, 2015, https://ctc.usma.edu/app/uploads/2015/06/Brooke_CTC_IslamicGroupSocialService_June20153.pdf.
8. Richard Gauvain, 'Salafism in Modern Egypt: Panacea or Pest?' *Political Theology* 10 (2010), 802–25; Richard Gauvain, *Salafi Ritual Purity: In the Presence of God* (Abingdon: Routledge, 2014).
9. Asya El-Meehy, 'Egypt's Popular Committees: From Moments of Madness to NGO Dilemmas', *Middle East Report* 265 (2012), 29–33.
10. This is akin to Ziad Munson's approach in his article 'Islamic Mobilization: Social Movement Theory and the Egyptian Muslim Brotherhood', *The*

Sociological Quarterly 42 (2001), 487–510, where he focuses on the interactions between the ideational and organisational components of the Brotherhood in its first decades. He writes: 'This study suggests that our existing understanding of the role of ideas in social movements must be deepened to consider the ways in which mobilization depends on the interactions among ideas, organization, and environments – not simply on one or the other of these three dimensions' (488).

11. Gauvain, *Salafi Ritual Purity*, 34.
12. Muhammad Fathi Muhammad, *Al-Fikr al-siyāsī lil-tayārāt al-salafiyya* (Cairo: Arab Library for Knowledge, 2013), 115.
13. Ibid., 103.
14. Ibid., 113.
15. Morroe Berger, *Islam in Egypt Today: Social and Political Aspects of Popular Religion* (Cambridge: Cambridge University Press, 1970), 94.
16. Mohamed Fahmy Menza, *Patronage Politics in Egypt: The National Democratic Party and Muslim Brotherhood in Cairo* (New York: Routledge, 2012), 73.
17. Gauvain, *Salafi Ritual Purity*, 37.
18. Brooke, 'Islamic Groups' Social Service Provision', 26.
19. Ibid., 15.
20. Ammar Ahmed Fayed, 'Al-Salafiyyun fī maṣr: min sharīʿah al-fatwa ila sharīʿah al-intikhāb', *Al-Jazeera*, 16 July 2012, http://studies.aljazeera.net/ar/reports/2012/07/201271103413876925.html (accessed 19 June 2019).
21. Human Rights Watch, 'Anatomy of a State Security Case: The "Victorious Sect" Arrests', vol. 19, no. 9 (2007), www.hrw.org/reports/2007/egypt1207/egypt1207web.pdf.
22. Doug McAdam, John D. McCarthy and Mayer N. Zald (eds), *Comparative Perspectives on Social Movements: Political Opportunities, Mobilizing Structures, and Cultural Framings* (Cambridge: Cambridge University Press, 1996), 3.
23. Dieter Rucht, 'The Impact of National Contexts on Social Movement Structures: A Cross-Movement and Cross-National Comparison', in *Comparative Perspectives on Social Movements: Political Opportunities, Mobilizing Structures, and Cultural Framings*, ed. Doug McAdam, John D. McCarthy and Mayer N. Zald (Cambridge: Cambridge University Press, 1996), 191.
24. Wael Ramadan, 'Wāqiʿ al-daʿwa al-islāmiyya fī maṣr baʿd ʿām min al-thawra. . .ʿaqbāt wa 'amāl', *al-Furqan*, 26 March 2012, www.al-forqan.net/articles/1882.html (accessed 19 June 2019).
25. Ansar al-Sunna, 'Bayān b-shu'n ma uthīr ḥawl talaqa al-jamʿiyya l-tamwīlāt

’ajnabiyya’, 9 May 2011, www.altawhed.net/article.php?i=534 (accessed 19 June 2019).

26. El-Meehy, ‘Egypt’s Popular Committees’.
27. Maurice Pinard, *Motivational Dimensions in Social Movements and Contentious Collective Action* (London: McGill-Queen’s University Press, 2011).
28. Muhammad, *Al-Fikr al-siyāsī*, 113.
29. *Asharq Al-Awsat*, ‘Egypt’s Salafist Ansar al-Sunna to form political group’, 11 April 2011, https://eng-archive.aawsat.com/theaawsat/features/egypts-salafist-ansar-al-sunna-to-form-political-group (accessed 19 June 2019).
30. Shura Council of Scholars, ‘Majlis shura al ‘ulamā’ al-bayān’ al-’awal’, 19 March 2011, www.ansaralsonna.com/web/play-5212.html (accessed 19 June 2019).
31. Stéphane Lacroix, ‘Egypt’s Pragmatic Salafis: The Politics of Hizb Al-Nour’, Carnegie Endowment for International Peace, 1 November 2016, https://carnegieendowment.org/2016/11/01/egypt-s-pragmatic-salafis-politics-of-hizb-al-nour-pub-64902.
32. Shura Council of Scholars, ‘Al-bayān’ al-thānī l-majlis shura al ‘ulamā’, 11 April 2011, www.ansaralsonna.com/web/play-5214.html (accessed 19 June 2019).
33. Muhammad, *Al-fikr al-siyāsī.*
34. Ahmed Abdel Fatah, ‘Al-gam‘iyya al-shar‘iyya tad‘ū lil-tansīq bayn al-firq al-islāmiyya taḥt raiyat al-azhar’, 25 September 2011, http://gate.ahram.org.eg/News/119700.aspx (accessed 19 June 2019).
35. David A. Snow, E. Burke Rochford, Jr, Steven K. Worden and Robert D. Benford, ‘Frame Alignment Processes, Micromobilization, and Movement Participation’, *American Sociological Review* 51 (1986), 467.
36. Salma Shukrallah and Yassin Gaber, ‘What was Religion Doing in the Debate on Egypt’s Constitutional Amendments?’ *Ahram Online*, 22 March 2011, http://english.ahram.org.eg/NewsContent/1/64/8267/Egypt/Politics-/What-was-religion-doing-in-the-debate-on-Egypts-Co.aspx (accessed 19 June 2019).
37. Shura Council of Scholars, ‘Majlis shura al ‘ulamā’ al-bayān’ al-’awal’, 19 March 2011, www.ansaralsonna.com/web/play-5212.html (accessed 19 June 2019).
38. Ismailia Online, ‘‘Ulamā’: al-kharūj lil-istifitā’ wājib shar‘ī wa al-taṣwīt lil-ta‘dīāt b-’na‘m’ maṣlaḥ lil-ummah’, 17 March 2011, www.ismailiaonline.com/pages.php?option=browse&id=54549 (accessed 19 June 2019).

39 Mena George, ‘سجد الجمعية الشرعية بأسيوط (أبو بكر الصديق) سمعتها في المايك, : لازم يوم السبت كلنا نروح و نصوت بـ(نعم) , #Egypt #Jan25’, 14 March 2011, https://twitter.com/MSGeorge_/status/47426110358683649 (accessed 19 June 2019).

40. Shukrallah and Gaber, ‘What was Religion Doing?’ [emphasis added].

41 Mohamed ElBaradei, ‘إعلان من الجمعية الشرعية بالصفحة الأولى بالأهرام بأن التصويت بنعم واجب شرعي!. أمر مخيف ومريب !’ 19 March 2011, https://twitter.com/ElBaradei/status/491502491676330336 (accessed 19 June 2019).

42. OTV, 2011, ‘Taṣḥīḥ ra’īs al-gam‘iyya al-shar‘iyya l-ma wa rad bil-ahrām’, www.youtube.com/watch?v=THythiQHagA.

43. al-Da‘wa al-Salafiyya, ‘Bayān min ‘al-da‘wa al-salafiyya’ b-shu’n al-istifitā’ ‘ala al-ta‘dīlāt al-dustūriyya’, 6 March 2011, www.alsalafway.com/cms/news.php?action=news&id=10522 (accessed 19 June 2019).

44. Muhammed Abdel Khaliq, ‘Salafīū al-iskandariyya: al-mushārika fī al-istifitā’ ‘ala al-ta‘d īāt al-dustūriyya wājib shar‘ī’, *Al-Ahram*, 7 March 2011, https://bit.ly/2IpResq (accessed 19 June 2019).

45. Muhammed Elesawy, ‘Al-taṣwīt b-’na‘m’ wājib shar‘ī fī rā’ī al-jamā‘a al-salafiyya bil-manūfiyya’, *Al-Ahram*, 19 March 2011, http://gate.ahram.org.eg/News/51014.aspx (accessed 19 June 2019).

46. The Egyptian parliament is now unicameral, comprising the House of Representatives alone.

47. Mahmoud Maqbool, ‘‘Al-islāmiyya’ wa ‘al-ikhwān’ wa ‘al-salafiyya’ wa ‘al-shar‘iyya’. . .’yid wāhida b-sūhāg’, *al-Yawm al-Sabaa*, 6 November 2011, https://bit.ly/2Xntw8H (accessed 19 June 2019)

48. Hamdy Debash and Osama al-Mahdy, ‘Masājid al-salafīīn wa ’aḍraḥat al-mutiṣawifat fī khidmat al-intikhābāt’, *al-Masry al-Yawm*, 10 November 2011, www.almasryalyoum.com/news/details/124782 (accessed 19 June 2019).

49. Egyptian Association for Community Participation Enhancement, ‘Al-bayān al-thāmin – al-yawm al-intikhābī al-thānī jawlat al- ‘iāda al-marḥala al-’ūla’, (6 December 2011), www.mosharka.org/index.php?newsid=426 (accessed 19 June 2019).

50 Ayman Ade, ‘يدعوكم حزب النور بالدقهلية لمسيرة ضخمة بعد صلاة الجمعة القادمة إن شاء الله تخرج المسيرة من أمام الجمعية الشرعية. . . http://fb.me/KSZaHQ3X’, 27 December 2011, https://twitter.com/AymanAde/status/151759069567397890; Bassem Tarek, ‘دعايه للمرشح ' حزب النور ' علي مسجد الجمعيه الشرعيه بشارع نادي امبابه الرياضي (امبابه الدائره الثالثه بالجيزه -. . . http://fb.me/14d9rP9NW’, 15 December 2011, https://twitter.com/Bassem_Tarek/status/147396668940230656; Gharbia Ikhwan Media, ‘مخالفات إنتخابيه وكسر للصمت الإنتخابي : 1 \ خيمة دعائية لحزب النور أمام مسجد الجمعية الشرعية بالدلجمون 2 \ خيمة. . . http://fb.me/ZnlrY5y9’, 2 January 2012, https://twitter.com/gharbiamedia/status/153892433879515137.

51. Brooke, ‘Islamic Groups’ Social Service Provision’, 21.

52. Hamdy Debash, ‘Al-taḥāluf al-islāmī yunāfis b-693 murshaḥan wa yurāhin ‘ala

muḥāfiẓin al-wajh al-baḥra', *al-Masry al-Yawm*, 26 October 2011, www.almasryalyoum.com/news/details/121440 (accessed 19 June 2019).

53. Brooke, 'Islamic Groups' Social Service Provision', 21.
54. European Parliament, 'Map of Egyptian Political Parties: First Phase of Parliamentary Elections', 25 January 2012, www.europarl.europa.eu/meetdocs/2009_2014/documents/dmas/dv/dmas20120125_02_/dmas20120125_02_en.pdf.
55. Saleh Ramadan, 'Al-shaykh moḥamed ḥassan 'mām 20 'alf shakhṣ bil-manṣūra: lisat 'aḍwa' fī ḥizb aw jamā'a', *al-Yawm al-Sabaa*, 9 December 2011, https://bit.ly/2IThQkR (accessed 19 June 2019).
56. Fatah, 'Al-gam'iyya al-shar'iyya tuṭālib b-murashaḥ wāḥid 'an al-tayār al-islāmī'.
57. Debash, 'Fashil al-tansīq bayn 'al-ikhwān' wa 'al-salafīīn''.
58. *Al-Ahram*, 'Khafāji yu'ayid mubādira 'al-da'wa al-salafiyya' lil-itifāq 'ala murashaḥ al-islāmī', 20 March 2012.
59. Awad, 'The Salafi Dawa of Alexandria'.
60. al-Gam'iyya al-Shar'iyya, 'Bayān mawqif al-gam'iyya al-shar'iyya ḥawwal al-aḥdāth al-jāriyya l-intikhāb r'īs al-jumhuriyya', 2012.
61. Shura Council of Scholars, 'Majlis shūrī al-'ulama' al-bayān al-thālith wa al-'asharūn', 30 May 2012, www.ansaralsonna.com/web/play-6537.html (accessed 19 June 2019).
62. Hosny Kamal, Emad Eddin Saber and Ahmed Atrji, 'Al-hay'a al-shar'iyya lil-ḥuqūq wa al-iṣlāḥ: muhimat al-r'īs ḥirāsat al-dīn', *Al-Ahram*, 2 May 2012, www.ahram.org.eg/archive/Al-Ahram-Files/News/146864.aspx (accessed 19 June 2019).
63. Kamal Kamal, ''Afīfī: ikhtiyyār al-r'īs al-qādim shahādat farḍ', *Al-Yawm al-Sabaa*, 1 May 2012, https://bit.ly/31GJZ74 (accessed 19 June 2019).
64. Carrie Rosefsky Wickham, 'Interests, Ideas, and Islamist Outreach in Egypt', in *Islamic Activism: A Social Movement Theory Approach*, ed. Quintan Wiktorl-ahramowicz (Bloomington: Indiana University Press, 2004), 232.
65. Ibid., 244.

6

SALAFI LEADERSHIP OUTSIDE SAUDI ARABIA: HAKIM AL-MUTAIRI AND THE UMMA PARTY OF KUWAIT

Kristin Diwan

This chapter for the first time pulls together a comprehensive overview of the Umma Party – from its origins in Kuwait and its spread to the neighbouring Gulf countries of Saudi Arabia and the United Arab Emirates, over its involvement in the Syrian war, to its current fractured existence in exile in the United Kingdom and Turkey.[1] Taken in its full scope, the Umma Party provides an interesting case of a movement fully conversant in Saudi Islamism but forged mostly outside of its confines, its organisational and ideational innovations reflecting back on Saudi Islam and broader Salafi circles. As such, it provides a window into the distinctive role that Kuwaiti Islamism – forged in a more open political environment and with considerable financial resources – has been able to play both within the field of Islamism and regional politics.

From its very beginnings, the Umma Party has pushed ideological and political boundaries. While emerging out of the tradition of political or *haraki* Salafis, the party took its commitment to politics further than its peers. It has pressed the objective of a Salafi-inspired political liberation above other concerns, including religious reform and religious activities. Its establishment in 2005 unmistakably announced this difference in its declaration as a *hizb* or party: a position which immediately put it in the crosshairs of both the state and other Salafi groups. It was, in fact, the first movement, liberal or Islamist, to declare itself formally a 'party' in the Gulf monarchies. Its innovations did not stop there, as the party distinguished itself with its emphasis on internal deliberations – not always fully realised – and its willingness to form political coalitions with ideological adversaries, including Shiʿi and liberal groups, in order to achieve its goals.

Still, the greater impact of the Umma Party was not in its party politics, where it never met with any political success, but more in the intellectual reach of its ideas – in particular, the writings of its main ideologue, Hakim al-Mutairi. These wed a political perspective grounded in Arabia's tribal order to a normative reading of Islam, which accentuates its political aspects and the promise of liberation from tyranny. In the hands of al-Mutairi and his acolytes, this has most often involved the promotion of self-government and a hard-line stance against perceived Western imperialism, justifying taking up arms under certain conditions.

This revolutionary aspect has come to the fore as the Umma Party and al-Mutairi became more radicalised by the Arab Spring of 2011, more formally expanding beyond Kuwait to the fellow Gulf states of Saudi Arabia and the United Arab Emirates, and on to Syria, where the movement supported, both financially and materially, the jihad against the Assad government. Today, the already depleted movement has further splintered: one faction is based in London where it has joined with other small groups in a united front openly calling for the overthrow of the Saudi monarchy and the liberation of the Arabian Peninsula from Western 'colonial' tyranny. Al-Mutairi still heads a diminished Umma Conference currently residing in Turkey, a state he supports as a Muslim bulwark against foreign incursions in the region.

Origins of the Umma Party: The Kuwaiti Political Scene

The Umma Party was established in Kuwait in 2005, emerging from within its dynamic political environment and fractious Islamist milieu. The relative openness of Kuwaiti politics and public life has provided a rich environment for Islamist organisation and mobilisation. This development has been augmented by Kuwait's status as one of the first states in the Gulf to develop its oil resources and to distribute oil revenues to the public, through the creation of a generous welfare state. This wealth has allowed Islamists, both Sunni and Shiʿi, to establish social organisations and charities that have not only reshaped politics within the emirate, but also supported missions abroad.

A number of scholars, both Western and Kuwaiti, have written about the development of the Salafi political field in Kuwait.[2] From its beginnings in the 1960s, Salafi thought and practice spread in the traditional ways; small groups and charismatic individuals attracted followers through mosques and through the Kuwaiti gathering halls known as *diwaniyas*, which offer the protection and inviolability of homes while supporting public dialogue. By the late 1970s the Salafi movement had gained a devoted following, centred in Kuwait City's urban districts and with the backing of wealthy merchants.[3] As in much of the Arab world, the government found its growth useful, initially as a counterweight to the leftist and Arab nationalist politics that captivated urban life in the 1970s, and later as a check against the rising power of the better-organised Muslim Brotherhood. This was particularly true after the Islamic revolution in Iran in 1979, which garnered supporters among Kuwait's influential Shiʿi community while further emboldening the Brotherhood.

By the early 1980s, the movement had expanded its presence in public organisations – youth centres, student associations and labour unions. With the support of the government, in 1981 the Salafis established the Revival of Islamic Heritage Society (RIHS), an umbrella organisation for their proselytising and charitable activities, mirroring – and rivalling – the Brotherhood's Social Reform Society. This provided a more unified front for its social activities, and a formal institutional structure for local organisation and mobilisation. While the Revival of Islamic Heritage Society offered a public face, the leadership of the political organisation, known informally as the al-Jama'a al-Salafiyya or Salafi Group, remained concealed.

Kuwait stands alone in the Gulf in having enshrined within its constitution a legislative body with some genuine powers. While Kuwait's parliament, the National Assembly, does not have the right to appoint the government, it can call ministers in for questioning, and if they lose a vote of confidence, remove them from office. Beyond this political oversight, parliamentarians have the ability to pass laws impacting the economic and social welfare of constituents and contributing to the religious character of society and state. They also perform 'service' roles facilitating their constituents' access to employment and benefits.

Cumulatively, these powers are enough to provide some real incentives for political groups and movements to participate. It is not surprising, then, that it is in Kuwait where Salafis participated in parliamentary elections for the first time. In 1981 they successfully elected two representatives to the National Assembly, the founding chairman of the Revival of Islamic Heritage Society and wealthy merchant Khalid al-Sultan, and the editor of the Salafi journal *Majallat al-Forqan*, Jassim al-Oun. These two members – whose links to the Salafi Group were kept informal due to Kuwait's ban on political parties – were re-elected in 1985.

The religious justification for this participation in electoral politics was provided primarily by the group's most important spiritual leader, Abdul Rahman Abdul Khaliq, an Egyptian national who settled in Kuwait. Through numerous books and weekly columns in the Kuwaiti newspaper *al-Watan*, he pressed for full political engagement, arguing that abandoning the formal political field would only empower the Salafis' religious and ideological opponents. He provided religious support for this stance in his book *Politics According to the Shar'ia*, arguing that even in the early Meccan period, the Prophet Muhammad used all available media to counter pagan beliefs and publicly change the social system.[4]

The relative unity in Kuwait's Salafi ranks ended after Kuwait's occupation by Iraq, due to the influence of debates emerging within the religious field in Saudi Arabia. There has always been an easy passage of both people and ideas across the border between Kuwait and Saudi Arabia, facilitated by the numerous tribal and familial ties that exist between the populations. This became amplified during the Gulf War, as many Kuwaitis sought refuge in the Kingdom. While there, many Kuwaiti Salafis came under the influence of the *Ṣaḥwa* movement and became adherents to its twin calls for political empowerment and the expulsion of foreign troops and influence from the Arabian Peninsula.

This sharper political rhetoric and stance splintered Salafi political organisation in Kuwait. Over time, the Revival of Islamic Heritage Society came under the control of Salafists who rejected this more hard-line stance against Gulf governments. The *Ṣaḥwa*-inspired Salafists left the Revival of Islamic Heritage Society and eventually formed their own organisation in 1997, initially called al-Haraka al-Salafiyya al-Ilmiyya, or the Scientific Salafi movement, and later simply the Salafi Movement.[5]

While both groups supported participation in the parliamentary life that returned after Kuwait's liberation, the two increasingly diverged in their political stances within the National Assembly, with the Revival of Islamic Heritage Society -linked al-Tajammaual-Islami al-Shaabi (Islamic Popular Gathering) most often deferring to the ruler under the principle of *wālī al-amr*, while the Salafi Islamic Movement frequently joined the political opposition.

The Umma Party emerged from a further division that occurred within the *Ṣaḥwa*-inspired Salafi Movement. Umma Party founder Hakim al-Mutairi had been one of the most prominent members of the activist Salafis, becoming Secretary-General of the Salafi Movement in 2000. However, after returning from studies in Birmingham, England, he disagreed with the direction of the movement prioritising transnational charity over national politics.[6] With the founding of the Umma Party in 2005, al-Mutairi was to go even further in championing the primacy of politics.

National Politics in the Service of Gulf Liberation

The Salafi movement in Kuwait had taken unprecedented steps engaging with the political system and participating in elections: steps well beyond the usual Salafi preoccupation with behavioural norms and deference to political authority. Under the Islamist intellectual Hakim al-Mutairi, the Umma Party would go even further, championing pluralism and pressing for the legalisation of political parties – positions that are usually anathema to Salafi adherents. Under al-Mutairi, the Umma Party would commit to the political field above all else, including religious reform.

The launch of the party, held not in Kuwait City but in the more tribal city of Jahra, was covered by local and Arab media and attended by representatives of the US embassy in Kuwait. In the opening press conference, al-Mutairi stressed the need for greater political development: 'The Gulf region still lives in a state of political backwardness. People must grasp the opportunity to practice their right to manage their own affairs'.[7] The brief founding statement was notable for its almost exclusive focus on the pursuit of political rights: the formation of political parties, peaceful assembly, free expression, free press, guaranteed human rights, as well as justice and equality before the law.

The announcement to form a political party caused a stir within Kuwaiti politics. Since Kuwait's liberation in 1990 and the restoration of Kuwait's parliament, Kuwaiti political societies had become more public in their organisation. The Muslim Brotherhood established a separate and more autonomous political wing, al-Haraka al-Disturiyya al-Islamiyya, or the Islamic Constitutional Movement. Within the Salafi field, the more purist Salafis began campaigning under the banner of the Popular Salafi Gathering, later simply Salafi Gathering, while the Salafi movement ran its own candidates. The Umma Party, however, was the first to declare itself a *hizb*, testing the tolerance of the Kuwaiti authorities, as well as of the Salafis, for this political advancement.

The reaction of the Kuwaiti government was immediate. Party leaders were summoned before the public prosecutor, on charges of violating the laws on assembly and publication, and for establishing a party calling for changing the system of government.[8] However, the party was successful in arguing that it was advocating peaceful reform and pluralism and thus did not run afoul of the constitution. A year later, when the constitutional court ruled the law restricting public gatherings itself to be unconstitutional, that charge was also dropped.[9] While the government did not go further in formally accepting political parties, the Umma Party was tolerated.

This did not end the innovations that the Umma Party introduced to the Kuwaiti political scene. The party consistently took positions pressing for the maturation of political life within the emirate. This led them to adopt unorthodox postures within Salafi ways of thinking on public morality, women's rights and sectarian divisions:

- The Umma Party declined to be drawn into the cultural battles that are the bread and butter of most Salafi religious movements. At times, it explicitly rejected campaigns infringing on publication and broadcast rights due to questions of morality – for example, issuing a statement opposing a government decision to block internet blogs that display anti-religious content.[10]
- In 2005, the Umma Party was the only Sunni Islamist political society to voice its support for granting women the right to both vote and run for office. While this position reportedly resulted from a division within

the party, with al-Mutairi opposing women's enfranchisement, the vote of the majority within the Shura Council was respected.[11] The party later defended this position in public seminars and debates.

- The party expressed an openness to non-Salafi members and demonstrated a capacity to avoid sectarian polarisation, especially when it threatened to undermine the cause of greater political empowerment of Kuwaiti citizens. In 2006, a Shi'i political movement drew sharp criticism for publicly mourning the assassination of the notorious Hizbollah operative Imad Mughniya. The Umma Party, however, issued statements denouncing the call for the arrest of the Shi'i members of parliament affiliated with that movement, charging that these measures violated freedom of opinion and the constitution.[12] In these early days of the party, al-Mutairi also voiced his support for the resistance against Israel in southern Lebanon, even in the face of Salafi criticism of Shi'a movements more generally in the midst of Iraq's civil strife.[13]

To understand how and why these heterodox political postures could emerge from a Salafi movement, one must look more closely at Hakim al-Mutairi's thought and his political programme. His central ideas are laid out in his influential treatise *Al-Hurriyya aw-l-tufan* (Freedom or the Flood), which was first published in 2004 and has gone through several reprints.[14] The book follows the Salafi method in its call for a return to the understanding of the righteous ancestors or Salaf in all matters of religion. Yet, it stands out for its single-minded focus on politics, mining the early history of Islam for an inspired mode of consultation and governance, and the failure to sustain it in the centuries that followed.

The book, subtitled 'An Objective Study of the Legitimate Political Discourse and Stages of History', lays out this argument by constructing a periodisation of Islamic political development. The first stage provides the ideal type, directed by the divinely revealed religio-political discourse from the time of the Salaf: an Islamic state headed by an Imam who is selected through the consultation and deliberation of the Umma. Al-Mutairi maintains that this consultation requires conditions of political freedom. He provides numerous examples of how dissent is tolerated at this time, from the hypocrites of Medina to the rebel groups under the Caliph 'Uthman. This, he argues, demonstrates that dissent and political pluralism are tolerated in this system.

For al-Mutairi, the first and most dangerous deviation from this revealed political system is the transition to monarchical Umayyad rule. This begins the second stage characterised by the expropriation of the right of the nation to choose the imam, turning the government from consultation to inheritance and confiscating the nation's right to express opinion and to advise. The 're-interpreted' religio-political discourse of this stage, with its emphasis on obedience to the ruler, decreases the nation's role in confronting injustice, despite the efforts of some independent religious scholars who fought to maintain the autonomy of the courts.

The proof of the degeneration that this engenders is the subjugation of the Islamic world by the West, which begins al-Mutairi's third stage of Islamic history. In this 'altered' stage, scholars again adopt a discourse that emphasises religion and legitimates those in power, evading the crucial question of politics. The failures of this third stage, however, exceed those of the prior, as central aspects of the Islamic system – the caliphate, *sharīʿa* law and defensive jihad – are now neglected or declared illegitimate.

Al-Mutairi argues that achieving the renaissance of the Islamic peoples requires re-capturing the political practices and principles of the early period. Most Salafis today fail to grasp the essential problem: it is the political system – not the religiosity of the population – that determines whether Islamic society prospers or declines. The backwardness from which the Islamic nation is suffering is a natural consequence of the deviation from the legitimate political discourse established at the time of the Salaf, stripping the *umma* of its right to choose its authority, the right of accountability and the right of resistance.

For al-Mutairi, the solution requires both intellectual and practical action. Every organised collective action to achieve these Islamic principles are legitimate acts. As Talal al-Rashoud has argued in an excellent unpublished paper on the Umma Party's founding, this 'revolutionary reordering of priorities within a Salafi framework', privileging political over religious reform, allows for broader political action: 'When religious issues take a back seat, the stage becomes clear for alliances with religiously opposed groups for the sake of political reform'.[15] This, fundamentally, helps to explain the surprising flexibility of the Umma Party. Heterodox political coalitions and social positions are tolerated, if they work towards the goal of consolidating an opposition programme and alliance for political empowerment.

These same principles of political consultation informed the structure of the Umma Party. The party continued the march of Salafi movements in the emirate towards more formal organisation and advanced it in transparency. Its founding document on the internal structure of the party, published in 2005, describes a relatively horizontal organisation with members electing a Shura Council, which in turn selects the General Conference, the highest authority in the party. There are plans for further branches, which would in turn elect members to the General Conference – and for specialised bureaus focused on women, research, public relations, politics and culture. The history of the party does reflect to some degree this commitment to elections and consultation, as demonstrated in the posture of the party towards the women's vote in Kuwait. However, in truth, the party never grew to a size that would test this organisation, and al-Mutairi often wielded authority over decision-making in a way more reminiscent of more traditional charismatic leadership within Salafi movements.

Yet, despite this transparency and tactical flexibility, the Umma Party found no electoral success in Kuwait. Its principled political stance prompted the party to forgo opportunities that other movements seized in elections, or, most often, prompted it to boycott elections altogether. This was the case in the first elections after the party's formation held in 2006, when the movement joined the protests demanding a change in electoral districts in Kuwait. After the government yielded to demands, reducing Kuwait's districts from twenty-five to five, the Umma Party contested its first and only elections in 2008. It ran a slate of eleven candidates – a large number by Kuwaiti political standards – but won no seats. This poor result reflected the very limited popular base that the party had established. But it may also have been impacted by the party's principled refusal to participate in the tribal primaries held in Kuwait's outer districts where the party has its social base. These primaries, illegal but informally tolerated, organise tribal support for candidates before general elections, overwhelmingly to the benefit of the government. During the 2008 elections, al-Mutairi went so far as to issue a controversial *fatwa* stating that oaths to vote for tribal candidates are not binding.[16]

Since that time, the Umma Party has refused to participate in elections altogether, arguing that the current system, where the parliament functions without adequate legal and political foundations, is only contributing to Kuwait's political instability. In 2011, as Kuwaitis took to the streets in protest against political corruption and as the opposition mounted a successful campaign to translate this popular mobilisation into parliamentary gains, the Umma Party demurred. It again boycotted elections on the basis that the state had provided none of the conditions necessary for political life, including: a reformed electoral system based on one electoral district; a law establishing political parties; an independent electoral commission; and enforcement against vote-buying, accompanied by a new campaign finance law.[17] By 2012, when Kuwait's political crisis had deepened with the court-demanded dissolution of the opposition-led parliament, accompanied by a change in the electoral system disadvantaging the opposition, many in Kuwait's opposition joined the Umma Party in calling for more fundamental political reforms. The Umma Party now upped the ante, demanding a new constitution enshrining popular government and an independent judiciary, while pressing for a more vigorous defence of Kuwait's sovereignty.[18] While most Kuwaiti opposition movements opted to return to political life, succumbing to the pressures of government prosecution and demoralised by the failures of Arab spring movements regionally, the Umma Party continued to hold out for more fundamental reform.

The Umma's Regional Projects

As the party lost faith in fundamental political reform in Kuwait – and perhaps despaired of any popular reception – al-Mutairi began eyeing more regional projects. His writings had proven influential amongst reform-minded Salafis, read not only in Kuwait but in other Gulf countries and farther afield in Egypt.[19] As early as 2008 al-Mutairi sought to organise with like-minded colleagues in fellow Gulf countries, through the formal establishment of a coordinating body called the Umma Conference.

This initial interest in extending his political agenda to other Gulf countries can be seen as a natural expression of al-Mutairi's sociological background and political perspective. A distinctive aspect of the Umma Party – and of al-Mutairi himself – is the communal grounding within Kuwait's tribal population. One of the most enduring cleavages in Kuwaiti politics separates the urban or *hadhar* population centred in Kuwait City from its more Bedouin outer constituencies. This cleavage sets the early settlers of the city, who benefitted from the wealth of the pearl trade and later the oil boom, against the later arriving tribesmen who settled in Kuwait's outer environs and are more dependent on state employment. This *hadhar-bedu* cleavage holds political relevance also in other Gulf states, particularly Saudi Arabia, where the tensions between settled tribes and nomadic Bedouin were instrumental in the emergence of Wahhabism itself.[20]

The more activist Salafi networks, and the Umma Party in particular, found great traction with the educated members of this tribal outer constituency, whose discontent is sowed by disparities in both wealth and social status. Tribal youth, long employed in security services and politically organised within loyalist tribal networks, are increasingly rejecting this in favour of more populist appeals, as crystallised in the rise of the Kuwaiti opposition leader Musallem al-Barrak, as well as in the rise of Hakim al-Mutairi.

This outsider perspective can be gleaned from a fascinating series of essays published on al-Mutairi's website and entitled 'Slaves without Shackles', in which he develops his own historical narrative of Arabia. These essays are analysed in an unpublished paper by the Saudi political theorist Sultan al-Amr, who explores the political epistemology of al-Mutairi's ideas, rooted in a tribal sensibility and grounded in a Gulf nativist perspective.[21] The essays present a revisionist history of the Ikhwan movement, which emerged in the Najd in the early 1900s and was a key component of the Saudi ruler Ibn Saud's military campaign and establishment of the modern Saudi state. In al-Mutairi's narrative, the Ikhwan arise in response to the supplanting of the Ottoman Islamic caliphate by the British Empire, which successfully conspires to divide Arabia into small states. The Ikhwan rebellion against this British project is itself thwarted by Ibn Saud, who sacrifices the Ikhwan in a compact made with the British. In this retelling, then, the tribal Ikhwan, instead of being reduced to tools within Ibn Saud's state-building project, are reinstated with historical agency as defenders of Arabian independence.

This critical perspective carries over into the regional political programme of the Umma Party. In a political treatise, al-Mutairi attributes the weakness of the Gulf states to their narrow political base. This renders the Gulf

Cooperation Council subject to tribal disputes among the ruling family-based leadership. As a transitional remedy, al-Mutairi supports the creation of a GCC parliament, which could provide a mechanism for transnational work to unify the peoples of the Gulf. And for al-Mutairi this includes all of Arabia, including Yemen, which shares a common tribal base.

The Arab revolutions changed the course of the Umma Conference and its incipient branches. Al-Mutairi and the party wholeheartedly supported the uprisings that began in Tunisia, then spread to Egypt and Libya, and later to Syria. One by one, constituent branches of the Umma Conference emerged from informality and announced their presence. Eventually all of the Umma activists were consumed by the escalation of the conflict in Syria, which drew in both their fundraising and, later, active participation.

On 10 February 2011, nine Saudis announced the establishment of the Saudi Islamic Umma Party – Saudi Arabia's first – and posted their manifesto on the internet.[22] The statement expressed the signatories' faith in Islam to address contemporary developments and their desire to advance a peaceful political reform movement in the kingdom, 'where all exercise their responsibilities in building their nation on a basis of equality'. The party likewise published a letter submitted the day before to the king announcing – not requesting – the establishment of the party, endeavouring to do so with 'transparency and frankness in practicing our political rights'.

The signatories were overwhelmingly professionals – professors, lawyers, businessmen, political activists – and, as in Kuwait, drew primarily from the aspirational educated tribal milieu. Some of the founders had personal connections with al-Mutairi from the time he studied at Umm al-Qura University in Mecca. The six-page political programme accompanying the founding statement delineated the reform vision of the party, including its political principles, goals and means of achieving them. This vision encompassed a holistic reform agenda: the expansion of political rights and government oversight within a framework of separation of powers, civil and economic rights, and political sovereignty. Yet the underlying principles – the Umma being the source of authority and the unification of the Umma a legal necessity – sit uneasily within the national framework.

The Saudi branch of the Umma Party did not find the political tolerance that the mother organisation had found in Kuwait. The reaction was immediate: within a week of publishing the manifesto, most of the founding members were detained.[23] One of the founders, Abdelaziz al-Wuhayby, was later tried and sentenced to seven years imprisonment after refusing to give up political activities.[24] The designated spokesman of the party, Muhammad al-Muffarih, fled the kingdom and later arrived in Syria just as the insurrection was building.

A little over a year after the announcement of the party in Saudi Arabia, a second correspondent party was announced, this time in the United Arab Emirates. The founding statement of the party was published on 8 August 2012.[25] The statement echoed the goals of its sister organisations, but with some distinctions tailored to the political reality and preoccupation of Emiratis. The statement frankly acknowledges the success of the country in achieving a high standard of living in comparison to others, including employment opportunities, education, healthcare and infrastructure. However, it argues that political development has not kept apace, allowing citizens to define the interests of the nation, choose its government and ensure its oversight. At the current stage, then, the founders see the necessity of establishing the country's first political party to pursue needed reforms. These are framed in general terms designed to have broad appeal – justice, freedom, rights and the protection of national wealth and identity. But while reference is made to pluralism and freedom of expression, these are couched in Islamic references such as expression being 'within the bounds of Islamic *sharī'a*', and foreign policies being guided by 'foundations of the *umma*'. Like in the other Umma parties, there is an emphasis on Gulf unity to resist the encroachment of regional and international powers. And there is a particular emphasis on preserving the equality of citizens across different emirates and to stop policies – in education and tourism – that negatively impact the Islamic character of the country.

The document was signed by the Secretary-General of the party, Hassan al-Diqqy. Al-Diqqy emerged as the leader of a more activist and politically hard-line faction of younger Islamists; he had been ejected from the Muslim Brotherhood movement due to his radicalism.[26] He came to the attention of the Emirati authorities in 2004 due to his establishment of a human rights organisation, the Emirates People's Rights Organisation. He also had an online presence denouncing political abuses while decrying the construction of Christian churches, Hindu temples and Western universities in the UAE.[27]

The announcement of the party came in the midst of a crackdown on political organisation, stemming from the increased political activism of the Arab Spring in 2011. A petition calling for expanding the election of the Federal National Council, the UAE's federal advisory body, and enlarging its powers to include law-making and oversight, garnered the support of a wide swath of Emirati intellectuals, both liberal and Islamist. The government prosecuted – and later pardoned – the five perceived backers of the petition. Yet, later, in 2012 the authorities launched a campaign of arrests targeting Islamists centred on the *Islah* organisation associated with the Muslim Brotherhood, conducting a mass trial in April 2013.[28] Since that time all independent Islamist organisations have been hounded out of existence. Most, including both the Muslim Brotherhood and Umma Party, were designated terrorist organisations in a decree issued by the cabinet in November 2014.

The Umma Party in Syria

Despite the ambitious agendas of these Umma franchises, by 2012, the attention of al-Mutairi and most of the remaining Umma activists was directed to a much more volatile political project – the political uprising in Syria. The Umma Party was to find a surprising level of influence given its small size. Working through the Popular Commission in Support of the Syrian Revolution, the party drew on its relationships at home and across the Gulf region to raise prodigious funds for the cause. Quite rapidly, they moved beyond fundraising to standing up or facilitating the organisation of militias and even fighting on the ground, coordinating their efforts through the Umma Conference based in Istanbul.

From the early days of the Syrian crisis, Kuwait played a role distinct from its Gulf neighbours.[29] As Saudi Arabia and Qatar intervened directly in the Syrian conflict, supporting different elements of the armed opposition, at times in competition, Kuwait restricted its support to humanitarian assistance. Yet, while the state moved cautiously, Kuwaiti society mobilised on both sides of the Syrian divide. With sympathy for the Syrian opposition running high in Sunni communities in Kuwait, private donations amounting to hundreds of millions of dollars were collected in informal gatherings and public fundraisers. These personal appeals and popular campaigns on social media reached across the Gulf, attracting contributions from donors in states where fundraising was restricted or forbidden.

As early as in the summer of 2011, Sunni Islamist networks began forging relationships with the sizeable Syrian expatriate community in Kuwait. In a thorough study based on interviews with participants, Elizabeth Dickinson describes how these expatriates provided the Kuwaiti donors with information and contacts on the ground in Syria, while the Kuwaitis applied their skills in fundraising and campaigning to the cause. [30] These campaigns drew fairly broad public support within Kuwait, with prominent public figures (including former parliamentarians) accepting donations in nightly *diwaniyas*, and tribes competing to see which family could raise the most funds. By the winter of 2011 Kuwaiti benefactors began channelling some of their funding towards the creation of armed groups.

Hakim al-Mutairi and the Umma Party launched themselves in the centre of these activities. As early as in September 2011, al-Mutairi publicly endorsed an armed uprising in Syria.[31] The party worked closely with the Popular Commission in Support of the Syrian Revolution, whose leadership included the young cleric Hajjaj al-Ajmi, alongside the head of the Umma Party's political office, Ershaid al-Hajiry.[32] Indeed, it seems that the close coordination between the party and the commission was the subject of an internal dispute within the party, which contributed to the ousting of the formal party leader and his Secretary-General in favour of al-Mutairi. Among the complaints reviewed by a party investigatory committee was a-Mutairi's decision to bring the Popular Commission's leadership into party Shura Council meetings, a move seen by some as a violation of party rules and organisational intent to focus on politics and not charity.[33]

The Popular Commission became one of the most prominent faces of the Kuwaiti involvement in the Syrian campaign. This is especially true for Hajjaj al-Ajmi who had gained popularity through an Islamic reality show and put this media recognition and his social media skills to use.[34] Al-Ajmi's daily *diwaniya* gatherings and appeals on social media recounted his frequent trips to the Syrian battlefield to personally deliver assistance and to demonstrate the need for further support. These postings, alongside others from militias expressing gratitude for the donations, map the commission's support for rebel groups and their attempted alliances: Liwa al-Umma, the Syrian Revolutionary Front and Ahrar al-Sham, among others.[35]

The Popular Commission recruited donors further afield than Kuwait. One of the members of the commission, Mubarak Al-Ajji, is Qatari, and the commission undertook targeted campaigns seeking Qatari donations.[36] Meanwhile, the Kuwaiti Umma Party actively solicited contributions for the Popular Commission from supporters in Saudi Arabia.[37]

The Syrian war provided a *raison d'etre* for the struggling Umma state franchises within the Gulf. Umma Party leaders facing prosecution in their home countries – Muhammad al-Mufarrih from Saudi Arabia, and Hassan al-Diqqy and Muhammad al-Abduwly from the UAE – all joined in the campaign along with al-Mutairi operating from the Umma Conference base in Istanbul.

Both the Umma Conference and the Popular Commission were on the ground early in the conflict while insurgent coalitions were just taking shape. The stakes were high, not only for Syrians fighting over the future of their country, but also for the foreign participants who believed that the outcome of the Syrian war would set the future political direction of the region. Alongside the states intervening to alter to course of the insurgency – Saudi Arabia, Qatar, Turkey – were a dizzying assortment of Islamist movements competing to determine which version of Salafism would prevail. This competition involved not only more state-aligned, 'quietist' movements against activist Salafis, but also competition among the different activist movements.[38]

Al-Mutairi addresses the implications of this chaotic landscape in a book he wrote on the Syria war, *Al-A'alam be ahkam al-jihad wa nawazilihi fe al-Sham*.[39] Rather than a recounting of his experience, the book focuses on Islamic doctrine, explaining how the laws of jihad can be applied in a conflict riven by factions, like Syria. He argues that Muslims have the right to jihad even if there is no imam or *wālī al-amr* to lead them. For an insurgency fought by dozens of brigades, this is an important point of justification, and a controversial one. In conducting the war, he further makes allowances for a limited loyalty or *bay'a* to a brigade leader, while holding ultimate loyalty to the caliph or imam of the *umma*. He rejects, however, blind loyalty to this group, which results in a conflict among Muslims and similarly forbids killing or punishing jihadis who leave the group.

The primary militias supported by the Popular Commission and Umma Conference shared their revolutionary populism and enthusiasm for the uprisings of the Arab Spring. The Liwa al-Umma or Umma Brigade established in the spring of 2012 in the area around Idlib came together after Syrian rebels approached a prominent Libyan revolutionary, Mahdi al-Harati, who led the Tripoli brigade in the overthrow of Muammar al-Qaddafi and was later elected mayor of the Tripoli Municipality. He offered to train them, bringing along some Libyan and other foreign fighters, but insisted that their participation was temporary: 'When the Syrians have achieved their revolution, our job will be done'.[40]

This more collaborative approach was achieved through attention to politics and organisation, another hallmark of Umma Salafism. The Liwa al-Umma developed a Syrian-led political wing with plans to transform the brigade into a political party. In December 2012, the brigade published its political manifesto, broadly in line with Umma Party objectives with its emphasis on elections, civil society organisation and categorical rejection of 'any foreign aggression on any Islamic country'.[41] Yet, while promising ethnic and religious pluralism with 'no compulsion in religion', the programme also gave the state a role in the 'prevention of vice and promotion of virtue'.

The other primary recipient of financial and political support from the Umma trend was the rebel group Ahrar al-Sham, which for a time became the most powerful non-ISIL faction in Syria and formed the anchor for the Islamic Front. Ahrar al-Sham announced itself publicly in early 2012, exhibiting a degree of political pragmatism and pursuing a more collaborative organisation which contrasts with the 'elite jihad' of Jabhat al-Nusra.[42] As argued by Jérôme Drevon in this volume, Ahrar al-Sham's institutional development enabled it to strategise: pursuing pragmatic alliances with both state and non-state actors, while maintaining connections with its Syrian base operating within their localities. Along the Salafi continuum, both Umma-backed militias demonstrated an ideological flexibility that earned them the attribution 'revisionist jihadism' or 'jihadi light'.[43] And both militias, like the Umma, fell squarely within the evolving Qatari-Turkish axis of influence.

It is difficult to discern whether this ideological consensus emerged due to a natural affinity between donor and beneficiary, or rather demonstrated the ability of the Umma Conference to shape their organisations and agendas.

While certainly not the sole source of funding for these militias, the donations from the Popular Commissions do appear to have been consequential.[44] In its trial in absentia of Emirati Umma Party operatives, Emirati prosecutors charged party leaders with forming the Umma Brigade and training Libyan and Syrian fighters militarily and ideologically.[45] Joseph Braude asserts that the brigade was 'co-founded and co-funded' by the Umma Party leadership, pointing to their demonstrated ties on social media.[46] It is true that the ties between the brigade and the party are substantial. The Syrian leader of the Liwa al-Umma went on to inaugurate the official branch of the Umma Party in Syria, with principles close to the other branches.[47] He, as well as Libyan founder Mahdi al-Harati, continued to participate in Umma Conference events.[48]

Several different sources also place the Umma Party leadership close to Ahrar al-Sham at a relatively early stage of its organisational development. Al-Mutairi was calling for donations to secure weapons for the group as early as in February 2012 and assuring donors that, according to his communications with the group, they were receiving donations from Hajjaj al-Ajmi regularly.[49] Aaron Lund goes further, quoting a source which contends that al-Mutairi helped unite the forces behind Ahrar al-Sham, placing him at a founding meeting in Istanbul: 'It was basically Hakim al-Mutairi from Kuwait and a number of guys from Qatar, Salafis all of them. They decided they wanted to start something really big and finance it really well'.[50] A source close to the Umma Party in Kuwait indicated that al-Mutairi went to Syria, keen to establish political brigades attached to the Umma Party, but that his expectations of loyalty were unfulfilled.[51] Al-Mutairi actually places that distinction elsewhere. In his funeral ovation for Muhammad al-Mufarrih, the head of the Saudi Islamic Umma Party who died in 2014, he relates that al-Mufarrih and Abu Abd al-Aziz al-Qatari visited Ahrar al-Sham in its early stages and extols his role in its formation.[52] Given the different sources, it is worth considering the role that the Umma Conference and affiliated charitable arm played in brokering relations between the militia and the regional governments, and in funding it in its early years.

Certainly, the Umma leadership provided more than funding for the Syrian insurgency. The Umma Conference established a separate initiative, the Consultative Commission, to support the Syrian Revolution, which essentially provided professional development for the *mujahidin.* According to their website, the Consultative Commission played a 'prominent role in providing the necessary support for the revolutionary fighters, including political and administrative training courses and workshops, preparing the leadership and developing their skills'.[53] This training and practice extended to the battlefield.

In March 2013, the head of the Emirati Umma Party, Muhammad al-Abduwly, was killed by a sniper while fighting for Ahrar al-Sham.[54] Abduwly was a former colonel in the UAE army from Fujairah and had been in Syria since 2012. In a tweet, Al-Mutairi praised his role in training Ahrar al-Sham and Umma Brigade troops, in addition to fighting himself.[55] His Umma Party colleagues honoured him by establishing a training centre for foreign fighters in his name.

There is a paradox to this deepening involvement of the Umma Conference in the Syrian war. Through its fundraising and collaboration with factions of the Syrian insurgency, it had an impact, enabling the early rise of militants and supporting a revisionist approach to jihad, more politically reflective and tied to its popular base. Yet, at the same time, this drew the movement ever further from its political work with its own constituencies. The elevation of the Umma Conference over the Umma parties sacrificed its own populist ties in favour of jihadi credentials.

The window for real influence by the private Gulf financiers and movements was brief. By late 2013, the growing role of international jihadists and their abuses in Syria eroded Gulf public enthusiasm for the Syrian insurgency, as did the falling fortunes of the revolutionary states across North Africa. Under increased international scrutiny and pressure from the US authorities, the Kuwaiti government passed new anti-money laundering legislation to address the absence of both legal and logistical means to counter terror-financing.[56] In August 2014, the United States Department of Treasury designated al-Ajmi as a terrorist financier, accusing him of providing financial support to the al-Qaida-linked al-Nusra Front, in exchange for installing Kuwaitis in leadership positions.[57] These accusations of links to al-Nusra, along with condemnations of the atrocities carried out by Popular Commission-backed militias, would continue to dog al-Ajmi; nonetheless, the Kuwaiti authorities only briefly detained him for questioning.[58] The charity continued functioning under al-Hajiri's leadership, but changed its name and work towards humanitarian relief, running operations with assistance from the Umma Conference offices in Istanbul.[59]

In any case, the tide in the Syrian war had turned, and states sought to re-assert their control over the besieged rebel coalitions. As Turkey became the lone refuge for Arab fighters, it was to Turkey that the Umma Conference would turn.

New Splits and New Turkish Loyalties

Today the Umma Conference continues activities from Istanbul, but its horizons are diminished, and its outlook has changed in the wake of the Syrian insurgency's impending defeat. Over the past several years, it has seen a depletion in its funds and a split among its already weakened ranks. With the hopes for a people's reform via election or a people's victory via jihad failing, al-Mutairi and the Umma have found yet another cause to champion: a Turkish-led caliphate.

The core leadership of activists from Kuwait, Saudi Arabia and the UAE suffered the loss of the Emirati Umma Party chief, Muhammad al-Abduwly, on the battlefield. Then, in 2014, the head of the Saudi Islamic Umma Party, Muhammad al-Mufarrih, passed away under what al-Mutairi insists are suspicious circumstances. Al-Mutairi alleges that al-Mufarrih had been under threat of assassination, and that the Turkish government had offered protection.[60]

Upon his death there opened up a split between the leadership of the Saudi Islamic Umma Party and the Umma Conference. The new head of the party, Abdullah al-Salem, set up in London and in 2017 suspended his party's membership in the Umma Conference, citing al-Mutairi's interference in the setting of local policies and the lack of real consultation among conference members.[61] Within months it was cooperating with a new opposition alliance, the Union of Opposition Forces in the Arabian Peninsula. This coalition of five organisations – including *Atiqal*, a group defending political detainees, and the Islamic renewal party under long-time Saudi opposition figure Muhammad al-Masary – supports self-determination of the Saudi people and openly calls for the fall of the Saudi ruling family.[62] There is no longer any cooperation between the Umma Conference in

Istanbul and this Saudi Islamic Umma Party, which al-Mutairi implies has been compromised.

The space for the particular Umma parties to operate within their respective countries has only closed further since the movement's participation in the Syrian war. In 2017, Emirati Umma co-founder Hassan al-Diqqy was sentenced, in absentia, by the UAE government to ten years' imprisonment.[63] The founding head of the Saudi Islamic Umma Party, Abd al-Aziz al-Wuhayby, and his deputy Ahmed al-Ghamdy remain imprisoned in Saudi Arabia. And the Saudi government continues to actively denounce the Umma activists, running educational campaigns warning students to avoid them and their writings.[64] Another campaign championed by the Saudi-backed Qatari dissident Khaled al-Ha'il and promoted though Saudi social media reached al-Mutairi's home state of Kuwait. Unsubstantiated leaked tapes of al-Mutairi speaking with the late Libyan President Muammar Al-Qadhdhafi implicated al-Mutairi in a plot to sow dissent and destabilize Gulf states taking advantage of "creative chaos" in Iraq. The Kuwait courts convicted al-Mutairi in absentia, sentencing him to life in prison.[65]

With popular avenues in their home-countries and Syria closing, al-Mutairi and his dwindling supporters have pivoted to a new political position, aligning their rhetoric and worldview with their Turkish hosts. This places al-Mutairi and the Umma within the broader Islamist camp that is siding with Turkey, in opposition to the quartet of countries – Saudi Arabia, the UAE, Bahrain and Egypt – that broke off relations and imposed a boycott on Qatar. Accordingly, in 2017 the quartet placed several individuals from the Umma Conference (al-Mutairi, al-Diqqy) and its associated networks (al-Ajmi, al-Harati) on its list of 'Qatar linked and based Al Qaida Terrorism Support Networks'.[66]

The new political alignment of the Umma Conference was accompanied by a re-balancing of emphasis from Arab Spring political empowerment to liberation from foreign powers – an element that, of course, had always been present in Umma doctrine. This is nicely summarised in al-Mutairi's tweeted response: 'Democracy is defined as rule by the people, and there is no rule by the people for those who have lost their sovereignty! States' sovereignty is fundamental and democracy is secondary'.[67] Al-Mutairi argues that strengthening the alliance with Turkey is essential for the protection of Arab Gulf states from both American and Iranian designs, and he depicts this protection as historic and natural: 'Turkey is returning once again to its strategic depth as a central Islamic power that has protected the Arabian Peninsula and the two Holy Mosques from the Crusader and Safavid danger for five centuries'.[68] The Umma Conference has, of course, supported Turkey's policies and Islamic leadership, including a proposal to replace the Organisation of Islamic Countries with an organisation under Turkish control.[69] In recognition of the central importance of this new partnership, al-Mutairi has opened a Twitter account to communicate in the Turkish language.[70]

From Domestic Reformer to Regional Revolutionary

The Umma Party and the ideologue behind its creation, the Kuwaiti Islamic intellectual Hakim al-Mutairi, have received only peripheral attention in academic and policy studies. This is likely due to the movement's small size and diffuse impact: it has never won formal representation through an election and often works transnationally in coordination with other groups to pursue its goals. Yet, I would argue that the influence of the party has been more extensive than appreciated. The originality of al-Mutairi's ideas, the Umma Party's innovations in Salafi political organisation and the reach of its material support have made their mark on Salafi thought and mobilisation across several countries, most notably in the Syrian jihad.

Tracing the personal history of al-Mutairi uncovers the influence of Saudi Islamist trends, especially the thinking of Muhammad Abdin al-Suroor and the Saudi *Ṣaḥwa* on his own thought. Yet, one can clearly discern the original element contributed by al-Mutairi: melding a tribal sensibility with Western political concepts, while working within the relative openness of Kuwaiti politics and the more revolutionary settings opened by the Arab spring uprisings. This overview of Al-Mutairi and the Umma Party thus presents the case-study of a relatively heterodox thinker and movement, adapting to regional politics and most often working against existing state orders.

This rejectionist posture places Al-Mutairi and the Ummah party in direct opposition to the regional trend in the Gulf. While states promote nationalism and an obedient state-centred Islam, al-Mutairi continues to champion an Islam that is transnational and rejects deference to the ruler.

Yet, the potency of the early Umma programme – a mix of Salafi methodology, tribal affirmation and self-government – has been lost. As the Umma Party abandoned its state projects in favour of armed insurgency and, more recently, protection under a Turkish caliphate, it has sacrificed what was always a limited popular base.

Notes

1. Some of the best explorations of the party and the thought of its founder Hakim al-Mutairi include Talal al-Rashoud. Talal al-Rashoud, 'An Unlikely Reformer? Kuwait's Salafi Umma Party', Paper Presented at *The Gulf Research Meeting*, Cambridge, UK (2012); Bjørn Olav Utvik, 'The Ikhwanization of the Salafis: Piety in the Politics in Egypt and Kuwait', *Middle East Critique* 23/1 (2014), 5–27.
2. Falah Abdullah Al-Mudarris, *Islamic Extremism in Kuwait: From the Muslim Brotherhood to Al-Qaeda and other Islamic Political Groups* (London: Routledge, 2010); Carine Lahoud-Tatar, *Islam et Politique au Koweit* (Paris: Presses Universitaires du France, 2015); Zoltan Pall, 'Salafi Dynamics in Kuwait: Politics, Fragmentation and Change', in *Salafism after the Arab Awakening*, ed. Francesco Cavatorta and Fabio Merone (Oxford: Oxford University Press, 2016), 169–87.
3. Zoltan Pall, 'Kuwaiti Salafism and its Growing Influence in the Levant', *Carnegie Endowment for International Peace*, May 2014, 5.
4. Abd al-Rahman 'Abd al-Khaliq, *Al-Muslimon wa-l-'amal al-siyasi* (al-Dar al-Salafiyya, 1985,) www.salafi.net/books/book26.html.
5. Al-Mudarris, 'Islamic Extremism in Kuwait', 93–94.
6. Pall, 'Kuwaiti Salafism', 31.
7. Ibrahim al-Saeedi, 'Al-Amyn al-ʿam Hakim al-Mutairi: Al-minṭaqa t'aysh fi takhalluf siyasiy wa al-shu'ub taḥkumuha Nuẓum al-Shumuliya', *al-Qabas*, 1 January 2005, https://alqabas.com/article/112260.
8. Husain al-Abdulla, 'Al-Niyaba tuwaṣil al-taḥqeeq maʿ Ḥizb al-Umma', *al-Qabas*, 8 May 2005, https://alqabas.com/154079/.
9 Husain al-Abdulla: 'Ḥezb al-Umma . . . Bara'a', *al-Qabas*, 17 May 2006, https://alqabas.com/article/201783-حزب-الأمة-براءة accessed on January 21.
10. 'Hizb al-Umma: al-Mudawanat al-Siyassia al-Kuwaytiyya Mafkhara Narfuth Muraqabatuha', *Ommah.net*, 5 April 2008; as cited in al-Rashoud, 19.
11. Al-Mudarris, 'Islamic Extremism in Kuwait', 111.
12. 'Hizb al-Umma Yarfuẓ Raf'al-Hasana 'an al-Na'ibayn', *Al-Rai*, 18 March 2008; 'Hizb al-Umma: li-Waqf Hamlat al-I'iʿtiqalat Dhid al-Tahaluf al-Islami al-Watani', *Al-Rai*, 12 March 2008; as cited in al-Rashoud, 20.

13. Hakem al-Mutairi, 'Ahkam al-Muqawmah wa al-Shahada: Bayan Wujub Nasrat al-Muqawamah fi Falastin wa Labnan' (The Rules of Resistance and Martyrdom: The Necessity of Supporting the Resistance in Lebanon and Palestine), Kuwait, undated. As cited in Al-Mudarris, 116.
14. Hakim al-Mutairi, *al-Ḥurriyya aw-l-ṭufan* (Beirut: al-Mu'assasa al-'Arabiyya li-l-Dirasat wa-l-Nashr, 2008).
15. Al-Rashoud, 'An Unlikely Reformer? Kuwait's Salafi 'Umma Party', paper presented at the Gulf Research Meeting, 2018.
16. Salim al-Shatti, 'Hakim al-Mutairi: Kul Suwar Qasam al-Nakhibin Ayman Batila', *Al-Rai*, 10 May 2008; as cited in al-Rashoud, 18.
17. 'Ḥizb al-Umma 'ila Muqaṭa'at al-Intikhabat li Fasad al-'Amaliyya al-Seyasiya', *Al-Jarida*, 7 December 2011, www.aljarida.com/articles/146197 0632163714400/.
18. 'Bayan Ḥizb al-Umma ḥawl al-'Azma al-Seyasiya fi-l-Kuwait', Gulf Centre for Development Policies, 2012, http://gulfpolicies.com/index.php?option=com_content&view=article&id=1222:-17-2012-&catid=158:2012-01-03-19-52-52&Itemid=266.
19. Stephane Lacroix, 'No Spring in Riyadh: Saudi Arabia's Seemingly Impossible Revolution', in *Taking to the Streets: The Transformation of Arab Activism*, ed. Lina Khatib and Ellen Lust (Baltimore: Johns Hopkins University Press, 2014), 298–322.
20. For more nuance on the construction of this *hadhar* and *bedu* divide, see Farah al-Nakib, *Kuwait Transformed: A History of Oil and Urban Life* (Palo Alto: Stanford University Press, 2016), and Abdelaziz al-Fahad, 'The 'Imama vs. the 'Iqal: Hadari-Bedouin Conflict and the Formation of the Saudi State', in *Counter-Narratives: History, Contemporary Society, and Politics in Saudi Arabia and Yemen*, ed. Madawi al-Rasheed and Robert Vitalis (New York: Palgrave-MacMillan, 2004), 35–75.
21. Sultan Alamer, 'The Myths of Ikhwan Movement', unpublished essay provided by the author, December 2013.
22. 'Albayan al-Ta'sisy li Hizb al-Umma-l-Islamy', *Ammon News*, 19 February 2020, www.ammonnews.net/article/80023.
23. 'Saudi Arabia: Free Political Activists Secret Police Crackdown on First Political Party', *Human Rights Watch*, 19 February 2011, www.hrw.org/news/2011/02/19/saudi-arabia-free-political-activists.
24. Amnesty International, *Amnesty International Report 2012: The State of the World's Human Rights* (London, 2012), 287f.

25. 'Al-Maktaba wa Bank al-Maʿluwmat,'Hizb al-Umma-l-Emaraty: Bayan al-Taʾsis, Gulf Center for Development Policies, https://gulfpolicies.org/index.php?option=com_content&view=article&id=1987:2019-07-10-07-45-42&catid=125&lang=ar&Itemid=1080.
26. Personal interview with author, February 2020; see also Courtney Freer, *Rentier Islamism: The Influence of the Muslim Brotherhood in Gulf Monarchies* (Oxford: Oxford University Press, 2018), 137.
27. Freer, *Rentier Islamism*, 131.
28. Lori Plotkin Boghardt, 'The Muslim Brotherhood on Trial in the UAE', *Washington Institute for Near East Policy*, Policy Watch 2064, 12 April 2013, www.washingtoninstitute.org/policy-analysis/view/the-muslim-brotherhood-on-trial-in-the-uae.
29. Elizabeth Dickinson, 'Playing with Fire: Why Private Gulf Financing for Syria's Extremist Rebels Risks Igniting Sectarian Conflict at Home', *Brookings Institution*, Analysis Paper No. 16, December 2013, www.brookings.edu/wp-content/uploads/2016/06/private-gulf-financing-syria-extremist-rebels-sectarian-conflict-dickinson.pdf.
30. Dickinson, 'Playing with Fire', 5–6.
31. Hakim al-Mutairi, 'al-Thawrat al-Suwriya wa-l-Khiyar al-Akhiyr', 19 September 2011, www.drhakem.com/Portals/Content/?info=TnpVMkpsTjFZbEJoWjJVbU1RPT0rdQ==.jsp; as cited in Dickinson, 6.
32 'Man Nahnu, 'Ommah Conference, accessed 19 April 2020, www.ommahconf.com/من-نحن-.
33. 'Hizb al-Umma al-Kuwayty, 'Tumuwhat wa Siraʿat al-Salafiyyat al-ʿIlmiyya,' 'Bawwabat al-Harakat al-Islamiyya, 18 May 2019, www.islamist-movements.com/26501.
34. Amiyn Hussayn, 'Maharat al-Taʿawun le-l-Shaiykh Hajjaj al-ʿAjmi', YouTube video, 18 January 2010, https://youtu.be/6aJyvjwH0h8.
35. Joby Warick, 'Private Money Pours into Syrian Conflict as Rich Donors Pick Sides', *Washington Post*, 15 June 2013, www.washingtonpost.com/world/national-security/private-money-pours-into-syrian-conflict-as-rich-donors-pick-sides/2013/06/15/67841656-cf8a-11e2-8845-d970ccb04497_story.html.
36. Dickinson, 10.
37. Ommah Party KW (@OmmahPartyKW), 'Akhy al-Suʿuwdy Idʿam Ikhwanak' Twitter feed, 29 May 2012, https://twitter.com/OmmahPartyKW/status/207516929492131840.

38. Thomas Pierret, 'Salafis at War in Syria: Logics of Fragmentation and Realignment', in *Salafism After the Arab Awakening: Contending with People's Power*, ed. F. Cavatorta and F. Merone (London: Hurst & Co, 2017), 3.
39. Hakem al-Mutairi, '*Al-A'alam be Ahkam al-Jihad wa Nawazilihi fe al-Sham*' (Mu'tamar al-Umma, 2013), https://ia800709.us.archive.org/31/items/alle3lam/alle3lam.pdf.
40. Mary Fitzgerald, 'The Syrian Rebels' Libyan Weapon', *Foreign Policy* 9 August 2012, www.foreignpolicy.com/articles/2012/08/09/the_syrian_rebels_libyan_weapon.
41. Asher Berman, 'The Umma Brigade Political Manifesto', *The Syria Survey*, 25 March 2013, https://syriasurvey.blogspot.com/2013/03/.
42. Pierret, 'Salafis at War in Syria', 17–18.
43. Sam Heller, 'Ahrar al-Sham's Revisionist Jihadism', *War on the Rocks*, 30 September 2015, https://warontherocks.com/2015/09/ahrar-al-shams-revisionist-jihadism/.
44. Joby Warrick, 'Private Money Pours'. See also Dickinson, 'Playing with Fire', 10.
45. 'Hizb al-Umma al-Emaraty Yatalaqqa Da'man Maliyyan min al-Kharij', *al-Bayan Newspaper*, 18 October 2017, www.albayan.ae/across-the-uae/accidents/2016-10-18-1.2737119.
46. Joseph Braude, 'The Muslim Brotherhood's More Frightening Offshoot', *The Atlantic*, 15 July 2013, www.theatlantic.com/international/archive/2013/07/the-muslim-brotherhoods-more-frightening-offshoot/277786/.
47. UmmaSyri, 'Al-bayan al-Ta'sisy li Hizb al-Umma al-Suwry', YouTube video, 28 December 2012, www.youtube.com/watch?v=jEBEDcgfa5s&feature=youtu.be; Hakem al-Mutairi (@Drhakem), 'Qa 'id Liwa' al-Umma wa Mumathil Hizb al-Umma al-Suwry', Twitter feed, 6 October 2013, https://twitter.com/DrHAKEM/status/386921110350336000?s=20.
48. Hakem al-Mutairi (@Drhakem), 'al-Qa'id al-Liyby Mehdi al-Harati', Twitter feed, 20 October 2013, https://twitter.com/DrHAKEM/status/392003284338483200?s=20.
49. Hakem al-Mutairi (@DrHakem), 'al-Sha'b al-Sury al-Yawm Ahwaj li-l-Silah', Twitter feed, 10 February 2012, https://twitter.com/DrHAKEM/status/167845036782927873?s=20; Hakem al-Mutairi (@DrHakem), 'Shahadaton li-l-Allah', Twitter feed, 26 April 2012, https://twitter.com/DrHAKEM/status/195622810821996544?s=20.
50. Aron Lund, 'Syria's Salafi Insurgents: The Rise of the Syrian Islamic Front', *Swedish Institute of International Affairs*, Occasional Paper 17 (March 2013),

30, www.ui.se/globalassets/ui.se-eng/publications/ui-publications/syrias-salafi-insurgents-the-rise-of-the-syrian-islamic-front-min.pdf.
51. Personal interview, 26 August 2019.
52. Aaron Zelin, 'The Syria Twitter Financer Post-Sanctions', *Jihadology*, 18 March 2015, https://jihadology.net/2015/05/18/guest-post-the-syria-twitter-financiers-post-sanctions/#sdendnote19anc.
53. 'Man Nahnu, 'Ommah Conference'.
54. Asher Berman, 'A Former UAE Colonel Dies in Syria', *The Syria Survey*, 5 July 2013, http://syriasurvey.blogspot.com/2013/07/a-former-uae-colonel-dies-in-syria.html.
55. Hakem al-Mutairi (Drhakem), 'Sharaka al-ʿAbduli fe Tadriyb Liwaʾ al-Umma', Twitter feed, 5 March 2013, https://twitter.com/DrHAKEM/status/308840466856701953?s=20.
56. Dickinson, 'Playing with Fire', 20.
57. 'Treasury Designates Three Key Supporters of Terrorists in Syria and Iraq', US Department of Treasury, Press Center, 6 August 2014, www.treasury.gov/press-center/press-releases/Pages/jl2605.aspx.
58. 'Kuwait Detains Muslim Cleric Suspected of Funding Militants: Security Source', *Reuters*, 14 August 2014, www.reuters.com/article/us-syria-crisis-kuwait-cleric/kuwait-detains-muslim-cleric-suspected-of-funding-militants-security-source-idUSKBN0GK25Q20140820.
59. Aaron Zelin, 'The Syrian Twitter Financiers Post-Sanctions'.
60. 'Hadiyth Dr. Hakem al-Mutairi ʿan al-Shaiykh Mohammad al-Mufarreh', Sawaʾih al-Fikir, YouTube video, 22 December 2014, www.youtube.com/watch?v=_e-um46fHPI.
61. Islamic Ommah Party (@IslamicOmmaPart), 'Bayan Hizb al-Umma al-Islamiy', Twitter feed, 7 April 2017, https://twitter.com/islamicommapart/status/850353994429906944?s=20.
62. Union of Opposition Forces (@UOFsAP), 'Nuʿlin ʿan Taʾsiys ʾIttihad Quwa al-Muʿarada', Twitter feed, 24 June 2017, https://justpaste.it/Unionofoppositionforces.
63. Hakem al-Mutairi (@Drhakem), 'Wa Akhtaru min dhalik ʾIghlaq Hisabat', Twitter feed, 8 November 2018, https://twitter.com/DrHAKEM/status/1060468971739275265?s=20.
64. 'Imam University Warns Students, Staff against Extremist Preachers', *Saudi Gazette*, 26 March 2018, http://saudigazette.com.sa/article/531337.

65. Khitam Al Amir, 'Kuwait: Hakim Al Mutairi sentenced to life imprisonment,' *Gulf News*, April 26, 2021, https://gulfnews.com/world/gulf/kuwait/kuwait-hakim-al-mutairi-sentenced-to-life-imprisonment-1.78785718.
66. '43 New Designations Specifically Address Threats Posed by Qatar Linked and Based Al Qaida Terrorism Support Networks', *Emirates News Agency*, 9 June 2017, http://wam.ae/en/details/1395302618259.
67. Hakem al-Mutairi (@drhakem), 'fa-l-dimoqratiyya hiya Hukm al-Sha'b', Twitter feed, 7 November 2018, https://twitter.com/DrHAKEM/status/1060127824206577667?s=20.
68. Hakem al-Mutairi (@drhakem), 'Ta'ziyz al-Khaliyj al- 'Araby 'Elaqatuh be Turkiyya', Twitter feed, 10 October 2018, https://twitter.com/DrHAKEM/status/1050040472935288833?s=20.
69. Hakem al-Mutairi (@drhakem), 'Fe Del 'Ajz Munadamat al-Ta 'awun al-Islamy', Twitter feed, 26 October 2018, https://twitter.com/DrHAKEM/status/1055890213388595200?s=20.
70. Hakem al-Mutairi (@HakemProf), Twitter account, created October 2018, https://twitter.com/HakemProf?s=20.

PART 3

SALAFI JIHADISM AND INTER-GROUP COMPETITION

7

WAHHABI SALAFISM VERSUS ISLAMIC STATE: AGE-OLD TRADITIONS APPROPRIATED BY MODERN-DAY TERRORISTS

Abdullah bin Khaled al-Saud

There are few terms today that are thrown around so casually, without being properly fathomed or employed, as *Wahhabism*, or *Salafism*, the two often being used interchangeably. In the field of Terrorism Studies, *Wahhabi Salafism* is a term that is often misused or poorly understood. Over the years, it has come to signify different things to different people. In the Western popular imagination, the term signifies the most radical, intolerant and violent variant of Islam. Some in the West believe that Wahhabi Salafism is actually 'the main source of global terrorism',[1] while others argue that 'there is nothing here that separates Wahhabism from ISIS'.[2] Indeed, there exists a mass of literature accusing Wahhabi Salafism of breeding radicalism and serving as the guiding ideology behind modern Islamist terrorism.[3] How much truth do these assertions hold? This chapter argues that Wahhabi Salafism differs in five significant ways, both historically and in its present form, from the ideology and practice of the self-described Islamic State (IS) and other modern-day jihadist terrorist groups. It also sheds light on the ideological roots of some of the most contentious concepts of contemporary Islamic radical thought, arguing that their roots lie in the theorisation of twentieth-century scholars and intellectuals rather than in eighteenth-century religious movements.

As noted in the introduction, to some the analysis presented in this chapter might appear as an apology piece for the Saudi regime. It is, however, important for researchers and students of Salafism to understand how the

Saudi Wahhabi scholars and the Saudi regime actively try to differentiate their reading of Salafi thought from those of the numerous jihadi groups that claim to draw on Salafi Wahhabi discourse. When delving into this discussion, it is important to begin by providing a precise definition of the term 'Wahhabism'.

What is Wahhabism?

Historically, Wahhabism refers to the eighteenth-century religious reformist movement led by Shaykh Muḥammad ibn 'Abd al-Wahhab, which was closely tied, through an alliance with Saudi rulers, to the establishment of the first, second and third Saudi states in 1744, 1824 and 1932, respectively. It is important to clarify that Wahhabism originated as a derogatory term that was first imposed on the eighteenth-century movement by its enemies. The term was intended to spread feelings of antipathy and antagonism towards the movement among the Muslim masses. Followers and supporters of the movement do not use the term to refer to themselves. They would rather call themselves 'unitarians' (*muwaḥḥidun*), in reference to their adherence to the concept of *tawḥīd* (God's unity); Salafis, in reference to the pious forefathers of the first three generations of Islam (*al-salaf al-ṣāliḥ*); or simply Muslims. This is primarily because they do not want to give credence to the notion propagated by opponents – that is, that Shaykh ibn 'Abd al-Wahhab introduced a new school of Islamic law and, thus, is a *mubtadi'* (a pejorative term that translates as 'innovator'). King Salman himself, in 2010, while he served as governor of Riyadh, weighed in on the debate surrounding the term with an article published in the newspaper *Al-Hayat*:

> The call of Shaykh Muḥammad ibn 'Abd al-Wahhāb is not a new school or approach (*manhaj*) or a new [way of] thinking (*fikr*), and I repeat here the call to whoever finds in the writings and letters of the Shaykh any departure or deviation from the Qur'ān and *sunnah* (the words and deeds of the Prophet Mohammad, peace be upon him) and the deeds or works of the *salaf* (forefathers) to highlight it and confront us with it.[4]

However, despite the dislike of the term on the part of the followers of the movement, the main justification for retaining it has always been to distinguish the specific Saudi context and strand from the many Islamic movements across the world. Logically, therefore, the term specifically refers to the religious reformist movement that started in the eighteenth century, as it evolved and is understood, practised and applied in the courts and religious institutions of its homeland of Saudi Arabia.

Indeed, there have been some radical statements and positions on the part of several past scholars of the Wahhabi mission.[5] However, movements such as Wahhabi Salafism[6] are not static, but rather are 'subject to the spatial and temporal developments that [they] live in, while committed to the absolute fundamentals'.[7] Two important points, one historical and the other methodological, are often ignored when dealing with the movement's rich heritage. First, its long history, spanning more than 250 years, witnessed different political realities and the rise and demise of two Saudi states before the 1932 establishment of what is Saudi Arabia today. Thus, the rich and diverse heritage of the movement was produced during different eras and in varied historical circumstances and contexts, which must be taken into account.

Second, and most important, is that the heritage of the Wahhabi movement should be divided, according to the nature of its content, into two distinct categories: one *ta'ṣīlī* (foundational) and the other *tawāṣulī* (communicative). The former consists of statements and declarations of creed, jurisprudence and rituals, through either authorship or annotations, whereas the latter comprises the many replies, epistles and discussions that engaged numerous past scholars of the movement. The contents of such communicative and proselytising efforts – which included the names of many individuals, regions and tribes – were products of specific historical contexts and, therefore, are more akin to personal communications than scientific references to the movement. Methodologically, it is the former, substantive part of the heritage that forms the basis of, and reference for, the movement's *manhaj* (path or approach).

Nonetheless, as I mentioned in a previous study, . . .

> IS and likeminded radical groups and ideologues tap into the heritage of the movement, just like they tap into the verses of the Qur'an itself, choose the most extreme verses and references, mainly from the communicative part, strip them of their historical contexts, ignore debates and disagreements surrounding them, even within the movement itself, and present them in

> an incantatory fashion in order to vindicate their preconceived convictions and theorizations.[8]

The claim by IS to what it describes as the 'true' legacy of the eighteenth-century movement and teachings of Muhammad ibn 'Abd al-Wahhab is clear in its many attempts to discredit the Saudi religious establishment and scholars, such as its fervent critique that . . .

> Hiding behind claims of being 'Sunni', 'Hanbali', 'Salafi' and especially descendants and students of Muhammad Ibn 'Abdil Wahhab, they are truly nothing more than slaves of *taghut*, waging war against the mujahidin in order to maintain the status quo. [. . .] When asked about the clear disparity between the Qur'an-backed creed of Muhammad Ibn 'Abdil Wahhab and the Saudi regime's constant coalition with crusaders against Muslims, palace scholar Hatim al-'Awni criticised Ibn 'Abdil Wahhab and considered this one of the reasons for a required revision of the texts written by the historic scholars of Najd.[9]

The attempt to masquerade as an extension of established Islamic traditions, in this case Wahhabism, rather than a recent metastatic and virulent ideology, is a calculated move the origins of which can be traced to long before the rise of Islamic State. As early as in the 1980s, one of the most dangerous ideologues of Salafi-jihadism and the godfather of Islamic State, the Jordanian Abu Muhammad al-Maqdisi, developed a number of ideas that drive the jihadist movement today. In his books *Millat Ibrahim* (1984) and the *Obvious Proofs of the Saudi State Infidelity* (1989), al-Maqdisi tapped into the heritage of the Wahhabi mission, employing the same cunning methods used by Islamic State decades later, in order to give his radical concepts a veneer of legitimacy by claiming that they were an extension of past and recognised lines of thought.[10] Ironically, through the powerful effects of selectivity, appropriation and repurposing, 'he tapped into the heritage of a Salafism that preaches political acquiescence and quietism in order to formulate a message that preaches the complete opposite'.[11]

Five Major Departures

There are five central concepts in the IS ideology and worldview that are completely alien to Wahhabism, both past and present. These key differences explain why traditional Wahhabism has very little to do with Islamic State and transnational jihadism in general. The first three concepts are unique to Islamic State, while the other two are shared with all the other jihadist groups.

The first concept is that of the global caliphate. While Islamic State relies heavily on this idea to paint a utopian picture that attracts and emotionally appeals to religious novices, Saudi Wahhabis have never aspired to, or advocated for, the establishment of a caliphate. The first Saudi state, which was established in the eighteenth century in the autonomous region of Najd, existed parallel to the Ottoman Caliphate, yet it did not promulgate itself as a base for a counter-caliphate despite their mutual enmity.

The second concept espoused by Islamic State that has no precedence in mainstream Saudi religious discourse is its apocalyptic dimension.[12] As opposed to Islamic State and other 'doomsday' groups, which believe they are witnessing and contributing to the end of times, Saudi Wahhabi scholars place this in the realm of *al-ghayb* (the unknown). Indeed, as a member of the Saudi Council of Senior Scholars recently warned, one should not try to find meaning and understanding in *ḥadīth*s related to the end of times following every new event or affliction.[13]

The third concept is that of barbarity and savagery. There is nothing in the history of the Wahhabi mission that comes even close to the level of brutality and bloodthirstiness displayed by Islamic State. Indeed, one of the most infamous acts of Islamic State barbarity – the burning in a cage of the captured Jordanian pilot Muath al-Kasasbah in 2015 – was decried by the mufti of Saudi Arabia as a 'horrendous crime' that is rejected by Islam because 'only the lord of fire can torment with fire'.[14] Although the early-twentieth-century campaign against deviance in the Arabian peninsula, in pursuit of the unification of what has become the Kingdom of Saudi Arabia, led to the deaths of between 10,000 and 25,000 persons,[15] the extreme violence of Islamic State lies in the legacy of Abu Musab al-Zarqawi, who founded the Islamic State precursor group al-Qaida in Iraq. However, one cannot talk about al-Zarqawi without acknowledging the role of 'the theological brains behind [his] ultraviolent brawn' – namely, Abu Abdullah al-Muhajir, the Egyptian radical ideologue whom he first met in Afghanistan around the year 2000, and whose influence on him cannot be overstated.[16]

Al-Muhajir's magnum opus, *Issues from the Jurisprudence of Jihad* (also known as *The Jurisprudence of Blood*), was printed by the Islamic State publishing house al-Himma Library in 2014 and has been celebrated in its circles. This tome included everything from 'ruminations on the merits of beheading, torturing, or burning prisoners to thoughts on assassination, siege warfare, and the use of biological weapons'.[17] Muhajir's intellectual legacy is an important component of the literary corpus of Islamic State. It helps the group to render practically anything permissible, as long as it is presented as contributing to the jihad.

If that were not damning enough, the fourth and fifth concepts, which are key tenets of all radical transnational jihadist groups, constitute the most important departures from the mainstream Saudi Salafi Wahhabi heritage and discourse, which will be examined in more detail in the following three sections. First is the concept of *ḥākimiyya* (the political sovereignty of God and his laws alone), and second is the necessity of rebellion against the Muslim rulers.[18] The danger of these two concepts lies in the fact that the former has come to form the basis of *takfīr* (excommunication) against all Muslim rulers, and the latter has become the consequence of that act. The ideological roots of these concepts can be traced to political Islamism and the theorisation of Sayyid Qutb,[19] the leading Egyptian Muslim Brotherhood figure and theorist of the 1950s and 1960s, who in turn was influenced by the writings of the jurist Abu al-Ala al-Maududi from the Indian subcontinent.[20]

The Ideological and Genealogical Roots of Contemporary Islamic Radicalism

The most dangerous seminal contributions to radical political Islamism were developed far from the control or influence of so-called Wahhabism and constituted the results of conflicts within specific environments; most importantly, Jamal Abdul Nasir's Egypt and the persecution of the Muslim Brotherhood. The following excerpt from one of Qutb's landmark publications, *In the Shadows of the Qur'an*, explains his conceptualisation of his two main contributions to political Islamism – namely, *jāhilīyya* (a state of pre-Islamic ignorance) and *ḥākimiyya*:

> People, at any time and place, either rule according to Allah's Law (*sharī'a*) – in its totality – accept it and surrender to it completely, in which case they

> are in Allah's religion; or rule according to man-made laws, in any way or form, and accept them, in which case they are in a state of *jāhilīyah* and in the religion of whomever they rule according to his law, and not in any case in Allah's religion.[21]

Qutb was not a Wahhabi, and his other landmark publication, *Milestones*, could not be more different from *Kitāb al-Tawḥīd*, ibn 'Abd al-Wahhab's most important book. While the latter was a legal discussion focused on the issue of monotheism and its implications for Muslims' daily lives, the former was more of a manifesto for action, describing the battle between good and evil and encouraging Muslims to take part in the battle against evil.[22] In *Milestones*, Qutb described 'all societies on earth today, including those that claim to be Islamic' as *jāhilī*s and, thus, in dire need of being Islamised once again.[23]

However, while Qutb stopped short of pronouncing *takfir* explicitly, Muhammad Abdul Salam Faraj, the main ideologue of the Egyptian extremist group *Tanzim al-Jihad* and the author of the 1980 tract *Jihad: The Absent Obligation*, took Qutb's ideas to their logical conclusions and made the leap towards the excommunication of all Muslim rulers, thus paving the way for armed rebellion.[24] About a year later, in the most dramatic manifestation of Qutb's ideas, Egyptian president Anwar al-Sadat was assassinated.[25]

What *The Absent Obligation* called for, in short, was the deposing of all apostate Muslim rulers through jihad, which, according to Faraj, has become a personal duty upon every Muslim, in order to establish the caliphate and institute God's *ḥākimiyya*. He stressed that the priority is to fight the near enemy (the apostate rulers) rather than the far enemy (Israel).[26]

Nonetheless, over the following decade, Abu Muhammad al-Maqdisi echoed the views of Faraj in a different context, through the publication of a number of books and treatises.[27] *Ḥākimyya*, as first articulated by al-Maududi, theorised by Qutb and espoused by Faraj, was also central to al-Maqdisi's new Salafi-jihadi ideology. According to him, the legislation of, application of and compliance with any man-made law are tantamount to *shirk* (association with God in worship), which is the gravest sin: 'The first duty upon the monotheist is to disavow of and disbelieve in the scattered gods and the many names that are being worshipped other than God, which in the past took the form of stones and primitive idols, and in our modern time are the rulers and legislators and their man-made laws and legislations'.[28]

Another central concept that, according to al-Maqdisi, 'distinguishes this current [Salafi-jihadism] from others'[29] is the concept of *al-walā' wa-al-barā'* (loyalty to Islam and Muslims and disavowal of unbelief and unbelievers). Few early scholars of Wahhabism who lived in the eighteenth and nineteenth centuries, during times of political loss and calamity, have voiced radical views regarding this concept.[30] Most prominent was Hamad ibn Atiq (d. 1883), whose uncompromising spirit was evident in his treatises during the Ottoman-Saudi wars.[31] However, it was the later developments during the twentieth century, particularly by al-Maqdisi, that weaponised the concept and made it into an offensive tool to target opponents.

The significant change that al-Maqdisi introduced to the concept of *al-walā' wa-l-barā'* is the connection he made between it and, not only monotheism (*tawḥīd*) and politics, but also excommunication (*takfīr*).[32] According to him, '[w]hile *tawḥīd*, which we spoke of, entails *al-bar*ā*'* [the disavowal of] and disbelief in these man-made laws and scattered idols, one of its most trustworthy ties is the subject of *al-walā' w-al-barā'*, which requires the disavowal of the authors of these laws and regulations and the people who are applying them'.[33]

Al-Maqdisi's understanding of *ḥākimyya* led him to equate the application of man-made laws, the willingness to abide by them and obedience to the rulers with un-Islamic worship. These acts violate the central principles of *tawḥīd* and *al-walā' wa-l-barā'*, which in turn warrants the application of *takfīr*.[34]

Mainstream Saudi Tradition and Understanding

Mainstream Saudi scholars have not adopted these ideas. The line of thought and argument regarding the essence of *ḥākimyya* and what constitutes *kufr* (disbelief) have remained fairly consistent from the early days of the movement to the beliefs of the present-day members of the Saudi Council of Senior Scholars.[35] The majority of these scholars argue that not all man-made laws are forbidden, as the issuance of new statutory regulations and laws by the government on matters that have no bearing on Islamic law is permissible – as long as they do not contradict the *sharī'a* (Islamic law).

Most importantly, however, these scholars require an important condition before ever pronouncing *takfīr* on those who do not rule according to God's revelation: a presence of *i'tiqād* or *istiḥlāl* (the belief or conviction on the part of the ruler or legislator that a man-made law, while seemingly contradicting *sharī'a*, may actually be a better choice and is in fact permissible in Islam). Otherwise, the act is regarded as *kufr aṣghar* (minor unbelief), which does not expel the person from the realm of Islam.

For instance, the former Saudi mufti Shaykh Muhammad bin Ibrahim (d. 1969), who seemed unyielding in some of his early statements regarding this issue, especially his 1960 *Risalah fi tahkeem al-qawaneen* (Letter in Applying the Laws), said in one of his *fatwa*s issued about five years later:

> Fulfilling the meaning of 'there is no God but God' and 'Mohammad is the messenger of God' [means]: Applying [God's] *sharī'ah* [laws], sticking to them, and disregarding all laws and situations that *oppose* them. He who rules according to [those opposing laws] or resorts to them *believing* the permissibility and acceptability of that is committing the kind of *kufr* that expels one from the fold of Islam. He, however, who does the same *without believing* in the permissibility of his action or superiority of such laws is committing a practical *kufr* that does not expel from Islam.[36]

Among a few past scholars of Wahhabism, there are some older radical interpretations regarding when the contentious principle of *al-walā' wa-l-barā'* constitutes apostasy. However, the mainstream understanding among the majority of past and especially present-day Saudi religious scholars runs contrary to the understanding of most modern-day extremists. According to these Saudi scholars, intent and what is in the heart are key. As a result, what determines the absence or presence of apostasy is whether there is *walā'* (loyalty) to or support for the unbeliever's religion. In other words, if seeking the support of non-Muslims against an aggressor, which is what Saudi Arabia did in the early 1990s to repel Saddam's invasion of Kuwait, is done out of necessity and for earthly purposes that have nothing to do with the religion or creed of the non-Muslim, then it is permissible, or at worst *kufr aṣghar* (minor unbelief), but does not constitute *kufr akbar* (major unbelief that expels the person from the fold of Islam). It only constitutes apostasy and major unbelief if it involves complete loyalty to the non-Muslim religion.

That was explained by the former mufti of Saudi Arabia, Shaykh Abdulaziz ibn Baz (d. 1999), who said, during one of his lectures regarding the liberation of Kuwait, that 'there is nothing wrong in what the [Saudi] state did in seeking support [from the United States] out of necessity and dire need of their help to Muslims. And because of the grave danger threatening the country if this oppressor [Saddam] continued in his aggression and invasion'.[37]

The current member of the Saudi Council of Senior Scholars, Shaykh Salih al-Fawzan, has also argued that lending support to non-Muslims against other Muslims willingly, and without force, coercion, or necessity, is no ground for *kufr* (apostasy) in itself unless it is accompanied by a love for, and loyalty to, the non-Muslims' religion. According to him, '*al-tawallī* [alliance or loyalty to unbelievers] is two different categories: The first is *tawallī* for the sake of their religion, and that constitutes *kufr* that expels from the fold of Islam. The second is *tawallī* for the sake of earthly rewards while disliking their religion, and that is forbidden but does not constitute *kufr*'.[38]

If one contrasts these statements with the writing of modern Salafi-jihadist ideologues, the difference becomes clear. Anwar al-Awlaqi, for instance, contends that 'we do not judge by what is in the heart . . . We judge by what is apparent'.[39] Moreover, Abu Abdullah al-Muhajir argues that 'what is apparent alone is the basis of passing judgments . . . [Therefore,] siding with the polytheists, supporting them and helping them against Muslims is major *kufr* that expels from the fold of Islam, even if it is done for a purely earthly purpose.'[40] Furthermore, in the early 1990s, Abu Muhammad al-Maqdisi wrote *Delighting the Sight in Exposing the Misconceptions of Contemporary Murji'as* with the express intention of refuting what he called the 'misconception' that those who 'rule by and obey man-made laws of *ṭāghūt*s [in reference to Muslim rulers] are not to be excommunicated [declared apostates] unless they are doing it with *juhoud* [in denial of God's law] and *istiḥlāl* [with the belief that they are permissible and superior to God's law]'.[41]

Takfir al-Mu'ayyan

Takfir is one of the most contentious issues and dangerous tools employed by jihadists to license the mass-killing of political or ideological opponents. It is important, however, to distinguish between two different types of *takfir*: *takfir bi al-naw'*, meaning the declaration of *kufr* on specific words or deeds, and *takfīr al-mu'ayyan*, meaning the declaration of a certain individual as *kāfir* (an apostate or unbeliever). Declaring *takfīr* on certain practices, words, or deeds, such as insulting God and his messenger or associating others with God in worship, is largely uncontroversial among past and present scholars. This is because it only requires the heartfelt disavowal from the deed and its perpetrator, and should not entail the physical application of the rulings of *takfīr* such as the spilling of the individual's blood. Declaring *takfīr* on a specific individual (*takfīr al-mu'ayyan*), however, is where most Salafi-jihadists diverge from the teachings of ibn 'Abd al-Wahhab and his followers.

Most past and present Wahhabi scholars realise the seriousness of *takfīr* and have a great appreciation for its numerous conditions and barriers. Therefore, they argue that one cannot practise *takfīr al-mu'ayyan* until all conditions, such as intent and free choice, are present, and all barriers, such as ignorance or error, are absent.[42] They also argue that it is not for an individual to decide whether the conditions are present and the barriers are absent. Ascertaining whether this is the case falls under the duty or prerogative of the ruler and the judiciary alone. Thus, if someone believes that a certain individual has committed an act of *kufr* or apostasy, the only thing they should, or can, do is to disavow the deed in their heart or, if it is possible to do so without causing further harm, by their words. In the eyes of the Wahhabi scholars, it is never the responsibility of the individual to go beyond that and carry out the application of the rulings of *takfīr*. According to Natana DeLong-Bas, who studied the work of ibn 'Abd al-Wahhab in depth, . . .

> However much he denounced certain practices or beliefs, Ibn Abd al-Wahhab never called for wholesale killing of people, not even apostates [. . .] In fact, declarations and accusations of or rulings against apostasy are quite rare in Ibn Abd al-Wahhab's works. His focus on the importance of education, knowledge, intent, and comprehension of God's expectations of humanity led him to restrict accusations of apostasy to a very few extreme cases [. . .] He further cautioned that evidence of apostasy must be very clear, so that the permissibility of seizing property and killing apostates will be neither rampant nor easily practiced.[43]

The fact of the matter is that Wahhabi scholars, both past and present, 'have been very cautious and restrained not to declare [*takfīr*] until all conditions are met and all barriers are absent'.[44] Islamic State, on the other hand, has never been shy about declaring certain individuals as apostates and blatantly calling for their murder. For instance, in February 2017, the group launched a media campaign called 'Kill the Imams of Kufr', whereby the names and pictures of many religious scholars, both Saudi and others, were published along with instructions to followers to kill them.[45]

Conclusion

It is clear that, as opposed to Islamic State and other modern-day radical jihadists, mainstream Saudi Wahhabi Salafi scholars place a premium on stability and on law and order, viewing rebellion as a source of discord and social strife. They state that two important conditions must be met before contemplating rebellion against the Muslim ruler – namely, his commitment of *kufr bawāḥ* (an obvious disbelief that is not open for interpretation or contestation) and the possession of the capabilities to depose him. This stands in complete contrast to the ideology and practice of Islamic State, al-Qaida and other transnational revolutionary jihadist groups.

What is evident is that the picture is more complicated than many are led to believe. Islamic State constitutes a departure from most Islamic traditions, and its deviation from the Wahhabi Salafi heritage and discourse specifically is evident. This deviation is continuously highlighted by the Saudi religious establishment. It also serves to explain why Islamic State is very hostile to and repeatedly targets Saudi scholars and clerics, declaring them 'apostates' and calling for their murder. As the following excerpt demonstrates, the discrediting of the Saudi religious establishment has always been a main priority and goal for Islamic State and its followers:

> [T]he palace scholars of the Saudi regime – from their "Grand Mufti" 'Abdul-'Aziz Al ash-Shaykh to the minions who spread deceitful pro-*ṭāghūt* propaganda atop the pulpits of their "kingdom" – are at the forefront of this effort to dissuade Muslims from jihad and from upholding the *Sharī'ah*, averting them from the path of Allah.[46]

In short, Wahhabism and Islamic State are very different from each other, and their understanding regarding key concepts, as shown above, diverge strongly. While some of ibn 'Abd al-Wahhab's followers may have used *takfir* as a defensive tool to safeguard the Muslim community from forms of *shirk* (association with God) or unbelief, Salafi-jihadists have used the concept in a very different way, politicising and weaponising it to use it as an offensive tool in their quest for authority and leadership against Muslim governments and other opposing entities.

Due to such clear divergence in tradition and understanding, and the apparent enmity between the true heirs of the Wahhabi Salafi mission in the religious institutions of its homeland and the extremist claimants to its past, it can be argued that the former are among the best suited to fight the latter's virulent extremist ideology and counter their appeal.

Notes

1. 'What Is Wahhabism? The Reactionary Branch of Islam from Saudi Arabia Said to Be "The Main Source of Global Terrorism"', *The Telegraph*, 19 May 2017.
2. Alastair Crooke, 'You Can't Understand ISIS if You Don't Know the History of Wahhabism in Saudi Arabia', *Huffington Post*, 25 May 2017.
3. See Hamid Algar, *Wahhabism: A Critical Essay* (New York: Islamic Publications International, 2002); As'ad Abukhalil, *The Battle for Saudi Arabia: Royalty, Fundamentalism and Global Power* (New York: Seven Stories Press, 2004); Robert Baer, *Sleeping with the Devil: How Washington Sold Our Souls for the Saudi Crude* (New York: Crown, 2003); Charles Allen, *God's Terrorists: The Wahhabi Cult and the Roots of Modern Jihad* (London: Abacus, 2006); Khaled Abou El Fadl, *Speaking in God's Name: Islamic Law, Authority and Women* (Oxford: Oneworld, 2001); Karen Armstrong, 'Wahhabism to ISIS: How Saudi Arabia Exported the Main Source of Global Terrorism', *The New Statesman*, 27 November 2014.
4. Salman bin Abdulaziz, 'Falyahthar Al Bahithoun min Fakh Mustalah Al Wahhabiyya' [Researchers, Beware of the Trap of the Term '*Wahhabiyya*'], *Al-Hayat*, 28 April 2010.
5. See Abdullah al-Askar, 'Al-Wahhabiyya Thaqafa Dieniyya Mahaliyya' [Wahhabism is a Local Religious Culture], *Alriyadh*, 26 May 2004; Cole Bunzel, 'The Kingdom and the Caliphate: Duel of the Islamic States', *Carnegie Endowment for International Peace*, February 2016, 4–8.
6. For a historical analysis of the relationship between Wahhabism and Salafism, see David Commins, 'From Wahhabi to Salafi', in *Saudi Arabia in Transition: Insights on Social, Political, Economic and Religious Change*, ed. Bernard Haykel et al. (New York: Cambridge University Press, 2015), 151–66.

7. Khalid al-Mushawah, *Religious Currents in Saudi: From Salafism to al-Qaeda's Jihadism and the Currents in Between* (Ar.) (Beirut: al-Intishar al-al-mushawah-rabi, 2011), 21.
8. Abdullah K. Al-Saud, 'Deciphering IS's Narrative and Activities in the Kingdom of Saudi Arabia', *Terrorism and Political Violence* (2017) DOI: 10.1080/09546553.2017.1378645.
9. *Dabiq*, 13 (19 January 2016), 7.
10. For more on al-Maqdisi, see Abdullah K. Al-Saud, 'The Spiritual Teacher and His Truants: The Influence and Relevance of Abu Mohammad al-Maqdisi', *Studies in Conflict and Terrorism* 41 (2017), 736–54.
11. Ibid., 740.
12. For more on IS's apocalyptic dimension, see William McCants, *The ISIS Apocalypse: The History, Strategy, and Doomsday Vision of the Islamic State* (New York: St. Martin's Press, 2015).
13. 'Udhu Hay'at Kibar al-Ulama al-Mutlaq: La Yajouz Tadawul Ahadith al-Fitan wa al-Istidlal biha fi Ghayr Makaniha' [Member of the Council of Senior Scholars al-Mutlaq: It Is Not Permissible to Circulate the *Hadiths* of *Fitan* (Discord) to Infer Misplaced Conclusions]), *Okaz*, 13 February 2015, www.okaz.com.sa/article/974016/.
14. 'Mufti al-Saudiyya: al-Harq bi al-Nar Haram wa Daesh la Deen laha' [Saudi *Mufti*: Burning with Fire is Forbidden and Daesh Has No Religion], *Alwasatnews*, 4 February 2015, www.alwasatnews.com/news/958934.html.
15. In his primary-source data study, Jeff Eden debunked the claim that 400,000–800,000 individuals were killed or wounded as a result of the 'Wahhabi conquest of the Arabian Peninsula between 1902 and 1925' and showed that the total number 'was probably somewhere between 10,000–25,000'. See Jeff Eden, 'Did Ibn Saud's Militants Cause 400,000 Casualties? Myths and Evidence about the Wahhabi Conquests, 1902–1925', *British Journal of Middle Eastern Studies* (2018) DOI: 10.1080/13530194.2018.1434612.
16. Charlie Winter and Abdullah K. Al-Saud, 'The Obscure Theologian Who Shaped ISIS', *The Atlantic*, 4 December 2016.
17. Ibid.
18. For more on those two concepts and how they have become central to the Salafi-jihadist ideology, see Shiraz Maher, *Salafi-Jihadism: The History of an Idea* (London: C. Hurst & Co., 2016), 169–206.
19. For a detailed account of his life and ideas, see John Calvert, *Sayyid Qutb and the Origins of Radical Islamism* (London: C. Hurst & Co., 2010).

20. For more on al-Maududi's theorisation of *ḥākimiyya* and his influence on Qutb, see Asyraf Hj. Rahman and Nooraihan Ali, 'The Influence of Al-Mawdudi and the *Jama'at Al Islami* Movement on Sayyid Qutb Writings', *World Journal of Islamic History and Civilization* 2 (2012), 232–36; Saleh Zahr al-Deen, *Al-Harakat wa al-Ahzab al-Islamiyya wa Fahm al-Aakhar* [Islamic Parties and Movements and the Understanding of the Other] (Beirut: Dar al-Saqi, 2012), 87–107; and Maher, *Salafi-Jihadism*, 178–81.
21. Sayyid Qutb, *Fi'Dhilal Al-Qur'an: Surat Al-Ma'idah* [In the Shadows of the Qur'an: *Surat Al-Ma'idah*], 114, available e at: www.ilmway.com/site/maqdis/MS_34.html.
22. Natana J. DeLong-Bas, *Wahhabi Islam: From Revival and Reform to Global Jihad* (London; New York: I. B. Tauris, 2007), 259.
23. Sayyid Qutb, *Ma'alim fi al-Tareeq* [Milestones], 10th ed. (Cairo: Dar al-Shurouq, 1983), 96.
24. Shahrough Akhavi (1997), 'The Dialectic in Contemporary Egyptian Social Thought: The Scripturalist and Modernist Discourses of Sayyid Qutb and Hasan Hanafi', *International Journal of Middle East Studies* 29 (1997), 377–401; Mohammad Abdul Salam Faraj, *The Absent Obligation*, 1st ed., edited and annotated by Abu Umamah (Birmingham, UK: Maktabah Al Ansaar Publications, 2000); Danny Orbach, 'Tyrannicide in Radical Islam: The Case of Sayyid Qutb and Abd al-Salam Faraj', *Middle Eastern Studies* 48 (2012), 961–72.
25. William Farrell, 'Sadat Assassinated at Army Parade as Men Amid Ranks Fire into Stands; Vice President Affirms "All Treaties"', *New York Times*, 7 October 1981, https://archive.nytimes.com/www.nytimes.com/learning/general/onthisday/big/1006.html#article.
26. Faraj, *The Absent Obligation*.
27. Abu Muhammad al-Maqdisi, *Millat Ibrahim wa da'wat al-'anbiya' wa al-mursalin* [The Religion of Abraham and the Mission of Prophets and Messengers] (1984), available at: www.ilmway.com/site/maqdis/MS_20383.html; *al-Kawashif al-Jaliyya fe Kufr al-Dawla al-Saudiyya* [The Obvious Proofs of the Infidelity of the Saudi State], 2nd ed. (1421 A.H.), 130, available at: www.ilmway.com/site/maqdis/MS_65.html.
28. See the interview by *Al-Asr*, an online magazine, with Abu Muhammad al-Magdisi in 1426 A.H. (2005 C.E.), available at: www.tawhed.ws/r?i=040309gb.
29. Ibid.

30. For more details, see Abdullah K. Al-Saud, 'Religious Radicalisation and Violence in Saudi Arabia' (unpublished PhD thesis, 2012, King's College London), 117–32.
31. See, for instance, Hamad ibn Atiq, *Sabil al-Najat wa al-Fakak* [The Path of Survival and Escape], edited by Alwaleed al-Frayyan (1415 A.H.), www.al-tawhed.net/Books/Show.aspx?ID=708.
32. See Joas Wagemakers, 'The Transformation of a Radical Concept: *Al-wala' wa al-bara'* in the Ideology of Abu Muhammad al-Maqdisi', in *Global Salafism: Islam's New Religious Movement*, ed. Roel Meijer (London: Hurst & Company, 2009), 81–106.
33. *Al-Asr*, interview with al-Magdisi.
34. Wagemakers, 'The Transformation of a Radical Concept', 92–93.
35. Official Saudi religious scholars have always argued that there are only three types of *tawḥīd* (belief in the oneness of God): *tawḥīd al-rububiyya* (the Oneness of Allah's Lordship), *tawḥīd al-uluhiyya* (the Oneness of Allah's Divinity) and *tawḥīd al-asma' wal-sifat* (the oneness of Allah's names and attributes). Accordingly, 'adopting a system of government that copes with Allah's Laws comes under *tawhid al-uluhiyyah* [. . .]. [M]aking *ḥākimīyah* a separate type of *tawḥīd* is an innovated act that no scholar ever adopted'. See 'The Fifth Question of Fatwa no. 18870', *The Permanent Committee of the General Presidency of Scholarly Research and Ifta*, www.alifta.net/Fatawa/fatawaDetails.aspx?languagename=en&BookID=7&View=Page&PageNo=1&PageID=10729.
36. The *Fatwa* is dated 9 Muharram 1385 A.H. (9 May 1965). See *Fatawa wa rasa'il samahat al-Sheikh Mohammad bin Ibrahim bin Abdullatif al-Shaikh* [*Fatwa*s and Letters of Shaykh Mohammad bin Ibrahim], 1st ed., edited and annotated by Mohammad bin Qasim (Makkah: Government Press, 1399 A.H.), 11, p. 9, https://al-maktaba.org/book/8476/2486.
37. Abdulaziz ibn Baz, 'Hawla ijtiyah hakim al-Iraq lil Kuwait' [On the Invasion of the Iraqi Ruler to Kuwait], *Majallat al-Buhouth al-Islamiyya* [Islamic Research Journal] 34 (1412 A.H.), 22–24, https://bit.ly/2pTDtIe.
38. Salih bin Fawzan al-Fawzan, *Duroos fi sharh nawaqidh al-Islam* [Lectures on Explaining the Nullifiers of Islam], ed. Mohammad al-Husayn, 3rd ed. (Riyadh: Maktabat al-Rushd, 2004), 172.
39. Cited in Maher, *Salafi-Jihadism*, p. 74.
40. Abu Abdullah al-Muhajir, *Issues in the Jurisprudence of Jihad* (Al-Himma Library, 1435 A.H.), 412, 418.
41. Abu Mohammad al-Maqdisi, *Imta' al-nathar fi kashf shubuhat murji'at al-asr*

[Delighting the Sight in Exposing the Misconceptions of Contemporary *Murji'as*], 2nd ed. (Ghurfat al-Fajr al-Islamiyya, 1420 A.H.), 3.

42. For a more detailed discussion on how Ibn Abdul Wahhab and his followers adhere to the established rules and principles regarding *takfir*, see Nasir al-Aqil, *Islamiyya la Wahhabiyya* [Islamic, not Wahhabi] (Riyadh: Dar al-Fadilah, 2007), 243–67.
43. DeLong-Bas, *Wahhabi Islam*, 82.
44. al-Aqil, *Islamiyya la Wahhabiyya*, 242–43.
45. For instance, on page 6 of issue 13 of the magazine *Dabiq*, under a heading that translates as 'Kill the Imams of Kufr', two red circles were drawn around the faces of Shaykh Abdulaziz al-Shaikh, the mufti of Saudi Arabia, and Shaykh Abdulrahman al-Sudais, the imam of the Holy Mosque in Mecca.
46. *Dabiq*, 13 (January 2016), 7.

8

FRATRICIDAL JIHADISM REVISITED: THE COMPLEX NATURE OF INTRA-JIHADI CONFLICT[1]

Tore Hamming[2]

Why do Sunni jihadis contest and kill each other? Despite the fact that they largely share the same ideology and objectives, they time and again engage in discursive attacks to undermine one another or, in some instances, even fight each other. The effects appear obvious: intra-jihadi conflict diverts focus away from their common enemy; it has a radicalising and polarising impact on the jihadi movement; it demobilises the jihadi masses, and it leaves high numbers of their fighters dead.[3] It has even been argued that it is the main reason why they lose their wars.[4] While the majority of scholarly and analytical focus is generally devoted to the threat that jihadi groups and individuals pose to (mainly) Western security, how they govern and mobilise, or their ideological specificities, less attention is devoted to the phenomenon of intra-jihadi contestation and infighting despite its growing occurrence and impact. This chapter offers some initial ideas and concepts to understand intra-jihadi contestation and infighting as a stepping-stone for further research on the topic.

Intra-jihadi discursive contestation and military infighting is captured by the Islamic notion of *fitna* (conflict). This term has its intellectual genealogy in the Qur'ān where, in one form or another, it is mentioned sixty times with varying meanings ranging from 'trial' to 'insanity'.[5] Although the original meaning of *fitna* may be 'testing' or 'trial' in relation to the believer's faith, it also signifies sedition, civil strife or conflict,[6] which poses a threat to the unity of the Muslim community.[7] The negative perception of *fitna* is not just based on the warnings in the holy sources, but also on its empirical genealogy from early Muslim history. The first *fitna* in Islam, known as the Great Schism (*al-fitna al-kubrā*), took place in 656–61 between the supporters and opponents of 'Uthmān, the third caliph after the Prophet Muhammad, beginning with the killing of 'Uthmān in 656.[8]

Since its emergence in the 1960s, the jihadi movement has suffered from internal tensions, sometimes boiling over and erupting in conflict.[9] Sayyid Qutb and Abdel Salam Faraj differed on whether jihad should be considered a method or a goal in itself, and on the importance of education.[10] The Egyptian groups Al Jihad and al-Jama'ah al-Islamiyyah disagreed on the strategy of how to topple the regime, while bin Laden and his mentor Abdallah Azzam had different visions for the jihadi project post-Afghanistan. The revisionist current in the 2000s, perhaps most famous for the controversy between Ayman al-Zawahiri and his former friend and superior Sayyid Imam al-Sharif, known as Dr Fadl, illustrated a critique from within. And in some instances, as in Algeria and Afghanistan in the 1990s and in Iraq during the 2000s, jihadis even fought and killed one another. In the contexts of both Algeria and Afghanistan, and now in Syria, *fitna* has been used by jihadis themselves to describe the events of jihadi infighting.[11]

The puzzle of the question of *why jihadis contest and kill each other* is based on three assumptions. First, on an ideological level, jihadis share more than what divides them. Second, it must be assumed that jihadis would (often) gain more from cooperation than from infighting. And third, jihadis are extremely isolated political actors with few other potential cooperative partners. Of course, jihadis are not the first or only example of isolated political actors contesting each other or engaging in infighting. Underground left- and right-wing groups,[12] rebel and insurgent groups in the context of civil wars,[13] and revolutionary groups like the Russian communist movement[14] have all had similar experiences of internal problems, either as intra- or inter-group fragmentation and infighting. But being so inherently fearful of *fitna*, jihadis should – theoretically – be different from other groups, as their loyalty lies in the religion and in following the path of Allah rather than in political agendas. Why would these servants of God, one could ask, become victims of silly internal conflicts that would risk derailing their ambition of reaching a shared (albeit in minor details divergent) social, political and religious objective?

The most dominant explanation in the existing literature on jihadism and Islamism appears to suggest that jihadi contestation and infighting is the result of ideological cleavages, extreme ideology,[15] or strategic differences.[16] However, studying the events of intra-jihadi dynamics in the context of Syria since 2013, we see contestation and infighting not only between groups that are ideologically very different (within the spectrum of the jihadi movement), but also between groups that are rather similar theologically, ideologically and in terms of strategic priorities. Differences in ideology or strategy also cannot account for the timing of internal conflict. The ambition of this chapter is not to argue that these differences do not matter. Rather, the objective is to suggest a more complex explanation as to how we can understand intra-jihadi contestation and infighting, which recognises the relative importance of religion and politics. It proceeds in five steps: (1) It briefly discusses the existing literature on intra-jihadi conflict and diversity. (2) It conceptually defines the Sunni Jihadi Movement, identifies its idiosyncratic character and outlines mechanisms of conflict and peace. (3) It then proposes a new typology of jihadis rationales towards internal cooperation and conflict, followed by (4) a brief illustration of how these rationales played out in the Syrian context in the period between 2013 and 2019. (5) Finally, it discusses the impact of conflict on the movement's cohesion.

Adding to the Literature on Intra-jihadi Conflict

The literature on internal contestation and conflict within the jihadi movement is relatively sparse.[17] Although new research on internal conflict in specific geographical areas is being published, it is mainly carried out with an empirical focus, largely leaving conceptual and theoretical considerations aside.[18] The main takeaway from this literature is that jihadis contest or fight one another as a result of *ideological* or *strategic* differences.

Some of the extant jihadism literature has offered typologies as a way to understand the differences in jihadis' political preferences or to highlight the importance of theology. Hegghammer rendered an important service when he developed a typology distinguishing between different forms of jihadism based on their guiding rationales and their manifestations, which has been extremely helpful in understanding the historical evolution of the movement and sources of intra-movement contestation.[19] Another example is Lahoud's pioneering research on intra-jihadi diversity, in which she distinguishes between *strategists* and *doctrinarians*, thus acknowledging a division between groups based on the importance they assign to politics and religion, respectively.[20] But while she makes an important distinction, it is also problematic since the terms imply a strict division between strategy and doctrine where there is none.

While these efforts help define the external political priorities, highlight some important internal fault lines and are incredibly helpful in understanding the diversity within the Sunni Jihadi Movement, they are less helpful in answering the question of why jihadis contest and fight each other. Intra-jihadi conflict does not only occur between *global jihadis* and *revolutionary jihadis*, or between *doctrinarians* and *strategists*. Another way to categorise jihadis is to distinguish between *Jihadi-Salafists* and *Qutbists* but, as will be explained later, such a distinction directs the focus to theology – which cannot account for internal conflict. Arguably the most relevant typology to understanding contemporary internal fault lines within jihadism is offered by Stenersen. In her article 'Jihadism after the "Caliphate": Towards a New Typology', she places jihadi groups on two scales: how they relate to society (integration versus separation) and whom they see themselves as fighting for (the nation versus the *umma*).[21] This typology offers an important framework tuned to a more fine-grained analysis of the internal diversionary issues within the movement, and it allows for a nuanced understanding of the internal diversity and dynamics *over time*. But although an understanding of jihadi groups according to these two scales offers the most precise explanation of contemporary intra-jihadi diversity, it falls short of explaining conflict that does not occur exclusively between groups at different positions on the scale, but also between groups that subscribe to similar positions. This chapter intends to add to this body of literature with concepts and theory to enhance our understanding of why jihadis engage in internal conflict, as well as the detrimental impact it has on the broader jihadi movement.

Explaining Intra-jihadi Conflict

Before we can hope to understand intra-jihadi conflict, we need properly to define the phenomenon and how it potentially distinguishes itself from conflicts within other movements. The following sections will define the Sunni Jihadi Movement, outline the idiosyncratic character of the movement and identify mechanisms of conflict and peace.

(De-)Constructing Terminology: The Sunni Jihadi Movement

What makes intra-jihadi conflict particularly interesting is that it qualitatively differs from, for example, infighting among *rebels* or *insurgents*,[22] as well as between movements and counter-movements,[23] for two important reasons. Unlike conflict between rebels or between movements and counter-movements, intra-jihadi conflict occurs between actors that are part of a narrowly defined movement.[24] Rebels often come from different movements – for example, nationalist, irredentist, Islamist, or perhaps the jihadi movement – which entails a certain distance between rebel actors. Movement and counter-movement conflict takes place between movements that are ideologically opposed to one another – such as extreme left- and right-wing factions – and as such are already opponents. But, in contrast, jihadis subscribe to the same broad ideology and generally view one another as the best of Muslims.

Defining the Sunni Jihadi Movement is no easy task, and it has only become more complicated because of the various, but often misleading, labels used to describe jihadis.[25] The movement should only include actors that have rather similar political priorities and motivations, while at the same time seek to include as many actors as possible.[26] In current discussions of jihadism, the term *jihadi-Salafi* (or Salafi-jihadi) is increasingly dominating. The proverb goes that, while not all Salafis are jihadis, all jihadis are Salafis,[27] and although most serious scholars and observers would easily accept the fallacy of this statement,[28] the jihadi-Salafi label is nonetheless becoming the preferred label as a reference to the entire jihadi current – or at least to describe specific groups.[29] One possible reason for the dominance of this label is that jihadism is often studied through a focus on Salafism.

I will argue that this development is problematic, because the jihadi-Salafi label involves a misrepresentation of the ideological orientation and cohesion within specific jihadi groups and only represents a segment of the broader jihadi movement.[30] Initially, no robust definition of the term 'jihadi-Salafi' existed, thus making it difficult to distinguish it from other ideological orientations within the jihadi current.[31] Indicative of this definitional issue, as Hegghammer writes, is that '[s]ome consider the Qutbist revolutionaries of 1970s Egypt and Syria as Jihadi-Salafis. Others consider that the origins of Salafi jihadism can be traced to the Muslim Brotherhood. Yet others see Jihadi Salafism as representing a mixture of Salafism and Qutbism'.[32] Later on, scholars such as Wagemakers and Maher have provided excellent descriptions of Jihadi-Salafism as a distinctive ideology, which in the words of the latter is based on the five concepts of *jihad, tawḥīd, ḥākimiyya, takfīr* and *al-walā' wa-l-barā'*.[33] Yet, despite their efforts, it remains problematic to apply the label to entire groups – not to speak of a whole *movement* – as it imposes an artificial, monolithic impression.[34]

As the aim here is to understand jihadi contestation and infighting more generally, and not just among jihadi-Salafi figures, it is necessary to capture the entirety of the current. In order to do so, we need to conceptualise the movement based on what unites the actors, be they groups or individuals. During an interview with Abu Qatada al-Filastini, one of the most senior al-Qaida-linked ideologues, the author was told that one needs to understand the history of jihad in order to define the movement.[35] From its emergence in the early 1960s, I identify four different jihadi currents that show its modern historical evolution and diversity, which together offer a broad definition of the Sunni Jihadi Movement that is not based on a certain theology or political preference, but on the foundation of jihad as a legitimate and necessary method in a political and social struggle.

The first current of the modern Sunni Jihadi Movement emerged in Egypt in the early 1960s – specifically in 1963, according to Abu Musab al-Suri – with Sayyid Qutb and later Muhammad Abd al-Salam Faraj as the intellectual and organisational pioneers. This current, which can be termed a *nationalist jihad* with an ideological foundation in the Muslim Brotherhood, viewed local governments as illegitimate since they were not ruling according to God's law, the *sharī'a*. While they did have their disagreements, both Qutb and Faraj considered jihad to be a means of achieving a certain objective – namely to topple the near enemy (*al-'aduww al-qarīb*) through the struggle of a vanguard movement – thus showing the influence of the ungodly Leninist movement. The second current, the *solidarity jihad*, started in 1979 and lasted until the mid-1990s. Led by Abdallah Azzam, the new current centred around the anti-Soviet struggle in Afghanistan. Its innovation was Azzam's reframing of jihad as an individual duty (*farḍ al-'ayn*) and his assertion that jihad was not a matter of a certain nationality, but the concern of the entire *umma*. It was also around this time that the debate emerged about whether to prioritise the near enemy (un-Islamic Arab governments) or the far enemy (Israel). Ayman al-Zawahiri, a senior member of the Egyptian Al Jihad, wrote that the liberation of Palestine goes through Cairo,[36] but in the mid-1990s other jihadis slowly started to doubt such an assertion.

This re-orientation towards the far enemy after the fall of the Soviets initiated the third current, the *global jihad*. It was now the US, not Israel, that was seen as the main far enemy – the head of the snake – that had to be defeated in order to facilitate successful national jihadi campaigns. There have been different accounts of whether this re-orientation was led by bin Laden or the Egyptian contingent represented by al-Zawahiri.[37] It appears likely, however, that it resulted from the confluence of al-Zawahiri becoming disillusioned with the unsuccessful struggle against the Egyptian regime, as well as bin Laden, being extremely preoccupied with the issue of Palestine, starting to see the US as the main obstacle to Palestinian liberation and as a transgression against Islam with its presence in the holy land of Saudi Arabia. The rise to prominence of Abu Musab al-Zarqawi, as a popular Jihadi leader in Iraq, implied a return to the prioritisation of the near enemy and, thus, does not represent a qualitative shift or evolution in the characteristics of the jihadi current. Salafi ideas were already a strong influence within al-Qaida, but they gained even more traction within al-Zarqawi's Iraqi movement, especially in terms of the impact of concepts such as *al-walā' wa-l-barā'* (loyalty and disavowal) and *takfir* (excommunication).

With the US invasion of Iraq, the ideas of bin Laden and al-Zarqawi coalesced to some degree, which eventually facilitated a union between the two in 2004. Striking the far enemy in the Middle East region thus became an acceptable substitute for striking in the far enemy's own countries. The fourth and most recent current, *statehood jihadism*, emerged with the Islamic State in 2014. Ideas such as controlling territory (*tamkin*) or establishing an Islamic political entity, whether a caliphate or an emirate, were not new, but were prioritised and taken to new heights by the Islamic State. The group concretised the jihadis' political project and developed a highly systematised governance structure unlike that of any previous jihadi project. In addition, the group adopted an unprecedented focus on both the near *and* far enemy, resulting in an extreme level of ideological hybridisation in terms of enemy hierarchies and ambitions.[38] This 'glocal' outlook is evident from its campaign of international terrorist attacks and its extensive establishment of provinces around the world.

Based on its historical trajectory, we can thus conclude that, rather than a theological orientation, it is the action of jihad, viewed as a legitimate and necessary methodology, that defines the jihadi movement and functions as the communality between groups as diverse as Ahrar al-Sham,[39] Hayat Tahrir al-Sham, the Taliban, al-Qaida and Islamic State. This also corresponds to how jihadis generally refer to themselves. Notions such as the 'jihadi movement' (*al-ḥarakat al-jihadiyya*),[40] the 'jihadi current' (*al-tayyar al-jihadi*),[41] 'global Jihad' (*al-jihad al-'alamīy*),[42] 'jihadist' (*mujāhid*) and 'jihadi Salafism' (*al-salafiyya al-jihadiyya*)[43] are terms regularly employed by jihadis to describe their movement.[44] With the exception of 'jihadi Salafism', all these endonyms place emphasis on *jihad* as the defining character. Just like we can talk about a specific *Salafi* DNA that comprises Salafists with diverging political preferences,[45] we can also talk about a *jihadi* DNA. This does not imply that there does not exist ideological or theological diversity within the Sunni Jihadi Movement, but the movement is nonetheless united by the political preference for jihad as a necessary methodology based on the motivation to establish an Islamic entity.

Ordinary Jihadis, Idiosyncratic Jihadis: The Intricate Relationship between Politics and Religion

The main theoretical argument proposed in this chapter is that jihadis are both ordinary and idiosyncratic in terms of their internal conflict processes, but in order to understand the respective characteristics it is necessary to unravel the intricate relationship between politics and religion. In much of the jihadism literature, ideological and theological cleavages are seen as the main driver of conflict, while the civil war literature mainly identifies political issues such as power struggles as the main source of infighting. I argue that intra-jihadi conflict is best conceptualised as a triangular relationship consisting of political interests, creedal and methodological differences, as well as diverging views of the political and social context, which is articulated through a religious discourse. While differences in creed, methodology and perceptions of the political and social context inform relations between groups and individuals, this research argues that the escalation from discursive contestation to military infighting is mainly driven by groups' political objectives, which are linked to distinctive rationales guiding intra-movement behaviour. Religious and ideological differences do matter, but just not in the way as it is assumed in the existing literature. Fault lines can be a source of tensions and contestation, but they are not the direct cause of conflict. An illustrative example is the split between al-Qaida and Hayat Tahrir al-Sham. A focus on ideology thus cannot in itself explain fratricide, as incidents of infighting do not correspond to ideological shifts.[46] Religion and ideology are therefore not the triggers, but rather *enablers* of internal conflict. In that way, the Sunni Jihadi Movement resembles other types of movements, be they insurgents, nationalist, secular or non-militant movements, in that political power struggles are the primary driving force of internal conflict.[47]

Despite a resemblance to key features of internal conflict in other movements, the Sunni Jihadi Movement distinguishes itself in several important aspects – and a central argument is that we cannot completely grasp the movement without understanding its specificity. This line of argument relates to the discussion about how 'sticky' or 'thick' a certain ideology or identity is. Brubaker makes a distinction between a particularising stance – arguing that religiously grounded conflicts are unique – and a generalising stance – rejecting the notion of uniqueness and claiming that religious identities are similar to other identities and ideologies, thus implying that religion does not require special analytical treatment.[48] Studying intra-jihadi conflict I tilt towards the particularising stance based on what I view as a strong influence of religion in informing the normative order of the Sunni Jihadi Movement,[49] which impacts not *why* internal conflict occurs but the process of *how* it does though specific mechanisms for violence and peace.

On an 'external' level, the Sunni Jihadi Movement distinguishes itself from other militant movements in that its objective is absolutist and that it considers politically negotiated solutions to be illegitimate.[50] In the context of nationalist and rebel movements, Krause and Fotini explain how intra-movement conflictual dynamics depend on groups' ambitions to achieve the most powerful position in a post-settlement context.[51] While this 'absence of a political process alternative' to victory clearly impacts groups' risk aversion and use of violence – as demonstrated by Islamic State[52] – it also infuses a different logic of intra-movement conflict dynamics, as the eruption of conflict cannot be explained by a group's standing during peace negotiations. Hence, we cannot expect the same dynamics in terms of alliances and conflict within the Sunni Jihadi Movement as in broader rebel or nationalist movements.

Movement characteristics on an 'internal' level are even more relevant to understanding the specific conditions of internal conflict dynamics. Jihadis' foundation in a literal and often extreme interpretation of religious sources induces a Manichean worldview between right and wrong, which unsurprisingly is a catalyst for volatile relations with other actors, including fellow jihadis. This leaves critical limitations on the diversity within the Sunni Jihadi Movement, as behaviour necessarily must be legitimised by religion. Religion also offers powerful concepts such as *al-walāʾ wa-l-barāʾ* (loyalty and separation) and *takfīr* (excommunication), which are handy tools with which to de-legitimise rivals. While the former is most often used to promote separation from non-Muslims, in some cases jihadis also rely on it to legitimise confronting other jihadis, either if they believe that they are acting against God's law or for instrumentalist purposes. In extreme cases, jihadis have excommunicated other jihadis. When it comes to ideological and theological diversity, such a Manichean attitude does make it challenging to handle the internal diversity that exists within the Sunni Jihadi Movement, or at the very least it offers jihadis a frame within which to religiously sanction internal conflict. This is particularly the case for doctrinally rigid groups like Islamic State.

Like other political actors, jihadis have ambitions of power. They struggle for dominance and leadership in order to spread and impose their ideology, but also, it appears, for the sake of power in itself, which occasionally transcends and overtakes the ideological tensions that may exist between groups or individuals. During his lifetime, Usama bin Laden was the predominant authority within the Sunni Jihadi Movement, but with him out of the picture and Ayman al-Zawahiri struggling to cement his authority within the broader movement, Abu Bakr al-Baghdadi eyed an opportunity to take over al-Qaida's dominating position. While the importance of power as an explanation for intra-jihadi conflict also can be taken too far,[53] it is important to recognise this more profane element: groups fight to dominate or to survive.

The struggle for power is arguably related to the issue of group identity. For example, in the struggle between al-Qaida and Islamic State, a valid argument can be made that the struggle is also about nationality. Al-Qaida is dominated by Saudis and Egyptians, and it appears that Islamic State and its predecessors – dominated by Iraqis, Syrians and Jordanians – were disgruntled with this external 'superiority'. Hence, clashes of identities can be a source of inter- or intra-group tensions that can potentially lead to competition, contestation or even infighting.

The emergence of infighting between jihadi groups does not happen in a vacuum but is closely connected to micro-level legitimation and macro-level events and structural changes, either because such micro- and macro-level factors function as triggers, or because they enable certain opportunities – for example, to challenge existing hierarchy structures. Context is thus important in understanding why infighting erupted between al-Qaida and Islamic State *when* it did. Tensions existed between the two groups for many years, but the death of bin Laden, which left a leadership vacuum in the Sunni Jihadi Movement, and the outbreak of civil war in Syria were important factors to explain the evolution from inter-group tensions to infighting. The interference of external actors militarily and diplomatically has also impacted jihadi infighting in several different ways.

On a micro-level, jihadi groups are particularly dependent on so-called *ideologues* to legitimise conflict with other jihadis. Ideologues are considered 'intellectual guardians'[54] within the Sunni Jihadi Movement, because of their (alleged) knowledge of Islamic sciences; thus, their support is considered important, especially in relation to extremely contentious issues such as jihadi infighting. On several occasions in the context of the Syrian civil war, ideologues issued *fatwa*s (religious rulings) on the legitimacy of engaging in infighting. While the exact importance of ideologues is difficult to measure, it testifies to their importance that groups prioritise receiving a *fatwa*, or at least ask for advice, before engaging in certain actions.[55] Foreign-fighter accounts from Syria also explain how the positions of leading jihadi ideologues were influential in the initial period of intra-jihadi conflict as a way of navigating in an extremely volatile environment.[56]

Just as religion and ideology are factors that facilitate conflict, they can also, as already mentioned, function as mitigating elements. The ideological closeness of groups and the general internal solidarity within the Sunni Jihadi Movement does make internal conflict less likely than conflict against outsiders who are considered ideological opponents. After all, the ideological differences between jihadi groups are relatively minor and often revolve around nuances such as the timing of establishing a caliphate, the criteria for choosing a caliph, or the legitimacy of allying with non-jihadi actors. These differences are mainly based on diverging views of reality (*wāqiʿ*) and interpretation of jurisprudence (*fiqh*), which translate into differences in methodology (*manhaj*). This implies that creed (*aqīda*) is usually not at the centre of conflict between jihadis. In contrast, the negative perception of *fitna*, the religious imperative of unity among believers, and the sanctity of Muslim blood are inciting peace among jihadis. Besides threatening unity (and God's commandments), what essentially makes *fitna* so sensitive is that it involves killing fellow Muslims and declaring others apostates in order to legitimise their killing.

Jihadis are required to label their rivals using specific categories such as apostates (*murtad*), which implies that the individual/group is considered outside of Islam, or as rebels (*bughāt*, sing. *bāghī*) or seceders (*khawārij*).[57] While the latter two categories do not take one outside of Islam, it is still considered legitimate to fight against them, albeit with certain restrictions. Hence, the contentious nature of fighting other jihadis necessitates a convincing effort to legitimise it. Islamic State's proclamation of *takfīr* on Jabhat al-Nusra is illustrative of this. During 2015, the group ran a series of articles in its English-language magazine *Dabiq* about the unholy alliances that Jabhat al-Nusra – and al-Qaida more generally – enjoyed with apostate factions, which, from the perspective of Islamic State, was a clear violation of *al-walā' wa-l-barā'*. These articles served to prime its proclamation of *takfīr* on al-Nusra, which finally came in November 2015.

A further mitigating factor is the strategic downside of opening a front against other jihadis. Jihadis usually have enough enemies to fight, and thus to open new and unnecessary battlefronts would most often just pose an unnecessary threat and mount pressure on the group and its fighters. It is no longer controversial to argue that jihadis are strategic actors, and we know that issues such as enemy prioritisation and the number of open battlefronts are being seriously considered internally within jihadi groups.[58] For instance, both bin Laden and al-Zawahiri have been explicit about limiting jihadis' active battlefronts in order to protect its primary struggles. Embarking on jihadi infighting is thus generally considered an unnecessary cul-de-sac resulting in jihadi casualties, demobilisation, fragmentation and polarisation that – besides its potentially illegitimate nature – has more strategic downsides than upsides.

Similarly, just as context and micro-level legitimation can be *triggers* of conflict, they can also be mitigating factors by confining behaviour in certain ways. Ideologues can choose to not embrace or even oppose infighting between two groups, which has the potential to actually prevent it from occurring or make it a one-sided affair. This illustrates ideologues' double role as *peacemakers* and *instigators of war* at the same time.

Towards a New Typology of Intra-jihadi Relation

Despite jihadism receiving increasing scholarly and analytical attention, intra-jihadi dynamics remain largely a black box. Arguably, this is partly due to the intense focus on group *ideology* and *strategy*, and the *security threat* that jihadism poses. Hence, there are no existing analytical categories available to help us understand *why* jihadis engage in internal conflict. To address this shortcoming, this research proposes the definition of three typologies to enhance our understanding of intra-jihadi relations. It does so by outlining three distinctive attitudes towards other groups within the movement, to help shed light on the conflictual dynamics so often raging between relatively like-minded groups.

Compared to existing ones, the typology proposed here takes an internal perspective and focuses on jihadi rationales guiding intra-jihadi relations. Part of the reason for this is that it is not possible to define one fault-line between jihadi groups as the cause of intra-jihadi conflict. For example, while in the 1990s[59] and in Saudi Arabia in the mid-2000s[60] the definition of the primary enemy was a contentious issue within the Sunni Jihadi Movement, it was never the only factor causing internal problems between jihadis, and it has since turned into an issue of secondary importance.[61] In the current context, the question of the role of the caliphate is undoubtedly important, as highlighted by Stenersen, but differences of opinion on the matter do not explain the infighting.

Table 8.1 Jihadi intra-movement rationales

Rationale	Logic behind intra-movement actions	Strategy towards other groups	Attitude to intra-movement infighting/*fitna*	Dominant attitude to ideological diversity
Hegemonist	Seeking to become a movement hegemon	Exclusivism,[64] co-optation & competition	Legitimate and necessary	Rigid
Unitarian	Seeking unity within the movement	Inclusivism/[65] cooperative	Illegitimate and only to defend	Pragmatic
Isolationist	Neutrality as a principle	Staying neutral	Illegitimate and only to defend	Pragmatic

In his doctoral research, Hegghammer elaborately reflected on the nature of typologies, their usefulness and limitations.[62] This section will rely on his reflections and add to them when needed. Typologies can be divided between *essentialist* and *interpretive*, with the former being based on a recognition of the idiosyncrasy of Islamic doctrines and using the actor's own terms, while the latter focuses on observable differences. As the ambition in this chapter is to suggest 'analytical categories which are rooted in observable political behavior and reflect differences in priorities and preferences',[63] I propose an interpretive and rationale-based typology.

Based on empirical observations in Syria in the period from 2013 to 2018, three distinctive rationales for intra-jihadi relations are suggested (see Table 8.1), namely: *hegemonist*, *unitarian* and *isolationist*. These distinctive rationales impact intra-jihadi collaborative and conflictual dynamics, as they inform the strategy that groups apply towards other groups and their attitudes regarding the legitimacy of infighting and ideological diversity. The two variables of interest are discourse and behaviour, since it is through how actors speak and act that we can understand their attitude to other jihadis. That said, the categories are ideal types, and one should thus expect some level of gradualism between the categories, not least in different geographical settings.

Hegemonist

A hegemonist's attitude to intra-jihadi relations is primarily driven by power ambitions and a desire to dominate the Sunni Jihadi Movement locally, regionally or globally. Based on the self-perception that it represents the sole, or most capable, jihadi authority in its territory of operations, other jihadi groups are seen as competitors, if not a threat that potentially needs to be fought. As its ambition is to dominate the movement, the hegemonist likely adopts an aggressive attitude towards other groups, leading to competitive dynamics that risk escalating into infighting. Obvious contemporary examples are Islamic State, whose caliphate declaration was an explicit demand for hegemony, and Hayat Tahrir al-Sham. Historical examples include the Algerian Armed Islamic Group (GIA) and al-Qaida in Iraq (AQI).

The presence of one or more hegemonist groups is arguably a prerequisite for intra-jihadi conflict to erupt, and it critically heightens the volatility of the movement. This is because it is less tolerant of the existence of other jihadi groups, although the level of tolerance differs among hegemonists. Other groups are expected to merge with, or at least be subservient to, the hegemonist rather than simply being a collaborator or a competitor. Such an exclusivist strategy stirs competitive dynamics based on the view that infighting is necessary and/or legitimate to reach its objective. However, while the desire to dominate is largely driven by political objectives, the justification for infighting is consequently framed through a religious terminology to legitimise the contentious action of *fitna*.

The way in which these typologies relate to the level of ideological rigidity, or extremism, is complicated. An argument can be made that ideologically rigid groups such as Islamic State, the Armed Islamic Group or Boko Haram are more inclined to have a hegemonic attitude because of their lesser toleration for ideological diversity within the jihadi movement and a general emphasis on concepts such as *al-walā' wa-l-barā'* and *takfir*. But in 2017–18 Hayat Tahrir al-Sham, a pragmatic and ideologically moderate jihadi group, started acting like a hegemonist in northwestern Syria, thus illustrating that it is not exclusively a phenomenon of ideological extremism. Hence, we conceive of ideological extremism as a contributing factor, but not the direct cause.

Unitarian

For a unitarian the main rationale is to seek unity within the movement. This rationale is founded in a self-perception as a group (*jamaa*), in contrast to an all-encompassing authoritative entity such as a state (*dawla*) or a caliphate (*khilāfa*). Unity is sought through an inclusivist attitude that is promoted through alliances and cooperation, while infighting with other jihadi groups is generally considered illegitimate and only justified to defend one's group from attacks. They tend to emphasise the impermissibility of shedding Muslim blood and caution against the practice of excommunication. Ideological rigidity is considered secondary to the objective of unity, which manifests itself in a more pragmatic approach. Hence, unitarians help to either prevent or de-escalate internal conflict by promoting peaceful co-existence and inter-group collaboration on a tactical and strategic level, as well as the importance of unity for jihadis to achieve their objectives. Unitarians can still seek authority within the movement and critique other jihadi groups in order to influence their ideology and behaviour, but their emphasis on unity and amicable relations prevents debate and criticism from devolving into infighting.

Al-Qaida in the post-2013 period is an example of a group with a unitarian rationale. It has consistently considered itself a *jamaa* (group) among *jamaat* (groups) – in contrast to Islamic State's exclusivist caliphate claim – and it has sought cooperation with groups whose ideology differs from its own. From the early days of the Syrian conflict onwards, al-Qaida leader al-Zawahiri has consistently promoted a discourse of jihadi unity, not just in relation to the conflict with Islamic State, but also when tensions emerged between Hayat Tahrir al-Sham and Hurras al-Deen, an al-Qaida-affiliated group in Syria established in February 2018. Another example is the Turkistan Islamic Party (TIP), who have consistently called for intra-jihadi reconciliation and unity while generally abstaining from participating in infighting.

Isolationist

The rationale of an isolationist is to entirely isolate itself from intra-jihadi infighting. Like unitarians, isolationists are in favour of unity and intra-jihadi collaboration, but their reaction to any act of aggression is isolation rather than retaliation. Such abstention comes from the view that infighting is illegitimate, and a refusal to take sides because of inferiority vis-à-vis the aggressor. The isolationist attitude appears to be the rarest, arguably because it is a challenging position to subscribe to after Islamic State rejected neutrality in its conflict with other jihadi groups. While hegemonists and unitarians are typically (but not exclusively) rationales of powerful groups, isolationists are likely to be more peripheral groups struggling to survive.

One example of such an isolationist group is Junud al-Sham, a Syrian-based group consisting mainly of Chechen fighters led by Muslim al-Shishani. Despite the intense pressure on jihadi groups operating in Syria to choose to be either with or against Islamic State, al-Shishani has consistently subscribed to a neutral position and categorically rejected the legitimacy of infighting, while referring to it as *fitna*. Another possible example consists of the Abdullah ibn Zubayr Battalions.[66]

Changing Rationales and Intra-group Divergence

Two central points about this typology concern the facts that rationales are not static but can change over time, and that it is possible to see different dominant rationales within a group in different geographical locations – effectively making them hybrids. Such dynamism and intra-group diversity would largely be absent if the emphasis were placed strongly on theology; however, when acknowledging that jihadi groups are strategic actors, we can analyse how their actions and logics are informed both by the context in which they find themselves and by group identity – including religious convictions. This once again highlights how entangled the political and the religious facets are within the Sunni Jihadi Movement. Two examples help illustrate these points. The group established as Jabhat al-Nusra but now known as Hayat Tahrir al-Sham has undergone a shift in rationales from 2014 to 2018. Initially, when conflict between Jabhat al-Nusra and Islamic State broke out, it followed a unitarian rationale, declining to escalate the intra-movement conflict while aligning with al-Qaida leader Ayman al-Zawahiri's unity discourse. But in early 2017, when it had split from al-Qaida and merged with a few other groups to establish Hayat Tahrir al-Sham, it started to act as a local hegemonist. Al-Qaida and its affiliate in Somalia, al-Shabab, offers an example of how different rationales can dominate within a single group. While al-Qaida's leadership, represented by al-Zawahiri, has consistently promoted unity and non-aggression, al-Shabab on two occasions cracked down on Islamic State elements in Somalia to maintain its domestic jihadi hegemony in the country.

Limitations and Challenges

Since the typologies are based on observations of events in conflict zones across the broader Middle East in the period from 2013 to 2018, their applicability more generally across geography and time should be cautioned, although not necessarily abandoned. Testing them thoroughly on the jihadi infighting in Afghanistan in the 1990s would be an interesting effort to see the extent to which they can explain other episodes of jihadi infighting. It also implies that they are developed from contexts where several jihadi groups are operating in a common territory, thus enabling direct confrontation and physical infighting. But intra-jihadi conflict is not limited to physical confrontations, and hegemonist and unitarian attitudes are similarly relevant on a global and de-territorialised scale through discourses. Hence, examining this de-territorialised aspect more closely should be another priority.

Hegghammer highlights two further challenges one should be aware of: why are there changes in rationales over time, and how can we distinguish between instrumental strategies and more lasting rationales?[67] While the first of these challenges will be discussed later in this chapter, I will briefly address the second challenge here. Our only method to determine the governing logic of intra-jihadi attitudes is to thoroughly research and scrutinise their discourse and behaviour over prolonged periods of time, by asking the questions 'how do jihadi groups talk about other groups?' and 'how do they behave towards other groups?' This requires studying the actors and their discourses closely on social media and, if possible, through conducting interviews, but only in this way can we verify the dominance of a certain rationale over time and distinguish it from short-term strategies.

Intra-jihadi Conflict in Syria, 2013–19

For current observers of jihadism, internal debates and infighting have become a common feature of jihadi activity. With the outbreak of the Syrian civil war, Sunni jihadism started to experience a critical fragmentation that was most vividly illustrated by the public break between al-Qaida and Islamic State, the latter until then known as the former's Iraqi affiliate. The effects of the split were not limited to the Levant but contaminated the entire global Sunni Jihadi Movement, affecting how jihadis from Nigeria to the Philippines view other jihadis and the legitimacy of fighting them. In Syria, a *jihadi* civil war broke out in early January 2014, with most groups finding common ground in their opposition to the aggressive behaviour of Islamic State. In the following years, jihadis fought on a regular basis, killing each other's senior figures, seizing territory and demonising the opposition (see Figure 8.1). This section discusses the intra-jihadi conflict in Syria in the period from 2013 to 2019 and identifies four slightly overlapping phases corresponding to the evolving dynamics of the conflict: *emergence and intensification*, *fragmentation and polarisation*, *radicalisation* and *internalisation*.

Although intra-jihadi conflict is not new, its most recent manifestations post-2013 have exposed some qualitative differences from past experiences, which stresses the importance of reaching a better understanding of intra-jihadi dynamics of conflict. Based on the period under study we can identify a 'typical' *conflict cycle* within the Sunni Jihadi Movement (see Figure 8.2). Initially, tensions emerge either as a result of ideological cleavages or power-related struggles for territory, resources or recruits, to implement their specific model, or strategy, of jihad, issues of nationality, or simply for the sake of power. Tensions are followed by discursive contestation where actors start criticising one another and, where the conflict is about to escalate, begin to rhetorically prime legitimations for infighting. Infighting will eventually erupt, and, in some cases, it will be preceded by group factionalism or splintering. After infighting has erupted, groups will typically attempt to establish supra-group institutions to de-escalate infighting and drive reconciliation, although such efforts have generally been unsuccessful.

First Phase: Emergence and Intensification

Over the spring and summer of 2013, tensions between jihadi groups in Syria were building as a result of Islamic State's expansion from Iraq and its aggressive posture vis-à-vis other groups. But it was in January 2014 that tensions escalated into conflict when the *jihadi civil war* broke out. It further intensified when al-Qaida and Islamic State officially cut relations in early February, and as a result of the latter's ensuing offensive in eastern Syria capturing territory from rivalling jihadi groups. The obvious culmination was Islamic State's caliphate declaration in late June, which was inherently a claim for global hegemony.

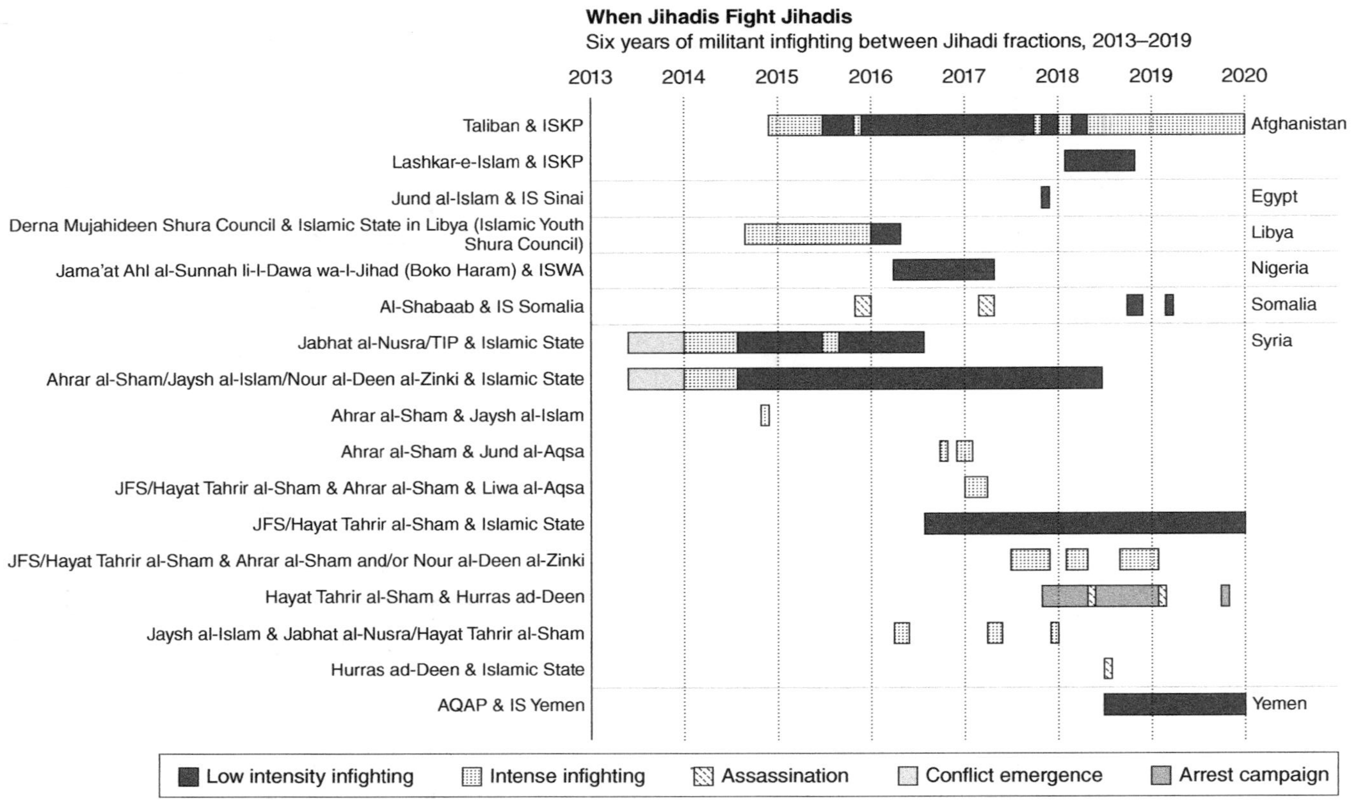

Figure 8.1 Overview of jihadi infighting globally

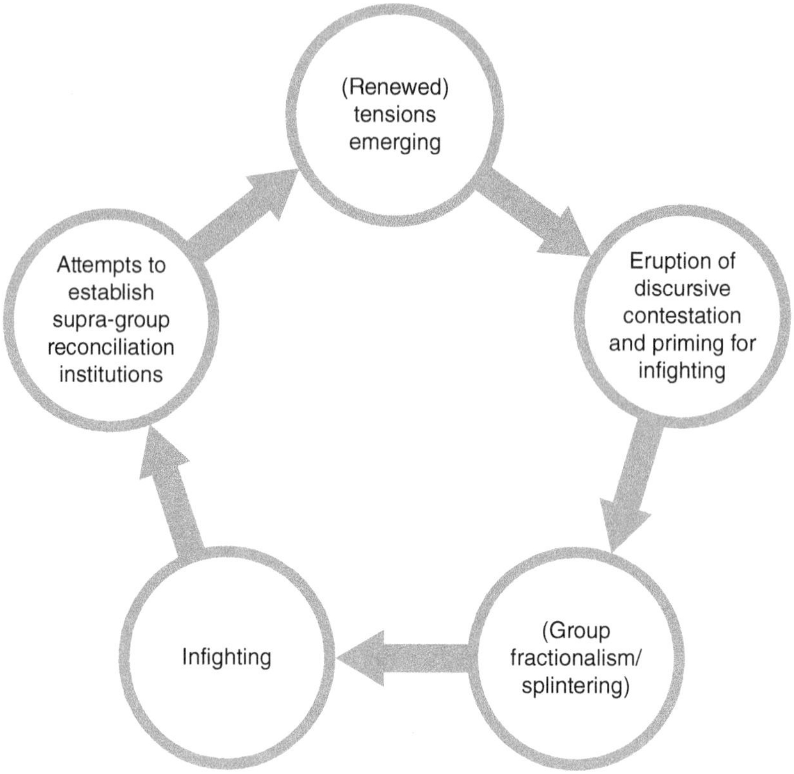

Figure 8.2 Intra-jihadi conflict cycle

From the inception of its Syrian venture Islamic State followed a hegemonist rationale. The group rejected all attempts at arbitration and sought to overpower competing jihadi groups to monopolise the jihadi struggle. Attacks against other jihadis were generally legitimised through reference to *al-walā' wa-l-barā'* and their alliances with apostate factions. When it declared the caliphate, it simultaneously ordered other groups to dissolve and merge into the caliphate. Other jihadi groups either followed a unitarian or isolationist rationale, but while the unitarians all promoted unity among the conflicting jihadis, they differed on how to respond to Islamic State's aggression. Groups like Ahrar al-Sham and Jaysh al-Islam were quick to respond militarily to Islamic State, while Jabhat al-Nusra was more hesitant to retaliate. Al-Qaida's global leadership also promoted a unitarian discourse, despite the continued aggression from Islamic State.

Second Phase: Fragmentation and Polarisation

The caliphate declaration led to the movement's fragmentation and polarisation. In late 2014 Islamic State initiated its global expansion process, resulting in the establishment of a range of new groups and a more dispersed power distribution within the Sunni Jihadi Movement. Already when announcing the caliphate, al-Adnani declared that all other groups were null. This discourse was further developed in its magazine *Dabiq*, where the group described the *extinction of the grey zone*, essentially leaving the Sunni Jihadi Movement in two camps: those with and those against Islamic State. Around this time, the jihadi civil war was turning global and the polarising logic cementing itself.

Ideologues and supporters aligned with the groups issued a wealth of publications attacking the opponent group, offering arguments and justification for a certain behaviour. While the Islamic State narrative remained aggressive and expansionist, al-Qaida-aligned figures mainly issued religious rulings that emphasised restraint in reaction to Islamic State, while working on reconciliation initiatives in private discussions. It was in this phase that the prospects of reconciliation and unity between al-Qaida and the Islamic State died out, however.

Third Phase: Radicalisation

The third phase is characterised by a radicalisation of the relationship between al-Qaida and the Islamic State, further polarising their respective positions vis-à-vis one another. In November 2015, Islamic State proclaimed *takfir* on Jabhat al-Nusra in its magazine *Dabiq*, thus legitimising conflict with the group under no uncertain terms.[68] Until then, al-Qaida leader Ayman al-Zawahiri had been lenient in his criticism of the Islamic State, but now he offered his first critical response to the renegade group in his *Islamic Spring* series running from March 2015 to June 2016. In the nine episodes, al-Zawahiri chastised al-Baghdadi's claim to be caliph, the group's aggressive attitude and its rejection of arbitration. In August 2016, he further escalated his rhetoric by applying the label *neo-khawārij* for the first time to refer to Islamic State. While this theoretically legitimised conflict with Islamic State, the al-Qaida leader continued a discourse of reconciliation and unity. It was also in this period that Islamic State began to publish photos and videos showing executions of fellow jihadis, including Jabhat al-Nusra, Jaysh al-Islam and Taliban fighters.

Fourth Phase: Internalisation

In the fourth and last phase both al-Qaida and Islamic State witnessed an *internalisation* of conflict. While the two groups remained bitter rivals and occasionally fought one another, internal problems began to overshadow their external challenges vis-à-vis rivalling jihadi groups. For only the second time in its thirty-year history, al-Qaida experienced an affiliate breaking its allegiance to the group when Jabhat al-Nusra in late July 2016 first re-branded itself as Jabhat Fatah al-Sham and then half a year later merged with several smaller groups to establish Hayat Tahrir al-Sham. In the aftermath of the creation of Hayat Tahrir al-Sham, a war of words between senior Hayat Tahrir al-Sham figures and al-Qaida loyalists in Syria turned public and a new conflict cycle initiated, albeit only involving small-scale infighting. Once again, al-Zawahiri would offer only subtle criticism of his former affiliate, instead focusing on the importance of unity among jihadi groups to counter their common enemy.

In Islamic State, internal tensions emerged already in 2014 when theological hard-liners questioned issues related to *takfir*. At this early stage, these hard-liners were suppressed either through imprisonment or execution, but the conflict would re-emerge in 2016 and escalate over the years, to detrimental effect on group cohesion. In the period from 2017 to 2019, the internal power struggle between two identifiable factions, often referred to as *Binaliyya* and *Hazimiyya* (eponyms derived from late Islamic State ideologue Turki al-Binali and Saudi theologian Ahmad al-Hazimi), intensified and resulted in open conflict for control over powerful institutions and the support of Abu Bakr al-Baghdadi. The group's general demise since 2017 and its internal problems thus largely turned its focus away from rivalling jihadi factions.

The Impact of Internal Conflict

This chapter poses the question why jihadis fight each other. But, as with so many others, it is a question with no simple answer. The literature tells us that jihadi infighting is the result of ideological or strategic cleavages or extreme ideology. While these are important factors, they are not sufficient to explain the highly contentious act of killing another jihadist. The argument presented here is that the process of engaging in infighting is much more complex, and this chapter identifies several factors that influence infighting, by either *facilitating* or *mitigating* conflict. Defining three rationales of intra-jihadi relations and offering a processual explanation of internal conflict stressing the importance of religion *and* politics, it suggests new conceptual tools to the study of intra-jihadi (and arguably more broadly 'non-state' actors) dynamics.

Having discussed the how and why of intra-jihadi conflict, the remaining pages briefly outline its effect on a movement level, namely *fratricidal killings*, *diversion from the main objective*, *fragmentation and polarisation*, *fratricidal socialisation*, *demobilisation* and *radicalisation*.

Fratricidal Killings

The most obvious direct negative consequence of this internal jihadi conflict is that infighting results in jihadis being killed. While numbers are difficult to determine precisely, a conservative estimate is that since 2014, more than 6,000 jihadis have died in Syria, Afghanistan, Somalia, Yemen, Egypt, Libya and Nigeria from the bullets (or bombs) of fellow, but rival jihadis.[69] While the numbers are relatively low in Egypt and Nigeria, they are more significant in Somalia and Yemen, while in Syria and Afghanistan the numbers exceed a thousand in each country. Fratricidal killings are problematic for any movement, but this is particularly the case for the jihadi movement. Despite their recent success in attracting large numbers of sympathisers, the militancy of jihadism still only appeals to a very small number of people around the globe. Bearing in mind the superiority of their common enemy, groups need all the resources possible. Killing off one another's most precious resource – dedicated fighters – thus leaves the movement as a whole worse off.

Diversion from the Main Objective

Jihadis largely share the same enemy. While jihadis traditionally have been divided between groups that prioritise the near enemy (local Arab regimes) and those prioritising the far enemy (Israel and the West), such distinction makes little sense on battlefields like Syria and Afghanistan, where both near and far enemy are present and, occasionally, fight on the same side. When jihadis train their guns on each other, it occupies critical resources and removes strategic focus from their fight against their primary enemies. Time and again, jihadis themselves have warned about this strategic cul-de-sac, which eventually distorts their greater ambitions. In his work on the Irish Republican Army (IRA), John Morrison wrote about organisational splintering and argued that the ensuing 'competition can often times distract the organizations from the pursuit of their purposive objectives with an over proportionate amount of time and energy being spent on competition between two groups who to many external observers may be regarded as indistinguishable in nature'.[70] A similar conclusion is valid for jihadism. Usama bin Laden stressed the danger of opening too many battlefronts, while al-Qaida's current leader, Ayman al-Zawahiri, consistently points to the detrimental impact of infighting in his attempts to steer the jihadi movement back to its main objective. It has been argued elsewhere that rebel infighting is in fact the main reason why rebels – including jihadis – lose their wars. Although such an assertion is probably too kind to jihadis, the strategic blunder of infighting is certain.

Fragmentation and Polarisation

Never since its modern resurgence in the 1960s has the Sunni Jihadi Movement been as fragmented or polarised as it currently is. Fratricide leads to intra/inter-group tensions, groups splintering and the establishment of new groups. The act of killing people ideologically close to oneself, sometimes even former brothers-in-arms, inevitably gives rise to some level of *communal distrust* that is hard to heal. Jihadi groups are military organisations and, as any officer would acknowledge, trust in the person standing next to oneself is essential. Islamic State required other jihadi groups to choose a side based on the Manichean idea that one is either with or against the group. In theory, neutrality was not tolerated. More recently, there has been lots of talk about potential alliances or mergers between jihadi groups. While not impossible, organisational collaboration is much harder to achieve if the groups in question have fought each other. The fear is that former jihadi brothers-turned-enemies-turned-brothers are 'Trojan horses' who will cause havoc if groups merge.

Fratricidal Socialisation

The act of killing another Muslim or of excommunicating someone from the religion is a highly sensitive issue; nonetheless, jihadis have spent considerable efforts since 2013 to make such actions acceptable in specific contexts. We know that socialisation into cultural narratives of violence is conducive to future waves of violence,[71] and thus the acts of intra-jihadi violence and their theoretical legitimation have major effects on the current and future generations of jihadis. A generation of (hopeful) jihadis currently grow up being accustomed to extreme violence and the normality of criticising and even attacking other jihadis. While jihadism has always been prone to internal conflict, this likely will be even more so in the future after such an intense period of socialisation, leaving the question of whether internecine conflict will be the new norm.

Demobilisation

For some jihadis, however, fratricide and the dynamics of radicalisation are intolerable. They rebel against these – in their eyes – illegitimate practices by abandoning the jihadi cause. Back in 2014, there circulated lots of stories of returning foreign fighters who were disillusioned with jihad. One reason they offered was that they had joined the jihadi struggle to fight the Assad regime, but ended up fighting other Muslims. This demobilising impact proved to be a problem on previous jihadi battlefields such as Afghanistan in the 1990s; it has also been a feature of other militant movements, as the example of Northern Ireland shows. Jihadis put major efforts into mobilisation, and so it is highly counterproductive when their own actions have demobilising effects. While some groups do pay attention to this problem, those driving internal conflict appear to consider it a necessary evil that is unavoidable while they are pursuing certain strategic objectives.

Radicalisation

Jihadis are generally considered *radicals*, but it appears that a competitive environment and infighting between jihadi groups does not just have a demobilising impact, but also carries the risk of radicalising ideas and behaviour even further. Competition and infighting forces jihadi groups to evolve and distinguish themselves from competitors. Take the example of the use of violence: the predecessors of Islamic State have always employed extreme violence, but in its new iteration the group relied even more on violence in the form of regular (filmed) mass beheadings, burning and sectarian massacres. On an ideational level, similar processes of radicalisation occurred, partly to legitimise political objectives. For instance, in order to enable attacks against fellow jihadis, Islamic State politicised the concept of *excommunication* to fit its operational needs. Needless to say, such politicisation is a slippery slope, with detrimental impacts on the internal radicalisation dynamics within the group.

Notes

1. This research is part of a larger project on intra-jihadi dynamics of conflict, mainly focusing on the struggle between al-Qaida and the Islamic State, but also on the more general repercussions that the dynamics between the two groups have on the Sunni jihadi movement.
2. This paper was presented at the conference 'The Future of Salafism' at the University of Oxford on 7 December 2018. The author would like to thank the participants for their questions and remarks. I would also like to thank Mona Kanwal Sheikh for discussing an early draft of this paper.
3. Tore Refslund Hamming, 'When Jihadis Kill Jihadis: The Implications of Militant Infighting', *World Politics Review* (13 December 2018).
4. Mohammed M. Hafez, 'Fratricidal Jihadists: Why Islamists Keep Losing Their Civil Wars', *Middle East Policy* 25 (2018), 86–99.
5. See Forum Q&A '22899: Meanings of the word fitnah in the Qur'aan', https://islamqa.info/en/22899.
6. See 'Fitna', in *Brill's Encyclopedia of Islam*, 2nd edition, ed. L. Gardet. A related notion is that of *inqisām* (schism).
7. See 'Civil War', in *The Princeton Encyclopedia of Islamic Political Thought*, eds Gerhard Bowering et al. (Princeton: Princeton University Press, 2013), 99–101.
8. Shiraz Maher, *Salafi-Jihadism: The History of an Idea* (London: Hurst & Company, 2016); Khaled Abou El Fadl, *Rebellion and Violence in Islamic Law* (New York: Cambridge University Press, 2001); Abu Jafar Muhammed bin Jarir Al-Tabari, *The History of Al-Tabari: The First Civil War*, ed. and trans. G. R. Hawting, vol. XVI, (Albany: SUNY Press, 1996); Patricia Crone and

Martin Hinds, *God's Caliph : Religious Authority in the First Centuries of Islam* (Cambridge: Cambridge University Press, 1986).

9. Tore Hamming, 'Polemical and Fratricidal Jihadists: A Historical Examination of Debates, Contestation and Infighting within the Sunni Jihadi Movement', International Centre for the Study of Radicalisation, (August 2019).
10. Aaron Y. Zelin, 'Al-Farida Al-Gha'iba and Al-Sadat's Assassination, a 30 Year Retrospective', *International Journal for Arab Studies* 3 (2012).
11. Author's discussion with Abdallah Anas.
12. Donatella Della Porta, *Social Movements, Political Violence, and the State: A Comparative Analysis of Italy and Germany* (Cambridge: Cambridge University Press, 1995).
13. Paul Staniland, 'Between a Rock and a Hard Place: Insurgent Fratricide, Ethnic Defection, and the Rise of pro-State Paramilitaries', *Journal of Conflict Resolution* 56/1 (2012), 16–40.
14. Philip Pomper, *Lenin, Trotsky, and Stalin : The Intelligentsia and Power* (New York: Columbia University Press, 1990).
15. Nelly Lahoud, *The Jihadis' Path to Self-Destruction* (New York: Columbia University Press, 2010); Hafez, 'Fratricidal Jihadists: Why Islamist Keep Losing Their Civil Wars'; Mohammed M. Hafez, 'Fratricidal Rebels: Ideological Extremity and Warring Factionalism in Civil Wars', *Terrorism and Political Violence* 32 (2020), 604–29, https://doi.org/10.1080/09546553.1389726.
16. John Turner, 'Strategic Differences: Al Qaeda's Split with the Islamic State of Iraq and Al-Sham', *Small Wars and Insurgencies* (Taylor & Francis, 2015), https://doi.org/10.1080/09592318.2015.1007563.
17. Exceptions are Assaf Moghadam and Brian Fishman (eds), *Self Inflicted Wounds: Debates and Divisions within Al Qa'ida and Its Periphery* (West Point: CTC Harmony Project, 2010); Nelly Lahoud and Muhammad Al-Ubaydi, 'The War of Jihadists against Jihadists in Syria', *CTC Sentinel* 7 (2014), 1–6; Lahoud, *The Jihadis' Path to Self-Destruction*; Hassan Abu Hanieh and Mohammad Abu Rumman, *The 'Islamic State' Organization: The Sunni Crisis and the Struggle of Global Jihadism* (Amman: Friedrich-Ebert-Stiftung, 2015); Tore Refslund Hamming, 'The Al Qaeda-Islamic State Rivalry: Competition Yes, but No Competitive Escalation', *Terrorism and Political Violence* 32 (2020), 20–37; Tore Refslund Hamming, 'Jihadi Competition and Political Preferences', *Perspectives on Terrorism* 11 (2017), 63–88. More general research on conflict between non-state Islamist actors includes Hafez, 'Fratricidal Jihadists: Why Islamist Keep Losing Their Civil Wars'; Hafez, 'Fratricidal Rebels'; Barak Mendelsohn, 'The

Battle for Algeria: Explaining Fratricide among Armed Nonstate Actors', *Studies in Conflict and Terrorism* (2019), https://doi.org/https://doi.org/10.1080/1057610X.2019.1580419.

18. See, for example, Turner, 'Strategic Differences: Al Qaeda's Split with the Islamic State of Iraq and Al-Sham'; Clint Watts, 'Deciphering Competition Between Al-Qa'ida and the Islamic State', *CTC Sentinel* 9 (2016), 1–6; Jacob Zenn, 'Boko Haram's Factional Feuds: Internal Extremism and External Interventions', *Terrorism and Political Violence* 31 (2019), 1–33, https://doi.org/10.1080/09546553.2019.1566127; Harun Maruf and Dan Joseph, *Inside Al-Shabaab: The Secret History of Al-Qaeda's Most Powerful Ally* (Bloomington: Indiana University Press, 2018); Antonio Giustozzi, *The Islamic State in Khorasan: Afghanistan, Pakistan and the New Central Asian Jihad* (London: Hurst & Company, 2018); Tore Hamming, 'Why Did the Jihadi Cold War in Yemen End?', *War on the Rocks* (November 2018). See also the research carried out on contestation between individuals such as Joas Wagemakers, '"Seceders" and "Postponers"? An Analysis of the "Khawarij" and "Murji'a" Labels in Polemical Debates between Quietist and Jihadi-Salafis', in *Contextualising Jihadi Thought*, ed. Deol Jeevan and Zaheer Kazmi (London: Hurst & Company, 2012), 145–64; Joas Wagemakers, 'What Should an Islamic State Look Like? Jihadi-Salafi Debates on the War in Syria', *The Muslim World* 106 (2016), 501–22; Joas Wagemakers, 'Contesting Religious Authority in Jordanian Salafi Networks', *Perseverance of Terrorism: Focus on Leaders* 117 (2014), 111–25; Joas Wagemakers, 'Protecting Jihad: The Sharia Council of the Minbar Al-Tawhid Wa-l-Jihad', *Middle East Policy* 108 (2011), 148–62, http://onlinelibrary.wiley.com/doi/10.1111/j.1475-4967.2011.00492.x/full.
19. Thomas Hegghammer, *Jihad in Saudi Arabia: Violence and Pan-Islamism since 1979* (Cambridge: Cambridge University Press, 2010).
20. Lahoud, *The Jihadis' Path to Self-Destruction*.
21. Anne Stenersen, 'Jihadism after the "Caliphate": Towards a New Typology', *British Journal of Middle Eastern Studies* (2018), 1–20, https://doi.org/10.1080/13530194.2018.1552118.
22. Hafez, 'Fratricidal Rebels'.
23. Mayer N. Zald and Bert Useem, 'Movement and Countermovement: Loosely Coupled Conflict', *CRSO Working Paper 302* (1983), 1–31; Graham Macklin and Joel Busher, 'The Missing Spirals of Violence: Four Waves of Movement – Countermovement Contest in Post-War Britain', *Behavioral Sciences of Terrorism and Political Aggression* 7 (2015), 1–16, https://doi.org/10.1080/19434472.2014.977329.

24. Mayer N. Zald and John D. McCarthy, 'Social Movement Industries: Competition and Cooperation Among Movement Organizations', *CRSO Working Paper 201* (1979), 1–32.
25. See also Jérôme Drevon, 'The Jihadi Social Movement (JSM): Between Factional Hegemonic Drive, National Realities and Transnational Ambitions', *Perspectives on Terrorism* 11 (2017), 55–62, who talks about the Jihadi Social Movement.
26. Thomas Hegghammer, 'Violent Islamism in Saudi Arabia, 1979–2006: The Power and Perils of Pan-Islamic Nationalism' (unpublished doctoral diss., 2007, Institut d'Etudes Politiques de Paris – Ecole Doctorale de Sciences Po), 53–79.
27. Olivier Roy, 'Who Are the New Jihadis?', *The Guardian*, 13 April 2017, www.theguardian.com/news/2017/apr/13/who-are-the-new-jihadis.
28. Joas Wagemakers, 'Revisiting Wiktorowicz', in *Salafism After the Arab Awakening*, ed. Francesco Cavatorta and Fabio Merone (London: Oxford University Press, 2017), 18.
29. Abu Mariyah al-Qahtani, a senior member of Hayat Tahrir al-Sham, claimed in 2015, when he was a member of al-Qaida's Syrian group Jabhat al-Nusra, that 'those who say that Al-Qaida is only Salafi Jihadist, he has made a mistake, rather the organization is a complete group with multiple schools of law (*madhāhib*), with those who carry the Salafi thought, and in it there are also Maturidis and Sufis. But some want to present al-Qaida as being Salafi Jihadist. See Abu Mariah al-Qahtani, 'Al-Qaida and Those Who Claim Adherence to It', *Al Minara* (2015), https://alminara.wordpress.com/2015/06/26/shaykh-abu-mariyah-al-qahtani-al-Qaedah-and-those-who-claim-adherence-to-it/.
30. Thomas Hegghammer, 'Jihadi-Salafis or Revolutionaries? On Religion and Politics in the Study of Militant Islamism', in *Global Salafism: Islam's New Religious Movement*, ed. Roel Meijer (London: Hurst & Company, 2014), 244–66.
31. For example, the Jordanian Jihadi ideologue Abu Muhammad al-Maqdisi once issued the following definition: 'the current which seeks to implement monotheism through jihad against the tyrants'. See 'Discussion with Sheikh Abu Muhammed al-Maqdisi' (*hiwar ma' al-shaykh Abu Muhammad al-Maqdisi*), 2002–3. This definition, however, would prove very controversial to many as it included only jihadis targeting the local regimes and thus not al-Qaida.
32. Hegghammer, 255; Hassan Hassan, 'The Sectarianism of the Islamic State: Ideological Roots and Political Context', Carnegie Endowment, 13 June 2016.

33. Maher, *Salafi-Jihadism: The History of an Idea*; Joas Wagemakers, *A Quietist Jihadi: The Ideology and Influence of Abu Muhammad Al-Maqdisi* (Cambridge: Cambridge University Press, 2012).
34. Nelly Lahoud, 'Beware of the Imitator: Al-Qa'ida through the Lens of Its Confidential Secretary', Combating Terrorism Center (2012), 41.
35. This is not a controversial view. Kepel has previously described the Sunni Jihadi Movement as a development of three distinctive *generations* (Cécile Daumas, 'Gilles Kepel: "Il Faut Écouter Les Prêches Du Vendredi"', *Libération*, 14 April 2016), while Jordanian analyst Abu Hanieh talks about three *schools of Jihadi thought* to capture not just the movement's modern genealogy, but also its internal diversity (Author's interview with Hassan Abu Hanieh, 18 June 2018, Amman). Even from within the Sunni Jihadi Movement, Abu Musab al-Suri has provided his account of the ideological composition of the movement (Moghadam and Fishman, *Self Inflicted Wounds: Debates and Divisions within Al Qa'ida and Its Periphery*, 108) and its methodological diversity in terms of strategy (Chapter 8, section 4 in Abu Musab al-Suri, 'The Global Islamic Resistance Call', 2004).
36. In my interview, Hassan Abu Hanieh explains how leftist groups in Jordan said even before al-Zawahiri that liberation of Palestine goes through Amman, which shows a clear line of inspiration.
37. In general, there seems to exist confusion about the authoritative relationship between bin Laden and al-Zawahiri, with some arguing that the latter was in fact the real thinker behind al-Qaida, while bin Laden was its poster boy. For instance, Gilles Kepel calls al-Zawahiri bin Laden's *mentor*; see Kepel, *Fitna: Guerre Au Cœur de l'islam*, 13.
38. Thomas Hegghammer, 'The Hybridization of Jihadi Groups', *Current Trends in Islamist Ideology* 9 (2009), 26–45.
39. An argument could be made that Ahrar al-Sham, which has been labelled as a Salafi-jihadi group, was by 2018 slowly leaving the Sunni Jihadi Movement, as the group appears increasingly open to a negotiated solution and perhaps even to participating in some sort of democratic setup.
40. Regularly used by Abu Mahmoud al-Filastini in his statements on Telegram. See http://t.me/abomahmd.
41. Abu Qatada Al-Filastini, 'Al-Tahawwulat-Al-Mutawaqqaah an Tahaadatha Fi Al-Tayyar Al-Jihadiyya' [The Expected Transformations to Happen in the Jihadi Movement], 3 March 2017.
42. Abu Muhammed Al-Adnani, 'Apologies, Amir of Al-Qaida', *Al-Furqan Media Foundation*, 11 May 2014, https://pietervanostaeyen.wordpress.

com/2014/05/12/new-audio-message-by-isis-shaykh-abu-muhammad-al-adnani-as-shami-apologies-amir-al-qaida/. A related term used by Jihadis is the 'global Sunni jihadi movement' (*ḥarakat al-jihad al-sunni al-ʿālamīy*). See Sami Al-Uraydi, 'Rasail Manhajiyya Min Al-Thughur Al-Shamiyyah' [Methodological Messages from the Syrian Front], May 2017.

43. Regularly used by Abu Muhammad al-Maqdisi and Abu Qatada al-Filastini.
44. Cole Bunzel, 'Jihadism on Its Own Terms', Hoover Institution (2017).
45. Jacob Olidort, 'Is Quietist Salafism the Antidote to ISIS?', Brookings Institute, 13 March 2015, www.brookings.edu/blog/markaz/2015/03/13/is-quietist-salafism-the-antidote-to-isis/.
46. Paul Staniland, 'Between a Rock and a Hard Place: Insurgent Fratricide, Ethnic Defection, and the Rise of pro-State Paramilitaries', *Journal of Conflict Resolution* 56 (2012), 16–40.
47. A similar conclusion emerges from Fotini's research on the Afghan civil war in the 1990s. She describes a constantly changing pattern of alliances and infighting, which shows that ideology, being relatively static, is not the main source. See Christia Fotini, *Alliance Formation in Civil Wars* (Cambridge: Cambridge University Press, 2012), 60.
48. Rogers Brubaker, 'Religious Dimensions of Political Conflict and Violence', *Sociological Theory* 33 (2015), 1–19.
49. Within Terrorism Studies, Gunning and Jackson make the argument that it is problematic to view religious terrorism as a distinctive type of terrorism, as is the tendency among many terrorism scholars, because of the difficulty of establishing a causal link between religion and a certain type of violence. See Jeroen Gunning and Richard Jackson, 'What's so "Religious" about "Religious Terrorism"?' *Critical Studies on Terrorism* 4 (2011), 369–88, https://doi.org/10.1080/17539153.2011.623405.
50. This distinction is also noted in Mark Juergensmeyer, *Terror in the Mind of God: The Global Rise of Religious Violence*, 3. ed., rev. and updated (Berkley: University of California Press, 2003), 157.
51. Fotini, *Alliance Formation in Civil Wars*; Peter Krause, *Rebel Power: Why National Movements Compete, Fight, and Win* (New York: Cornell University Press, 2017).
52. Krause, 22–27.
53. Christoph Reuter, 'The Terror Strategist: Secret Files Reveal the Structure of Islamic State', *Der Spiegel*, 18 April 2015, www.spiegel.de/international/world/islamic-state-files-show-structure-of-islamist-terror-group-a-1029274.html.

54. Wagemakers, 'What Should an Islamic State Look Like? Jihadi-Salafi Debates on the War in Syria'.
55. In an interview, Labib Nahhas explained to this author how jihadi groups, including his own (Ahrar al-Sham), always sought religious support in the form of a *fatwa* before engaging in contentious acts (author's interview, 15 April 2018, London).
56. Author's interview with a Danish Foreign Fighter who fought with an al-Qaida-affiliated group in Syria in the period from 2012 to 2015, conducted on 28 June 2017, Copenhagen.
57. John Kelsay, 'Muslim Discourse on Rebellion', *Ethics and International Affairs* 27 (2013), 379–91, doi:10.1017/S0892679413000348; Khaled Abou El Fadl, *Rebellion and Violence in Islamic Law* (New York: Cambridge University Press, 2001). For a jihadi discussion of rebels (*bughat*), see Muhammed Abd al-Salam al-Faraj, 'The Neglected Duty', §43 in the translation by Johannes J. G. Jansen, in *The Neglected Duty: The Creed of Sadat's Assassins and Islamic Resurgence in the Middle East* (New York: Macmillan, 1986).
58. Brynjar Lia and Thomas Hegghammer, 'Jihadi Strategic Studies: The Alleged Al Qaida Policy Study Preceding the Madrid Bombings', *Studies in Conflict & Terrorism* 27 (September 2004), 355–75, https://doi.org/10.1080/10576100490483642.
59. Hegghammer, 'Violent Islamism in Saudi Arabia, 1979–2006', 68; Fawaz A. Gerges, *The Far Enemy: Why Jihad Went Global* (Cambridge: Cambridge University Press, 2005).
60. Thomas Hegghammer, 'Global Jihadism after the Iraq War', *The Middle East Journal* 60 (2006), 11–32.
61. This does not imply that enemy prioritisation is no longer a contentious issue. For example, it plays a role in the competition between groups; see Hamming, 'Jihadi Competition and Political Preferences'.
62. Hegghammer, 'Violent Islamism in Saudi Arabia, 1979–2006'.
63. Ibid., 69.
64. Exclusivism means that groups consider alliances and cooperation with other jihadi groups less attractive or even illegitimate, while preferring that other groups join them.
65. Inclusivism means that groups consider alliances and cooperation between Jihadi groups attractive and legitimate.
66. Aymenn Jawad Al-Tamimi, 'Abdullah Ibn Zubayr Battalions of Deir Az-Zor Reject Fighting ISIS', *Syria Comment*, 25 April 2014.

67. Hegghammer, 'Violent Islamism in Saudi Arabia, 1979–2006', 78.
68. There is evidence that the Islamic State proclaimed *takfir* on Jabhat al-Nusrah as early as January 2015, as per Aymenn Jawad al-Tamimi's sources.
69. Tore Hamming, 'Jihadi Politics: Fitna within the Sunni Jihadi Movement 2014–2019', PhD Dissertation (European University Institute, 2020).
70. John F. Morrison, *The Origins and Rise of Dissident Irish Republicanism: The Role and Impact of Organizational Splits* (New York: Bloomsbury Press, 2014), 000.
71. Donatella Della Porta, *Clandestine Political Violence* (New York: Cambridge University Press, 2013), 72.

9

AHRAR AL-SHAM'S POLITICISATION DURING THE SYRIAN CONFLICT

Jérôme Drevon

A substantial number of independent Salafi armed groups emerged after 2011.[1] This remarkable development contrasts with the affiliation of most Salafi-jihadi groups to al-Qaida in the 2000s.[2] The most widely covered case was the Islamic State (IS), which emancipated from al-Qaida and claimed to revive the caliphate with uninhibited violence.[3] But Islamic State only represents the most extreme trajectory. Many Salafi armed groups have distanced themselves from al-Qaida and developed more realistic political approaches during the conflicts that have plagued Libya and Syria since 2011. These illustrate the polarisation of armed Salafism, the dissociation of many Salafi armed groups from al-Qaida and the Islamic State's coup over al-Qaida's international leadership. This chapter defines the most perceptible trend characterising armed Salafism after 2011 as *politicisation*. This concept empirically accounts for the development of realistic tactical and strategic objectives, durable alliances with other actors including foreign states and non-state armed groups, as well as the normalisation of these groups' interactions with the population.

Salafi-jihadi groups such as al-Qaida or Islamic State pursue political objectives. Fighting the US presence in the Middle East and re-establishing the caliphate are inherently political ambitions. But the choice of the term 'politicisation' accentuates armed groups' involvement in political matters,[4] in contrast to the pursuit of utopian and ultimately unreachable objectives.

Politicisation underlines the alignment between clear political and military objectives, beyond al-Qaida's excessive focus on the military dimension of jihad, or Islamic State's uncompromising internal theological debates. The concept instead stresses armed groups' engagement with other armed groups (especially non-Salafi) and the international system of states, which jihadi-Salafism vilifies on theological grounds.[5] While the politicisation concept can be contested, it reflects these groups' own internal discourse on balancing political versus military objectives and means.[6] It is also more appropriate than the concepts of moderation,[7] or de-radicalisation,[8] which are not applicable to armed groups that still use violence.

The Syrian Salafi armed group Ahrar al-Sham epitomises the most prominent case of politicisation. By 2014, Ahrar al-Sham was the leading insurgent group in Syria, with the largest number of soldiers, presence throughout Syrian opposition-held areas and relatively strong ties to foreign countries, including Turkey and Qatar. Ahrar al-Sham explicitly rejected al-Qaida's legacy and developed a more inclusive approach to other groups and the population. This chapter traces the group's emergence and development to demonstrate how pre-war developments and a de-centralised alliance-based expansion underpinned its politicisation over the years. This case-study also contends that politicisation was sustained by the group's internal institutionalisation, which ultimately explains its successes and failures during the conflict. This chapter is based on extensive field research interviews in Turkey and northwest Syria in 2019 with an array of leaders and members of Ahrar al-Sham, armed opposition groups and independent Syrian Islamists.

Ahrar al-Sham's Roots in the Syrian Islamist Social Movement

Ahrar al-Sham is largely the off-shoot of the Syrian Islamist Social Movement (ISM). The group's embeddedness in the Islamist Social Movement facilitated its expansion, in comparison with other armed opposition groups that could not rely on any type of structured organisation given the weakness of Syrian civil society before 2011. Embeddedness in the Islamist Social Movement has framed Ahrar al-Sham's ideological developments and shaped its de-centralised organisational structures. It has eased the group's initial expansion in contrast to local armed groups that failed to expand beyond their geographical areas, but also in comparison with Jabhat al-Nusra (Front of Support), which initially embraced a covert mode of organisation.

The Syrian Islamist Social Movement has been historically formed around many individuals, conservative families and informal groups sharing a broad collective identity and politico-religious views despite internal ideological divergences.[9] While repressive state policies prevented its public consolidation, low-level informal connections throughout the country existed between informal groups of friends, students, university graduates and locals. The Islamist Social Movement pervaded most of Syria. It was particularly influential in some areas around Aleppo, Hama and the neighbourhood of Duma in Damascus. Although the regime had long tried to divide Syrian Islamists by manipulating the clergy[10] and supporting Sunni Islamists abroad – such as Hamas in Palestine – the Islamist Social Movement had the potential to transform into a 'radical milieu', defined as a local environment that 'shares [insurgents'] perspective and objectives, approves of certain forms of violence, and (at least to a certain extent) supports the violent group morally and logistically'. [11]

The founding military units (brigades, *katā'ib*) of Ahrar al-Sham emerged in the Islamist Social Movement of northern Hama and Idlib before expanding throughout the country. This region was the epicentre of the repression of the Muslim Brotherhood in the 1970s, which peaked in 1982 when the city of Hama was ravaged by regime forces causing up to 40,000 casualties.[12] State repression effectively incapacitated the Brotherhood in the region at the time, but subsequent constraints on political Islam curbed neither the religiosity of the population, nor the emergence of new religious trends not affiliated with the organisation. The next Islamist generations, including Muslim Brotherhood families formerly repressed by the regime, were influenced by domestic and regional debates on matters ranging from the *Ṣaḥwa* religious movement in Saudi Arabia[13] to the American-led invasion of Iraq in 2003.[14]

Emerging in northwest Syria was a comparative structural advantage. Other geographical areas, especially around the cities of Damascus and the opposition stronghold of Homs, were quickly besieged by regime forces or proved unable to maintain strong connections with one another and with foreign supporters of the opposition (both states and individuals). Syrian insurgents in the south of Syria were restrained by strong Jordanian control, while the east of the country was ultimately swayed by Islamic State, benefitting from its Iraqi strategic depth. Northwest Syria was comparatively widely connected to foreign supporters and logistical support from the early days of the uprising and benefitted from the Turkish *laissez-faire* attitude.

In comparison to other armed groups which similarly emerged in northwest Syria, Ahrar al-Sham was the first group to agglomerate the majority of early Islamist brigades that spread in the region after 2011. These Islamists created the first military brigades in their villages and cities by gathering together friends, neighbours and trusted contacts – a mobilising pattern shared with non-Islamist groups at the beginning of the uprising. But, in contrast to the nationalist and less-ideological groups that only gradually endorsed violence to protect the mass protests and in reaction to repression, the Islamist brigades wanted to face the regime from the onset, since they believed that non-violence would not lead to regime change. More importantly, they (1) shared similar ideas and world-views and (2) were already connected through loose social networks. These characteristics contrast with other local factions that emerged in certain geographical areas or for the purpose of specific military battles, but which were quickly plagued by administrative issues.[15]

Ahrar al-Sham's characteristics shaped the group's early ideological and organisational construction. The group's early cells emerged before the congregation of many independent brigades into the Free Syrian Army. The Syrian Islamists who created Ahrar al-Sham in northwest Syria started with clearer objectives and worldviews that contrasted with more nationalist and local gatherings, which did not necessarily embrace a coherent political project. Ahrar al-Sham's early brigades convened many meetings at the beginning of the conflict in order to coordinate their efforts and gather resources. Early interactions between an array of Islamists from diverging ideological backgrounds required a consensual approach to prevent internal dissent. Considering their lack of organisational experience, the leaders of Ahrar al-Sham's early cells had to agree that they should define their ideological principles and make decisions in consensus in order to remain united.

This choice imposed a horizontal hierarchy among the group's early brigades, whose leaders gained a seat in the group's newly formed leadership council and were thus endowed with responsibility for strategic decision-making (Ahrar al-Sham's *majlis al-shūrā*).[16] This contrasted with most brigades, which remained centred on one geographical stronghold (for example, a city or inter-connected villages) and did not easily share power with brigades from other areas, often splitting up over people and resources. Ahrar al-Sham's early networking structure moreover developed a mainstream ideological frame that every sub-leader could embrace. It positioned the group in mainstream Islamism, despite pre-2011 divergences of opinion. Although widely labelled as 'Salafi-jihadist', differences of religious traditions between more scholastic or jihadi approaches to Salafism, for instance, became irrelevant when the immediate objective was to face a regime committed to repressing a popular uprising. This choice was reinforced by the joining of many Syrians who previously fought jihad abroad while opposing al-Qaida's choice to confront Western countries.

These key features explain the network effect underpinning Ahrar al-Sham's quick development during the first year of the conflict. The network effect reflects a self-fulfilling dynamic that bolstered Ahrar al-Sham's expansion: being a large group helps to gather more funding, recruits and popularity, which in turn boosts the group's attractiveness to other armed factions and sustains further organisational growth. Not relying on a single geographical stronghold or a strongman who had gathered local social networks into a single faction notably facilitated the integration of new sub-groups, which could quickly find their place under Ahrar al-Sham's broader umbrella network. Moreover, Ahrar al-Sham's mainstream approach to Islamism did not imply the imposition of strict ideological demands on newcomers, in contrast to other groups such as Jabhat al-Nusra where stronger ideological commitments and a personal individual allegiance (*bay'a*) to the group were initially required.

Ahrar al-Sham gradually institutionalised by formalising pre-existing agreements into the group's newly created organisational structures. During the first year, Ahrar al-Sham's military brigades worked independently and only used the name 'Ahrar al-Sham' when claiming responsibility for specific armed attacks. Individual leaders maintained connections to sub-groups situated in Syrian provinces disconnected from northwest Syria. Ahrar al-Sham started to become a tangible group when sub-brigades began to provide each other with weapons and resources.[17] Cross-brigade interactions reinforced solidarity with one another, and this feeling of belonging to a shared entity developed the group's *esprit de corps*. After one year, growing administrative issues motivated Ahrar al-Sham's *majlis al-shūrā*'s decision to create additional institutional structures inspired by state entities. The collective leadership therefore ordered the creation of administrative, financial, military, development and political offices, each with their own internal regulations to manage the group, clarify existing problems and provide solutions.[18] An external consultant was hired explicitly for that purpose.

Ahrar al-Sham's features encapsulate and refine two arguments often developed to explain the success of Syrian Islamist groups during the conflict. The first argument holds that Islamists were primarily bolstered by the liberation of prisoners that occurred throughout 2011, which would have been ordered by the regime to tarnish the reputation of the uprising. According to this view, the regime would have liberated Islamist prisoners to marginalise the non-violent component of the uprising and to equate the resistance to al-Qaida. Others add that the groups, including Ahrar al-Sham, were simply created by former prisoners when they returned to their localities.[19] In reality, while Ahrar al-Sham managed to gather most newly liberated prisoners, the group's early developments and expansion actually preceded the liberation of Islamist prisoners that occurred from mid-2011 onwards. The liberated prisoners were joining a group to whom they had previously been connected – since they often stemmed from the same Islamist milieu – or simply the main Islamist early riser. Prison liberation reinforced existing dynamics; most of Ahrar al-Sham's early brigades were not formed by former prisoners.

The second argument contends that Syrian Islamist brigades succeeded with financial support provided by their supporters in Gulf countries – states as well as individuals.[20] Although many armed groups (including Ahrar al-Sham) did receive extensive support from Gulf countries from the early days of the conflict, this argument is incomplete. Foreign support that is not provided through a unified structure is likely to aggravate armed groups' internal divisions. A plurality of armed factions and sub-groups can contend over resources and try to secure their own direct external support. External sponsors can upset a group's internal balance of power and cause it to split.[21] Only non-state armed groups that are more institutionalised around clearer organisational structures can exploit external funding without worsening internal rivalry. Moreover, foreign states and supporters are not necessarily willing to support local armed groups that cannot form a real alternative to the regime. When thousands of groups compete for support, the most militarily and politically potent groups are the most attractive choices for foreign patrons. The success of Ahrar al-Sham in gathering external support can therefore be explained for two reasons. First, the large diversity of Ahrar al-Sham's supporting networks signified that, more so than the localised military units, the group was capable of brokering multiple ties to foreign supporters – from mainstream Salafis in Kuwait to independent preachers and jihadi sympathisers worldwide.[22] Second, Ahrar al-Sham was the largest and most appealing Islamist group in northwest Syria. Prison liberation and foreign support therefore significantly sustained existing trends.

Becoming the Largest Insurgent Group through Factional Alliances

By 2012, the Syrian armed opposition had grown in size and sophistication. The opposition gradually seized large geographical areas located primarily in the country's periphery. The eastern part of the city of Aleppo, as well as the border control of Baab al-Hawa with Turkey, switched to the hands of the opposition in the summer of 2012, which contributed to the unification of northwest Syria. The regions of Ghuta in the suburbs of Damascus and eastern Syria were similarly lost by regime forces and transferred to armed opposition groups by mid-2013. The transformation of the conflict from low-scale guerrilla attacks against military checkpoints and infrastructures to the stabilisation of relatively wide front-lines transformed the Syrian opposition. The small and geographically localised armed groups realised that they had to coordinate their efforts to gather more extensive resources, develop a credible alternative political project that could sway the population and create local structures of governance while limiting inter-factional fighting.

As the main Islamist early riser, Ahrar al-Sham was favourably positioned to take the lead. The group's early agglomeration of an array of sub-groups around a culture of ideological and organisational consensus (*tawāfuqiyya*) facilitated its transformation into a mass movement alongside the liberation of large geographical areas. Early interactions between the groups' composing brigades shaped the foundations of Ahrar al-Sham's political project, reinforced internal solidarity and sustained the collaboration of many sub-groups not merely confined to a single locality. Ahrar al-Sham transformed into a more institutionalised group, structured around shared decision-making processes that enabled its leaders to share internal resources and make strategic decisions more adequately than competing groups.

The diversity of Ahrar al-Sham's constituting networks helped the group to present political initiatives to unify the Syrian opposition. The integration of well-experienced leaders with extensive ties abroad hastened the group's learning processes. When other groups focused on their survival after the successive deaths or replacement of their leaders and prominent commanders, Ahrar al-Sham's early political officers in Turkey were opening channels of communication with an array of countries and non-state actors to articulate the group's positions regionally and internationally.[23] In contrast to networks of deserting officers or locals fighting to protect their communities, Ahrar al-Sham's brokerage with wide social networks was more conducive to the articulation of a clearer political approach to the conflict. Brokerage later included other factions with a more urban, middle-class outlook, such as Liwa al-Haq in Homs, which further bolstered Ahrar al-Sham's politicisation, since these factions would figure prominently in the group's political bureau.[24]

Ahrar al-Sham expanded throughout insurgent-held areas through a strategy of cross-group alliances that reinforced its consensual decision-making at the leadership level. Ahrar al-Sham initiated major attempts to unite the armed opposition inside Syria. The group repeatedly attempted to include most Islamist-leaning brigades in larger fronts (*jabha*) that would pave the way for a meaningful organisational merger throughout Syria,[25] although many initiatives failed to achieve their objectives. The liberation of vast geographical areas, especially in northwest Syria, facilitated the process, but important obstacles remained. Ideological differences of views between various Islamist groups persisted. New opposition-held areas were not geographically contiguous, and their strategic significance was not understood similarly by the groups in control. For instance, while northwest Syria could be more easily stabilised through its connection to foreign countries, the periphery of Damascus in the Ghuta region was more threatening to Syria's capital. Other regions conversely remained under siege and could not easily coordinate with other provinces.

The transformation of Ahrar al-Sham into a large movement occurred through three successive initiatives. The first initiative was the creation of the Jabha Thuwar Suriyya (Front of the Revolutionaries of Syria) with several smaller Islamist factions. The front failed to yield its objectives since contending groups did not endorse Ahrar al-Sham's lead and, more importantly, Ahrar al-Sham suffered from internal impediments. Ahrar al-Sham's leaders abroad tried to present an acceptable political programme that was not well understood by group members on the ground, who often had a different understanding of the conflict.[26] Although Ahrar al-Sham benefitted from the more refined political understanding of its leaders abroad, the latter recognised that they were developing a mainstream political programme too quickly, without clarifying and legitimising their rationales to the foot soldiers.

Then, Ahrar al-Sham created the Syrian Islamic Front in December 2012, with Al-Haqq Brigades in Homs, the Al-Fajr Islamic Movement in Aleppo, Ansar al-Sham in Latakia, Jaysh Al-Tawhid in Deir ez-Zor and the Hamza ibn Abd al-Muttalib Brigade in Damascus.[27] This front paved the way to these groups' subsequent unification – with the exception of al-Haq Brigades – under the name 'Islamic Movement of Ahrar al-Sham'. Ahrar al-Sham leaders recognised that many new sub-groups had a more Salafi-jihadi approach to Islam than themselves; yet, they acknowledged that in a competitive environment where Salafi-jihadi groups like Jabhat al-Nusra were expanding, it was necessary to co-opt and integrate smaller Salafi-jihadi brigades rather than abandon them to their contenders.[28] Integrating less experienced groups was an opportunity to challenge their approach to the conflict and integrate them into Ahrar al-Sham's mainstream.[29]

Ahrar al-Sham's organisational expansion and associated transformation into a movement consolidated the group's outreach. All the new factions were successfully integrated into the group's consultative council, regardless of their size,[30] and endowed with responsibility for strategic decision-making, while their leaders were given specific missions and responsibilities in opposition-held areas. Externally, a charter expressing the group's political positions and its willingness to include new factions in the group was published.[31] Some group leaders felt that the charter sent a signal of inclusiveness that contrasted with Salafi-jihadi groups. For example, Ahrar al-Sham describes its *manhaj* (method or approach to Islam) to be in the middle and moderate. Although Ahrar al-Sham subsequently clarified further its willingness to be considered a main actor of the revolutionary process, the charter had already positioned the group in Syria's mainstream opposition.

The final major step occurred with the emergence of the Islamic Front in late 2013. Ahrar al-Sham's objectives were to unite the major Islamist groups throughout the country into an all-encompassing umbrella, before integrating them organisationally. The emergence of the Islamic Front occurred in parallel to growing tensions with Islamic State, a few months before Syria's mainstream opposition launched a war against Islamic State and expelled the group from many regions in northwest Syria. The creation of the IF eased the future integration of several groups into Ahrar al-Sham, including Liwa al-Haq and Suqur al-Sham,[32] but did not achieve broader unity with a major actor such as Jaysh al-Islam for geographical, ideological and administrative reasons pertaining to each group's new responsibilities, power and share of resources in the new entity.[33] In addition, discussions with Jabhat al-Nusra did not lead to the group's inclusion in the Islamic Front, since its leaders believed that the Front was not a meaningful unification of the opposition.[34]

By 2014, Ahrar al-Sham maintained a dual structure on the ground. The group's sub-brigades maintained their geographical location and local embeddedness, which positioned Ahrar al-Sham at the core of local Syrian communities. At a more hierarchical level, the group promoted these brigades' leaders into the group's overall leadership according to their strength or specific skills. Ahrar al-Sham did not sever its brigades' connection to their local leaders and local constituencies, which helped to sustain the group's popular grounding at the possible cost of organisational cohesion. In contrast to more Salafi-jihadi groups like Islamic State, where sub-groups were more easily recomposed and isolated from their commanders, Ahrar al-Sham did not impose tight control over its brigades and could not prevent them from leaving the group. This choice meant that Ahrar al-Sham's leadership had to be more responsive to the needs and expectations of its sub-units. Ahrar al-Sham could not impose top-down decisions without risking the departure of its sub-component for competing groups.

Ahrar al-Sham's characteristics and choices explain why, by 2013–14, the group had become the most successful one in Syria. Its military strengths and broad alliance system with other groups surpassed its main competitor, Jabhat al-Nusra, which would be critically weakened at the beginning of

2013, due to its split from Islamic State. Whereas other groups were struggling to survive the disappearance of their leaders, Ahrar al-Sham managed to develop relatively advanced internal institutions within a short time-span. Although internal issues remained, the group was able to conduct internal reforms more so than the groups that were only unified by foreign support or a succession of military victories.

The Politicisation of an Insurrectionary Revolutionary Project

The politicisation of Ahrar al-Sham occurred gradually during the war. This process was sustained by pre-war factors as well as in-war dynamics, which urged Ahrar al-Sham to clarify its ideological positions and embrace the revolutionary agenda of the opposition. These factors gradually informed Ahrar al-Sham's dissociation from jihadi Salafism, although the next section reveals the existence of real institutional impediments.

The first notable factor underpinning Ahrar al-Sham's politicisation is the nature of its popular constituency (*hadina sha'biyya*). As noted above, Ahrar al-Sham emerged in northwest Syria from the bottom up, in contrast to many Salafi-jihadi groups spearheaded by foreign fighters or nationals coming home from lands of foreign jihad.[35] Ahrar al-Sham, meanwhile, has been manned primarily by local fighters originating from a mostly Sunni region, often connected to the families that militarily opposed the regime in the late 1970s and early 1980s.[36] In contrast to smaller groups mobilised around a shared foreign nationality – for instance, being Moroccan or Chechen[37] – Ahrar al-Sham has relied primarily on local rather than foreign manpower. Relying on the local support of the population rather than an external support network constrains insurgent actions and can, for instance, restrict their use of violence.[38]

At the same time, some of the group's members had been socialised into the Salafi-jihadi trend before 2011. According to several interviews, they stem from a plural array of backgrounds and various levels of religiosity, but eventually embraced the Salafi-jihadi approach to Islam in response to the changing regional and international environment.[39] The US-led wars in Afghanistan and Iraq, as in other countries in the region,[40] boosted the sympathy for this approach to Islam, in response to the external threats to the Muslim world. This is particularly true for the younger generations, who often mobilised in support of the Iraqi resistance to the American occupation of the country. The youths became Salafi-jihadi when this ideological trend was perceived as the only credible alternative in the region.

Many future Ahrar al-Sham leaders had already started a process of revising Salafi-jihadi ideas in prison prior to 2011. According to prison leaders connected to Ahrar al-Sham, thousands of individuals were arrested in the mid-2000s and imprisoned in Saydnayya.[41] Some of them had been or tried to go to Iraq in support of the anti-American armed resistance, provided logistical support to the insurgents, or simply sympathised with them. Prison regrouped different generations of Islamists, from the first generation of the late 1970s to young al-Qaida supporters. The prisoners had to organise themselves and make decisions as a group. Notable discussions concerned jihad and its practicalities in Syria. Against the backdrop of al-Qaida's spiral of violence in Iraq, prisoners reflected on their objectives in Syria and the complementarity of political and military means to achieve them. They notably contested al-Qaida's main military focus and the contradictions between Salafi-jihadi ideas and their real-life implementations. A prison uprising in 2008 made some prisoners move in favour of a military solution, but the majority asked for negotiations and formed the core group of former prisoners that joined Ahrar al-Sham in 2011 and 2012.[42] As a result, Ahrar al-Sham members who were close to the group's first leader, Hassan Aboud, confirm that he insisted they would never join al-Qaida when they left prison. While some Ahrar al-Sham supporters were Salafi-jihadis relatively sympathetic to the group, the early leaders had an antagonistic stance towards al-Qaida early on.

Ahrar al-Sham's multi-level networking structure reinforced this dynamic at the beginning of the conflict. The joining of Syrians fighters who participated in foreign jihad while opposing al-Qaida's agenda further distanced Ahrar al-Sham from jihadi Salafism. Prominent individuals such as Iyyad al-Sha'ar and, later, Abul-Abbas al-Shami warned the group against al-Qaida's influence. Al-Sha'ar notably argues that the he wrote the group's initial political programme, although it was not initially embraced by other leaders.[43] These Syrians were well connected abroad and, in Istanbul, liaised with many Islamist groups dwelling in Turkey, from Hamas to the Egyptian Islamic Group (*al-Jamaa al-Islamiyya*), to learn from their experience, to develop Ahrar al-Sham in Syria and to achieve the right balance between political and military means and objectives.[44]

The first few years of the conflict further bolstered the politicisation of Ahrar al-Sham. The main factor was the de-centralised structure of the opposition, especially in Syria's northwest, where Ahrar al-Sham was particularly powerful. Geographical, sociological and ideological divisions impacted the militarisation of the conflict and prevented the emergence of a unified front, despite Ahrar al-Sham's attempts to unite the opposition. Ahrar al-Sham leaders recognised that, among the opposition, they still needed to coordinate military battles, share spoils of wars and recognise each other's legitimacy. Only Islamic State refused to do so, declaring that, as a state, it could not accept the prerogatives of independent courts of justice manned by independent or factional preachers. A related element was practical. Once the armed opposition became the *de facto* ruler of extensive geographical areas, how to govern the population? None of the armed group had the experience to set up local structures of governance. They had to collaborate with other groups in Islamic committees and courts designed to support the population and stabilise security, which sometimes competed with civil-society-led initiatives.[45] External assistance provided by foreign non-governmental organisations (NGOs) also became a new reality that groups like Ahrar al-Sham had to acknowledge.

Furthermore, the armed opposition, and Ahrar al-Sham in particular, faced the rise of Islamic State. Despite Ahrar al-Sham's antagonistic position on al-Qaida, Islamic State could initially prosper and mobilise in opposition-held areas after the split from Jabhat al-Nusra. But, less than a year later, Islamic State imposed its hegemonic control over the eastern province of Raqqa, which had initially been liberated from the regime by Ahrar al-Sham and other groups. In addition to Islamic State's military danger, the regional and international threat posed by the group forced Ahrar al-Sham to further clarify its positions. Inside Syria, Ahrar al-Sham members were often reluctant to fight fellow Muslims.[46] Outside Syria, Islamic State's behaviour started to draw international attention to the Syrian Islamist armed groups opposed to the regime. Ahrar al-Sham leaders did not want to be assimilated into the group in people's minds and, therefore, had to demonstrate that they were fully part of Syria's mainstream opposition and embraced its revolutionary objectives.[47] They presented the revolutionary covenant of honour of the fighting brigades (*Mithaq sharaf thawri li al-kataib al-muqātila*) for that purpose and to oppose the dichotomy between Syrian Islamists and the Free Syrian Army.[48] The group confirmed its willingness to collaborate with foreign countries for the sake of the revolution, and this process was accompanied by growing international public relations efforts.

Ahrar al-Sham then tried to weaken Islamic State by providing direct assistance to Jabhat al-Nusra to help it survive the split between the latter two groups. Not helping Jabhat al-Nusra to survive would have benefitted Islamic State, which would have eventually gathered all of the former's resources and soldiers.[49] Although Ahrar al-Sham initially wanted to use Jabhat al-Nusra as a counterweight to Islamic State and encouraged it to join the Islamic Front, Jabhat al-Nusra subsequently became a threat in its own right. Jabhat al-Nusra tried to set up its own governing structures and successively dismantled several opposition groups.[50] But Jabhat al-Nusra's threat to Ahrar al-Sham was also ideological. When Jabhat al-Nusra started to become a larger group, its ideological proximity to Ahrar al-Sham threatened the latter's internal cohesion. Ahrar al-Sham leaders recognised that, after socialising young fighters around ideological concepts stemming from a shared approach to Islam, it became easy for Jabhat al-Nusra to recruit them. Ahrar al-Sham therefore had to develop a new distinctive identity around a flag, musical chants (*nashīd*) and shared history to protect the group's internal cohesion. Despite military collaboration with Jabhat al-Nusra, Ahrar al-Sham refused to unite with the group as long as Jabhat al-Nusra's ties to al-Qaida remained. Jabhat al-Nusra's affiliation to al-Qaida indeed warranted increased military strikes from foreign countries, such as the United States, and justified the narrative articulated by the regime.

Ahrar al-Sham additionally refined its religious approach by re-emphasising internally the importance of the Islamic schools of jurisprudence (*madhhab*), arguing that the Salafi reticence to recognise their role has severed the ties between Muslims and their scholars. Ahrar al-Sham's scholars published an array of publications justifying its political pragmatism considering the group's weakness and for the interest (*maṣlaḥa*) of the community, by aligning its position with *siyāsat al-sharīʿa* (*sharīʿa* politics), which is partially associated with the tradition of Ibn Taymīyyah, a mainstream Salafi reference.[51] But Jabhat al-Nusra's embeddedness in the Syrian opposition meant that these efforts were not sufficient to contain the group. In contrast with

Islamic State's expulsion from opposition-held areas, Jabhat al-Nusra continued to expand alongside the other armed opposition.

Institutional Constraints and Power Politics

Ahrar al-Sham expressed the desire to unite all the armed opposition by summer 2014, in collaboration with the main armed groups present throughout Syria. The initiative sought to create the council of the leadership of the revolution (*Majlis Qiyādat al-Thawra*), which would comprehensively unite the opposition's political and military structures and present a common front to the regime. The initiative nonetheless stumbled when other groups presented a competitive similar initiative; more importantly, cross-factional negotiations collapsed when most of Ahrar al-Sham's leaders were killed in an explosion in September 2014. The date marked the beginning of Ahrar al-Sham's institutional decay, which inhibited the group's decision-making process at the leadership level.

The killing of the group's leaders in September 2014 was a major institutional setback. The first and second leadership tiers of Ahrar al-Sham were decimated during a group meeting. Most *shūrā* members were killed, and the remaining leaders had to name the new leadership in a hurry to form a new *majlis al-shūrā*. While Ahrar al-Sham's relatively advanced institutions eased its survival in comparison to the groups that disappeared after the killing of one or two figureheads, the killing delayed its politicisation for the next two years.[52]

The core issue pertained to the newly named leadership. The new leaders were not all part of Ahrar al-Sham's early core membership. The three main figures were Hashim al-Shaykh (general leader), Abu Muhammad al-Sadiq (religious authority) and Abu Saleh al-Tahhan (military commander). Al-Shaykh had only joined the group in a latter phase and, along with al-Tahhan, froze group membership before the killing of Ahrar al-Sham leaders. Al-Sadiq was a newcomer to the group. These individuals were lesser known internally and did not enjoy the same level of sympathy as the former leadership. Moreover, although not affiliated with al-Qaida, their ideological positions were not necessarily aligned with the revisionist positions gradually endorsed by the assassinated leadership. They initially tried to impose their authority by isolating many Ahrar al-Sham founders and dictating their views. Internally contested decisions marginalised early Ahrar al-Sham leaders, some of whom split to form a new group, Jaysh al-Sham (Army of the Levant), which fully embraced the Syrian revolutionary agenda.[53]

For the next two years, two revisionist and obstructing factions contended to sway the group in their direction.[54] The revisionist faction included most of Ahrar al-Sham's early members who remained in the group and increasingly embraced the Syrian revolutionary agenda. They wanted to forge closer ties to foreign countries, especially Turkey, and other armed opposition groups. The obstructionists opposed this choice and prioritised a military strategy that was suspicious of the revisionists' political agenda. The obstructionists managed to control the group for the next six months while the revisionists vied to internally strengthen their position to isolate the new leadership. The revisionists notably exploited the integration of new factions as well as internal bureaucratic quarrels to reposition themselves step by step. They gradually seized the initiative through the group's political bureau and their majority in the group's *majlis al-shūrā*, which led to the election of a figure situated between the two sides the following year – Muhannad al-Masri. The new leader used his administrative authority to further marginalise the obstructing faction and gradually demote them of their prerogatives.[55] The head of Jaysh al-Sham lamented that the group had become clogged by lobby politics (*lūbbyāt*) since the September 2014 death of its top leadership. The existence of bureaucratic feuds instead of large-scale splits or a violent internal purge nonetheless substantiates that both sides accepted the group's key institutional features.[56]

The group's religious voice was a notable object of administrative dispute. A single controversial religious cleric, al-Sadiq, was designated after 2014 and subsequently attempted to obtain a veto over the group's strategy. While Ahrar al-Sham's key religious figures before September 2014 broadly endorsed the same revisionist views, religious divergences between the revisionist faction and al-Sadiq imposed an internal reconfiguration when the former reasserted themselves. They notably decided that having a single religious authority antagonistic to Ahrar al-Sham's unfolding political agenda was an impediment to the group's development.[57] They created instead an office composed of several figures who would make decisions based on the opinion of the majority. The designation of several individuals diluted the role played by a single cleric and was more amenable to the group's pragmatism.[58] Some of Ahrar al-Sham's religious figures, especially three Egyptians,[59] nonetheless continued to oppose the group's rapprochement with foreign countries, in particular Turkey. Moreover, they strongly condemned the efforts of the head of Ahrar al-Sham's international relations to reach out to Western countries from summer 2015 onwards.[60] When Ahrar al-Sham published a *fatwa* legitimising collaboration with Turkey in the north of the country,[61] these clerics were removed from their positions for opposing the group's political choices and ultimately presented their resignation.[62]

Bureaucratic quarrels delayed Ahrar al-Sham's full embrace of Syria's mainstream revolutionary path despite real steps forwards. Ahrar al-Sham remained plagued by internal divisions until the end of 2016. The group's consensual decision-making process at the *majlis al-shūrā* prevented the group from articulating clear positions on an array of issues, including the conference of Riyadh organised in December 2015. Paradoxically, the consensual and inclusive features that sustained Ahrar al-Sham's appeal during the first three years of the conflict burdened the group in the following two years. As a result, although Ahrar al-Sham became closer to Turkey henceforth, the group was an ally burdened by serious internal concerns. An armed opposition group that cannot take a clear stance on decisive strategic developments does not make a potent alternative.

Ultimately, the loss of Aleppo by the Syrian opposition at the end of 2016 helped to settle Ahrar al-Sham's internal conflicts. In September 2016, Ahrar al-Sham revisionists elected a new leader associated with their faction, Ali al-Omar. The obstructing faction disputed the outcome of the elections since they believed that they were now entitled to the leadership. They temporarily froze their membership in the *majlis al-shūrā*[63] and intensified internal pressure with an unauthorised decision to create a new military sub-group, Jaysh al-Ahrar (Army of the Free), to demonstrate their internal strength and change the outcome of internal elections.[64] It is notable that they did not resign immediately, but still sought to control the group. But they ultimately failed to impose their views and used the opportunity presented by Jabhat al-Nusra's new iteration, Jabha Fath al-Sham (Front of the Liberation of the Levant), to attempt to unite the opposition by leaving Ahrar al-Sham and joining a new group, Ha'ya Tahrir al-Sham (The Committed for the

Liberation of the Levant). They departed with less than a thousand soldiers but extensive military supplies.[65] Most of Ahrar al-Sham's cadres remained in the movement.

Retrospectively, the timing of the obstructionist faction's departure from the group can be explained by three main reasons. First, the last internal elections demonstrated that they did not enjoy the support of the majority of the *majlis al-shūrā* and that it would be difficult to ever control the group again. Second, Jabha Fath al-Sham's overture meant that they would not lose everything. Staying inside Ahrar al-Sham was previously rationalised by the understanding that the incumbent would keep control over the group's resources and supporting networks. It was better to remain in Ahrar al-Sham and try to change the balance of power from inside. But Jabha Fath al-Sham was a potent alternative in early 2017. Finally, the battle of Aleppo was a strategic turning point that imposed a political and military choice – between a decisive rapprochement and collaboration with Turkey on the political front versus an emphasis on the military dimension of the revolution, which required unity with Jabha Fath al-Sham.

The departure of Jaysh al-Ahrar reinforced Ahrar al-Sham's politicisation, but an intra-factional conflict with Haya Tahrir al-Sham then fractured northwest Syria. At the beginning of 2017, Ahrar al-Sham embraced the Syrian opposition's flag and the Arab penal code that was to be implemented in the areas controlled by the Syrian opposition.[66] Shortly thereafter, a factional confrontation with Haya Tahrir al-Sham throughout opposition-held areas in northwest Syria turned in favour of the latter, which significantly weakened Ahrar al-Sham. Although Ahrar al-Sham was initially reinforced by the joining of smaller armed opposition groups that sought protection,[67] it was not sufficient to maintain control over several strategic areas including the lucrative border with Turkey in Baab al-Hawa. The groups that joined Ahrar al-Sham were not fully integrated in the *majlis al-shūrā*,[68] and the localised structure of Ahrar al-Sham was exploited by Haya Tahrir al-Sham; the latter systematically isolated Ahrar al-Sham's geographical strongholds by creating sub-groups and relying on local agreements to isolate these areas from the larger confrontation.[69] Ahrar al-Sham's central military force was weakened by the internal split and mostly unable to mobilise against its contender. While Ahrar al-Sham's local embeddedness was a strength when facing an external enemy, the conflict with Haya Tahrir al-Sham demonstrated that it could backfire when an opponent had geographically movable military forces more efficient than Ahrar al-Sham's. The conflict resumed one year later, in spring of 2017. Ahrar al-Sham's new alliance with another local group, the Nour al-Din Zinki Movement, the formation of the Syrian Liberation Front and the naming of a new leader changed the outcome of the final confrontation and re-equilibrated the balance of power with Haya Tahrir al-Sham.

Meanwhile, the Syrian conflict became increasingly dominated by big power dynamics. From the beginning of the Russian-led Astana process, Turkey and Russia asserted their dominance over the political process and designated several de-escalation zones throughout Syria. These zones were gradually re-occupied by the regime through military pressure, internal divisions and the limited reintegration of former fighters under the so-called 'reconciliation' processes. The opposition stronghold of Ghuta in the suburbs of Damascus was reconquered by regime forces in April 2018, while the south of Syria followed suit by the end of July. Turkey simultaneously encouraged the formation of a united opposition front, the National Front for Liberation, which could pave the way to the development of a national army in the north of the country as well as in the province of Idlib. But a new round of conflicts ultimately gave the upper hand to Haya Tahrir al-Sham, which imposed its administrative control over all of northwest Syria and substantially weakened all remaining opposition groups, including Ahrar al-Sham.

Conclusion

Ahrar al-Sham is a singular case of a Salafi group that politicised during a civil war by articulating increasingly realistic political objectives, engaging with foreign states and non-Islamist groups and adopting a moderate position vis-à-vis the population. This development is rooted in the group's embeddedness within the Syrian Islamic social movement before 2011, which extensively debated al-Qaida's negative legacy on the jihadi movement and looked for an alternative Islamist project that would be different from the Muslim Brotherhood as well as al-Qaida. This process was subsequently bolstered by in-war factors, especially the unprecedented diversity of the armed opposition and the negative consequences of al-Qaida and Islamic State's behaviour both inside and outside Syria. The peculiarities of the Syrian conflict forced Ahrar al-Sham to confirm and cultivate its politicisation in response.

This case-study further suggests that Salafi armed groups can transform during a civil war, but that successful transformation is contingent on their institutionalisation. Existing research excessively focuses on Salafi armed groups' ideologies or individual leaders, without exploring more thoroughly the institutional factors faced by these groups. Analysing the consolidation of Salafi armed groups' organisational structures and ideational norms is critical to contextualising internal debates, decision-making processes and armed groups' internal cohesion beyond the study of their theological commitments only.

Notes

1. This chapter was presented at several conferences and workshops. I would like to thank Souhail Belhadj, Véronique Dudouet, Abdulla Erfan, Karin Goldner-Ebenthal, Tore Hamming, Sam Heller, Fouad Ilias, Aron Lund, Mona Sheikh, Nagwan Soliman and Isak Svensson for commenting on previous versions of this chapter. I also received financial support from the Swiss National Science Foundation (SNSF) and the Project on Middle East Political Science (POMEPS).
2. Barak Mendelsohn, *The al-Qaeda Franchise: the Expansion of al-Qaeda and its Consequences* (Oxford: Oxford University Press, 2015); Jérôme Drevon, 'The Jihadi Social Movement (JSM) Between Factional Hegemonic Drive, National Realities, and Transnational Ambitions', *Perspectives on Terrorism* 11 (2017), 55–62; Hassan Hassan, 'Two Houses Divided: How Conflict in Syria Shaped the Future of Jihadism', *CTC Sentinel* (2018).
3. Ahmed S. Hashim, *The Caliphate at War: The Ideological, Organisational and Military Innovations of Islamic State* (Oxford: Oxford University Press, 2018).
4. As emphasised by two common definitions: https://dictionary.cambridge.org/dictionary/english/politicize and www.collinsdictionary.com/dictionary/english/politicize.
5. Joas Wagemakers, *A Quietist Jihadi: The Ideology and Influence of Abu Muhammad al-Maqdisi* (Cambridge: Cambridge University Press, 2012), 147–90.
6. During field research, armed groups repeatedly emphasised their engagement with political matters over time, in contrast to pure military objectives. They often associated it with pragmatism more than moderation or de-radicalisation, terms they do not use.

7. Jillian Schwedler, *Faith in Moderation: Islamist Parties in Jordan and Yemen* (Cambridge: Cambridge University Press, 2006).
8. Omar Ashour, *The De-Radicalization of Jihadists: Transforming Armed Islamist Movements* (Abingdon; New York: Routledge, 2009).
9. Interviews with a large range of Syrian Islamists and insurgents. See also Arnaud Lenfant, 'L'évolution du salafisme en Syrie au XXe siècle', in *Qu'est-ce que le salafisme*, ed. B. Rougier (Paris: Presses Universitaires de France, 2008), 161–78; Line Khatib, *Islamic Revivalism in Syria: The Rise and Fall of Ba'thist Secularism* (Abingdon: Routledge, 2011); Muhammad Mustafa, *Jabhat al-Nusra li-ahl al-sham: Min al-ta'sif ila al-inqisam*, Arab Center for Research and Policy Studies (2012); Abd al-Rahman Al-Haj, *Al-Salafiyya wal-salafiyun fi suriya: Min al-islah ila al-jihad*, Al-Jazeera Center for Studies (2013); Teije H. Donker, 'Islamic Social Movements and the Syrian Authoritarian Regime: Shifting Patterns of Control and Accommodation', in *Middle East Authoritarianisms: Governance, Contestation, and Regime Resilience in Syria and Iran*, ed. S. Heydemann and Raymond Leenders (Palo Alto: Stanford University Press, 2013), 107–24; Raymond A. Hinnebusch, 'State and Islamism in Syria', in *Islamic Fundamentalism* (London: Routledge, 2018), 199–214; Dara Conduit, *The Muslim Brotherhood in Syria* (Cambridge: Cambridge University Press, 2019); Abd al-Rahman Al-Haj, *Thawahir al-islam al-siyasi wa tayarato fi suriya isti'ada khiyar al-dimuqrati* (n. d.).
10. Thomas Pierret, *Religion and State in Syria: The Sunni Ulama from Coup to Revolution*, vol. 41 (Cambridge: Cambridge University Press, 2013).
11. Stefan Malthaner and Peter Waldmann, 'The Radical Milieu: Conceptualizing the Supportive Social Environment of Terrorist Groups', *Studies in Conflict & Terrorism* 37 (2014), 979.
12. Raphael Lefèvre, *Ashes of Hama: The Muslim Brotherhood in Syria* (London: Hurst, 2013).
13. Stéphane Lacroix, *Awakening Islam: The Politics of Religious Dissent in Contemporary Saudi Arabia*, trans. George Holoch (Cambridge, MA: Harvard University Press, 2011).
14. Hinnebusch, 'State and Islamism in Syria'. See also note 9.
15. Adam Baczko, Gilles Dorronsoro and Arthur Quesnay, *Civil War in Syria: Mobilization and Competing Social Orders* (Cambridge: Cambridge University Press, 2018), 103–17.
16. Khaled Abu Anas, interview with the author; Abu Abd al-Rahman al-Suri, interview with the author; member of Ahrar al-Sham political bureau, interview with the author. Ahrar al-Sham's leader cannot take strategic decisions without a

majority in the *shura* council and cannot name new *shura* members without the council's approval.

17. Abu Abd al-Rahman al-Suri, interview with the author.
18. Khaled Abu Anas, interview with the author.
19. Ahmad Abazeid and Thomas Pierret, 'Les rebelles syriens d'Ahrar al-Sham: Ressorts contextuels et organisationnels d'une déradicalisation en temps de guerre civile', *Critique Internationale* 1 (2018), 63–84.
20. On the limits of foreign influence, see also Thomas Pierret, 'States Sponsors and the Syrian Insurgency: The Limits of Foreign Influence', in *Inside Wars: Local Dynamics of Conflicts in Syria and Libya*, ed. Luigi Narbone, Agnes Favier and Virginie Collombier (Florence: European University Institute, 2016), 22–28.
21. Henning Tamm, 'Rebel Leaders, Internal Rivals, and External Resources: How State Sponsors Affect Insurgent Cohesion', *International Studies Quarterly* 60 (2016), 599–610.
22. Thomas Pierret, 'Les Salafismes dans l'insurrection syrienne: Des réseaux transnationaux à l'épreuve des réalités locales', *Outre-Terre* 3 (2015), 196–215.
23. Husam Tarsha, interview with the author.
24. Labib and Kenan al-Nahhas from Liwa al-Haq joined Ahrar al-Sham's *majlis al-shūrā* when their group joined Ahrar al-Sham. They later became Ahrar al-Sham's heads of international relations and of the political bureau, respectively.
25. Munir al-Sayyal, interview with the author; Khaled Abu Anas, interview with the author.
26. Khaled Abu Anas, interview with the author; Husam Tarsha, interview with the author.
27. On the Islamic Front, see Aron Lund, 'Syria's Salafi Insurgents: The Rise of the Syrian Islamic Front', *UI Occasional Papers* 17 (2013).
28. Husam Tarsha, interview with the author.
29. The leader of al-Fajr Islamic Movement, Abu Yazan al-Shami, famously apologised in September 2014 for his affiliation with jihadi Salafism. See https://justpaste.it/gybk. See also Sam Heller, 'Ahrar al-Sham's Revisionist Jihadism', *War on the Rocks* 30 (2015).
30. The situation changed for the factions that joined Ahrar al-Sham subsequently, according to Khaled Abu Anas.
31. Ahrar al-Sham, *Mithaq harakat ahrar al-sham al-islamiyya* (2012).
32. Suqur al-Sham left subsequently.

33. Munir al-Sayyal, interview with the author; Khaled Abu Anas, interview with the author; Abu al-ʻAbbas al-Shami, interview with the author. Islam Alloush, interview with the author.
34. Abu Abdullah al-Shami, interview with the author.
35. Most Islamist insurgencies where Salafi-jihadi groups have been active were partially launched by nationals who had been in Afghanistan in the late 1980s (as in Algeria in the 1990s), or by international fighters (as in Iraq in the 2000s).
36. According to many testimonies, including that of Rami Dalati, interview with the author. See also 'Film ahrar al-sham', *al-Jazeera Arabic*, www.youtube.com/watch?v=_lydv7dr6qE.
37. For instance, Junud al-Sham (Soldiers of the Levant), primarily manned by Chechens, or Harakat Sham al-Islam (Islamic Movement of the Levant) recruiting Moroccan fighters.
38. Monica D. Toft and Yuri M. Zhukov, 'Islamists and Nationalists: Rebel Motivation and Counterinsurgency in Russia's North Caucasus', *American Political Science Review* 109 (2015), 222–38.
39. Munir al-Sayyal, interview with the author. See also 'Film ahrar al-sham'.
40. Drevon, 'The Jihadi Social Movement'.
41. Abul-ʻAbbas al-Shami, interview with the author; Rami Dalati, interview with the author. See also Khatib, *Islamic Revivalism*.
42. Rami Dalati, interview with the author.
43. Ayyad al-Shaʻar, interview with the author.
44. Ibid.
45. On insurgent courts, see also Baczko, Dorronsoro and Quesnay, *Civil War in Syria*; Regine Schwab, 'Insurgent Courts in Civil Wars: The Three Pathways of (Trans)Formation in Today's Syria (2012–2017)', *Small Wars & Insurgencies* 29 (2018), 801–26. On the local council, see Akram Kachee, 'Les conseils locaux syriens face à la militarisation du conflit', *Confluences Méditerranée* 4 (2016), 31–45.
46. For example, see the communiqué by Ahrar al-Sham on the exclusion of two subgroups for refusing to fight Islamist Social Movement in Ahmad Abazeid, *Ahrar al-sham baʻd ʻam tawil: Markaz ʻumran lil dirasat al-istratijiyya* (2015), 50.
47. Husam Tarsha, interview with the author; Munir al-Sayyal, interview with the author.
48. Ahrar al-Sham, *Mithaq sharaf thawri li al-kata'ib al-muqatila* (17 March 2014).
49. Husam Tarsha, interview with the author; Khaled Abu Anas, interview with the author.

50. Charles R. Lister, *The Syrian Jihad: Al-Qaeda, The Islamic State and the Evolution of an Insurgency* (Oxford: Oxford University Press, 2016), 223–25; Charles R. Lister, *Profiling Jabhat al-Nusra* (Washington DC: Brookings Institution Press, 2016), 16–18.
51. Ahrar al-Sham, *Al-uṣul al-shar li-l'amal al-islamī al-mu'asir* (n. d.); Ahrar al-Sham, *Al-istid'af wal-tamkin bayna mu'tayat al-waqi'a wa aḥkam al-dīn* (n. d.); Ahrar al-Sham, *Al-qawl al-mubin fi tartib maqāsid al-sharī'ah wa maṣlaḥah al-nafs wa al dīn* (n. d.); Ahrar al-Sham, *masā'il fi al-siyāsat al-sharī'ah* (n. d.).
52. For a study of the group in the year following the killing, see Abazeid, *Ahrar al-sham ba'd 'am tawil: Markaz 'umran lil dirāsat al-istratijīyah* (2015).
53. Abu Abd al-Rahman al-Suri, interview with the author. On this group, see also Ahmad Abazeid, *Jaysh al-Sham: Harakiyya al-shimal al-suriyya al-mustadama: Markaz 'umran lil dirasat al-istratijiyya* (2015).
54. Revisionists referred to the concept of *murāja'āt* (revisions), emphasised by Ahrar al-Sham's leaders.
55. See the details in Abazeid and Pierret, 'Les rebelles syriens d'Ahrar al-Sham', 72–73. See also Ahrar al-Sham, *qarar idari 84/a* (7 May 2016); Ahrar al-Sham, *qarar idari 86/a* (2 June 2016); Ahrar al-Sham, *qarar idari 89/a* (18 June 2016).
56. There have been limited internal altercations, including kidnappings, but the scale has remained very limited compared to other cases of internal factional purges.
57. Khaled Abu Anas, interview with the author.
58. The institutionalisation of a religious clergy in opposition to the influence of a single religious authority has an interesting comparable precedent in Saudi Arabia with the creation of the Council of Senior Scholars in 1972: Nabil Mouline, *The Clerics of Islam: Religious Authority and Political Power in Saudi Arabia* (New Haven: Yale University Press, 2014).
59. Abu al-'Abd Ashida, Abu Fath al-Farghali and Abu Yaqthan al-Masri.
60. See, for instance, an op-ed published in the US by Labib al-Nahhas, 'The Deadly Consequences of Mislabeling Syria's Revolutionaries', *Washington Post* (10 July 2015).
61. Ahrar al-Sham, *Fatawā bikhusus qitāl da'ish bi al-tanfiq ma' al-jaysh al-turki* (20 September 2016).
62. Ahrar al-Sham, *Mujahidu ashida* (20 September 2016); Aranews, 'Inshiqaq fi ahrar al-sham ba'd fatwā jawaz al-tansiq ma' al-atrak did da'ish' [Splits in Ahrar al-Sham after the *Fatwa* allowing coordination with the Turks against ISIS] (22 September 2016).

63. Ahrar al-Sham, 'Freezing Membership' (2016).
64. Ahrar al-Sham, 'Creation of Jaysh al-Ahrar' (12 December 2016); Ahrar al-Sham, 'Joining Jaysh al-Ahrar' (12 December 2016). See also Haid Haid, 'Why Ahrar al-Sham is Fighting Itself – And How This Impacts the Battle for Syria', *Middle East Eye* (2016).
65. Husam Tarsha, interview with the author.
66. Ahrar al-Sham, *Hukm raf' 'alam al-thawrah al-suriyya, ha'ya al-da'wha wa al-rishad* (2017).
67. Ahrar al-Sham, *Bayan mushtarak min kubra al-fasa'il al-thawriyya fi al-shimal* (26 January 2017); Ahrar al-Sham, 'Joining of New Factions' (26 January 2017).
68. Khaled Abu Anas, interview with the author.
69. Abu Abd al-Rahman al-Suri, interview with the author; Ahmad Abazeid, *Kayf anharat harakat ahrar al-sham? Markaz 'umran lil dirasat al-istratijiyya* (2017).

10

FILLING GAPS LEFT BY THE MUSLIM BROTHERHOOD: THE EXPERIENCE IN PALESTINE

Belal Shobaki

Islamists have never been a separate entity in the Palestinian national movement – ever since it began to take shape in the middle of the last century they have been very much part of the national fabric and of the revolution against the occupation, without any discrete ideological considerations to distinguish them. For example, since its inception the Fatah faction included prominent Palestinian Islamist figures. However, many factors, at the national and regional levels, subsequently contributed to the emergence of separate Islamic movements. These factors included the role reversal of the Palestine Liberation Organization (PLO) after its problems with Jordan and Lebanon, the collapse of its alliance with Saddam following his defeat in the Gulf War that later led to the loss of the Gulf's support and the outbreak of the first Palestinian Intifada in 1987. The most prominent of the Islamic movements to emerge in the wake of these contributing factors was the Islamic Resistance Movement (Hamas). Since its formation, Hamas has been eminently placed as the second-largest Palestinian faction after Fatah.

Through its ideological and organisational links with the Muslim Brotherhood, Hamas has remained the strongest Islamic movement in Palestine, even in the presence of the Islamic Jihad, the Islamic Liberation Party and the Salafi Da'wa groups. It functioned for decades – as a faction adopting military resistance against the Israeli occupation – without the existence of Salafi-jihadists in the Palestine region. However, since Hamas's participation in the 2006 legislative elections, Salafi-jihadists have begun to appear dramatically, particularly in Gaza.

This chapter argues that the emergence of the Salafi-jihadism in Palestine results from the gap between the political formation of Hamas's members over the course of the last two decades and its modern political behaviour. Hamas originally adopted a religious and non-reconciling discourse in educating its cadres, mostly young people. Then, it geared a new version of political discourse towards a democratic outlook – a discourse open to elections, political partnership with secular and Marxist parties, and political settlement with the Israeli occupation. But some of the movement's long-standing affiliates considered this new political trend to deviate from the norms on which they had been raised. Consequently, these individuals sought a new dynamic framework in line with their religious and intellectual upbringing – resulting, as this chapter argues, in a drift towards Salafi-jihadism.

Additional cofactors that led to the emergence of Salafi-jihadism will also be highlighted in this chapter, including those that contributed to the decline of the Muslim Brotherhood in general in the region after the Arab Spring, alongside the absence of the active role of the Salafi daʿwa in Palestine, which has opened up Palestine to regional changes. The spread of radical hatred discourse in the Arab media between followers of different sects and religions has also impacted Palestine, dividing its people who have fallen victim to this racist discourse.

The Roots of the Muslim Brotherhood in Palestine

The Muslim Brotherhood refuses to consider their activity in Palestine to be linked to the emergence of the Islamic Resistance Movement (Hamas). However, they are primarily referring to the latter's anti-Zionist activism. Although the emergence of Hamas in 1987 is considered to be the moment at which the Brotherhood made its strongest appearance in Palestine, the Brotherhood insists that it has in fact been present since the beginning of the British mandate. They consider themselves an extension of the Islamic groups that preceded their establishment, such as the 1919 Fedayeen Association, which included Haj Amin al-Husseini and Izz al-Din al-Qassam.

Before the establishment of Hamas and its vigorous work in the first Palestinian uprising (Intifada I), its founders had spent many years working with the Muslim Brotherhood in activities that were mostly seen as missionary work. Until 1952, the Brotherhood had enjoyed popularity and respect in Palestine; however, they were obliged to work secretively thereafter, due to Jamal Abdel Nasser's campaign against them in Egypt.[1] The secret activity, of a military nature, continued through the so-called 'Special Organisation' in Gaza, led by Abu Jihad Khalil al-Wazir, Abu Usama Khairy al-Agha and Muhammad al-Najjar, who were in contact with the Brotherhood leadership in Egypt through an intermediary named Muhammad Abu Sido. While the brothers of the West Bank were part of the Jordanian Brotherhood after the Jordanian annexation of the West Bank in 1950, they could do no more than some military training.

The Brotherhood's secret work did not lead to an evolution in their ability to influence – Jamal Abdel Nasser's campaign had pushed them into isolation. As a result, some of the Brotherhood members in Palestine wanted to join organisations aligned with a specific national identity, rather than organisation centred on Islamic identity. Therefore, they tried to establish a new national framework in which they would avoid confronting the Egyptian regime. However, Khalil al-Wazir, who carried the idea of establishing a new national framework to the Brotherhood leadership in the Gaza Strip, failed to receive their approval.

Despite this, Khalil al-Wazir continued to work on his idea away from the Muslim Brotherhood, with the participation of Yasser Arafat. Later, the Palestinian National Liberation Movement (Fatah) was founded and attracted a number of Brotherhood activists. Although the Muslim Brotherhood sought to present their own historical narrative by stating that it was part of the establishment of Fatah, the Brotherhood's rejection of Khalil al-Wazir's proposal had in fact heralded an important shift in the philosophy of influential leaders such as al-Wazir, Kamal Adwan and Salah Khalaf. This shift implanted a new faith in the need to form a Palestinian political framework free of the regional Arab burden.

However, in 1962 the Brotherhood attempted once again to establish its influence in Palestine and formed the Palestinian Brotherhood. Hani Bseiso was elected as a public observer.[2] This led to a change in the leadership hierarchy of the Brotherhood in Palestine. Their organisational work connected to Egypt continued, without any military role against the Israeli occupation, except for individuals participating under the umbrella of the Fatah faction between 1968 and 1970.

The 1970s witnessed a remarkable step by the brothers of Palestine, when the Palestinian organisation in Kuwait decided to spend 75 per cent of its budget on student activism. This enabled the Brotherhood to build a mass support base comprised mainly of university students. The students' activity in Kuwait was particularly prominent under the leadership of Khaled Mashaal because of the freedom offered by Kuwait to the Palestinians living there.[3] Meanwhile, in Egypt, Musa Abu Marzouq, Bashir Nafie and Fathi Shikaki succeeded in organising the Palestinian Islamic Movement in Egyptian universities. However, Shikaki left the Brotherhood influenced by the Iranian revolution and later established the Islamic Jihad Movement.

Back then, it seemed that the Muslim Brotherhood was also affected by the Iranian post-revolution period. Furthermore, it could be implied that they felt the danger of focusing solely on missionary and student-led activities without having a military presence with which to face Israeli occupation. This led them to establish a military wing (the Palestinian *mujāhidīn*, or the Palestinian Fighters) and a security wing (*majd*, meaning 'glory') in the early 1980s, later reconstructed between 1985 and 1986.[4]

At that point, the idea of participating in the military confrontation against the occupation had matured among the Brotherhood in Palestine. Their leadership made the decision to participate in future confrontations, but with caution so as not to be held responsible for the resulting turmoil if they failed. They ultimately waited for nearly three years before acting on this decision, until an incident on 8 December 1987, when four Palestinian workers were rammed by an Israeli truck. The Brotherhood leadership met in the Gaza Strip in the presence of Shaykh Ahmed Yassin, Abdel Aziz Rantissi and Abdel Fattah Dukhan, and they decided to initiate confrontations in various areas of the Gaza Strip. These began after Fajr (dawn prayer) on 9 December 1987, when demonstrations started in Jabalia Camp.

The Rise of Hamas

The Islamic Resistance Movement, Hamas, is a Palestinian movement founded in 1987 as a reaction to Israeli policies, specifically the beginning of the first Palestinian Intifada. Hamas is considered an intellectual extension of the worldwide Muslim Brotherhood movement. It was founded with the efforts of senior members of the Muslim Brotherhood in Palestine, most notably the late Shaykh Ahmed Yassin, Abdel Aziz Rantissi, Abdel Fattah Dukhan and Salah Shehadeh, who led the movement for a long time politically and militarily. In 1988, Hamas issued its political charter, which clarified its ideology; its relations to other political currents, the Arab and Islamic worlds and the international community; as well as its position on the occupation.[5]

Since 1988, Hamas has emerged mainly as a resistance movement with an interest in social action. Militarily, the activity of Hamas has evolved from its participation in popular confrontations to armed encounters with the occupation, using small arms and then suicide bombings, most notably in the mid-1990s. The movement has been criticised by all Western powers, culminating in Hamas being listed as a terrorist organisation by the United States and the European Union. In its social context, Hamas has been active in charitable activities through its provision of medical clinics, orphanages, *zakāt* committees and sport clubs. It offered services to the public freely or for a token charge which increased its popularity. Hamas's political role was limited to issuing statements illustrating the position of the movement on various policies of the occupation or of the PLO, the Palestinian Authority and other Palestinian factions.

When it was first established, Hamas benefitted from a number of external factors that aided its strength and presence. From a military perspective, one of these factors was the absence of the PLO and its most prominent constituent force, the Fatah movement, from the military scene in Palestine by 1987. The PLO and Fatah had originally launched the armed struggle from Jordan, but when they were expelled as a result of a crisis with the Jordanian monarchy, they moved to Lebanon, only to face the same fate after the 1982 war. As such, the Palestine Liberation Organisation (PLO) lost its ability to act militarily from neighbouring countries. Its transfer to Tunisia and the distribution of its cadres in North Africa ended its ability to act militarily at all against the Israeli occupation.

Politically, it was more complicated. The late Yasser Arafat's alliance with former Iraqi president, Saddam Hussein, and his support for the invasion of Kuwait led to the PLO losing other regional powers. The increasing weakness of the PLO coincided with the emergence of Hamas and the first Palestinian uprising (Intifada I); at a time when Hamas was growing rapidly within Palestine, the PLO was moving to negotiations with the Israeli occupation. It was weak militarily, politically and financially. This, in turn, created a vacuum on which Hamas was able to capitalise. Hamas's success in building regional alliances and eliciting support from Syria, Iran and Hezbollah has made it an influential political force with many facets.

Salafi-jihadism in Palestine

Based on the circumstances surrounding the emergence of the Muslim Brotherhood, Fatah, Hamas and Islamic Jihad as described above, Salafist ideology had no chance of spreading widely in Palestine. It did not have a considerable presence in the region until the late 1970s according to estimates, and this came about when graduates who had studied Islamic law at Saudi universities returned to Palestine, bringing with them Salafi ideas. However, despite their activism in mosques and some associations, they could not compete with Islamic Jihad and Muslim Brotherhood.

Since their inception, Hamas and the Islamic Jihad movements have adopted a political discourse that falls in line with the reality of their being under occupation. Hamas benefitted from previous decades of the Brotherhood's activity in Palestine, and their strong participation in the first Palestinian Intifada led to their accumulating a large popular support base. For Salafi-jihadists, the difficulty of communicating with supportive countries such as Saudi Arabia at that time and the lack of contact with countries that had such Salafi organisations, such as Afghanistan, hindered their ability to work effectively. Therefore, Salafi-jihadism, as opposed to Salafism as an ideology, had no strong presence in Palestine until the beginning of the third millennium. By the onset of the new millennium, the political settlement proposals with the occupying state were witnessing a dramatic collapse that resulted in the outbreak of the second Palestinian Intifada in 2000. After this and other developments on the ground, such as the implementation of the Israeli disengagement plan with the Gaza Strip, the participation of Hamas in the elections, the spread of violence between the Palestinian factions, and the Hamas takeover of the Gaza Strip, Palestine witnessed the beginning of the formation of Salafi-jihadist organisations.

The school of Salafi-jihadism holds that jihad and military action are the only ways to lead change. The movement became global after its leaders, most notably Ayman al-Zawahri in the mid-1980s, moved to Afghanistan, where al-Qaida was established in 1988. The organisation had branches in several Arab and Muslim countries, such as Yemen, Egypt, Nigeria and Somalia. The jihadist organisations continued to appear under different names after the 2003 Iraq war and then after the beginning of the Arab Spring, most notably that known as Islamic State in Iraq and Syria (ISIS).

This school also adopts the concept of 'global jihad', which combines the struggle against the (mainly Western) enemies occupying Muslim countries and the fight against local authoritarian regimes in all Arab and Islamic countries. It therefore does not differentiate a local enemy from any other, although, perhaps, its philosophy puts fighting the local 'apostate' regimes before the external enemy. In addition, it adopts the principle of 'overcoming' and considers it a legitimate method for reaching power. This makes it easy for Salafi-jihadism to fight its opponents, subjugate them, establish the state and impose *sharī'a* law by force. This has been evident in ISIS's actions in Iraq and then in Syria.

Despite its weak presence in Palestine, Salafi-jihadists began to attempt attacks on Israel from the West Bank. For its part, Israel pursued a cell south of Hebron and killed its members, while the Palestinian security forces arrested other Salafi-jihadists. But these indicators of the *beginning* of the transformation of Salafi-jihadism – from the circulation of ideas to the exercise of military activities on the ground – are not enough to say that formal Salafi-jihadist organisations existed. Rather, they are evidence of groups of young people who took up their ideas and exploited the insecure situation post-2000, but without having the capacity to build a strong organisation capable of polarising large numbers.[6] However, in 2015, drawing on Palestinian sources, Israeli media reported that Palestinian security forces had launched a campaign to arrest a dozen young Palestinians in the West Bank, due to their alleged association to Islamic State in Palestine. Those arrested were suspected of planning attacks on both Palestinian and Israeli targets. A spokesman for the Palestinian security forces, Adnan Dimarri, denied the existence of ISIS in the West Bank. However, pro-ISIS slogans were observed in the city of Al-Bireh.[7]

Unlike the West Bank, Gaza had an older and more systematic growth of

Salafi-jihadist groups. The most prominent of these was the Army of Islam, which was founded in 2005 by Mumtaz Dughmush, with most of its members hailing from the Dughmush family. The organisation was famous for its participation in the abduction of Israeli soldier Gilad Shalit in the Gaza Strip; yet, despite this cooperation its relationship with Hamas deteriorated in 2007. After that, the organisation announced its support for ISIS in 2015 and, since its foundation, the organisation has launched numerous attacks against foreign journalists and Christian associations. The period after the Israeli withdrawal from Gaza and the beginning of the siege also witnessed the emergence of other organisations, such as the Army of the Nation, Soyuof al-Haq (Swords of Righteousness) and Jaljalat in 2007, as well as Jund Al-Ansar in 2008. The latter organisation declared an Islamic Emirate in Gaza in 2009. This led Hamas to assassinate Jund al-Ansar's leader, Abdul Latif Musa, who was holed up inside the Ibn Taymiyyah Mosque in the Gaza Strip.[8]

This chapter argues that this appearance of Salafi-jihadist organisations in Palestine was caused by factors unrelated to Salafi-jihadism itself, in that it had not been systematically planned. Rather, it came about organically from the supportive enabling environment and from local circumstances that paved the way for them to form and organise. This will be discussed in the section below.

Internal Frictions within Hamas and the Rise of Salafi-jihadism

In 2005, the military resistance against the Israeli occupation forces began to retreat. Meanwhile, Palestinians took a different path towards organising their own internal affairs after five years of the Al-Aqsa Intifada that brought absolute absence of stability and the widespread destruction of institutions. All political parties in Palestine agreed on the importance of administrating the general affairs of the region with the inclusion and participation of all political parties, and in 2005 an agreement was signed in Cairo to hold a legislative election and reform the PLO.[9] The agreement received majority approval, with the exception of the Islamic Jihad Movement. This was a stepping-stone for Hamas, as it would now participate for the first time in managing Palestinian institutions at the national level after successfully participating in local elections.

Hamas officially announced its intention to participate in the legislative elections held on 21 March 2005, through its political bureau member, Dr Muhammad Gazal.[10] This news was welcomed by all stakeholders except for Israel, but they did not hinder the election process. The polls, however, indicated a clear victory for Fatah in the election, explaining Israel's lack of concern over Hamas's participation. It also explained the American stance on the issue, whereby they aspired to reform Hamas from a military organisation to a purely political party. This was evident in former US Secretary of State Condoleezza Rice's statement declaring that 'when people start getting elected and have to start worrying about constituencies and have to start worrying not about whether their fire-breathing rhetoric against Israel is being heard, but about whether or not that person's child down the street is able to go to a good school or that road has been fixed or life is getting better, that things start to change'.[11] Condoleezza Rice's statement displays her full understanding of the reality of the Palestinian Authority, its financial status and the ability of donors to manipulate it.

On 25 January 2006, the Palestinian Legislative Council (PLC) election was held under international supervision affirming its transparency.[12] The importance of this election lay in its alignment with the Israeli withdrawal from the Gaza Strip, as well as Hamas's decision to participate, having boycotted the first election in 1996.[13] Hamas won the majority, claiming 74 of the 132 seats.[14] It became a player that could no longer be ignored.[15] The result was a shock, not only for Hamas's opponents and the international community, but for Hamas itself; it was evident that Hamas had been aiming to play the opposition party, preventing the Palestinian Authority from submitting to international pressure during the political negotiations with the Israeli government. This, at least, was the conclusion drawn from Dr Muhammad Gazal during a political summit held in Amman in 2005.[16]

Until the results of the PLC election, criticism of Hamas's Charter was a minor subject, mainly of concern to political powers involved in the Palestinian-Israeli conflict. However, after Hamas's victory, the fear rose that Hamas will dominate the Palestinian Authority and all of its institutions. Hamas's national and international opponents thus began to criticise its charter and ideology publicly. The international community and other national parties demanded, directly and indirectly, that Hamas change or reform its charter in order to be accepted as a political party and enable work with the newly formed government. Hamas refused these demands and paid the price with an international siege and a political and financial boycott.

Khalid Alhoroob, a scholar of Islamic political movements, argues that Hamas's discourse was no longer aligned with its ideology. Its leaders began to praise the coexistence of the Islamic-Jewish-Christian religions throughout history in Palestine as well as in the Arab world, but this was fundamentally opposed to its charter. Writing at the time, Alhoroob noted: 'Hamas charter must change as it is no longer a representation of the Palestinian resistance against the Zionist project, and it adopts a narrative that Hamas abandoned a long time ago. The charter focuses on Jews as the follower of a religion and declares enmity to them for that and not just as occupiers and tends to adopt all European anti-Semitic statements'.[17]

Alhoroob was convinced that Hamas should not rely on its charter in its discourse, and that Hamas should take the peculiar stance of insisting on its charter as a holy text. However, scholars within the movement have not agreed that Hamas views its charter in this way. Al-Sawwaf argued that 'Hamas continuously revises its charters and changes its discourses as well as tactical changes that serve its long terms strategies. This continuous process takes place during any national and international political landscape changes as the movement puts forwards some tactics, retreat some or write it off altogether'.[18]

Ramzi Baroud believes that Hamas considers the experience of the Turkish AK Party a model to follow. He affirms that the party has proven its ability to change and grow since its inception in 1987, and the period of Arab revolutions must push Hamas for change. He said in a statement:

> Hamas should now re-think its charter of 1988, which was once an almost impulsive rally cry, and which will always be used in the interests of those seeking to discount Hamas' credibility. The language of the charter might have served a purpose in the past, but it fails to live up to the expectations of a people who wish for unity and to see past the confines of Oslo, its 'peace process' and its wealth-amassing elites.[19]

While al-Sawwaf and Baroud indicate the potential for change in Hamas's charter, Shoal Mishal argues that there has in fact been a shift in Hamas's political discourse without conflict with its ideology. He understands Hamas's acceptance of the 1967 border, admitted by Ahmed Yassin during the second Intifada 'as merely a pause on the historic road of jihad, Hamas achieved political flexibility without losing its ideological credibility. Acceptance of a political settlement in the short run was interpreted as being complementary, not contradictory, to long-term desires'.[20]

Along the same lines, Steven Simon and Jonathan Stevenson note Hamas's difficulty in accepting any political concession or reaching a common ground with other stakeholders in regard to a two-state solution. The main obstacle is that their charter states that Palestine is an Islamic state and land. They added that Hamas also was not willing to dispense with its military forces, viewing the Hizballah's experiment in forcing Israel to retreat from Southern Lebanon in 2000 as a success story; yet, they are aware that Israeli political strategies differ between the West Bank and Lebanon.[21]

On the other hand, Jeroen Gunning claimed that Hamas 'has scaled down expectations regarding one of its core goals, the creation of an Islamic state, and it has increasingly sought to find a pragmatic way out of its absolutist insistence on the liberation of all of Palestine'.[22] However, Jeroen Gunning changed his mind four years later, when he began to view Hamas's pragmatism as evidence of contradiction within the party.[23]

Despite the demand to change or modify Hamas's charter, questions remained concerning Hamas's reluctance to address the issue. The clear gap between the movement's charter and its statements and political behaviour indicated that Hamas was happy to bypass the charter and did not obey its principles; the charter was essentially a historic document that did not have any practical application in the present or the future. For years, the movement reinforced its contention that it determines its ideologies pragmatically and not by rigid ideological stereotypes. However, the movement was unable to repudiate its ideologies for an extended period of time, as it feared the consequences of doing so on its levels of public support. The main indications of the gap between the movement's charter and its political behaviours are summarised below.

First, following recent Hamas speeches there have been many statements by its high-level leaders asserting that the charter no longer determines its policies. When Khalid Mashal was the head of the movement's political bureau, he stated: 'They believe we belong to the Muslim Brotherhood which causes a sensitivity. Today, we are a national liberation movement with no ties with the Brotherhood'. With this statement, he ignored a fundamental principle of the charter stating that Hamas is a branch of the Muslim Brotherhood in Palestine. If Mashal's statements were not clear evidence of the party's neglect of its charter, Musa Abu Marzooq's statement in the Jewish newspaper *The Forward* clearly confirms the diminishment of the charter as a reference to its policies: 'We have many policies that are not going with the charter and there were people within Hamas who were talking about changing it'.[24]

Some analysts see these statements as a representation of the external pressure facing the party. The facts that the party had long been headquartered in Jordan and Syria and that it is currently dispersed across multiple locations means that outside leaders' remarks do not necessarily accurately represent the direction of the party within Palestine. However, this view can be countered by the notion that leaders inside Palestine also imply a similar neglect of the movement's charter.

Second, Hamas's political behaviour at the end of the second Intifada began to reflect pragmatic instability and a lack of commitment to the charter's principles, especially when Hamas decided to participate in the 2006 election, which resulted from the Oslo Accords that had actually been rejected by Hamas. According to its charter, Hamas also rejects any political settlement in the conflict with Israel. Hamas, however, does not see any contradiction between rejecting the Oslo Accords and its participation in the Palestinian Authority, nor does it consider this an act of bypassing its charter. Hamas states that its participation in the legislative council election was due to the practical end of the Accords when Israel destroyed Palestinian organisations and institutes, as well as the inability of the current Israeli government to meet the timeline of the Oslo Accords. Furthermore, it holds that its participation in the election was not the result of the Oslo Accords, but of the new agreement signed between the Palestinian political parties in Cairo in 2005, whereby all stakeholders agreed on the need for a reform of the PLO and the inclusion of Hamas, the Jihadi Organisation and the Palestinian National Initiative (Al-Mubadara).

Despite the fact that Hamas does not see its participation in the election as a contradiction of its charter in terms of the Oslo Accords, it also violated another principle of its charter, this time regarding the PLO. According to the Cairo Agreement, the reform of the PLO must be political and structural, including all the parties, but without any ideological changes. In Hamas's charter, however, Article 27 states that the involvement in the PLO requires the institute to adopt Islamic laws: 'When the Palestine Liberation Organisation adopts Islam as its system of life, we will be its soldiers and the firewood of its fire, which will burn the enemies'.[25]

Third, after Hamas's election victory in 2006 and the formation of its government, its political stands began to show some flexibility. This can be taken as an indicator of Hamas's belief that its charter does not represent the party's actual political views. Some noticeable incidents between 2006 and 2012 are the following:

- Khalid Mashal's confirmation of what was circulated among media outlets by other party leaders – that is, that Hamas agrees to establishing Palestine with 1967 borders.[26] Hamas argues that this solution does not contradict its charter principles, since it is a temporary solution and not a permanent one. Yet, the contradiction with the charter also appears from a different perspective: accepting 1967 borders means accepting a non-violent solution and a political settlement – which is a violation of the charter's principles.
- Hamas showed new willingness to abandon its charter when it led the tenth Palestinian government in an indirect way that absolved them of any responsibility to their supporters. Hamas agreed to sign the National Accord Document in 2006 in an effort towards national reconciliation. The document clearly focuses the resistance movement on 1967 borders, giving an initial indication that Hamas would give up any resistive movement with Israel inside 1948 borders.[27]
- When Hamas signed the Mecca Agreement for national reconciliation in Saudi Arabia in 2007, causing a clear contradiction with the charter. It led to the formation of the eleventh Palestinian government, which decided to respect agreements previously signed by the PLO.[28] The charter considers the abdication of any part of Palestine a violation of the *sharīʿa* law and thus unacceptable. Yet, Hamas welcomed the Mecca Accords and confirmed its agreement with all previously signed agreements.
- Hamas supported Mahmoud Abbas's efforts to gain Palestine non-member

> observer state status at the UN General Assembly in 2012. Hamas issued an official decree, giving its full support to President Abbas in his endeavour.[29] In fact, however, this step relied on the acceptance of previous UN resolutions such as 194, 242 and 338 – which are all rejected in Hamas's charter.

All these steps taken by Hamas – starting from its participation in local elections, the signing of the Cairo Agreement in 2005, its repudiation from the Muslim Brotherhood, its acceptance of the 1967 borders and participation in the legislative council election – contributed to forming a new picture for Hamas. The party was hoping to change its image in the eye of the international community who besieged it and refused to deal with it. However, Hamas remains inadmissible and besieged, and the new image only affects its members.

Hamas's new image, formed over a period of ten years, conflicted with that presented to their followers, especially through Islamic education in mosques, where young members were brought up in line with Hamas's charter and taught to adopt many Islamic theories and ideas. Some of these ideas led members to sympathise with Osama bin Laden and to believe that they held more in common with him than with local Palestinian parties. As a result, many young followers of Hamas began to discover the gap between what they believed the movement stood for and its actual actions.

This gap was one of the main reasons driving some of Hamas's members to withdraw from the party and join some of the other Salafi and jihadi movements gradually forming in Gaza. Some of Hamas members who grew up in a conservative environment were now unable to understand the movement's pragmatics and were willing to join parties better suited to their Islamic upbringing and beliefs. The Israeli withdrawal from Gaza in 2005 provided a safe environment for new Islamic movements to recruit Hamas dissidents, as well as those with Salafi and jihadi ideologies who had not previously had the chance to organise themselves.

The gap between Hamas's political behaviour and the upbringing it delivered to its young members deepened when the movement announced a new political document in 2017, which acted as official confirmation and documentation for every change in the party's political behaviour since 2005.[30] In the original charter, the movement presented itself as an Islamic movement, requiring an Islamic declaration to join and mandating a purely military resistance to the occupation. In the new document, the party declared itself a Palestinian movement without any organisational extensions. It requires organisational reform, confirms the necessity for democratic laws and does not exclude any form of resistance, as set out in article 29, 23 and 28. This implies a shift in the party's priorities, allowing for the formation of new alliances to ignore the Oslo Accord and to call for popular resistance in all Palestinian territories.

Even if the introduction of a new charter document tempered some of the damage done to Hamas's internal cohesion, it did not stop some of its followers from defecting to radical Salafi and jihadi movements. This created opportunities for radical Salafi movements to form in Palestine. Meanwhile, Hamas lost its conventional platforms in the West Bank, with all of its offices being closed by the Palestinian security force in 2007 and the detention of many of its leaders and members. In Gaza, Hamas partially abandoned its conventional platforms such as charity organisations and mosques, deciding instead to use government institutions and media outlets as new platforms.

Hamas's approach to the political and religious upbringing it delivered to its younger members had exposed the religious population to a radical Islamic paradigm, where the Salafi-jihadi movement flourished in the light of the Arabic Spring. The Salafi media then filled the space Hamas had left behind, widely growing and disseminating their ideology in the region. In addition, a more racist and discriminating discourse was being introduced around the Islamic world, and Palestine was no exception. In the midst of the Arab Spring, doctrinal and religious conflicts grew to reach Palestine, including hate speeches against the Shiʿi community. Politically, Hamas kept ties with Hizballah and Iran; yet, Hamas's ties with the Shiʿi community in Lebanon and Iran were rejected by many of its members who were influenced by the sectarian conflicts in the region. This in turn made the Salafi-jihadist movements even more appealing to many Hamas members whose ideology was better suited to a narrative and discourse of hatred.

All of the above was concurrent with the siege on Gaza and the humanitarian disasters it entailed; this assisted the growth of the Salafi-jihadist movement due to the following factors:

- First, Hamas was in charge of Gaza under the siege, and its failure to break the siege or improve life in Gaza weakened the perception of its ability to rule.
- Second, an environment under siege, along with economic and social crises, is considered an ideal milieu in which to adopt and spread new radical ideologies. This holds true anywhere in the world, and Palestine is no exception.

Even when Hamas repudiated its relationship with the Muslim Brotherhood and did not mention it in their new charter document, the ideological link between the two was still strong, and Hamas linked its faith to that of the Brotherhood in the midst of the Arab Spring. Hamas was hopeful of reconciling their relationship with the Muslim Brotherhood, especially after their success in Egypt following the fall of Mubarak's regime and the victory of Muhammad Morsi in the presidential elections. However, al-Sisi's coup against Morsi's administration weakened the Muslim Brotherhood across the Arab world, including Palestine, raising questions among members of the Brotherhood over the need for a gradual change in their ideologies. This debate saw some of their members eager to join more radical movements; thus, the military coup in Egypt is considered a further major factor in the increase of Salafi-jihadist movements in the region.

The loss of the Muslim Brotherhood in Egypt after the coup led by al-Sisi put Hamas in a difficult position. Hamas denied its relationship with the Muslim Brotherhood, but its members still considered themselves a part of this international organisation, even intellectually; they had an emotional bond with them. However, Hamas's political bureau believed that, as long as it was running the Gaza Strip, it must continue its security and political relations with the new Egyptian regime under al-Sisi. This came as a shock to the Brotherhood members in Egypt. For them, the issue was primarily ethical; while the political bureau considered it essential to focus its discourse on its political interests.

The behaviour of the Hamas political bureau – in maintaining a relationship with Egypt under al-Sisi – prompted some Hamas members at the lower levels to withdraw and join the jihadist movements – and even more so after

Hamas cooperated with the Egyptian regime to fight Salafi-jihadism in Gaza and Sinai.

Akram al-Natsheh, a specialist in Arabic Studies and an expert in Palestinian affairs, stated in an interview with the researcher that the growth of Salafi-jihadism in Palestine is mainly due to the behaviour of the Muslim Brotherhood in Palestine, and not directly related to Salafi-jihadism itself. The latter has occupied the vacuum left by the Muslim Brotherhood and Hamas as their political behaviour developed in a direction different from the educational and religious foundations with which their members had grown up. Al-Natsheh clarifies that 'many of the notable members of the Muslim Brotherhood in Palestine received their religious education in Saudi Arabia'. He adds that 'they came back with a rather Salafi mentality, but they joined the Brotherhood. This has given the brothers of Palestine many Salafi attributes for a long time, and now the impacts appear dangerous. Hamas is no longer capable of embracing this school of thought'.[31]

The latest factors contributing to the growth of extremist currents are the policies of the Palestinian Authority in Ramallah towards the Gaza Strip. The Fatah-Hamas dispute has been going on for years, but the Fatah leadership in Ramallah has now begun to enact a collective punishment on the Gaza Strip, to push Hamas into stepping down from power there. In other words, it aims to provoke the Palestinian mainstream in the Gaza Strip to take up arms against Hamas. Regardless of the precise purpose of the sanctions imposed by Palestinian President Mahmoud Abbas on the Gaza Strip, the results will gradually worsen the entire situation in a way that will facilitate the Salafi-jihadists in attracting the youth of Gaza. Abbas punishes the Gaza Strip, resulting in the Palestinians there feeling alienated and further without a national identity. As a result, Gazan youth will be more willing to join groups – such as ISIS – that do not believe in national identity and do not recognise national borders.

All these factors combined – alongside the problems of the Muslim Brotherhood in Palestine, Hamas's political behaviour, other regional developments and Israel's withdrawal from Gaza – have created a suitable environment for the formation of jihadist organisations. Many are currently in existence. They have carried out many activities against both Hamas and Israel, as well as some minor activities in the West Bank.

In the Gaza Strip, activities have become more dangerous. The journalist Alan Johnston was kidnapped by the Army of Islam in 2008, leading Hamas security forces to strike hard at the organisation until the captive was released. On 14 April 2011, a jihadist group abducted journalist Vittorio Arrigoni and demanded that the government in Gaza release Salafi detainees in exchange for their prisoner.

Arrigoni was executed before the deadline, and his body was found in an abandoned house in the northern Gaza Strip. The Tawhid and Jihad Group denied its connection to the murder but justified it by saying: 'It is the natural result of government policy [of Hamas] against the Salafis'.[32] However, Hamas chased the group and clashed with them in the Nusseirat Refugee Camp in the central Gaza Strip, killing two of the group and a Jordanian named Abd al-Horman al-Buraizat, while a third person was arrested and brought to trial.[33]

Between the kidnappings of Johnston and Arrigoni, another, most dangerous development occurred in the relationship between Hamas and the Salafi-jihadist groups. The establishment of an Islamic emirate in the Gaza Strip was announced on 14 August 2009 at the Ibn Taymiyyah Mosque, which was attacked and besieged by Hamas.[34] After this incident, Hamas faced a media campaign against them, with armed jihadist groups accusing Hamas of apostasy, infidelity and aggression against the *mujāhidīn* (Islamic fighters). This clearly shows that the priority of these Salafi-jihadist groups was to control the government, rather than to fight the Israeli occupation.

Although these groups fired rockets on Israel in 2015, this was merely to increase pressure on Hamas, which had agreed to a truce with the Israeli occupying forces that the rocket fire broke. This pressure was intended to force Hamas to release the Salafis detained by the Gaza government; otherwise, so the Salafi groups threatened, they would drag the Gaza Strip into confrontation with Israel. This was accompanied by bombings carried out by jihadist groups against Palestinian civilian targets such as internet cafés, beauty salons and entertainment venues. These attacks have prompted Hamas to apply tougher policies in dealing with Salafi groups, carrying out more arrests and seeking a return to calm.[35]

In 2015, Palestine began a new confrontation with the Israeli occupation in the West Bank, in what was then called the 'Intifada of Jerusalem'. ISIS came out with video recordings calling on Palestinians to distance themselves from the Fatah and Hamas movements and to join the Caliphate of al-Baghdadi. They stated that '[the people of Palestine] know that there is no difference between Fatah and Hamas, and that every party is looking for its own interests. Some of them serve as agents of the crusaders and Safavids, as you know'. They added: 'Hamas and Fatah are two faces of the same coin, and their disbelief is clear and explicit, we have from God a proof about that'.[36]

Differences in Ideologies: Hamas versus Salafi Jihadists

In addition to military conflict between the two in the Gaza Strip, there exists a clear difference between the ideologies of the Muslim Brotherhood (as adopted by Hamas) and the Salafi-jihadists (adopted by a few small movements in Palestine).

It is relevant to start out by saying that this is not the case in the eyes of the international community, which has tended to conflate the two movements in political discourse. Hamas was listed as a terrorist organisation in many countries, in the United States and the European Union, where they were compared with ISIS. However, this was more of a political move than a legal one, and the General Court of the European Union issued a bill on 17 January 2014 to remove Hamas from the list, following the argument that Hamas had been listed as a terrorist organisation based on media articles and not on independent evidence.[37] Hamas's stance was, in fact, purely political, especially when they met with distinguished political figures in Europe and the United States, including European Parliament members – such as in the meeting held between the former US president Jimmy Carter and Ismail Hania in Gaza in 2009, as well as with Khalid Mashal in Damascus 2008 and Cairo 2012.[38] Israel, for its part, has tried to capitalise on the political discourse of Hamas as a terrorist organisation by further promoting the idea that Hamas and ISIS are two sides of the same coin during congress speeches and AIPAC conventions.[39]

Yet, the international community's tendency to put Hamas and ISIS in the same basket neglects major differences between the two. The main difference between them lies in Hamas's identity as a moderate Islamic movement that adopts jurisprudence in the interpretation of religious texts, whereas Salafi-jihadists insist on the literal meaning of these texts.[40] This literal approach construes a movement such as Hamas as secular and infidel from the point of view of jihadists. In 2009, this difference erupted into an armed confrontation between the two parties, in which Hamas eradicated the Islamic emirate declared by Jund Ansar Allah.

Mahmoud al-Zahar, a prominent Hamas leader, declared that 'Daesh's threats can be felt on the ground, and we are handling the situation from a security standpoint. Whoever commits a security offense shall be dealt with in accordance with the law, and whoever wants to debate intellectually shall be debated intellectually; we take this matter seriously'.[41] Hamas has been able to contain Salafi-jihadist organisations because of their small number. However, some polls indicate that 24 per cent of Palestinians exhibit a positive attitude towards jihadist ideas.[42] This is not due to their belief in these movements, but their feeling towards the destructive role of the United States and their endless support for Israel.[43]

Hamas and ISIS differ in their definition of a modern democratic state, in both theory and behaviour. Yusef al-Qaradawi, a scholar of the Muslim Brotherhood resident in Qatar, has published books on this subject, including *The Jurisprudence of the State in Islam*, in which he claims that an Islamic state is not mentioned in Islam and that the modern state is based on respect for the opinion of the people with reference to Islam. It is based on the principles of accountability and acceptance of political pluralism. Hamas put this theoretical stance into practice when it participated in the local and legislative elections in 2006. When it won the elections, it called for the formation of a coalition government with the participation of secular and Marxist parties, and its parliamentary list included many women. Their first government included both Muslim and Christian ministers. By contrast, ISIS rejects democracy and any kind of participation in it, regarding it as an infidel regime.

The difference between the two groups also manifests in their respective definitions of the enemy. The only enemy of Hamas is the Israeli occupation, while ISIS considers everyone who disagrees with it to be an enemy. ISIS has committed many crimes against civilians in the areas which it controls and against its prisoners. ISIS's worst incident was the burning of the Jordanian pilot Moaz Kassab, while the behaviour of Hamas during the kidnapping of Gilad Shalit was of an entirely different nature.[44]

Conclusion

The factors that led to the emergence of Salafi-jihadist organisations in Palestine, mainly in the Gaza Strip, are numerous. They include all the internal changes that have taken place in the Hamas movement, particularly in its political behaviour and its discourse, alongside all the external factors that the movement has faced in terms of pressure, siege and boycott. Some of these factors relate to Israeli policies after 2000, such as the failure of political settlement projects and the unilateral withdrawal from the Gaza Strip; others are linked with regional variables such as the strengthening of armed jihadist organisations such as ISIS and the spread of hate speech in the Middle East. The most powerful of these factors was the siege on Hamas. This pushed Palestinians to support radical currents in place of secular trends – an expected behaviour in all places of siege and poverty. People opt for violence in the absence of a political horizon. Both Israel and the leadership of the Authority in Ramallah are responsible for providing an enabling environment conducive to the growth of Salafi-jihadism.

More importantly, a series of attacks conducted by Salafi-jihadists targeting citizens and foreigners in the Gaza Strip do not indicate any ability to sustain such attacks or expand on them. The question of its wider spread is linked to the persistence of the factors mentioned above. If Egypt can help Hamas break the siege and renew the truce with the occupying forces, the chances of jihadist groups spreading will decrease. However, the absence of any indicators of the success of Palestinian reconciliation, alongside the Israeli policy of separation of the Gaza Strip from the West Bank, will increase the chances of these jihadist groups to flourish. It is key to mention here that these organisations reflect the interests of tribal forces empowered in the Gaza Strip, and the more the strength of these tribes increases, the more democratic party competition diminishes.

Finally, Salafi-jihadism is not just an armed group that can be suppressed militarily; hence, reducing its chances of proliferation does not depend solely on violent confrontations. In Arab societies, including Palestine, religion is still a strong component in the formation of identity and culture and, consequently, religious currents will always find members willing to join them. It is, therefore, vital to rethink international attitudes towards Islamic currents;

so far, international political discourses have effectively prevented the involvement of the Islamic centralists in modern political paradigms, even where they have participated in democratic and fair elections. It is essential for the international community to understand that the current policy adopted to suppress moderate Islamic movements has done nothing but strengthen extremist Islamists.

Notes

1. Mohsin Salih, 'The Path from the Palestinian Muslim Brotherhood to Hamas', *Aljazeera*, 28 December 2016, www.aljazeera.net/home/print/6c87b8ad-70ec-47d5-b7c4-3aa56fb899e2/d9514581-9c15-40e6-b094-1893cac9246e.
2. Ibid.
3. Khalid Mash'al and Gassan Sharbal, *Ḥarakat Ḥamās wa-taḥrīr Filasṭīn* (Hamas and the Liberation of Palestine) (Beirut: Dār al-Nahār, 2006).
4. Khalid Abu al-Omarain, *Ḥarakat Ḥamas: Judhuruha, nasha'atuha wadawruha* (Hamas: Its Roots, its Origins and its Role) (Khartoum: Khartoum University, 1994), 221.
5. Ziad Abu-Amr, 'Hamas: A Historical and Political Background', *Journal of Palestine Studies* 22 (1993), 10.
6. Awni Faris, 'Salafi Jihadism in Palestine', *Journal of Palestinian Studies* 101 (2013), 45–57, www.palestine-studies.org/sites/default/files/mdf-articles/045-057.pdf.
7. Mohsin Salih, *Salafi Jihadist Group and the Possibilities of Proliferating Among Palestinians* (Beirut: Al-Zaytouna Center, 2015), http://eng.alzaytouna.net/2015/11/16/strategic-assessment-82-salafi-jihadist-groups-and-the-possibilities-of-proliferating-among-palestinians/.
8. Shlomi Eldar, 'Will Salafi Groups Trigger Israel-Hamas Clash?' *Al-Monitor*, 11 October 2016, www.al-monitor.com/pulse/originals/2016/10/israel-gaza-salafi-groups-provoke-hamas-israel-clash.html.
9. Björn Brenner, *Gaza under Hamas: From Islamic Democracy to Islamist Governance* (London: I. B. Tauris, 2017), 33–44.
10. Shamir Hassan, 'Hamas: A New Phase of Palestinian Resistance', *Proceedings of the Indian History Congress* 66 (2005), 1316–22.
11. Condoleezza Rice, Interview by Washington Times Editorial Board, *Washington Times*, 11 March 2005, http://2001-2009.state.gov/secretary/rm/2005/43341.htm.

12. Ryad Malki, 'Beyond Hamas and Fatah', *Journal of Democracy* 17 (2006), 131–37.
13. Mahjoob Zweiri, 'The Hamas Victory: Shifting Sands or Major Earthquake?' *Third World Quarterly* 27 (2006), 675–87.
14. Central Elections Commission-Palestine, 'The Second 2006 PLC Elections, Central Elections Commission-Palestine' (2006), www.elections.ps/tabid/818/language/en-US/Default.aspx.
15. Baudouin Long, 'The Hamas Agenda: How Has It Changed?' *Middle East Policy* 17 (2010), 131–43.
16. Ishtiaq Hossain and Belal Shobaki, 'Hamas in Power: A Study of Its Ideology and Policies 2006–2012', in *Islamic Resistance Movement-Hamas: Studies of Thought and Experience*, ed. Mohsin Saleh (Beirut: Al-Zaytouna Center, 2017), 375–416.
17. Khalid Hroub, 'How the "Hamas Charter" Will Not Become a Burden on the Palestinian National Project', *Alhayat*, 9 May 2007, www.alhayat.com/article/1339737.
18. Mahmoud Sawwaf, 'Hamas bayn alththabit walmutaghiir', *Alaqsa Voice*, 6 December 2009, www.alaqsavoice.ps/index.php/news/details/46716.
19. Ramzy Baroud, 'A New Charter for Hamas?' *Counterpunch*, 25 March 2011, www.counterpunch.org/2011/03/25/a-new-charter-for-hamas/
20. Shaul Mishal, 'The Pragmatic Dimension of the Palestinian Hamas: A Network Perspective,' *Armed Forces & Society* 29/4 (2003), 578.
21. Steven Simon and Jonathan Stevenson, 'Confronting Hamas', *The National Interest*, 1 December 2003, https://nationalinterest.org/article/confronting-hamas-1133
22. Jeroen Gunning, 'Peace with Hamas? The Transforming Potential of Political Participation', *International Affairs* 80 (2004), 253.
23. Jeroen Gunning, *Hamas in Politics: Democracy, Religion, Violence* (Columbia: Columbia University Press, 2008), 310.
24. Larry Cohler-Esses, 'Hamas Wouldn't Honor a Treaty, Top Leader Says', *The Forward*, 19 April 2012, https://forward.com/news/155054/hamas-wouldn-t-honor-a-treaty-top-leader-says/.
25. Muhammad Maqdsi, 'Charter of the Islamic Resistance Movement (Hamas) of Palestine', *Journal of Palestine Studies* 22 (1993), 122–34.
26. Elior Levy, 'Mashaal Agreed to 2-State Solution', *Yedioth*, 30 January 2013, www.ynetnews.com/articles/0,7340,L-4339225,00.html.
27. Palestinian political prisoners in Israeli jails, 'National Conciliation Document of the Prisoners', *Jerusalem Media and Communication*

Centre, 26 May 2006, https://unispal.un.org/DPA/DPR/unispal.nsf/0/CE3ABE1B2E1502B58525717A006194CD.

28. Middle East Gateway, 'Palestinian Unity Government Platform – Complete Text and Introduction', *Middle East Gateway*, 17 March 2007, www.mideast web.org/paunitygovernment.htm.
29. The Jerusalem Post, 'Hamas Lends Support to Abbas's UN Statehood Bid', *The Jerusalem Post*, 26 November 2012, www.jpost.com/Middle-East/Hamas-lends-support-to-Abbass-UN-statehood-bid.
30. Hamas, 'A Document of General Principles and Policies', 2017, http://hamas.ps/en/post/678/a-document-of-general-principles-and-policies.
31. Akram Natshah, interview with the author, 12 March 2018.
32. Asian News, 'In Gaza and West Bank Protest Marches and Mourning for the Italian Activist Killed', *Asian News*, 16 April 2011, www.asianews.it/news-en/In-Gaza-and-West-Bank-protest-marches-and-mourning-for-the-Italian-activ ist-killed--21325.html.
33. Maan News Agency, 'Arrigoni Murder Trial to Resume Monday', *Maan News Agency*, 8 October 2011, www.maannews.com/Content.aspx?id=426126.
34. Salih, 'The Path from the Palestinian Muslim Brotherhood to Hamas'.
35. Ibid.
36. Ibid.
37. Adam Withnall, 'Hamas Removed from List of Terrorist Organisations by EU court', *Independent*, 17 December 2014, www.independent.co.uk/news/world/middle-east/hamas-removed-from-list-of-terrorist-organisations-by-eu-court-9930124.html.
38. AP Television, 'Former US President Carter Presser with Hamas PM Haniyeh', *AP Television* [video] (2009), www.aparchive.com/metadata/youtube/d6c2060dc05c70f4424ad9468d07c95e; see also: Maan News Agency, 'Mashaal to Meet Former US President Carter', *Maan News Agency*, 24 May 2012, www.maannews.com/Content.aspx?id=488774; Robert Worth, 'Defying Israel, Carter Meets Hamas Leader', *New York Times*, 19 April 2008, www.nytimes.com/2008/04/19/world/middleeast/19carter.html.
39. Charlotte Alter, 'Netanyahu Tells World Leaders "Hamas is ISIS and ISIS is Hamas"', *Time*, 29 September 2014, http://time.com/3445394/netanyahu-un-general-assembly-hamas-abbas/.
40. Sameer Suleiman. *Islam, Demokratie und Moderne* (Herzogenrath: Shaker Media, 2013), 302.

41. Quds Net News Agency, 'Al-Zahar: ISIS Threats to Gaza Are Part of an International Campaign', *Quds Net News Agency*, 1 July 2015.
42. Samar Batrawi, 'What ISIS Talks About When It Talks About Palestine', *Foreign Affairs*, 28 October 2015, www.foreignaffairs.com/articles/israel/2015-10-28/what-isis-talks-about-when-it-talks-about-palestine.
43. Nabil Kukali, 'Poll No. 196', *The Palestinian Center for Public Opinion*, 10 February 2015, www.pcpo.org/index.php/polls/120-poll-no-196.
44. B. Ben Caspit, 'Gilad Schalit's Capture, in His Own Words: Part I', *The Jerusalem Post*, 30 March 2013, www.jpost.com/Features/In-Thespotlight/Gilad-Schalits-capture-in-his-own-words-Part-II-308198.

CONCLUSION
SALAFISM IN THE TWENTY-FIRST CENTURY

Itzchak Weismann

At the turn of the twenty-first century, Salafism was still largely *terra incognita*. The vast amount of research produced up to that point on the Islamic revival since the 1970s focused on Islamist political movements like the Muslim Brotherhood and the Jamaat-i Islami, and especially on their militant off-shoots – the jihadi organisations that fought their governments and the West under the inspiration of the radical Egyptian ideologue Sayyid Qutb. On the Shiʿi side, academic attention was directed by the nature of things to the Islamic revolution in Iran and to its Lebanese extension, Hizballah.[1] The major theoretical debates of the time raged around the appropriateness of the term 'Islamic fundamentalism' and the relation of Islamism to modernity and globalisation.[2] The term 'Salafism', at least in the scholarly literature, was mostly confined to the historical modernist movement of the turn of the twentieth century and to those considered its main protagonists: Jamal al-Din al-Afghani, Muhammad 'Abduh and Muhammad Rashid Rida.[3]

This began to change in the wake of the terror attacks in New York and Washington on 11 September 2001. It then transpired that there was another major theological/ideological force behind the contemporary Islamic revival from which global Islamic radicalisation imbibed. Al-Qaida and its ilk were accordingly portrayed as jihadi-Salafi organisations. The roots of this trend were traced to Saudi Arabia, from which fifteen out of the nineteen perpetrators of 9/11 originated, and to its puritan brand of Islam – Wahhabism.[4] Western public attention was turned to the obscurantist and xenophobic tenets of the Wahhabi creed and their worldwide propagation under Saudi aegis and with petrodollars funding.[5] Others put the blame on the internal dissent of the 1990s (the Saudi Islamic Awakening), which, inspired by the ideas of the Muslim Brotherhood, protested against the subservience of the senior Wahhabi scholars to the ruling house and its alliance with the United States.[6] The influential typology of the Salafis into purists, politicos and jihadis[7] stems from such perceptions, hence reflecting the state of this trend at the turn of the twentieth century.

Salafism has emerged from 9/11 on as one of the hottest issues in the study of contemporary Islam and among the public at large. The present volume, with its fine mixture of ethnographic and textual perspectives, makes a valuable contribution to this burgeoning research, and is thus a worthy sequence to the previous volumes on the topic edited by Rougier, Meijer, and Cavatorta and Merone.[8] In the following, I will try to pull together the various issues raised by its ten chapters and place them within the larger context of the evolution and diversification of the Salafi trend during the first two decades of the twenty-first century. I begin with a short discussion of the problematics of the concept Salafism and the debates it evokes between protagonists and detractors. I then move on to examine the trajectory of its factions against the backdrop of the major religio-political developments of the period: the opening up of Saudi Arabia, the Arab Spring and the rise of jihadism from al-Qaida to Islamic State (ISIS). These developments are embedded in the underlying processes of globalisation, and especially the spread of social media,[9] which the Salafis have proved to be highly apt in using. My conclusion points to a perceptible weakening of the current rigid forms of Salafism associated with the Wahhabi creed and a cautious revival of its earlier, more open version.

Salafism and Anti-Salafism

The first task that faces students of contemporary Salafism (Arab. *salafiyya*) is to define it. This has proved to be trickier than might appear at first, and the issue is still not satisfactorily resolved. The general idea is quite simple. The term *salafiyya* refers to the call to return to the exemplary model of the pious ancestors – *al-salaf al-ṣāliḥ* – in their understanding and application of the Qur'ān and the Prophet's way (*sunna*). This implies the rejection, to some extent or another, of latter-day harmful innovations (sing. *bid'a*) and aims at restoring the glory of Islam – so that God's word be supreme. Yet, beyond this apparent simplicity lie a bewildering array of thinkers and movements that differ on almost every point. Even among the Salafis themselves there is no consensus on who is to be included among the ancestors, what exactly constitutes the legacy they left behind and, most importantly, which ways should be adopted in realising their model in the present condition. The wide differences on such questions have often led to bitter controversies, acrimonious denunciations and mutual accusations of deviation and disbelief (*takfir*) among the Salafis, as well as between them and other streams in the Muslim community. It is thus even difficult to decide who is to be considered a Salafi and who is not.[10]

In view of this situation, it is no wonder that scholarly works on the topic habitually begin with the question of 'what is Salafism?' Beyond noting its derivation from the concept of *al-salaf*, they usually dwell on the primacy in its teachings of God's unity (*tawḥīd*), its literalist interpretation of the Qur'ān, preoccupation with the science of *ḥadīth*, rejection of traditional legal methodology, rational theology and Sufism, and its special way of being in the world (*manhaj*).[11] Some also refer to the division within the Salafi camp between adherents of the Hanbali school and those who dismiss the whole system of law schools. These are the characteristics of the hegemonic form of contemporary Salafism, which consists of the Wahhabis and their affiliates outside Saudi Arabia, on one hand, and the modern *Ahl al-Ḥadīth*, especially the followers of the *ḥadīth* scholar Nasir al-Din al-Albani, on the other hand.[12] Yet, in the scholarly literature one often comes across the epithet 'Salafi' in relation to a myriad of other Islamic movements such as the Muslim Brothers, the Tabligh-i Jama'at, Deoband, the Taliban, Islamic modernists and whatever else.

Elsewhere, I suggested solving the confusion by distinguishing between a broad and a narrow meaning of Salafism. In its broader sense it refers to the ideology-*cum*-theology that underlies practically all modern Sunni Islamic movements, as all of them strive, in some way or another, to keep a balance between an authentic Islamic identity and a quest for modernisation. In its narrow sense, it points to the current usage of the term, which is associated with the combined Wahhabi/ *Ahl al-Ḥadīth* ultra-conservative version, and with its political and jihadi off-shoots. The term 'modernism' refers, in this scheme, to the intellectually oriented non-Wahhabi/ *Ahl al-Ḥadīth* Salafis, which began with the nineteenth century Islamic reformers, while 'Islamism' denotes their politically oriented counterparts, first and foremost the Muslim Brotherhood. Both are Salafis in the broader sense. The motor for change in the Salafi trend are the hybrid forms, which combined the types: the early modernist Salafis and the Saudi *Ṣaḥwa*.[13]

Accordingly, of the four anti-Salafi groups that Fouad Hazim presents in the opening chapter of this volume, the first two – the traditional *'ulamā'* and the Sufis – are opposed to Salafism at large, although they too, by their very engagement, are influenced by its vocabulary and methodology. His other two groups – the modernists and the reformists – are themselves part of the broader Salafi camp, so that their criticism is directed only at its current Wahhabi/ *Ahl al-Ḥadīth* narrow brand. The essential commonalities and differences among these groups are mirrored in their respective arguments. The *'ulamā'* in their legal and theological schools reproach the core Wahhabi-Salafi methodology of relying solely on the Qur'ān and *sunna*, which in their eyes is the cause of their exclusivity, rigidity and rigor. They likewise reject the modernist rational judgment (*ijtihād*) and Islamist enmeshment in politics as sources of deviation. The Sufis in their brotherhoods follow suite in denouncing the Wahhabis for denying the Prophet Muhammad's lofty spiritual status and deriding the celebration of his *mawlid*, and the modernists and Islamists for relying on books and for forming political parties in the Western style.

On the other side, the modernists challenge the relevance attributed by the Wahhabis and *Ahl al-Ḥadīth* to the *ḥadīth* collections in solving contemporary problems and demand the embracing of modern ethics in place of their archaic corporal punishments and hate speech. The reformists in Hazim's definition are intellectuals/academics living in the Western diaspora, who add their criticism of Salafi formalism and stagnation and the Salafi degradation of women. I would rather combine the last two categories under the rubric of modernists and pose as the fourth group the Islamists, who censure the Wahhabis for their shunning of the political and their subservience to the rulers.

Saudi Arabia Opening Up

In view of the salient place of the Wahhabiyya in the contemporary Salafi movement, the opening up of Saudi Arabia may be regarded as the sole most influential factor in its evolution in the twenty-first century. Its roots lie in the endeavour of the Saudi ruling house to ward off international incriminations concerning the kingdom's responsibility for the attacks of 9/11 and in the subsequent wave of terror that swept the country in 2003–6.[14] Crown Prince, later King Abdallah (r. 2005–15) introduced a set of reforms that touched upon most aspects of life in the conservative kingdom: school curricula, higher education at home and overseas, the consultative councils, the status of women, and national and international dialogue.[15] The reforms were greatly accelerated with the announcement in April 2016 of Crown Prince Muhammad bin Salman's ambitious Vision 2030. In her chapter, which is based on extensive fieldwork and interviews in Saudi Arabia, Masooda Bano records the revolutionary nature of the reforms envisioned by the General Entertainment Authority, as well as the surprising speed at which such programmes became a reality. This she attributes to the growing pressure for change coming from the educated and media-savvy youth, and to the correspondingly weakening appeal of conservative Wahhabi-Salafi conceptualisations of society.

To be sure, the practice of religion continues to dominate the Saudi public scene, as I myself could witness during a tour of the country in February 2020. Shops and restaurants close during prayer times, buses are segregated, and the great majority of women stick to the black *niqab* covering everything but their eyes (and sometimes to the *burqa* covering even them). Still, the notorious religious police (*muṭaawwi'*) have now been withdrawn from the streets; women are allowed to work and drive; and foreign tourists are welcome. Apart from politics and subject to the prevailing social norms, information flows relatively freely, with smartphone shops being the busiest enterprises these days. People I talked with, especially the young, were enthusiastic about Muhammad bin Salman and his policies, Khashoggie's brutal murder notwithstanding, while older people showed themselves resigned to the winds of change. All were eager to demonstrate Islam's moderation and tolerance towards others.

The paradoxical situation of liberalisation by autocratic fiat is reflected in the reconfiguration of the Saudi Salafi camp. The religious establishment under Grand Mufti Abd al-Aziz Al al-Shaykh and Salih al-Fawzan, which in the past half century had been gradually subdued to the political authority and turned quietist, had no choice but to acquiesce to the reforms. Under Muhammad bin Salman even their legitimisation is no more asked, while scholars who proactively preach loyalty to the rulers in whatever they deem right are on the rise. On the other side of the fence, the activist Salafi dissent movement split into rival factions under the contradictory pressures of the socio-cultural opening up and political repression. Some have joined the government in its anti-terrorism campaign, while others have enlisted to al-Qaida or ISIS in their quest to turn Saudi Arabia into an Islamic state. In between the loyalists and the militants are those Salafis who seek to influence the course of reforms by peaceful means. These, too, have split over the past few years, into two opposing camps: conservatives who strive to turn the tide of liberalisation, with a special focus on the issues of religious education and women's segregation, and progressives who in the name of democracy and freedom of speech wish to see liberalisation extended to the political and intellectual fields.[16]

To the latter group belong the veteran activist Shaykh Salman al-Awda, whose arguments are expounded in this volume by Usaama al-Azami, and the theologian Hatim al-Awni, whose ideas Bano analyses towards the end of her chapter. Both use the Salafi methodology but combine it with a tacit acceptance of Western concepts. Al-Awda's assertion in the wake of the Arab Uprisings that obedience to the ruler is ultimately contingent on freely and willingly pledging allegiance (*bayʿa*) to him amounts to an advocacy of the liberal ideas of popular revolution and democracy in the face of the Saudi autocracy. Al-Awni's emphasis on the importance of openness and deliberation in mattes of creed (*ʿaqīda*), along with his claim that a rigid understanding of the concepts of *takfīr* and *al-walāʾ wa-l-barāʾ* (loyalty [to Muslims] and disavowal [of non-Muslims]) plays into the hands of the jihadists, challenges the core creed of Wahhabism.[17] Bano and her team refer to the progressive wing of the dissent movement by the term 'post-Salafism'.[18] Yet, from the longer perspective of the whole twentieth century, it rather represents a revival of the political and intellectual ideas of the early non-Wahhabi modernist Salafis, such as ʿAbd al-Rahman al-Kawakibi and Jamal al-Din al-Qasimi.[19] This occurred to me while perusing the Islamic shelf in a prominent bookstore in Medina, where I was delighted to find the works of Kawakibi, the subject of my latest book, in place of the usual Wahhabi stock.

The Arab Spring Effect

The so-called Arab Spring was a major watershed in the trajectory of the contemporary Salafi trend, as in the recent history of the Middle East at large. The mass demonstrations that spread like wildfire throughout the region in 2010–11 were motivated by civil and economic rather than purely religious concerns. Already by early 2012, however, Islamic movements, both Islamist and Salafi, became principal players in the events, either through the ballot box (as in Tunisia and Egypt), or through armed resistance (as in Syria, Yemen and Libya). The train of events differed considerably from one Arab country to another, although the monarchies – Saudi Arabia and the Gulf Emirates, Morocco and Jordan – generally proved better disposed to contain the unrest than presidential systems, partly due to their higher Islamic credentials. Among the Arab republics, the hardly contenting outcomes ranged from 'flawed democracies' over restored autocratic governments to civil wars and chaos.[20]

Salafism had been on the rise in many countries of the region already on the eve of the uprisings. Its quietist wing was favoured by autocratic regimes, and in some cases it penetrated even the Muslim Brotherhood;[21] jihadist militancy found a wide scope for action in areas of conflict: Algeria in 1990s, Lebanon, and Iraq in the aftermath of the American invasion of 2003. Under the impact of the Arab Spring Salafism underwent major modifications, realignments and mutations. The quietists were split between the Madkhali loyalists, who followed the Saudi lead in declaring any defiance of the government (not sparing even the opposition to the Alawite Assad) *fitna*, and the more political elements who showed themselves ready to play the democratic game in order to Islamise society and state. Once the democratic trail seemed to falter, some of the politicos were quick to return to the quietist fold, while others joined the jihadi-Salafi militias, which gathered under their banner veteran global jihadists and all sorts of local disaffected protestors.[22]

Many chapters in this volume testify to the centrality of the Arab Spring in the development of today's Salafism. Each chapter is situated in a particular country and engages with the peculiarities of one or more of the local Salafi groups. Yet, together they allow us to form some more general conclusions about the motivations that animated the Salafis, the inner dynamics and rivalries among their factions, their shifting relations with the state and with the Islamists, and the changes they underwent in the process.

From Guy Eyre's ethnographic study of the Moroccan Salafi scene, we can learn how monarchies manipulated the politicisation of the quietists in their endeavour to contain the unrest. Relations between the state and the Salafis were tense since the Casablanca bombings of 2003, which led to a crackdown on all Salafis and the imposition of an official version of traditional 'Moroccan Islam'. After the breaking up of the protests, the Moroccan regime introduced them back to the public sphere, hoping to harness them for its side in the upcoming parliamentary elections of 2012. Quietist Salafis such as Muhammad al-Maghraoui, head of the widespread Dor al-Quran network, dutifully disavowed their habitual rejection of participation in politics, but tended to support the Islamist Justice and Development Party (PJD), rather than the government's choice. As the authorities again turned against them in 2013, some reverted to their former quietist positions, while others attempted to join the PJD or form their own Salafi party, steps which the government was adamant to prevent. Similar tendencies in the relations between the monarchy and the Salafis are observable in the Jordanian case as well.[23]

Neil Russell's study of the Salafis of Egypt indicates which strategies quietists in the Arab republics could adopt during their short-lived democratic period. It focuses on the almost century-old Ansar al-Sunna al-Muhammadiyya, which decided to expand its activities of *da'wa* and charity works, rather than form a political party. This, however, did not mean that it forwent the democratic game. Reformulating its understanding of *da'wa* to include engagement in the political arena, it played a central role in the creation of a Salafi-Islamist bloc to foster Egypt's Islamic identity in the face of the secular revolutionary forces. Although disappointed with Morsi's Muslim Brotherhood government and professing fealty to al-Sisi's military coup, Ansar's posture as the flag-bearer of supra-factional Islamic activism made it a target of the new authoritarian regime. In comparison with Tunisia

– where quietist Salafism was less entrenched, the al-Nahda Islamist government more prudent and the jihadi-Salafi faction stronger – a closer look at Ansar is bound to add important insights on each of these variables.[24]

Kristin Diwan's study of Kuwaiti Salafism demonstrates what formidable pitfalls awaited the politicos over the course of the Arab Spring. Activist Salafis in this relatively open constitutional monarchy predated the Saudi Islamic Awakening and, in contrast to their less fortunate comrades, were allowed to participate in the elections to the National Assembly as early as 1981, winning two seats. In the 1990s they splintered between pro-government and opposition factions, the more progressive among the latter regrouping in 2005 under Hakim al-Mutairi in the Umma Party. Al-Mutairi prioritised political liberation over religious reform and ritual, and advocated pluralism, freedom of expression and the protection of human rights, which were translated in the party programme into a rejection of religious censorship and women's enfranchisement. Such positions made it a prototype of the political wing of neo-modernist Salafism. The 2011 demonstrations prompted al-Mutairi to demand profound constitutional reform. The ensuing political crisis led him to forge a regional Umma Conference, even though its protagonists in Saudi Arabia and the UAE were immediately detained. It nevertheless immersed itself in fundraising and later organising militias and even fighting on the Sunni side in the Syrian civil war, but this put it on the terrorist organisations list. As the tide turned against the rebels, the Umma Party's remnants in exile espoused the cause of a Turkish-led caliphate. Here a comparison with the North American and European Salafi scenes is most pertinent.[25]

The Challenge of Jihadism

The rise of jihadi violence – from Sadat's assassination, over the atrocities of the Groupe Islamique Armé (GIA) in the Algerian civil war, to 9/11 and ISIS's barbarities – has shocked world public opinion and generated havoc among the Arab and Muslim peoples. The dispersal of al-Qaida following the American invasion of Afghanistan led to a decentralisation of Islamic terrorist operations, with eventual autonomy for local entrepreneurs. Among these were al-Qaida regional networks, most notably in the Arabian Peninsula (AQAP) and in Iraq (AQI) – the precursor of IS; local jihadi groups such as al-Shabab in Somalia, Boko Haram in Nigeria, or Ansar Bayt al-Maqdis in Sinai; and all sorts of home-grown terrorists and lone wolves that spread throughout the Muslim world and in the West.[26] The Arab Spring brought in its wake a militarisation of the jihad, as armed militias were formed in countries in which peaceful demonstrations descended into civil war and chaos. Although hunted down and defeated in the Middle East and in the global arena, militant jihad is not going to disappear as long as the political and socio-economic conditions that nourish it continue to prevail.

Jihadi-Salafism had been shaped in the 1980s and 1990s on the battlefields of Afghanistan, through the merger of the radical Islamist ideas of Sayyid Qutb and Abd al-Salam Faraj with the militant creed of the original Wahhabiyya. Its quintessential prototype, al-Qaida, turned the priority of the jihad from the 'near enemy' – 'infidel' Muslim rulers and societies – to the 'far enemy' – the United States.[27] Jihadi-Salafism, even more than Salafism in general, remains a poorly defined and loose-end concept. It denotes a faction that, on one hand, is part of a broader jihadist camp that encompasses indigenous purely Qutbist organisations and that, on the other hand, includes Wahhabi-inspired ideologues of jihad, such as the highly influential Abu Muhammad al-Maqdisi.[28] On the operational side, jihadi-Salafi groups differ widely in terms of their political behaviour and goals, social bases and organisation, strategic considerations and tactical alliances.[29] Their recruits come from veteran jihadis, disillusioned quietist and activist Salafis, and civil elements who long for security, livelihood and dignity.

The final section of this volume demonstrates the extent to which the enormous escalation of violence over the past twenty years has destabilised the Salafi field and the Islamic movement at large. Each of the chapters tackles one particular arena of the ideational and actual antagonisms that reign the interactions of Salafi-jihadis among themselves and with other groups. Their critical reading urges us to think over the adequacy and applicability of the concept of jihadi-Salafism, the relative weight of strategy and tactics versus ideology and theology in the conduct of jihadi-Salafis, the opportunities and constrains that condition their activity, as well as the prospects for the (re)emergence of an alternative, more tolerant Salafi vision.

For the Saudi loyalist quietists, jihadi-Salafism poses a double, theological as well as political, challenge. Both al-Qaida and Maqdisi have declared the Saudi regime infidel, not least because of its alliance with the West, at the same time that they claim to derive their jihadi principles from 'true' Wahhabism, a claim that since 9/11 finds an echo in the West. The Wahhabi establishment's response as presented by Abdullah bin Khaled Al-Saud, is thus the other side of Saudi Arabia opening up. The gist of it is to de-emphasise Ibn 'Abd al-Wahhab's use of *takfir* against fellow Muslims and the mainstream Wahhabi adoption of the principle of *al-walā' wa-l-barā'* after him,[30] while attributing the key jihadi conceptualisations – whether ISIS's violent eschatological caliphate or the more generally applied excommunication and rebellion – to Muslim Brotherhood militancy. Against the quietist partisan discursive strategy, one may recognise both militant and quietist interpretations within the Wahhabi tradition and examine the actual religious socio-political conditions that made Qutb's and Faraj's formulations so attractive for young Saudis.

The greatest challenge to jihadi-Salafism from within the Islamic field, however, comes from internal jihadi debates and infighting. Violence has soared since the arrival on the scene of ISIS and its endeavour to monopolise the jihadi struggle in the Syrian civil war and other arenas. Tore Hamming employs in his chapter the social movement approach in an attempt to construct a general theory of intra-conflict in the overall Sunni Jihadi Movement. He locates the process of escalation in the intersection between political calculations and theological differences, and describes ISIS as a hegemonist group that has legitimated its fight against other jihadis first through *al-walā' wa-l-barā'* and then through its pretentions to the global caliphate.[31] No less important, however, is to establish criteria for distinguishing the jihadi-Salafi groups from other jihadis and to determine whether al-Qaida and ISIS, as well as their local and global militant rivals, are to be counted among the Salafi camp.

Jérôme Drevon's chapter shifts the spotlight to the 'jihadi light' group of Ahrar al-Sham (Freedmen of Syria). In his historical narrative, the group's success is ascribed to its rapid organisation as an inclusive network of local brigades operated through a consensual consultative council and a corresponding broad ideological frame that positioned it in mainstream Islamism. This pragmatic approach enabled it to unite the major Islamist groups throughout the country into a larger popular Islamic Front and propelled it to seek cooperation and funding from Western countries and foreign Islamic groups, among them al-Mutairi's Umma Party. Concomitantly, it was careful to dissociate itself from the extremist doctrinaire jihadi-Salafi groups of ISIS and the al-Qaida-affiliated Jabhat al-Nusra, and to emphasise its adherence to a moderate middle way and to the living Muslim tradition. Drevon argues that Ahrar al-Sham underwent a gradual process of politicisation during the Syrian civil war, yet his analysis proves that this was equally a process of de-Salafisation.

In Palestine, the main rival of jihadi-Salafism is the Islamist organisations of Hamas and Islamic Jihad. As Belal Shobaki shows in the last chapter of this volume, jihadi-Salafi organisations appeared especially in the Gaza Strip following the Israeli withdrawal and subsequent Hamas takeover in 2007, and they further strengthened in the aftermath of the Arab Spring, after Hamas decided to maintain relations with al-Sisi's government in Egypt, despite its harsh repression of the Muslim Brotherhood. This special case of intra-jihadi conflict he attributes to the disappointment of Salafi-oriented elements within Hamas at the politicisation of their movement – namely, its retreat from its erstwhile uncompromising positions in favour of a more pragmatic approach towards democratic procedures, the sharing of government and a political settlement with Israel. The firm reaction of Hamas and the Palestinian Authority on the West Bank concerning the declaration of an Islamic Emirate in Gaza in 2009 and the wave of bombings against civilian targets in 2015 demonstrates the crucial role that governments, however fragile and hampered, have in containing the jihadi-Salafi menace.

* * *

The picture that emerges from the different studies in this volume of the Salafi phenomena in the first two decades of the twenty-first century is of a highly diversified and dynamic field. The adaptation of the Wahhabi religious establishment to the expedited opening up of Saudi Arabia, the prompt organisation of political parties by the Egyptian Salafi groups after the outbreak of the Arab Spring and the formation of a myriad of armed militias by jihadi-Salafis in Iraq and Syria, Libya and Yemen testify to the remarkable resilience of Salafism in its various forms. These, however, cannot conceal the unbound servility of the loyalists to repressive governments, the lack of palpable achievements on the part of the politicos, the unspeakable atrocities perpetrated by al-Qaida and ISIS, and the utter defeat of jihadi opposition forces.

Against this general weakening of the Salafi camp over the past twenty years stands a cautious revival of the older non-Wahhabi version of Salafism. The obstacles to this neo-modernist-Salafi trend are indeed formidable. In Saudi Arabia, al-Awda has long been detained and may face the death penalty, and al-Awni has difficulties finding an audience for his views; the Kuwaiti al-Mutairi and his Umma Party's involvement in the Syrian civil war put them on the international terrorist list, while Ahrar al-Sham was decimated by a bombing that killed its entire command. Very different is the case of the American Salafi preacher-*cum*-academic Yasir Qadhi, to whom Masooda Bano turns at the end of her chapter. His reasoned use of the Salafi methodology to inculcate notions of citizenship, deliberation and tolerance of the other has found great appeal among Muslim minorities in the West. More than the political, theological or militant perspectives that have failed, it may be this practical legal approach that will enable the modernist-Salafi faction, which has been kept at bay for so long, to finally make its contribution to the realisation of a liberal and democratic Middle East.

Notes

1. See, for example, Sami Zubaida, *Islam, the People and the State: Political Ideas and Movements in the Middle East* (London; New York: I. B. Tauris, 1993); Gilles Kepel, *Jihad: The Trail of Political Islam* (London: I. B. Tauris, 2002).
2. Roxanne L. Euben, *Enemy in the Mirror: Islamic Fundamentalism and the Limits of Modern Rationalism* (Princeton: Princeton University Press, 1999); S. N. Eisenstadt, *Fundamentalism, Sectarianism, and Revolution: The Jacobin Dimension of Modernity* (Cambridge: Cambridge University Press, 1999).
3. Basheer M. Nafi, 'The Rise of Islamic Reformist Thought and its Challenge to Traditional Islam', in *Islamic Thought in the Twentieth Century*, ed. Suha Taji-Farouki and Basheer M. Nafi (London; New York: I. B. Tauris, 2004), 28–60.
4. See David Commins, *The Wahhabi Mission and Saudi Arabia* (London; New York: I. B. Tauris, 2006), 155–90.
5. Reinhard Schulze, *Islamischer Internationalismus im 20. Jahrhundert: Untersuchungen zur Geschichte der Islamischen Weltliga* (Leiden: Brill, 1990), part 2.

6. Stéphane Lacroix, *The Islamic Awakening: The Politics of Religious Dissent in Contemporary Saudi Arabia* (Cambridge, MA; London: Harvard University Press, 2011).
7. Quintan Wiktorowicz, 'The Anatomy of the Salafi Movement', *Studies in Conflict and Terrorism* 29 (2006), 207–39.
8. Bernard Rougier (ed.), *Qu'est-ce que le salafisme?* (Paris: Presses universitaires de France, 2008); Roel Meijer (ed.), *Global Salafism: Islam's New Religious Movement* (New York: Columbia University Press, 2009); Francesco Cavatorta and Fabio Merone (eds), *Salafism after the Arab Spring* (London: Hurst, 2016).
9. Olivier Roy, *Globalized Islam: The Search for a New Ummah* (New York: Columbia University Press, 2004); Dominique Thomas, 'Le Role d'Internet dans la diffusion de la doctrine salafite', in *Qu'est-ce que le salafisme?* ed. Rougier, *le salafisme*, 87–102.
10. Muhammad Abu-Rumman, *Al-Sira' 'ala al-salafiyya: qira'a fi al-idiulugiyya wa'l-khilafat wa-kharitat al-intishar* (Beirut: al-Shabka al-'arabiyya li'l-abhath wa'l-nashr, 2016).
11. See Bernard Haykel, 'On the Nature of Salafi Thought and Action', in Meijer, *Global Salafism*, 33–57.
12. On him, see Stéphane Lacroix, 'Between Revolution and Apoliticism: Nasir al-Din al-Albani and his Impact on the Shaping of Contemporary Salafism,' in Meijer, *Global Salafism*, 58–80.
13. Itzchak Weismann, 'A Perverted Balance: Modern Salafism between Reform and Jihad', *Die Welt des Islams* 57/1 (2017), 50.
14. Thomas Hegghammer, *Jihad in Saudi Arabia: Violence and Pan-Islamism since 1979* (Cambridge: Cambridge University Press, 2010).
15. David Commins, *Islam in Saudi Arabia* (London: I. B. Tauris, 2015), ch. 5.
16. See Stephane Lacroix, 'To Rebel or Not to Rebel: Dilemmas among Saudi Salafis in a Revolutionary Age', in Cavatorta and Merone, *Salafism after the Arab Spring*, 61–82.
17. See also Madawi al-Rasheed, *Muted Modernists: The Struggle over Divine Politics in Saudi Arabia* (London: Hurst, 2015).
18. Christopher Pooya Razavian, 'Post-Salafism: Salman al-Ouda and Hatim al-Awni', in *Modern Islamic Authority and Social Change, Volume 1: Evolving Debates in Muslim Majority Countries*, ed. Masooda Bano (Edinburgh: Edinburgh University Press, 2018), 172–94.
19. See David Dean Commins, *Islamic Reform: Politics and Social Change in Late*

Ottoman Syria (New York: Oxford University Press, 1990); Itzchak Weismann, *Abd al-Rahman al-Kawakibi: Islamic Reform and Arab Revival* (London: Oneworld, 2015).

20. For an overview see, for instance, Mark L. Haas and David W. Lesch (eds), *The Arab Spring: The Hope and Reality of the Uprisings* (Boulder, CO: Westview Press, 2017).
21. Husām Tammām, *Tasalluf al-Ikhwān: ta'ākul al-uṭrūḥa al-ikhwāniyya wa-ṣu'ūd al-Salafiyya fī jama'āt al-Ikhwān al-Muslimīn* (Alexandria: Maktabat al-Iskāndariyya, 2010).
22. Cavatorta and Merone, *Salafism after the Arab Spring.*
23. See Joas Wagemakers, *Salafism in Jordan: Political Islam in a Quietist Community* (Cambridge: Cambridge University Press, 2016).
24. Emmanuel Karagiannis, 'The Rise of Electoral Salafism in Egypt and Tunisia: The Use of Democracy as a Master Frame', *Journal of North African Studies* 24 (2019), 207–25.
25. See, for instance, Sadek Hamid, *Sufis, Salafis and Islamists: The Contested Ground of British Islamic Activism* (London; New York: I. B. Tauris, 2016).
26. Marc Sageman, *Leaderless Jihad: Terror Networks in the Twenty-First Century* (Philadelphia: University of Pennsylvania Press, 2008).
27. Fawaz A. Gerges, *The Far Enemy: Why Jihad Went Global* (Cambridge: Cambridge University Press, 2009).
28. Joas Wagemakers, *A Quietist Jihadi: The Ideology and Influence of Abu Muahmmad al-Maqdisi* (Cambridge: Cambridge University Press, 2012).
29. See Thomas Hegghammer, 'Jihadi-Salafis or Revolutionaries? On Religion and Politics in the Study of Militant Islamism,' in Meijer, *Global Salafism*, 244–67.
30. For such a 'liberal' view of Wahhabism, see Natana J. DeLong-Bas, *Wahhabi Islam: From Revival and Reform to Global Jihad* (London; New York: I. B. Tauris, 2007).
31. For a similar approach to the Algerian civil war of the 1990s, see Mohammed M. Hafez, 'From Marginalisation to Massacres: A Political Process Explanation of GIA Violence in Algeria', in *Islamic Activism: A Social Movement Approach*, ed. Quintan Wiktorowicz (Bloomington & Indianapolis: Indiana University Press, 2004), 37–60.

INDEX

Note: f indicates a figure, n indicates a note

Abbas, Mahmoud, 259–60, 263–4
'Abduh, Muhammad, 6, 22n28, 29
Abdulaziz bin Abdul Rahman Al Saud (Ibn Saud), King of Saudi Arabia, 150
Abdullah bin Abdulaziz al-Saud, King of Saudi Arabia, 45, 73, 99, 276
al-Abduwly, Muhammad, 158, 159
Aboud, Hassan, 233
Aboullouz, A., 106n9
Abu al-Dardā', 71
Abū Dāwūd, 40n7
Abu Hanieh, Hassan, 218n35
'Abu Ḥanifah, 40n8
Abu Ismail, Hazem Salah, 132
al-Adnani, Abu Muhammed, 209
al-Afghani, Jamal ad-Din, 22n28
Afghanistan, 189, 211–12, 219n47, 232
al-Afifi, Talaat, 122, 133
Ahl-i Ḥadīth movement, 6–7
Aḥmad bin Hanbal, 73
al-ʿAjmi, Hajjaj, 154, 157, 158
al-Albani, Nasir al-Din, 51
Algeria, 189, 202
Alhoroob, Khalid, 256
'Alī, 71
al-Amr, Sultan, 150
'Amr b. al-'Aṣ, 62
apostasy, 12, 179, 180, 181, 182
ʿaqīda, pl. *ʿaqā'id,* 50, 51, 52, 53, 277
Arab Spring, 50, 72, 89, 278–80
Arafat, Yasser, 249, 251
Arrigoni, Vittorio, 264
al-Awda, Salman, 50, 63–4, 65, 68–9, 74–5, 79, 80, 277, 284
al-Awlaqi, Anwar, 180
al-Awni, Hatim, 51–3, 56, 174, 277, 284
Azzam, Abdallah, 189, 193–4
Azzim, Sayyid Abdul, 123

al-Baghdadi, Abu Bakr, 197, 209
Bana'ma, Adil, 64, 66
El-Baradei, Mohamed, 128
Baroud, Ramzi, 256
al-Bayhaqī, 71
Bin Bayyah, 'Abdullah, 64, 65
  and counter-revolution, 75–6, 79

Bin Bayyah, 'Abdullah *(cont.)*
and democracy, 78
on obedience, 76–7
and royalism, 65, 80
bin Laden, Usama, 189, 194, 197, 200, 212
Bishr bin Marwān, 71
Bonnefoy, L., 90
Borhamy, Yasser, 122
Braude, Joseph, 157
Brooke, Steven, 117
Brubaker, Rogers, 196
Buhairi, Islam, 32–3, 34
al-Bukhārī, 65–6, 68, 69, 74
al-Buti, Said Ramadan, 27, 29–30

clerics
Islamic State (ISIS) and, 182
religious authority, 238–9, 245n58
companions of the Prophet, 21n8, 62, 65, 69–70, 71, 72

Dabiq (ISIL magazine), 187n45, 199, 209
al-Dadaw, Muhammad al-Hasan Wuld, 63, 64, 66–8, 69–74, 79, 80
da'wa movements, 2, 5, 92, 96, 114, 115, 123–6
Delgado, J., 106n9
DeLong-Bas, Natana, 181
democracy
Bin Bayyah and, 78
al-Dadaw and, 72
Morocco, 94, 95, 96, 97, 101, 102, 103, 104
al-Mutairi on, 160
Qadhi and, 54
and *sharīa*, 98
Devji, Faisal, 58n18
Dickinson, Elizabeth, 154
al-Diqqy, Hassan, 152–3, 160
Eden, Jeff, 184n15
Egypt
Ansar al-Sunna, 114–34, 279–80; and *da'wa*, 114, 116, 119, 120, 124, 126; expansion, 120–1; formation, 118–19; political participation, 117, 129–31; social welfare work, 117, 118, 121
al-Azhar University, 34, 38
da'wa movements, 114, 123–6
al-Daw'ah al-Salafiyyah, 115, 116, 121, 124, 128, 131, 132
al-Gama'a al-Shari'a, 115, 116, 124–5, 127, 129, 130–1, 132, 134
elections, 116, 129–33
al-Fadila Party, 116
'first Salafi conference' (2011), 121–2
Freedom and Justice Party (FJP), 117, 121, 129, 131
al-Gama'a al-Islamiyya, 115, 117–18, 129
al-Gama'a al-Salafiyya, 128
and Hamas, 267
Islamic Action League, 129
Islamic movement, 121–3, 124, 126–7, 128
modernists, 34, 38
Muslim Brotherhood, 114, 115, 130, 132, 134, 135n10, 176, 193, 262
al-Nour Party, 4, 114, 116, 129, 130, 131
preaching training institutes, 120
referendum on constitutional amendments (2011), 126–8
security services, 119, 120
shahāda, 116, 128, 133
Sharī'a Body of Rights and Reformation (SBRR), 122, 131, 132
Shura Council of Scholars, 115, 122–3, 123–4, 127, 132–3
Sunni Jihadi Movement, 193–4
al-Tawhīd (magazine), 119

European Union: and Hamas, 265
excommunication *see* takfir

El Fadl, Khaled Abou, 36, 37
Faisal bin Abdulaziz al Saud, King of Saudi Arabia, 7
Faraj, Muhammad Abdul Salam, 24n54, 177, 189, 193, 281
fatwas, 29
  Ahrar al-Sham, 238
  jihadi groups and, 220n55
  Kuwait, 148
  Morocco, 93
  Qatar, 81n5
  Saudi Arabia, 48, 180
  Syria, 198
al-Fawzan, Salih, 180
al-Filastini, Abu Qatada, 193
al-Fiqqi, Mohamed Hamid, 117, 118
fitna, 188–9, 199; *see also* jihadi groups: intra-jihadi conflict
Fizazi, Mohammed, 89
Forum for Promoting Peace in Muslim Societies (FPPMS), 64
Fotini, Christia, 196, 219n47
Futuh, Abdel Monem Abul, 132

Gauvain, Richard, 117
Gaza, 253–4, 260–2, 263, 264, 267, 282
Gazal, Dr Muhammad, 255
gender
  and education, 46
  Morocco, 93, 108n37
  see also women
Gesink, Indira, 40n11
al-Ghazali, Muhammad, 39n4
globalisation, 2, 44
Gulf Cooperation Council, 150–1
Gunning, Jeroen, 219n49, 257

hadiths
  interpretations, 4, 5, 28, 275
  modernists and, 33
  and obedience, 65–6, 66–8, 70, 73–5
  see also Ahl-i Ḥadīth movement
al-Hajiry, Ershaid, 154
ḥākimiyya, 12, 177–8
  and *takfir*, 176, 178
al-Harati, Mahdi, 156
Hassan, Muhammad, 123, 130
Hayat Tahrir al-Sham, 195, 196, 202, 210; *see also* Syria: Jabhat al-Nusra
Haykel, Bernard, 6
Hegghammer, Thomas, 190–1, 193, 201, 205
Hudhayfah bin al-Yamān, 73
human rights, 32, 50, 53, 280

Ibn ʿAbd al-Wahab, Muhammad, 8, 11, 172
  and apostasy, 181
  Kitāb al-Tawḥīd, 177
  and *takfir*, 282
  and *tawḥīd*, 9
  see also Wahhabis/Wahhabism
Ibn Atiq, Hamad, 178
Ibn Baz, Abdulaziz, 180
Ibn Hajar al-ʿAsqalānī, 77
Ibn Ḥazm, 74
Ibn Mājah, 40n7
Ibn Masʿūd, 70
Ibn Saud *see* Abdulaziz bin Abdul Rahman Al Saud (Ibn Saud), King of Saudi Arabia
Ibn Taymī yyah, Ahmad, 8, 28, 50, 62
Ibn Zubayr, Abdullah: Abdullah Ibn Zubayr Battalions, 204
ideologues, 198, 200, 209
ijtihād, 6, 29, 32, 275
Ikhwan movement, 150

India: *Ahl-i Ḥadīth* movement, 22n32
International Union of Muslim Scholars (IUMS), 63, 64
Iraq
invasion of, 194
jihadis, 189, 232–3
al-Qaida (AQI), 202
Irish Republican Army (IRA), 212
Isa, Ibrahim, 32–3, 33–4
Islam: political development, 146–7
Islamic renewal party, 159
Islamic State (ISIS)
and apostasy, 182
basis in Islam, 266
and caliphate, 74, 202
global expansion, 209
and global jihad, 253
and Hamas compared, 266
and internal conflict, 197, 198, 206, 209–10
and 'Intifada of Jerusalem', 264–5
political objectives of, 222–3, 281
and al-Qaida, 4
and *statehood jihadism*, 194–5
and Syria, 208, 234, 235
and *takfir,* 52, 209, 210, 213, 214
and violence, 175, 182, 210, 211, 213, 214, 266, 282
and Wahhabism, 12, 173–6
Islamists/Islamism, 23n33, 275
Ismail, Mamdouh, 130
Ismail, Walid, 33
Israel, 253, 264, 265, 267
istiḥ lāl, 12, 179, 180
i'tiqād, 12, 179, 180
'Iyād b. Mūsā, 62

Jackson, Richard, 219n49
Jaysh al-Islam, 207f, 208
jihad, 52
global, 194, 253
legitimisation of, 11–13, 155, 193–4
militarisation of, 281
origins of, 281
statehood jihadism, 194–5
jihadi groups
appeal of, 267
and *fatwas*, 220n55
intra-jihadi conflict, 188–214, 264; explaining, 191–5; global overview, 207f; impact, 210–14; literature, 190–1; Palestine, 283; politics and religion, 195–200; rationales, 200–5; Syria, 189, 190, 198, 205–10, 211–12; typology of, 190–1
legitimisation of, 177
militancy, 92, 278
mobilisation, 3, 6, 10
and rebellion, 182
Sunni Jihadi Movement, 192–5
and takfir, 180, 181, 183
and violence, 280–1
see also Hayat Tahrir al-Sham; Islamic State (ISIS); al-Qaida; Syria: Jabhat al-Nusra
Johnston, Alan, 264
jurisprudence, 5
Hamas and, 265
schools of, 235

al-Kasasbah, Mu'ath (Moaz Kassab), 175, 266
al-Kawakibi, 'Abd al-Rahman, 278
Kepel, Gilles, 218n35
Khaliq, Abdul Rahman Abdul, 143
Khashoggi, Jamal, 20n3, 58n14, 61
Krause, Peter, 196
Kuwait
constitution, 142, 149
and counter-terrorism, 158

elections, 142–3, 148
and Gulf liberation, 144–9
Muslim Brotherhood, 145
politics, 141–4
protests (2011), 149
Revival of Islamic Heritage Society (RIHS), 142, 143, 144
Salafi Movement, 143–4, 145, 280
and Saudi Arabia, 143
student activism, 250
and Syrian crisis, 153–5
al-Tajammau ʾal-Islami al-Shaʾabi (Islamic Popular Gathering), 144
Umma Party: elections, 148–9; origins, 140–1, 144, 145–6, 161–2, 280; political position, 145–6, 148; and reform, 149; structure, 148
women's enfranchisement, 146, 148

Lacroix, Stéphane, 124
Lahoud, Nelly, 191
law, Islamic, 28, 180
sharīa, 4, 36, 73, 98, 176–7; *see also* Egypt: Shari'a Body of Rights and Reformation (SBRR); *madhhabs*
Libya, 50
Lund, Aaron, 157

madhhabs, 4–5, 6, 235
al-Madhkali, Rabi, 118
Madkhalis, 4, 278
al-Maghraoui, Muhammad bin Abdul Rahman, 90, 279
criticism of AJS, 93–4
and democracy, 98, 102, 104
and Dor al-Qurʾan, 91, 97, 100–1
and family law, 93
and social injustice, 103
support for constitutional reform, 95–6
support for Saudi monarchy, 92, 99
al-Mahdy, Osama, 125–6, 127, 128
Maher, Shiraz, 9–10, 193
Mahir, Ahmad Abduh, 32–3
Maijer, Roel, 20n5
Mālik b. Anas, 62
al-Maliki, Muhammad Ibn Alawi, 27, 29–30
al-Maqdisi, Abu Muhammad, 174, 177–8, 180, 217n31, 281–2
marriage, 58n12, 93
martyrs, 74–5
Marzooq, Musa Abu, 258
Masbah, M., 90, 91–2, 105
Mashal, Khalid, 257–8, 259, 265
al-Masri, Muhannad, 237
el-Meehy, Asya, 117
Mishal, Shoal, 256–7
modernists/modernism, 7, 22n28, 34, 38, 275, 284
Mohammad, Prophet *see* Muhammad, Prophet
Mohammed VI, King of Morocco, 92
al-Mohsin, Mohsin Muhammad, 61
Morocco, 89–105, 279
'20 February protest movement', 92–4
Authenticity and Modernity Party (PAM), 99
constitution, 108n37
democracy, 94, 95, 96, 97, 101, 102, 103, 104
Dor al Qurʾān ('Association for the Quranic Call and for the Sunnah'), 90–1, 92–3, 95, 97–9, 100, 101, 102, 103, 104
'evolution' of Salafism in, 91–2
family law, 93
Ibn Tachfeen Institute for Modern Studies and Heritage Research and Intellectual Creativity, 101, 104

Morocco *(cont.)*
'Justice and Development Party' (PJD), 89, 96–7, 98, 100, 101, 102, 103, 279
Justice and Spirituality Association (AJS), 93, 94, 95, 100–1
military coup (2013), 104
al-Nour Party, 99
'Renaissance and Virtue Party', 89
Morrison, John, 212
Morsi, Muhammad, 132–3, 262
Mubarak, Gamal, 118
Mubarak, Hosni, 81n5
al-Mufarrih, Muhammad, 152, 157, 160
al-Muhajir, Abu Abdullah, 175–6, 180
Muhammad, Prophet
authority of, 67
on martyrdom, 74
on obedience, 73
on preferential treatment, 70
use of media, 143
Muhammad bin Ibrahim (d. 1969), 180
Muhammad bin Salman, Crown Prince of Saudi Arabia
and Khashoggi affair, 61
and 'moderate Islam', 1, 2, 50
and social reform, 44, 45, 47, 48, 49, 57n2, 276
Munson, Ziad, 135n10
Muslim Brotherhood
Egypt, 114, 115, 130, 132, 134, 135n10, 176
Kuwait, 145
militancy of, 11
Palestine, 248–68
and quietism, 278
rise of, 142
Saudi Arabia, 7, 10, 99, 100
United Arab Emirates, 153
Muslim ibn al-Hajjaj, 65, 68, 69
Ṣaḥiḥ Muslim, 74, 75
al-Mutairi, Hakim
and al-Abduwly, Muhammad, 158
Al-Al`alam be ahkam al-jihad wa nawazilihi fe al-Sham, 155
and Gulf Cooperation Council, 151
Al-Ḥurriyya aw-l-tufan (Freedom or the Flood), 146–8
importance of, 161
'Slaves without Shackles', 150
and Syria, 154, 157
and Turkey, 160–1
and Umma Party, 141, 144, 149–50, 280, 284

al-Nahhas, Kenan, 243n24
al-Nahhas, Labib, 220n55, 243n24
Nais, Ali, 123
Nasser, Gamal Abdel, 118, 249
al-Natsheh, Akram, 263
al-Naysābūrī, al-Ḥākim, 66
Nigeria: Boko Haram, 202
Nodah, Hisham, 131

obedience, 61–2
bin Bayyah and, 75–7
hadiths on, 65–6, 66–8, 70, 73–5
pro-revolutionary Islamic discourses on, 66–71
The Prophet on, 73
Qu'ran and, 65–6, 67, 76–7
and rebellion, 63–6, 68, 72–3, 182
right and wrong, 63, 71–3
Oslo Accords, 258
al-'Oun, Jassim, 143

Palestine
elections, 255–6
Hamas, 247–8, 248–9, 252, 267–8, 283; charters, 251, 255, 256–7, 258–9; and Egypt, 262–3; and elections, 254–6,

259, 266; image post-2005, 260–5; and Muslim Brotherhood, 262; rise of, 250–2; and Salafi jihadis, 265–6
Intifadas, 251–2; 'Intifada of Jerusalem', 264–5
liberation of, 194
Muslim Brotherhood, 248–50, 257–8
Palestine Liberation Organization (PLO), 247, 251, 254, 258–9
Palestinian National Liberation Movement (Fatah), 249, 251, 263
Salafi-jihadism, 252–4, 263, 266
Phillips, Bilal, 39n4
prisoners, 227, 233

al-Qabbaj, Hammad, 91, 97, 98, 99, 100, 101–2, 104
Qadhi, Yasir, 51, 53–4, 284
al-Qahtahi, Abu Mariyah, 217n29
al-Qaida, 196
and apostate factions, 199
opposition to, 233
and plurality, 4
political objectives, 222–3
Al-Qaida in Iraq (AQI), 202
regional networks, 280–1
and Salafism, 194, 272
and Saudi Arabia, 281–2
split with Hayat Tahrir al-Sham, 197
struggle with Islamic State, 198, 206, 208, 209–10
as a unitarian group, 203
see also Syria: Jabhat al-Nusra
al-Qaradawi, Yusef, 266
al-Qasimi, Jamal al-Din, 278
Qatar, 160
al-Qatari, Abu 'Abd al-'Aziz, 157
quietism, 275, 278, 281
Egypt *see* Egypt: Ansar al-Sunna
Morocco, 89–105
see also al-Maghraoui, Muhammad bin Abdul Rahman
Qur'ān
on disputes with rulers, 69
and *fitna*, 188
interpretations of, 4, 5, 6, 275
Light Sura, 100
and Moroccan constitution, 96
and obedience, 65–6, 67, 76–7
on sales contracts, 69
*see also hadith*s
Qutb, Sayed, 11, 12, 176–7, 189, 193, 281

radicalism, 176–8
al-Rasheed, Madawi, 9
Rashid Rida, Muhammad, 6, 7, 10, 22n28
al-Rashoud, Talal, 147
Razavian, Christopher Pooya, 52, 55
Reffouch, Adil, 97, 98, 99, 104
reformists, 34–7, 275
revolutions
counter-, 75–6, 80
French, 80
see also Arab Spring
Rice, Condoleezza, 255
Russia: and Syria, 240

al-Sadat, Anwar, 177
al-Sadiq, Abu Muhammad, 236, 237
Ṣaḥwah movement, 2, 10–11, 50, 56, 143
al-Ṣaḥwah al-Islāmiyya, 10–11, 20n6
Salafism
and anti-Salafism, 273–5
appeal, 5–6
critiques, 1–2, 27–38; modernist scholars, 32–4, 37, 38; reformist scholars, 34–7; Sufi *ṭuruq*, 30–2, 38; traditional *'ulamā'*, 28–30, 37–8
defining, 272–3
as a global movement, 56

Salafism *(cont.)*
origins, 3–4
reasoning, 4–6
resilience, 283–4
Saudi Arabia, 3–4, 6–8
transformation, 13
see also Egypt: Ansar al-Sunna; Wahhabis/Wahhabism
al-Salem, ʿAbdullah, 159
Salman bin Abdulaziz Al Saud, King of Saudi Arabia, 172
Saudi Arabia
dissent, 64, 277
education, 7, 46; International Islamic University (Medina), 7; King Abdullah University of Science and Technology (KAUST), 46
entertainment, 45, 47
establishment of, 150
hadhar-bedu cleavage, 150
independent scholars, 51–5
Islamic revival, 272–3
and Kuwait, 143, 179–80
mainstream tradition and understanding, 178–80, 182
mawlid, 31
political tensions, 45
religious authority, 49–50, 276
religious police, 47, 276
Salafism, 3–4, 6–8
social liberalism, 1, 2, 44–9, 55–6, 276–8, 277; Vision 2030, 45, 57n2
Umma Party, 151–2, 159, 160
Wahhabism, 9, 48, 49–50, 273, 282
women, 46, 47–8, 276
al-Sawaaf, Mahmoud, 256
al-Shaʿar, Iyyad, 233
Shafik, Ahmed, 132
el-Shahat, Abdel Moneim, 129–30
Shakir, Abdullah, 118, 120, 122, 123
Shalit, Gilad, 254, 266
al-Shami, Abu Yazan, 243n29
al-Sharif, Sayyid Imam (Dr Fadl), 189
al-Shater, Khairat, 122, 132
al-Shaykh, Hashim, 236
Shikaki, Fathi, 250
al-Shishani, Muslim, 204
Shoman, Hazem, 130
Simon, Steven, 257
Somalia, 204
Stenersen., Anne, 191
Stevenson, Jonathan, 257
Sufism
India, 23n32
and Salafism, 27, 30–2, 37, 38
and Wahhabism, 36, 275
al-Sultan, Khalid, 143
Sunni Muslims
jihadi *see under* jihadi groups
Kuwait, 141, 153
and obedience, 66, 67–8
and Salafism, 1, 4–5, 27, 28
Saudi Arabia, 7–8, 154; *see also* Saudi Arabia: Umma Party; Wahhabis/Wahhabism
al-Suri, Abu Musab, 193, 218n35, 218n36
Syria
Ahrar al-Sham, 156, 157, 207f, 208, 223–41, 282–3, 284; expansion, 228–32; politicisation, 232–6; politics, 230–1, 236–40; roots, 223–8
de-escalation zones, 240
Free Syrian Army, 225
Haʾya Tahrir al-Sham, 238–9, 240
Hurras al-Deen, 203, 207f
Islamic Front, 230, 231
Islamic State (ISIS), 208, 234, 235
Islamist Social Movement (ISM), 224
Jabha Fath al-Sham, 238, 239
Jabha Thuwar Suriyya, 230

Jabhat al-Nusra, 156, 158, 199, 204, 207f, 208, 209, 210, 224, 226, 231–2, 235–6, 237; *see also* Hayat Tahrir al-Sham
Jaysh al-Ahrar, 238
Jaysh al-Sham, 237
jihadis, 189, 190, 198, 205–12
Junud al-Sham, 204
Liwa al-Haq, 229, 231
Muslim Brotherhood, 224
Nour al-Din Zinki Movement, 240
prisoners, 227
Umma Conference, 156, 157–8
Umma Party, 151, 153–9, 284
uprising, 40n13, 50

al-Tabarani, Abu al-Qasim, 62
al-Tahhan, Abu Saleh, 236
takfir
al-Awni and, 52, 277
definition, 1
and ḥākimiyya, 176, 178
Ibn al-Wahhab and, 282
Islamic State and, 209, 210, 213, 214
Jabhat al-Nusra, 199
jihadis and, 197, 202
takfīr *al-mu*ʾ*ayyan*, 12, 180–2
takfīr *bi i-naw*180 ,12 ,ʿ
Wahhabis and, 9–10, 13
taqlīd, 5, 29
tawhīd, 1, 53
Ibn ʿAbd al-Wahhab and, 8–9, 10, 11
al-Maqdisi and, 178
Saudi Council of Senior Scholars and, 186n35
Wahhabis and, 172
al-Tayyib, Ahmad, 30
terrorism, 219n49
al-Thawri, Sufyān, 62
al-Tirmidhī, 40n7

Tunisia, 279–80
Turkey
strategic importance of, 160–1
and Syria, 240
Umma Conference, 153, 159–60, 161
Turkistan Islamic Party (TIP), 203

ʿUbādah b. al-Ṣāmit, 65, 69, 72
ʿ*ulamā*, 5
independent, 51–5
modernist, 6–7, 32–4, 37, 38
reformist, 34–7
traditional, 7–8, 9–10, 11, 28–30, 37–8
ʿUmarah bin Ruwaybah, 71
al-ʿUmari, ʿAli, 64–5
Umma Brigade, 156
Umma Conference, 149, 151, 280
Syria, 156, 157–8
Turkey, 153, 159–60, 160–1, 161
Union of Opposition Forces, 159
United Arab Emirates: Umma Party, 152, 153, 157
ʿUthmān, caliph, 70, 71, 189

violence
Islamic State, 175, 182, 210, 211, 213, 214, 266
jihadi, 280–1, 282
justification for, 176
political, 33–4
and rebellion, 63
and religion, 219n49

Wagemakers, J., 135n3, 193
Wahhabis/Wahhabism, 7, 8–11, 29, 171–83
heritage, 172–4
and Islamic State, 173–6
Saudi, 11–12, 48, 49–50, 273, 282
and Sufism, 36

Wahhabis/Wahhabism *(cont.)*
  and *takfir*, 52, 181–3
  see also Ibn ʿAbd al-Wahab, Muhammad
al-walāʾ wa-l-barāʾ, 10, 52–3, 178, 179, 197, 199, 202, 277, 282
al-Wazir, Abu Jihad Khalil, 249
Wickham, Carrie, 134
Winter, Tim, 5
women
  Kuwait, 146, 148
  Palestine, 266
  Saudi Arabia, 1, 46, 47–8, 276
al-Wuhayby, ʿAbd al-ʿAziz 152, 160

Yacoub, Mohamed Hussein, 123
Yassin, Shaykh Ahmed, 250, 251, 257
Yusuf, Hamza, 81n3

al-Zahar, Mahmoud, 266
al-Zarqawi, Abu Musʿab, 175–6, 194, 197
al-Zawahiri, Ayman, 189, 194, 200, 203, 209, 210, 212, 252

EU representative:
Easy Access System Europe
Mustamäe tee 50, 10621 Tallinn, Estonia
Gpsr.requests@easproject.com

www.ingramcontent.com/pod-product-compliance
Lightning Source LLC
Chambersburg PA
CBHW050203240426
43671CB00013B/2235
* 9 7 8 1 4 7 4 4 7 9 1 3 4 *